Fairness and Rights in
International Criminal Procedure

For my mother, Victoria Rigney (1950–2008)

and

For my children, Archibald Clark and Dorothea Clark

Fairness and Rights in International Criminal Procedure

Sophie Rigney

EDINBURGH
University Press

Edinburgh University Press is one of the leading university
presses in the UK. We publish academic books and journals
in our selected subject areas across the humanities and social
sciences, combining cutting-edge scholarship with high
editorial and production values to produce academic works
of lasting importance. For more information visit our website:
edinburghuniversitypress.com

Cover image: Flight from Reason by Stella Bowen (1941).
Courtesy of the Australian War Memorial.
Cover design: riverdesignbooks.com

Edinburgh University Press Ltd
The Tun – Holyrood Road
12(2f) Jackson's Entry
Edinburgh EH8 8PJ

Typeset in 10/12pt Goudy Old Style
by Cheshire Typesetting Ltd, Cuddington, Cheshire, and
printed and bound in Great Britain

A CIP record for this book is available from the British Library

ISBN 978 1 4744 6630 1 (hardback)
ISBN 978 1 4744 6632 5 (webready PDF)
ISBN 978 1 4744 6633 2 (epub)

Contents

Acknowledgements

I acknowledge the Wurundjeri people of the Kulin Nation, and the palawa/ pakana of lutruwita, the sovereign owners of the lands on which much of this book was written. Any royalties from this book will be paid directly to the organisations for these sovereign owners as a small gesture towards paying the rent I owe.

The cover image for this book is from the painting 'Flight from Reason', by Australian artist (and later official war artist), Stella Bowen. In this painting, Bowen depicts the wreckage of German bombing raids on London in 1941, and in particular she shows the sculptures and monuments of The Inner Temple (one of the four professional associations for barristers in England and Wales). To her, these monuments appeared 'untouched and complacent, amid the wreckage'. From this description, we are invited to consider law's place and complacency in the midst of conflict and desecration – a theme I try to take up in this book. I am grateful to the Australian War Memorial for permission to use this image.

Some of the arguments made in this book have appeared in an earlier form in the following publications: Sophie Rigney, '"The Words Don't Fit You": Recharacterisation of the Charges, Trial Fairness, and *Katanga*' (2014) 15 *Melbourne Journal of International Law* 515; Sophie Rigney, '"That a Trial is Fair": The Centrality and Incoherence of Fairness in International Criminal Trials' in Arman Sarvarian et al (eds), *Fairness in International Criminal Proceedings* (British Institute of International and Comparative Law, 2015); and Sophie Rigney, 'The Fractured Relationship between Fairness, the Rights of the Accused, and Disclosure at the International Criminal Court' in Jadranka Petrovic (ed), *Accountability for Violations of International Humanitarian Law* (Routledge, 2015).

This book has lived in many spaces. It emerged first as an experience of being an international criminal lawyer in The Hague; it continued in the form of a doctoral thesis at the University of Melbourne; and it was re-written as a monograph while I was living in London, Dundee and Hobart. In each of these places, I have been fortunate to have significant material support in the form of employment or financial assistance, union membership, healthcare, childcare and housing – all of which has made this book possible. In the decade that has now passed since commencing my doctoral work, I have also fallen in love, had a miscarriage, had a child, and as I write this, my second child is just a few weeks old, cooing at my side. In the middle of a pandemic, our wee family left Scotland suddenly and returned to Hobart. Such significant events affect research and writing, and there are many people – friends, colleagues, comrades and loves – who have supported me in many ways, and who have therefore also been integral to this work, and also to making my life outside of work something that I am very proud of and grateful for.

At Edinburgh University Press, my thanks to Laura Williamson and Sarah Foyle, who gave useful feedback on the initial proposal, supported the work and were gracious in providing me with extensions to the timeframe when 2020 proved more challenging than many of us could ever have imagined. In the production phase, Judith Mackenzie provided expert oversight of the manuscript; Luke Turner was a fantastic copy-editor; and Elske Janssen did a wonderful job of providing an index. I am very thankful for their excellent work. I am also grateful to the University of New South Wales for providing funds to support the index. I am also very grateful to the anonymous reviewers who provided very helpful insights on this book at both the proposal stage and the manuscript stage; and to Carsten Stahn (Leiden University) and Elies Van Sliedregt (Leeds University), who examined my doctoral thesis and provided helpful insights for redrafting the thesis into a monograph.

At Melbourne Law School, I acknowledge Tim McCormack (now University of Tasmania) and Peter Rush, who supervised my doctoral thesis. I was very fortunate to have a number of people guide my research and develop my abilities during this formative time at Melbourne: my particular thanks to Hilary Charlesworth, Alison Duxbury, Ann Genovese, Kirsty Gover, Cathy Hutton, Rain Liivoja (now University of Queensland), Shaun McVeigh, Ian Malkin, Chantal Morton, Anne Orford, Di Otto, Sundhya Pahuja and Gerry Simpson (now London School of Economics). I am also grateful to the Australian Government for funding my research through an Australian Postgraduate Award, and to Melbourne Law School for additional research funding to support field work in The Hague and London in 2013 and 2014.

My experiences working at the International Criminal Tribunal for the Former Yugoslavia provided the genesis for this work. I am thankful to the University of Tasmania for providing me with the Tim Hawkins Memorial Scholarship, which funded my initial Internship at the ICTY. Everyone I worked with at the ICTY influenced this work and the person I have become, and I am very grateful to all those very talented lawyers. A special thanks to Richard Harvey, who has taught me so very much, including teaching me about the importance of creating a space for optimism and always thinking through how to make a better world.

For their participation in interviews, their candour and their enthusiasm, I thank Carmel Agius, Danya Chaikel, Adrian Fulford, Gregor Guy-Smith, Joanna Korner, Justice Bakone Moloto, Howard Morrison, Alphons Orie, Rod Rastan, Patrick Robinson, Peter Robinson, Colleen Rohan, Cuno Tarfusser, Stefan Trechsel, and those interviewees who wished to remain anonymous.

I am especially grateful to Jane Hwang, who provided me with a home in The Hague while I undertook the interviews. Jane is exceptionally generous and kind, and this book would look very different but for her warm creation of a home for me at that time. My thanks also go to Lara Renton, and to Richard Harvey and Sarah Burton, who opened their homes to me during my research trips.

I am grateful to Sergey Vasiliev for his thoughtful comments on preliminary parts of this book, and to Yvonne McDermott Rees for suggesting some litera-ture at an early stage. Ideas in this book have benefitted greatly from feedback provided at workshops and conferences. For their thoughtful engagement, I thank Philippe Sands, Martti Koskenniemi, Mark Antaki, Kevin Heller, Philip Alston, Ralph Zacklin, and the participants and organisers of the 2013 Australia New Zealand Society of International Law Postgraduate Workshop, the 2014 ATLAS Agora Symposium, the 2013 and 2014 International Criminal Law Workshops at Melbourne Law School and the University of New South Wales, the 'Procedural Fairness in International Courts and Tribunals' workshop (University of Surrey, 2014), the 'International Law's Objects' workshop (QMUL 2016), the 'International Criminal Justice On/ And Film' workshop (LSE, 2016), and the 'Towards a Counter-Aesthetic of International Law' workshop (Liverpool, 2017).

At the Universities of Melbourne, Dundee, and New South Wales, I am indebted to all the professional and administrative staff who assisted me, par-ticularly the Research Offices and the Libraries. Megan Anderson provided some research assistance for this book, and I am very thankful to her and to the University of Dundee for funding Megan's work.

I am grateful to the University of Dundee branch of the University and Colleges Union (DUCU). The support of the Union – and particularly of Carlo Morelli and Iain Ellis – was hugely valuable. There's strength in a union, and a union makes us strong. The writing of this manuscript was interrupted, at various points, by the industrial action of the University and Colleges Union (UCU) related to pensions, workloads, equality pay gaps, and casualisation. It was a privilege to stand on the picket line with such talented individuals as my comrades at the University of Dundee.

There are no words to express the gratitude I owe to the National Health Service (NHS) and particularly the NHS Tayside, Ninewells Hospital in Dundee, and the Neonatal Intensive Care Unit there. I am also grateful to the Royal Hobart Hospital's Maternity Services and Women's Health Tasmania. Without the care of the NHS and of public healthcare in Australia, I would not have been able to write this book. Thanks to the Department of Work and Pensions, who provided me with the state pension when I was informed that I would not be provided paid Maternity Leave while at Dundee.

I am grateful to the Early Childhood Educators at my child's childcare centres. They provide me with the space and time to write, and I would not have been able to complete this work without them. Much more importantly, they provide Archie with care, education, play and emotional support, and I am grateful to them every day.

In truth, it was a struggle to finalise this book while working full-time on a separate funded research project, and with a toddler at home (and in the middle of strike action and then a global pandemic and then while being pregnant). At various points, Martin Clark took over all parenting duties to allow me little writing retreats in different places around the world (Edinburgh, Montpellier and Launceston). These gasps of extended writing time allowed me space, time, light, chocolate and uninterrupted early morning starts with coffee and fruit toast. I don't acknowledge this to glorify Martin's parenting (I also take over, from time to time, to allow his work to be done), but rather to make visible the reality of writing work: for me, it necessitated brief spells away from my family and the usually shared domestic labour of home, and I am glad that Martin could enable my writing in this way. Many mothers, in particular, continue to suffer significant structural impediments to the realities of academic and writing work; it is why mothers, as a category of writer and of academic, have only really emerged in recent decades. We have things to commit to paper, though; and so universities, publishers, partners, and governments and communities all need to work harder to address these structural constraints and enable our writing to exist.

For their mentorship over many years, I thank Dianne Nicol, Lisa Butler Beatty, and Terese Henning (all currently or formerly at the University of Tasmania), and Penny Green (QMUL). Mark McMillan (formerly Melbourne Law School) has given me so much and has changed the course of my life – thank you, Mark. Damien Short provided me with wonderful mentorship, support and friendship at the Institute of Commonwealth Studies in London. I am also grateful for the support of Megan Davis and George Williams, with whom I currently work at the University of New South Wales, and all my colleagues at the Indigenous Law Centre and in the Office of the PVC Indigenous at UNSW. While undertaking this work at UNSW, I have been fortunate to work closely with the members of the Uluru Dialogue, and I have learned a huge amount from their dedicated and passionate work.

Academic work has a particular pleasure, which is discovering the company of people who become not just colleagues but good friends. Thank you to Gabrielle Appleby, Paul Bradfield, Michelle Burgis-Kasthala, Edzia Carvalho, Madelaine Chiam, Monique Cormier, Sara Dehm, Debolina Dutta, Maria Elander, Luis Eslava, Yvonne Evans, Rosemary Grey, Rob Knox, Tor Krever, Kevin Heller, Jessie Hohmann, Anna Hood, Dani Larkin, Dylan Lino, Simon McKenzie, Golnar Nabizadeh, Emma Palmer, Rose Parfitt, Charlie Peevers, Laura Petersen, Isobel Roele, Anna Saunders, Oishik Sircar, Christine Schwöbel-Patel, Joe Spooner, Rebecca Sutton, Ntina Tzouvala, Lars Waldorf and Henrietta Zeffert.

For their love, laughter and friendship, I thank Paula Antley, Jason Antley, Pauline Barton, Boglárka Benko, Luke Boenisch, Anica Boulanger-Mashbourg,

Kirraley Bowles, Kate Cashman, Ness Chapman, Felicity Ey, Kate Fitzgerald, Jo Flanagan, Charlotte Frew, Megan Gayford, Elli Göetz, Robert Grey, Sara Gul, Catriona Holmes, Lisa Claire Hutchison, Jane Hwang, Mardie Landvogt, Mak Livingston, Lea McInerney, Christina Marsden, Rikki Mawad, Phoebe Miller, Amanda Molesworth, Katie O'Byrne, Marie O'Leary, Annie O'Reilly, Candice Parr, Alice Ramsay, Lara Renton, Alex Rigozzi, Charmaine Roberts, Vaughn Rogers, Sophie Shugg, Kirsten Sjøvoll and Mirjana Vukajlović.

I am grateful to my family: Hannah, Sam and Ruby Lewis; Ruth Jedryka and Sam and Zoe Calleija; Patrick Carroll, Ange Crane, and Hamish, Maxwell and Olivia Carroll; Angie Carroll and Ryan Robertson; Libby Robinson; Annette Carroll; Julie Prideaux, Peter Clark, Patrick Clark and Natalia Barker. My grandparents – Betty Rigney, Lance Rigney and Stefan Jedryka – all influenced this work (and everything else) in profound ways.

When we left Scotland in the middle of the pandemic, with only 48 hours' notice, we had to leave our darling bulldog Hugo in the UK, pending a flight to Australia. Hugo came to me as a 12-week-old puppy in the months between leaving The Hague and starting my PhD. He has been with me – and then, as I met Martin and had Archie and now Dorothea, with us – through all this process of writing this book. It is not an exaggeration to say that I owe so much of my happiness and my life to Hugo. Because of the difficulties of the pandemic, we waited 17 months for him to join us in Australia, and our hearts were broken every day he was not with us. But this story has a happy ending: as I finalise these acknowledgements, we have just been reunited with Hugo, and our home feels whole once more. We are so grateful to Fletch Williams and John Gallagher, Tracy Papiccio and Mo Hoseini, and Laura Waterman for their assistance in taking care of Hugo in 2020–2021.

To my love, Martin: 'I'll tak your trusty haun / and lead you over the haw – hame, ma darlin.' (Jackie Kay).

To my son, Archie: thank you for your abundant love. Thank you for your boundless curiosity and your exuberant storytelling. Thank you for the snuggles, for the laughter, and for making every day sparkle. We love you, darling heart.

To my daughter, Dorothea: you, my love, are a blessing. Thank you for your beautiful smiles; your insistent wails (which suggest you have strong views on important matters); your delight in cuddles; your companionship on long walks and in the middle of the night. We love you so, we love you so.

And to my mother, Victoria Rigney, who raised me wrapped up in her love and in a love of learning, in a home that valued justice, writing, and seeking to understand complexity. She is in every word of this book and in everything I do.

Introduction
Why fairness and rights matter, and what this book sets out to do

This book examines two of the most fundamental precepts of international criminal justice: fairness and the rights of the accused. These two ideas – and the relationship between them – are central, contested and misunderstood. What exactly is 'fairness'? How do we know whether or not a trial is 'fair'? Can a trial still be 'fair' if the rights of the accused are undermined? This book particularly examines procedural decisions made in recent trials at the International Criminal Court (ICC) and the International Criminal Tribunal for the Former Yugoslavia (ICTY).[1] The primary question in this book is, how are fairness and the rights of the accused connected in procedural decision-making in contemporary international criminal trials? Trial Chambers have a responsibility to 'ensure that a trial is fair and expeditious and conducted with full respect for the rights of the accused and due regard for the protection of victims and witnesses'.[2] Fairness, rights and procedure are therefore closely aligned. However, I show that in making decisions about how these trials are run, Trial Chambers routinely invoke the idea of fairness – in order to justify decisions that may undermine the rights of the accused. Thus, although fairness and rights are supposed to be closely related, in fact, we can observe a distancing between them in judicial decisions. This book ultimately calls for a renewed close association between fairness and the rights of the accused, particularly when making determinations on matters of procedure in international criminal trials.

Despite the interconnectivity of fairness, rights and procedure, in this book, I argue that they are also rightly conceived of as separate and separable aspects of international criminal trials. It is important to examine each of fairness, rights and procedure as discrete entities to properly appreciate how they are connected and their significance (both separately and collectively) to international criminal trials. Fairness is the overriding requirement of international criminal trials. Fairness is given content by the rights of the accused, and these rights are operationalised and ensured

---

[1] At the end of 2017, the ICTY was replaced by the United Nations Mechanism for International Criminal Tribunals (MICT). This book will examine the jurisprudence of both the ICTY and MICT from 2008–2018.

[2] *Rome Statute of the International Criminal Court*, opened for signature 17 July 1998, 2187 UNTS 90 (entered into force 1 July 2002) ('*Rome Statute*') Art 64(2); SC Res 827, UN SCOR, 48th sess, 3217th mtg, UN Doc S/RES/827 (25 May 1993), as amended by SC Res 1877, UN SCOR, 64th sess, 6155th mtg, UN Doc S/RES/1877 (7 July 2009) ('*ICTY Statute*') Art 20.

by procedure. However, fairness consists of more than the rights of the accused – but, as I demonstrate, there is little agreement about precisely what else this entails. In this book, the rights of the accused are examined as procedural rights (gained by virtue of being an accused in a criminal process) rather than human rights. Procedure is to be understood as the rules and practice of the procedural order of international criminal trials – found in the relevant *Rules of Procedure and Evidence* and statutes of the international criminal institutions, along with the *Regulations* at the ICC, and the relevant jurisprudence. While procedure operationalises the rights of the accused, as I show in this book, procedure is also the site where we can understand the separation between fairness and rights, and how it is that rights may be balanced away in the name of fairness.

First, though, I would like to offer a brief pause to set the scene for this book. This book originated from my experiences as a junior lawyer at the ICTY, where I was an Intern (in the Trial Chambers) and then, for two years, a Case Manager and Legal Assistant for the Defence. During that time, I had the opportunity to observe and, in a small way, participate in the workings of international criminal law. Like many others, I had come to the project of international criminal law with a desire to 'do good'. When I arrived in The Hague as a twenty-three-year-old, directly after finishing my law degree, I wanted to help 'end impunity' and 'bring war criminals to justice'.[3]

Yet as time went on, I became uneasy with what I saw and experienced at the ICTY. In particular, the way that the accused (and their defence) was treated seemed inconsistent with the principles I had thought the international criminal legal mission held dear: fairness, rights, due process. I could not understand how my experiences could be reconciled, either with these principles or with the stated law.[4] This book emerged as an attempt to theorise, understand and respond to those experiences. There are two moments, in particular, that stand out as emblematic: I call these 'the photocopier' and 'the acquittal'.

On an otherwise entirely unremarkable day in the defence room, I find myself yelling at a recalcitrant photocopier that has, yet again, stopped working. I stun myself. I no longer recognise the person that I have become. I am not a person who yells at office equipment – so how did this come to pass? In this moment, I see how this work has weighed me down, changed me and adversely affected my ability to defend my client. I leave The Hague

---

[3] For more on the 'bringing war criminals to justice' narrative in international criminal law, see Sophie Rigney, 'Postcard from the ICTY: Examining International Criminal Law's Narratives', Daniel Joyce and Jessie Hohmann (eds) *International Law's Objects* (OUP, 2018).

[4] For more on how I came to move 'from believing in an international criminal law "mission" to engaging in critical conversations about the project', see Sophie Rigney, 'You Start to Feel Really Alone: Defence Lawyers and Narratives of International Criminal Law in Film' (2018) 6(1) *London Review of International Law* 97.

soon after, exhausted not only from the heavy work of helping to defend those accused of committing international crimes, but also from constant negotiations with broken photocopiers, the stigma attached to being a 'red pass holder' (a defence lawyer), and the insecurity of working conditions.[5]

I had been working for the defence team representing Lahi Brahimaj, accused in the first-ever retrial of an acquittal in international criminal law.[6] Two years after the incident with the photocopier, on 29 November 2012, I returned to The Hague to watch the verdict in that case. Brahimaj and his co-accused were again acquitted on the charges of the retrial. Our team of defence lawyers travelled to Kosovo to be with Brahimaj as he returned to his village for the first time in eight years. Witnessing his homecoming to his family, community and country, reinforced to me the need for a robust process in international criminal law. Any deprivation of liberty – and any removal of a community member – must be justified. Charges of international crimes are, of course, a strong and worthy justification. Yet with this justification comes also a need for a robust process. This is, as Gerry Simpson has noted, an area of law that is 'thoroughly politicised, culturally freighted and passionately punitive', and as such, 'there is a need for even greater protections for the accused'.[7]

In reading the judgment, I could see the importance of the Rules of Procedure and Evidence. Without enough evidence, adduced and admitted according to law, the presumption of innocence remains. Unless a prosecutor can bring this evidence, they cannot discharge their burden. Yet the apparent straightforwardness of 'the presumption of innocence', 'the

---

[5] Every ICTY employee holds a security pass, which allows them to access the building. The security pass of defence employees has a red border. These passes only allow access to limited areas in the building, and there are signs on doors and walls in the Tribunal which read 'Red Pass Holders Not Allowed Beyond This Point'. Defence lawyer Peter Robinson has described the frustration of being a 'red pass holder': 'I feel [inequality] every day at the ICTY, when you go into the building and there are bunch of signs of door [sic] that say people with red passes are not allowed to enter': Frédéric Mégret, 'The Legacy of the ICTY as Seen through Some of Its Actors and Observers' (2011) 3 *GJIL* 1011, 1024. As I have said, the red pass system was about 'being tolerated and yet not really welcome' as defence lawyers (Rigney (n 4)).

[6] *Prosecutor v Haradinaj, Judgement* (IT-04-84-A, 19 July 2010). In the first trial, two of the accused (Ramush Haradinaj and Idriz Balaj) were acquitted on all counts, while Lahi Brahimaj was convicted on two counts and sentenced to six years imprisonment, and acquitted on the remaining charges (*Prosecutor v Haradinaj, Judgement* (IT-04-84-T, 3 April 2008). The charges that Brahimaj was convicted of were not the subject of the retrial proceedings. On 29 November 2012, this retrial resulted in the acquittal of all three of the accused on all the counts they faced. The complexities of the case will be examined in later Chapters.

[7] Gerry Simpson, 'War Crimes: A Critical Introduction' in Timothy McCormack and Gerry Simpson (eds), *The Law of War Crimes: National and International Approaches* (Kluwer Law International, 1997) 1, 15.

burden of proof', 'the rights of the accused' and 'fair trial' obscures significant complexity.

My work at the ICTY revealed shortcomings of the international criminal legal system. These shortcomings made the work of the defence more difficult. Standing over a photocopier, frustrated at it not working, sounds trivial – but this was not an isolated incident. More accurately, this should be understood as a symbol for all the various challenges that coalesced into an almost impossible situation. The other challenges include the time when I was not paid for six months; the limited computer space that led to arguments in the defence room; a basic lack of office equipment; days where you would work for fourteen hours straight, with no guarantee that you would be paid at the end of it (and certainly no other workplace entitlements like annual leave or sick pay).[8] How can a lawyer adequately defend their client when this is what they must contend with? These shortcomings were procedural and substantive; structural and endemic. They appeared to occur regardless of the case, the composition of the Trial Chamber, or of the parties prosecuting and defending. These elements seemed to be felt by all defence teams. I struggled to understand how this could be the reality of international criminal law. This seemed so at odds with the legal mission I had wanted to work with: one I had thought would be fair. Instead, this reality felt like an affront to the workings of the entire system of law.

These challenges were usually related to a procedural right of an accused. Difficulties with defence team funding and the resources of the defence room; challenges in securing translations of documents or an interpreter; disclosure of evidence coming late or not at all – these are all examples I experienced at the ICTY, and all directly relate to the rights of the accused. They reveal challenges to the rights to time and facilities to prepare a defence, to the free assistance of an interpreter, to potentially exculpatory material, and to the principle of equality of arms. I wanted to better understand what I perceived to be the failure of the institution to adhere to these principles. This was the genesis of this book.

This is a book about the rights of the accused in international criminal trials, both because that is the story I know best and because it is the area I wanted to understand in more detail. Nonetheless, I have deep sympathy for the victims of these atrocities. Writing this book in 2020, with resurgent

---

[8] Dov Jacobs writes about the 'balancing away of the defence' which is a 'daily, practical reality' at the ICC, embodied in experiences including inadequate office space, exclusion on mailing lists, and an inability for the defence to directly book a conference room to meet visitors: Dov Jacobs, 'Neither here nor there: the position of the defence in International Criminal Trials', in Kevin Heller et al. (eds), *The Oxford Handbook of International Criminal Law* (OUP, 2020) 67, 82. On issues relating to the pay and working conditions of defence lawyers compared to other staff in international criminal courts and tribunals, see Till Gut et al., 'Defence Issues', in Göran Sluiter et al. (eds), *International Criminal Procedure: Rules and Principles* (OUP, 2013) 1202, 1226–7.

genocide denial and the rise of the far-right,[9] I am somewhat reticent about my work: I do not wish anything I write to be construed as an apologia for acts of mass violence. However, equally, these times of reinvigorated fascism remind us of the importance of rights, of fair trials, and of a structurally robust system of law.

The photocopier and the acquittal demonstrate the power and importance of fairness, rights and procedure in international criminal trials. The photocopier represents the nadir of how international criminal trials can treat the accused and their lawyers; but the acquittal demonstrates the possibility of what can happen when fairness, rights and procedure work in tandem. Acquittals are often not the right result in these trials: frequently, guilt is clear and established beyond a reasonable doubt. Acquittals should not necessarily be aspired to or advocated for. But a conviction simply should not be entered if a trial is not fair, if rights are curtailed, or if process is not adhered to. This book interrogates the space between the photocopier and the acquittal: where fairness, rights and procedure intersect – or fail to meet. In doing so, this book hopes to reveal more about the conditions of possibility – and, perhaps, impossibility – of international criminal law. The ultimate aim is to imagine and consider what international criminal law might meaningfully be able to aspire to.

Such a desire to understand the hope and the reality of international criminal law appears to be shared by many scholars. The fields of international criminal law and procedure are now firmly established. We have moved past the questions of old – whether international criminal law is law; what international criminal procedure is; should international criminal law exist? – into a space of evaluation and critique. Scholars are calling for, and undertaking, examinations of the history, politics and ideologies underpinning international criminal law, as well as its 'conceptual flaws and ontological limits'.[10] In addition, much recent literature has addressed the imperfections and apparent impossibilities of international criminal law.[11]

---

[9] See, for example, Martti Koskenniemi 'International Law and the Far-Right: Reflections on Law and Cynicism' Fourth Annual Asser Institute Lecture, <https://www.asser.nl/upload/documents/20191121T165243-Koskenniemi_web.pdf> (last accessed 9 December 2021); Anne Orford, 'International Law and the Populist Moment: A Comment on Martti Koskenniemi's Enchanted by the Tools? International Law and Enlightenment' (2020) 35(3) *AUILR* 427.

[10] Dov Jacobs, 'Sitting on the Wall, Looking in: Some Reflections on the Critique of International Criminal Law' (2015) 28 *LJIL* 1, 2. For examples, see particularly Christine Schwöbel (ed), *Critical Approaches to International Criminal Law* (Routledge, 2014); on the 'critical turn', see Sergey Vasiliev, 'The Crises and Critiques of International Criminal Justice', in Heller et al. (eds) (n 8) 626.

[11] See Payam Akhaven, 'The Rise, and Fall, and Rise, of International Criminal Justice' (2013) 11 *JICJ*, 527; Joseph Powderly, 'International Criminal Justice in an Age of Perpetual Crisis' (2019) 32 *LJIL* 1; Elies van Sliedregt, 'International Criminal Law: Over studied and Underachieving?' (2016) 29 *LJIL* 1, 5; Frédéric Mégret 'The Anxieties of International

Such critiques were unusual until relatively recently – with international criminal law enjoying a position of confidence that was almost evangelical – but in the last decade, critical views have become ubiquitous.[12] As Carsten Stahn writes, 'there is a growing sense that the time of experiments is over',[13] with a move from pure 'faith' in international criminal law (which Stahn defines as the 'belief in the value and worthiness of the project')[14] to a desire for more 'facts' (an 'actual and demonstrable record').[15] There is often a tension between 'faith' and 'facts' – and in particular, 'the fundamental question as to how and by what standards one should assess success or failure remains unanswered. International criminal justice is still partly in search of its "identity"'.[16] However, Stahn urges an understanding of faith and facts as complementary: while a factual understanding of international criminal justice is required, it is also important to 'acknowledge the limitations' of such a fact-based assessment of international criminal justice.[17]

This book attempts to use both factual and normative understandings of international criminal law to provide an account of one particular aspect: how fairness, rights and procedure interact. In light of the search for the 'identity' of international criminal justice and the uncertainty regarding how to measure the success or failure of international criminal justice, an evaluation of the relationships between fairness, rights and procedure in international criminal trials is necessary. Against this backdrop, it is also a ripe moment to build a critical and normative approach to the field of international criminal procedure: an approach which examines procedural rules within a sustained enquiry into 'the very foundation, the context – including economic, political, and social conditions – and the limitations' of international criminal law and procedure.[18] A critical approach (rather

Criminal Justice' (2016) 29(1) *LJIL* 197; Sergey Vasiliev, 'On trajectories and destinations of international criminal law scholarship' (2015) 28(4) *LJIL* 701.

[12] See, e.g., Schwöbel (n 10); Jacobs (n 10); Tor Krever, 'International Criminal Law: An Ideology Critique' (2013) 26 *LJIL* 701; Pádraig McAuliffe and Christine Schwöbel-Patel, 'Disciplinary Matchmaking: Critics of International Criminal Law Meet Critics of Liberal Peacebuilding' (2018) 16(5) *JICJ* 985. This scholarship, growing rapidly since 2012, drew on earlier important contributions to critical approaches to international law, including Immi Tallgren, 'We Did It? The Vertigo of Law and Everyday Life at the Diplomatic Conference on the Establishment of an International Criminal Court' (1999) 12 *LJIL* 683; Immi Tallgren, 'Sensibility and Sense of International Criminal Law' (2002) 13 *EJIL* 561; Gerry Simpson, *Law, War, and Crime* (Polity Press, 2007); and Mark Drumbl, *Atrocity, Punishment and International Law* (CUP, 2007).

[13] Carsten Stahn, 'Between "Faith" and "Facts": By What Standards Should We Assess International Criminal Justice?' (2012) 25 *LJIL* 251, 253.

[14] Ibid. 254.

[15] Ibid.

[16] Ibid.

[17] Ibid. 257.

[18] Mikael Baaz, 'Review Essay: Dissident Voices in International Criminal Law' (2015) 28 *LJIL* 673, 688.

than mere criticism) attempts to consider not just 'success and failure' but instead also the 'underlying presumptions and conditions of possibility'.[19] For some, 'this translates into a project of developing a more just legal field ... to improve from within, "through a sustained process of critique and reflection"'.[20] While the discipline of international criminal law has undergone a 'critical turn', the same cannot easily be said of international criminal *procedure*, a sub-discipline that tends to be more focused on both doctrine and technique. This book attempts to undertake a small part of building that critical and normative approach to procedural questions by contextualising international criminal procedure concerns in a broader framework of international criminal law's current conditions of possibility. This book hopes to shed greater light on the structural limits and potentials of international criminal law, particularly surrounding fairness, rights and procedure. I do not seek to 'solve' these issues, prescribe a check-list for judges in their decisions, or offer policy solutions. Instead, it is my intention to identify the issues, link them to questions of power and the 'place' of contemporary international criminal law in both the scholarship and practice, and provide some utopian thinking for what this suggests about the future of international criminal law as a system.

Such an intervention is plainly needed, as we see a lack of clarity around fairness, rights and procedure regularly in international criminal trials – sometimes, with dramatic consequences, as can be seen in a recent example. At the end of the timeframe examined in this book, the controversial acquittal of Jean-Pierre Bemba Gombo at the ICC showed that, even in 2018, there is little agreement on the position of fairness and rights in international criminal law. This judgment was divided and incohesive, with four separate opinions provided by the Appeals Chamber: a majority decision issued by three judges, a dissenting opinion from two judges, and then two separate opinions from different judges in the majority (one Joint Separate Opinion from Judges Morrison and Van den Wyngaert; one Separate Opinion from Judge Eboe-Osuji). These opinions raised 'questions about Pre-Trial and Trial Chamber procedures, the standard of Appellate Chamber review, and the scope of command responsibility', and revealed 'sharp disagreements between ICC judges and created considerable confusion about the state of ICC law and procedure'.[21] In their Joint Separate Opinion, Judges Morrison and Van den Wyngaert offer a blistering view on their fellow judges, which goes to the heart of how fairness and rights are understood in international criminal trials. They write:

---

[19] Sara Kendall, 'Critical Orientations: A Critique of International Criminal Court Practice', in Schwöbel (n 10) 59, citing Mark Drumbl, 'Pluralising International Criminal Justice' (2005) 103 *MLR* 101, 133. See also Drumbl (n 12).

[20] Ibid.

[21] Leila Sadat, 'Prosecutor v. Jean-Pierre Bemba Gombo' (2019) 113(2) *AJIL* 353, 353–4.

it is important to recognise that the strong divergence in how we evaluate the Conviction Decision is not just a ... difference of opinion, but appears to be a fundamental difference in the way we look at our mandates as international judges. We seem to start from different premises ... it is probably fair to say that we attach more importance to the strict application of the burden and standard of proof. We also seem to put more emphasis on compliance with due process norms that are essential to protecting the rights of the accused.[22]

This quote is emblematic of what I call, in this book, the incoherence of the idea of fairness in international criminal law. We see, here, judges fundamentally disagreeing with how fairness is understood – how closely it must be linked to the rights of the accused, how it relates to the burden and standard of proof, and how this impacts on matters of procedure. One reading of this statement is that Judges Morrison and Van den Wyngaert have articulated a concern that trial fairness and the rights of the accused have been separated too far. As I will go on to develop, when we consider procedural decisions over the decade ending in 2018 (around the time this opinion was voiced), this concern is a reasonable one, whether or not one agrees with the Appeals Chamber's decision in the Bemba case.[23]

In the remainder of this Introduction, I will set out the significance of this area of enquiry with reference to the surrounding 'fairness and rights' literature; delineate the scope and boundaries of the book, with particular respect to sources and methodology; and set out the structure for the rest of the book.

---

[22] *Prosecutor v Bemba Gombo, Judgment on the appeal of Mr Jean-Pierre Bemba Gombo against Trial Chamber III's "Judgment pursuant to Article 74 of the Statute"* (ICC-01/05-01/08-3636-Red, 8 June 2018), Separate Opinion of Judge Van den Wyngaert and Judge Morrison.

[23] For more on the Bemba Appeals Case, see Joseph Powderly and Niamh Hayes, 'The Bemba Appeal: A Fragmented Appeals Chamber Destablises the Law and Practice of the ICC' (26 June 2018) <https://humanrightsdoctorate.blogspot.com/2018/06/the-bemba-appeal-fragmented-appeals.html> (last accessed 9 December 2021); Leila Sadat, 'Fiddling While Rome Burns? The Appeals Chamber's Curious Decision in Prosecutor v Jean-Pierre Bemba Gombo' (12 June 2018) <https://www.ejiltalk.org/fiddling-while-rome-burns-the-ap peals-chambers-curious-decision-in-prosecutor-v-jean-pierre-bemba-gombo/> (last accessed 9 December 2021); Alexander Heinze, 'Some Reflections on the Bemba Appeals Chamber Judgment' (18 June 2018) <http://opiniojuris.org/2018/06/18/some-reflections-on-the-bemba-appeals-chamber-judgment/> (last accessed 9 December 2021); Diane Marie Amann, 'In Bemba and Beyond, Crimes Adjudged to Commit Themselves' (13 June 2018) https://www .ejiltalk.org/in-bemba-and-beyond-crimes-adjudged-to-commit-themselves/> (last accessed 9 December 2021); Michael Karnavas, 'The Reversal of Bemba's Conviction: What Went Wrong or Right?' (19 June 2018) <http://michaelgkarnavas.net/blog/2018/06/19/bemba-rever sal/> (last accessed 9 December 2021).

A. PLACEMENT OF THIS WORK IN THE EXISTING LITERATURE

Fairness and the rights of the accused have both been traditionally under-examined in international criminal law scholarship. However, we can understand the 'fairness and rights' scholarship which does exist as falling (roughly) into three key 'generations'. Respectively, these generations have established questions of fairness and rights as important questions of international criminal procedure; explored the details of how fairness and rights might be operationalised in international criminal procedure; and more recently, scholarship reveals the gaps and identifies possibilities for how fairness and rights are treated in international criminal procedure.

The early literature that examined questions of fairness and rights as important questions for international criminal procedure emphasised the primacy of human rights law to developing a system of international criminal procedure and to ensuring trial fairness. For example, Christoph Safferling used both human rights and comparative law to suggest an appropriate model for international criminal procedure.[24] He argued that both the civil and common law systems of criminal procedure shared 'an overlapping goal: to actualize fundamental human rights within a fair procedure';[25] and therefore, that human rights 'can and should serve as a common denominator in the search for a conclusive procedural structure'.[26] Likewise, Salvatore Zappalà argued that human rights are an important element of international criminal procedure, with a focus on the rules and practice from the *ad hoc* tribunals.[27] These volumes importantly placed rights and fairness as key considerations for international criminal procedure scholarship.

A second generation of scholarship, from the mid-to-late 2000s, shifted its focus to operationalising procedure in international criminal trials. The emphasis was more on procedure than on fairness or rights: fairness and rights tended to be implicit or backgrounded in the scholarship here. Emblematically of this generation of scholarship, Frédéric Mégret suggested that the most important questions facing international criminal procedure had moved 'beyond fairness': that while earlier procedural work had focused on fairness concerns, there was a need to look to other questions regarding how international criminal procedure had developed.[28] This development in the scholarship matched a maturation in the procedure at the *ad hoc* tribunals: as the trial procedures became more complex, there was

---

[24] Christoph Safferling, *Towards an International Criminal Procedure* (OUP, 2001).
[25] Ibid. 2.
[26] Ibid. 3.
[27] Salvatore Zappalà, *Human Rights in International Criminal Proceedings* (OUP, 2003).
[28] Frédéric Mégret, 'Beyond "Fairness": Understanding the Determinants of International Criminal Procedure' (2009) 14 *UCLA JILFA* 37.

a need for the scholarship to examine the content of these procedures and how they related to fairness and rights.

In more recent years, scholars have returned to the issue of fairness. As the questions of identity and measures of success or failure of the international criminal justice project have become more pressing, there have been increasing examinations of the promise of fairness and rights in international criminal procedure and whether this promise is being fulfilled. As a result, there is a significant body of literature emerging on these issues.[29] The present book is aligned with other contemporary scholarship of this third generation, particularly Yvonne McDermott's *Fairness in International Criminal Trials*[30] and Sergey Vasiliev's work on a normative theory of international criminal trials.[31]

McDermott makes the argument that 'international criminal tribunals should set the highest standards of fairness'.[32] By this, she means 'full respect for the rights of the accused as established by international human rights standards and repeated in the statutes of the tribunals in a manner that is consistent with the principles of fairness, such as neutrality, equality, and consistency'.[33] Vasiliev also offers a normative approach for international criminal trials, but in doing so, he examines 'whether and why "fairness" is a suitable parameter for evaluating international criminal justice and its procedural law'.[34] Vasiliev approaches the fairness question within the framework of international human rights law.[35] I do not undertake a similar examination of human rights law at institutions beyond the international criminal courts and tribunals, but rather seek to expand upon the concept of fairness as it is invoked in international criminal trials.

I seek to further explain the nature of fairness and rights, and the relationship between them, in contemporary international criminal trials.

---

[29] For some recent contributions on fairness and rights in international criminal trials, see Jonathan Hafetz, *Punishing Atrocities Through a Fair Trial* (CUP, 2018); Caleb H Wheeler *The Right to be Present at Trial in International Criminal Law* (Brill, 2018); John Jackson and Sarah Summers (eds), *Obstacles to Fairness in Criminal Proceedings: Individual Rights and Institutional Forms* (Hart, 2018); Arman Sarvarian, Filippo Fontanelli, Rudy Baker and Vassilis Tzevelekos, *Procedural Fairness in International Courts and Tribunals* (British Institute of International and Comparative Law, 2015); Joanna Nicholson, '"Too High", "Too Low", or "Just Fair Enough"? Finding Legitimacy Through the Accused's Right to a Fair Trial' (2019) 2 *JICJ* 17, 351.

[30] Yvonne McDermott, *Fairness in International Criminal Trials* (OUP, 2016).

[31] Sergey Vasiliev, *International Criminal Trials: A Normative Framework* (PhD Thesis, University of Amsterdam, 2014).

[32] McDermott (n 30) 125. See also Yvonne McDermott, 'Rights in Reverse: A Critical Analysis of Fair Trial Rights under International Criminal Law' in William A Schabas, Yvonne McDermott and Niamh Hayes (eds), *The Ashgate Research Companion to International Criminal Law* (Ashgate, 2013) 165.

[33] McDermott (n 30) 34.

[34] Vasiliev (n 31) 89.

[35] Ibid. 90.

McDermott and Vasiliev both emphasise fairness and rights as being closely linked.[36] While I agree that this close alignment *should* be the case, in this book, I demonstrate that they are separable, and I address them as separate spheres of enquiry, to permit an examination of how fairness and rights interact. Conceiving fairness and rights as separate, but related, areas of investigation could possibly be criticised as a false dichotomy by those who might argue that fairness and rights are not separable. However, as I show, fairness and rights are indeed separated in procedural decision-making in contemporary international criminal trials: this is, therefore, not a false dichotomy but a real one. I seek to analyse further this separation and its implications. While I argue that we can observe a divide between fairness and rights, I also argue for a renewed closeness between fairness and rights. In order to make this claim, this book engages with questions that McDermott and Vasiliev have not examined in depth: what constitutes fairness; why fairness and rights matter; and, importantly, the ways in which fairness can be invoked to challenge the rights of the accused.

B. SCOPE AND BOUNDARIES OF THIS BOOK

This book analyses a particular, contemporary, point in time in relation to international criminal law and procedure. The cases analysed were in trial between the years 2008–18. This decade provides both a significant timeframe, but also gives the book current relevance, and the contemporary nature of the study highlights the urgency of resolving the issues raised in the book for the future of the international criminal law project. The ongoing search for the identity of international criminal justice and the questions of the appropriate standards against which to measure the international criminal justice project make this timeframe an important one for the examination of fairness, rights and procedure. Understanding how these areas have been approached, linked and separated in contemporary trials should assist us in addressing the questions of identity and evaluation of international criminal justice. The limited timeframe allows for an in-depth examination of the procedural motions and decisions; a longer span would have necessitated a shallower analysis of these documents, as there would have been too many to engage with in the way I do in this book. Furthermore, this timeframe is appropriate because many of the issues that have arisen with respect to the areas examined in the case studies in this book – disclosure, adjudicated facts and the protection of witnesses – have increased in their urgency over this decade, particularly with the start of the trials at the ICC and the larger cases at the ICTY.

---

[36] For another example, I would argue that Hafetz also elides the separation between fairness and rights (Hafetz (n 29)).

This book particularly examines practice at the ICC and the ICTY. These institutions provide an interesting juxtaposition of practice and approaches to questions of fairness, rights and procedure. The ICTY – as the first international criminal tribunal established in the modern era of the 'accepted history'[37] of international criminal justice – now has a wealth of procedural jurisprudence to draw upon and to compare to the approach at the more recently established ICC. The limited geographical and temporal jurisdiction of the ICTY also provides a counterpoint to the more expansive mandate of the ICC. How do questions of fairness, rights and procedure differ at these institutions, or are similar issues arising at both? For the purposes of this book, a detailed examination limited to two key institutions was preferable to an examination of a multitude of different international criminal institutions that would necessarily be restricted in its depth. Nonetheless, the findings of this book and the analysis of the jurisprudence of these two institutions will undoubtedly be useful for new institutions, like the Kosovo Special Chambers and the International Impartial and Independent Mechanism for Syria, which are likely to draw on the approaches of the ICC and the ICTY.

Not every case from 2008–18 at the ICTY and ICC has been examined in detail. Instead, this book focuses on the key cases where questions of fairness and rights have particularly emerged in the context of procedural litigation and decision-making. The cases that have been examined include *Lubanga*,[38] *Bemba*,[39] and *Katanga*[40] at the ICC, and *Karadžić*,[41] *Mladić*,[42] *Stanišić and Župljanin*,[43] *Šešelj*[44], and *Haradinaj*[45] at the ICTY. These cases were particularly relevant to the procedural case studies which are used in this book to examine the question of how fairness and rights are addressed in procedural decision-making: disclosure, the use of adjudicated facts, and the protection of victims and witnesses.

The procedural case studies provide a narrow scope of inquiry and therefore a detailed analysis. This is quite a different approach from the literature that attempts to examine all procedural rules comprehensively but in a less detailed way.[46] There were a number of controversial issues and cases that

---

[37] Sarah Nouwen, 'Justifying Justice' in James Crawford and Martti Koskenniemi (eds), *The Cambridge Companion to International Law* (CUP, 2012) 327–8.

[38] *Prosecutor v Lubanga* (ICC-01/04-01/06).

[39] *Prosecutor v Bemba* (ICC-01/05-01/08).

[40] *Prosecutor v Katanga* (ICC-01/04-01/07).

[41] *Prosecutor v Karadžić* (IT-95-5/18-T).

[42] *Prosecutor v Mladić* (IT-09-92-T).

[43] *Prosecutor v Stanišić* (IT-08-91-T).

[44] *Prosecutor v Šešelj* (IT-03-67-T).

[45] *Prosecutor v Haradinaj* (IT-04-84bis-T).

[46] See, e.g., Zappalà (n 27); Safferling (n 24); Christoph Safferling, *International Criminal Procedure* (OUP, 2012); Gideon Boas et al. (eds), *International Criminal Law Practitioner Library: Volume III, International Criminal Procedure* (CUP, 2011).

arose during the timeframe of this book, which have not been examined.[47] However, the case studies of disclosure, the use of adjudicated facts, and the protection of witnesses were selected for examination because they are particularly integral to the operation of rights in these trials and are key areas of concern for practitioners, judges and scholars. They also provide illuminating divergences and convergences. Disclosure, considered to be 'at the heart of criminal trials',[48] has proved to be one of the most highly litigated areas of international criminal procedure at all international criminal courts and tribunals. In contrast, the use of adjudicated facts – the admission to the trial record of facts in the instant proceedings but which have been previously adjudicated in other proceedings at the institution – has emerged relatively recently as a highly contentious issue at the ICTY and has not yet received much academic analysis. Although the use of such facts has not yet been problematic at the ICC, there is increasing concern about the admission of written evidence in place of oral testimony. This permits an examination of the differences between the institutions and also identifies problems that have occurred at the ICTY in order to suggest 'best practice' for the ICC. Finally, the protection of witnesses has been highly contentious at both the ICTY and ICC and has had a profound impact on how cases are litigated and how fairness and rights are understood and given content in these trials.

These three case studies are also chosen because they are very closely linked and will influence each other. A defence case and strategy – including whether and how to examine witnesses in order to adduce evidence to rebut an admitted adjudicated fact – will be determined partly by the material disclosed to a defence team and by when that disclosure occurred. The ability to cross-examine a witness will be influenced by the disclosure of the identity of the witness, of key documents related to the witness, or of other documents which may help clarify the exact contours of the prosecution's case. Late or incomplete disclosure of this information – perhaps undertaken in order to protect the identity of a witness – will affect cross-examination strategies, and ultimately of the ability to address material adduced through

---

[47] This includes retrials of acquittals generally (the matter of the *Haradinaj* case is examined due to its relationship to fairness, rights and procedure issues; but the case of *Stanišić and Simatović* is not included, as the decision was made on a question of substantive rather than procedural law, and did not explicitly raise fairness or rights issues). Another example would be the role and composition of Chambers staff and their influence on judicial impartiality, as in the *Mladić* case (see *Prosecutor v Mladić, Decision on Defence Motion for a Fair Trial and the Presumption of Innocence or, in the alternative, a Mistrial* (IT-09-92-T, 4 July 2016); *Decision on Interlocutory Appeal Against Decision on Defence Motion for a Fair Trial and the Presumption of Innocence* (IT-09-92-AR73.6, 27 February 2017).

[48] Kate Gibson and Cainnech Lussiaà-Berdou, 'Disclosure of Evidence' in Karim Khan, Caroline Buisman, and Christopher Gosnell (eds), *Principles of Evidence in International Criminal Justice* (OUP, 2010) 306.

adjudicated facts. For these reasons, it was important to analyse these procedural areas together.

This book is bounded by the field of international criminal procedure.
I do not undertake a comparative analysis between international criminal
procedure and the procedures of other legal systems. Nor do I examine the
jurisprudence regarding the rights' of the accused and trial fairness at human
rights institutions. Such examinations have already been undertaken.[49]
As the rights of the accused are effectively copied from Article 14 of the
International Covenant on Civil and Political Rights[50] and are set out in a myriad
of other human rights documents, drawing on other human rights jurisprudence or undertaking a comparative approach would be valid. However,
given the now firm establishment of international criminal law and procedure, it is important to examine the jurisprudence of international criminal
trials as areas of enquiry whole in themselves. If we are interested in the
search for the identity of international criminal justice, we must examine
international criminal law and procedure on its own terms.

Rather than considering these rights from a human rights perspective, I
instead examine them as procedural rights, attaching to a person by virtue
of their being an accused in a criminal trial. Yvonne McDermott makes
explicit the difference between these two categories, or what she calls 'status
human rights' and 'pure human rights'.[51] She points out that there is a
distinction in international law between the additional rights that attach to
people by virtue of their holding a particular status – for example, a refugee,
a combatant, or a prisoner – and the rights that attach to them by virtue of
their simple humanity.[52]

I do not engage with the question of whether international criminal
procedure is an adversarial or inquisitorial system, but rather take as a
starting point that international criminal procedure is a *sui generis* system,
with both adversarial and inquisitorial elements.[53] The question of whether

---

[49] See Ryan Goss, *Criminal Fair Trial Rights: Article 6 of the European Convention on Human Rights*
   (OUP, 2014); Piero Leanza and Ondrej Pridal, *The Right to a Fair Trial: Article 6 of the European
   Convention on Human Rights* (Kluwer Law International, 2014); Vasiliev (n 31); Robert Roth
   and Françoise Tulkens (eds), 'Symposium: The Influence of the European Court of Human
   Rights' Case Law on (International) Criminal Law' (2011) 9 *JICJ* 571; William Schabas,
   'Synergy or Fragmentation? International Criminal Law and the European Convention on
   Human Rights' (2011) 9 *JICJ* 609.

[50] *International Covenant on Civil and Political Rights*, opened for signature on 16 December 1966,
   999 UNTS 171 (entered into force 23 March 1976).

[51] McDermott (n 32) 166.

[52] Ibid.

[53] See John Jackson, 'Transnational Faces of Justice: Two Attempts to Build Common
   Standards Beyond National Boundaries' in John Jackson, Máximo Langer and Peter Tillers
   (eds), *Crime, Procedure and Evidence in a Comparative and International Context: Essays in Honour
   of Professor Mirjan Damaška* (Hart Publishing, 2008) 221; Safferling (n 24); Elies van Sliedregt,
   'Introduction: Common Civility – International Criminal Law as Cultural Hybrid' (2011)

international criminal procedure is mainly adversarial, mainly inquisitorial, or mixed, is perennial but uninspiring.[54] It has also been essentially answered: there is widespread agreement that international criminal procedure has tended to be predominantly based on adversarial understandings but with a gloss of inquisitorial elements.[55] This inquisitorial gloss has increased in recent years, as I will examine in greater detail in Chapter Five. In responding to the pressures, issues and questions placed before it, international criminal law has had to create its own approach to procedure.[56]

I also do not examine the implications for complex trials occurring in national jurisdictions, such as trials for major corporate crimes, corruption, or transnational crime (including drug trafficking or modern slavery). There is undoubtedly much to be learned from the procedure of these trials for trials of international criminal law and vice versa. Surely these trials could gain from international criminal procedure. For these reasons, this would be a fruitful area of future research. However, as I have deliberately limited this book to international criminal procedure and trials, this is outside the scope of this study.

This book engages with debates that are occurring in two settings. First, I engage with the existing scholarship, particularly to address questions of the political and ideological underpinnings of international criminal law and procedure, and the flaws, limits and potential of this legal system. This allows me to undertake a factual and normative analysis of fairness, rights and procedure in international criminal trials. Secondly, I use the primary texts of the ICTY and ICC (the statutes, *Rules of Procedure and Evidence*, and *Regulations*), as well as selected procedural motions and decisions at both trial and appellate level in contemporary international criminal trials held at the ICTY and ICC. I examine this law and related motions and decisions

---

24 *LJIL* 389; Mégret (n 28); Vasiliev (n 31); Gideon Boas, *The Milošević Trial: Lessons for the Conduct of Complex International Criminal Proceedings* (CUP, 2007) 286; Jens David Ohlin, 'A Meta-Theory of International Criminal Procedure: Vindicating the Rule of Law' (2009) 14 *JILFA* 77.

[54] This question has been described as 'sterile' (Máximo Langer, 'The Rise of Managerial Judging in International Criminal Law' (2005) 53 *AJCL* 835, 836), 'outdated' (Boas (n 53) 286), and 'well-worn' (Boas et al. (eds) (n 46) 14). Boas suggests that the question must now be 'abandoned' (Boas (n 53) 287).

[55] John Jackson, 'Finding the Best Epistemic Fit for International Criminal Tribunals: Beyond the Adversarial–Inquisitorial Dichotomy' (2009) 7 *JICJ* 17. See also Jackson (n 53); Frédéric Mégret, 'International Criminal Law: A New Legal Hybrid?' (2003) <http://papers.ssrn.com /sol3/papers.cfm?abstract_id=1269382> (last accessed 9 December 2021) 39; Boas (n 53) 286; Richard Vogler, 'Making International Criminal Procedure Work: From Theory to Practice' in Ralph Henham and Mark Findlay (eds), *Exploring the Boundaries of International Criminal Justice* (Ashgate, 2011) 105; Zappalà (n 27) 2.

[56] See, e.g., Mirjan Damaška, 'Negotiated Justice in International Criminal Courts' (2004) 2 *JICJ* 1018, 1019; Bert Swart, 'Damaška and the Faces of International Criminal Justice' (2008) 6 *JICJ* 87, 94.

to understand how fairness and rights are addressed in the international criminal procedural framework. I analyse both the relevant Chamber's approach and the effect of the decisions. In doing so, I have asked: 'how has the Chamber addressed fairness concerns?'; 'how has the Chamber accounted for the rights of the accused?'; and 'what have been the implications of this decision for the rights of the accused?' These documents permit an analysis of what procedural questions have arisen and how they have been resolved in relation to both fairness and rights. This ultimately facilitates an analysis of how fairness, rights and procedure interact.

In order to complement the doctrinal and academic writings with which I engage, I undertook interviews with judges, prosecutors and defence lawyers based at both the ICTY and the ICC.[57] I approached judges who had written on the topic of fairness or the rights of the accused (either in judicial decisions or extra-judicially). Prosecutors and defence lawyers were approached chiefly if they had been involved with a case where disclosure and the use of adjudicated facts had been particularly at issue.[58] Interviews were semi-structured, and questions were both expansive (for example, 'what do you think the aims of an international criminal trial are?') and focused (for example, 'what is your view on the argument that there should be increased provision for sanctions against prosecutors for disclosure violations?'). The interviews are limited in the sense that it was not possible to interview all the judges, prosecutors and defence lawyers at the ICTY and ICC. The interviews are therefore not intended to be a source of comprehensive empirical data. Rather, they are designed to provide greater context and explication to the existing doctrinal and academic writings. The insights of these judges and practitioners are woven throughout the book and connect practical realities to the theoretical analysis.

C. STRUCTURE OF THIS BOOK

In order to examine how fairness and rights are connected in procedural decision-making in contemporary international criminal trials, this book examines the aims of international criminal trials (Chapter One); the nature of rights and fairness in international criminal trials (Chapters Two and Three); and procedural decision-making in these trials (Chapters Four, Five and Six). Thus, the book offers a conceptual and normative analysis

---

[57] Interviews were conducted in person. All views expressed are personal, and do not represent the institution the individual is, or was, affiliated with. Consistent with the ethics approval granted by the University of Melbourne, I have identified participants where they consented to being identified, and have provided pseudonyms where they have consented to pseudonyms instead of identification by name.

[58] At the time of interviews being conducted, these were the two case studies examined; the case study on the use of written evidence was not primarily considered at the time of interviews.

of fairness, rights and procedure in international criminal trials. Chapters One, Two and Three build the theoretical framework for an understanding of how rights, fairness and procedure interact in contemporary international criminal trials. This is then deployed in relation to the particular case studies of disclosure (Chapter Four), the use of adjudicated facts (Chapter Five), and the protection of witnesses (Chapter Six), to analyse how procedural rules interact with fairness and the rights of the accused, in these trials. This book argues that there is a separation between fairness and rights in international criminal procedure, and in the final chapter (Conclusions and Looking to the Future), I argue for a closer relationship between fairness, rights and procedure.

In Chapter One, I analyse the aims of international criminal law and argue that there is a lack of clarity around the aims of international criminal law, institutions and trials. The aims of these three levels have been conflated, and several of the aims that have been placed on the level of the trial are problematic. I argue for a recalibration of the aims of international criminal trials and suggest that the primary aim of the *trial* should be the forensic determination of the accused's guilt or innocence. This chapter thus argues that the individual accused is at the heart of the trial process, and this has implications for how we understand the role of rights and of fairness in the trial process.

In Chapters Two and Three, I examine both rights and fairness in international criminal trials. Chapter Two commences with an examination of rights in international criminal trials – what they are, who they attach to, and why they are considered to be important. The chapter then moves to examine the concept of fairness and why fairness is understood as central to international criminal trials. I outline various perspectives on, and challenges to, fairness: what it is, why it is important, who it is owed to, and how to ensure it. I outline the centrality of fairness in international criminal trials and why fairness is considered to be so important. As a point of convergence between most scholars and practitioners of international criminal law, the centrality of fairness offers an opportunity for a shared vision and approach – but it also brings the potential for greater friction if conceptions of fairness are in conflict. A coherent understanding of the concept of fairness is thus required.

Yet, as I show in Chapter Three, there is presently no coherent understanding of the concept of fairness. In fact, there is a multitude of different views regarding what fairness is and how it manifests in trial proceedings, which has led to the concept being incoherent and unstable. I argue that the concept of fairness is incoherent for three main reasons: a conflict over what legal protections are required by fairness; a conflict over who should be the key beneficiary of fairness in trials; and a lack of certainty around how to ensure fairness in a *sui generis* procedural system. In other words, there is a lack of shared understanding around *what* fairness includes, *whom* fairness is owed to, and *how* fairness can be assured. I conclude this chapter by arguing that there is a separation between fairness and the rights of the accused in international criminal trials, which emerges from, and adds further to, the conceptual incoherence of fairness.

In Chapters Four, Five and Six, I examine this disconnection between fairness and the rights of the accused in international criminal trials in relation to three case studies: disclosure, the use of adjudicated facts, and the protection of witnesses. These case studies ground and contextualise the interplay between fairness, the rights of the accused, and procedure in contemporary international criminal trials. In relation to each of these three case studies, I ask: how has fairness been used by Trial Chambers when making procedural decisions? What have been some of the outcomes of these decisions? How do these outcomes reconcile with the rights of the accused? These questions allow an examination of how the procedural decisions of Trial Chambers – often made with reference to the fairness of the trial – in fact interact with the rights of the accused.

In Chapter Four, I undertake a doctrinal analysis of two main issues related to the way disclosure is undertaken in international criminal trials. First, I examine the effect on the rights of the accused of large volumes of disclosed material. Second, I argue that at the ICC, there is an environment that permits non-disclosure of material (particularly exculpatory material) by both victims and the prosecution. I argue that while Trial Chambers often emphasise the importance of disclosure to ensuring a trial that is fair, the way that Trial Chambers regulate disclosure creates a trial environment where the rights of the accused are not upheld. There is thus a separation between the way that disclosure occurs – as permitted by procedural decisions – and the rights of the accused. This may, in turn, have implications for the fairness of the trials.

In Chapter Five, I examine how concerns regarding fairness and rights were used to expand the use of adjudicated facts beyond the literal meaning under the *Rules*. I then examine how the shifting evidential burden permitted by this rule may affect the equality of arms. Finally, I examine the potential issues around consistency and clarity in decision-making on this issue. I argue that while Trial Chambers often reiterate the importance of fairness in their decisions on the use of adjudicated facts, the use of this mechanism facilitates an environment where the rights of the accused are not upheld.

In Chapter Six, I examine the particularly challenging issue of balancing trial fairness, the rights of the accused, and the protection of witnesses. This is an unusual procedural issue because it is clear that the rights of the accused may, sometimes, need to be adversely affected in order to ensure the protection of witnesses and, therefore, trial fairness. Nonetheless, as I show in this chapter, judicial decision-making has frequently extended procedural mechanisms (like redactions and written evidence) and has done so without any sustained examination of how these mechanisms will affect the accused's rights. We, therefore, again see the separation between fairness and rights here.

Thus, in the three case studies, I demonstrate that there is a disconnection between the use of the concept of fairness and the rights of the accused in procedural decisions. The implications of this disconnection are examined in the Conclusions to this book. There, I argue that fairness and rights should be more closely aligned in international criminal trials (particularly when considering procedural matters) and that there should be a renewed association between fairness and rights. I outline what this closer relationship might ensure in the trial process. In order to ensure the conceptual coherence of fairness, rights must be afforded a significant place in fairness considerations. As I demonstrate throughout this book, where 'fairness' is used as a rubric for decisions that ultimately undermine the rights of the accused, both fairness and rights suffer. Not only are the rights of the accused diminished, but the coherence of the concept of fairness is also challenged further. I also demonstrate the continuing relevance of this question of the relationship between fairness and rights and the importance of this question for the future of procedure in these trials.

This book, therefore, answers the question 'how are fairness and the rights of the accused connected in procedural decision-making in contemporary international criminal trials?' by demonstrating that fairness and rights are separable and separated in contemporary international criminal procedural decisions. While fairness, rights and procedure are closely linked in principle, and Trial Chambers are meant to 'ensure that a trial is fair . . . and conducted with full respect for the rights of the accused',[59] when procedural decisions are examined, we witness a separation between fairness and rights. This disconnection both emerges from and adds further to the conceptual incoherence of fairness. However, this separation is not consistent with the duties of a Trial Chamber or the appropriate aims of international criminal trials, and thus fairness and rights should be realigned to enjoy a closer connection.

---

[59] *ICTY Statute* Art 20; *Rome Statute* Art 64(2).

Chapter 1

The particular place of international criminal trials: aims and procedure

. . . rather like saying, "What is the aim of the universe?"[1]
– International criminal judge, when asked about
the aims of international criminal trials

Why do international criminal trials exist? In this chapter, I examine the aims of international criminal law in order to better understand the system of international criminal law, its institutions and its processes. Identifying the aspirations, values and underpinnings of international criminal law is key to analysing its achievements: does international criminal law do what it says it aims to? We can then move to a space of critical engagement and of examining structural causes for success and limitation. Analysing these aims is also crucial to securing a strong examination of international criminal procedure: without understanding the rationales behind international criminal law and its trials, it is difficult to understand their operation.

Given the centrality of aims to these questions of achievement and limitation, discussions around the aims of international criminal law have been persistent – and have only increased in recent years with the 'critical turn' of international criminal law scholarship.[2] However, as I show, this discourse regarding the aims of international criminal law and procedure suffers from a lack of clarity. In the first part of this chapter, I argue that there has been a conflation of three levels of analysis: the system of law, its institutions of courts and tribunals, and its trial processes. I argue that it is important to understand these as three separate levels of analysis – capable of supporting different aims or of supporting the same aims in different ways. This division into three levels of analysis (the system of law, its institutions and its trials), and sorting the aims against these levels, is a new way of understanding how international criminal law, and its aims, interact.

---

[1] Interview with Judge Adrian Fulford (5 June 2014).
[2] See, e.g., Pádraig McAuliffe and Christine Schwöbel-Patel, 'Disciplinary Matchmaking: Critics of International Criminal Law Meet Critics of Liberal Peacebuilding' (2018) 16(5) *JICJ* 985; Caleb H Wheeler, 'The Scales of Justice: Balancing the Goals of International Criminal Trials' (2019) 30 *CLF* 145; Darryl Robinson, 'Inescapable Dyads: Why the International Criminal Court Cannot Win' (2015) 28 *LJIL* 323; Barrie Sander, 'The Expressive Turn of International Criminal Justice: A Field in Search of Meaning' (2019) 32 *LJIL* 851; Sara Kendall, 'Commodifying Global Justice: Economics of Accountability at the International Criminal Court' (2015) 13 *JICJ* 113.

However, several of the aims that have been placed on the level of the trial are problematic; and in the second part of this chapter, I demonstrate this with reference to three aims: ending impunity, giving a meaningful voice to victims, and the search for the truth. In the final section of this chapter, I then argue that a recalibration of the aims of international criminal trials is needed and that the aims of the *trial* should properly emphasise the aim of a forensic determination of the accused's guilt or innocence. In this way, the individual accused is correctly placed at the heart of international criminal procedure.

A. THE AIMS OF INTERNATIONAL CRIMINAL LAW: VARIETY, DIVERGENCE AND PROMISES UNFULFILLED

As is frequently noted, there is a proliferation of aims of international criminal law. These include ending impunity, the restoration or maintenance of peace, reconciliation, giving victims a meaningful voice, deterrence, a socio-pedagogic or didactic function, ensuring an accurate historical record, and setting out the 'truth' of events.[3] The number of goals is partly due to the fact that international criminal law is given both 'classical domestic' and 'international' aims, and thus 'may have to deal even more than other branches of law with a functional problem of "goal variety" and "goal ambiguity"'.[4] As a system of law, international criminal law is very much a Western and liberal construct[5] but has been influenced by various approaches to justice – criminal, cosmopolitan and international justice, with elements of retributive, distributive and transitional justice.[6] These

---

[3] See Martti Koskenniemi, 'Between Impunity and Show Trials' (2002) 6 *Max Planck Yearbook of United Nations Law* 1; John Jackson, 'Finding the Best Epistemic Fit for International Criminal Tribunals: Beyond the Inquisitorial–Adversarial Dichotomy' (2009) 7 *JICJ* 17; Mirjan Damaška, 'The Competing Visions of Fairness: The Basic Choice for International Criminal Tribunals' (2001) 36 *NCJILCR* 365; Mark Klamberg, 'What are the Objectives of International Criminal Procedure? – Reflections on the Fragmentation of a Legal Regime' (2010) 79 *NJIL* 279; Bert Swart, 'Damaška and the Faces of International Criminal Justice' (2008) 6 *JICJ* 87; Minna Schrag, 'Lessons Learned from the ICTY Experience: Notes for the ICC Prosecutor' (2004) 2 *JICJ* 427. See also *Rome Statute of the International Criminal Court*, opened for signature 17 July 1998, 2187 UNTS 90 (entered into force 1 July 2002) ('*Rome Statute*') preamble; SC Res 827, UN SCOR, 48th sess, 3217th mtg, UN Doc S/RES/827 (25 May 1993), as amended by SC Res 1877, UN SCOR, 64th sess, 6155th mtg, UN Doc S/RES/1877 (7 July 2009) ('*ICTY Statute*') preamble.

[4] Carsten Stahn, 'Between "Faith" and "Facts": By What Standards Should We Assess International Criminal Justice?' (2012) 25 *LJIL* 251, 260. On 'goal ambiguity', see Yuval Shany, 'Assessing the effectiveness of International Courts: A Goal-based Approach' (2012) 106 *AJIL* 225, 233.

[5] See particularly Mark Drumbl, *Atrocity, Punishment and International Law* (CUP, 2007); Kamari Maxine Clarke, *Fictions of Justice: The International Criminal Court and the Challenge of Legal Pluralism in Sub-Saharan Africa* (CUP, 2010).

[6] See Frédéric Mégret, 'What Sort of Global Justice is "International Criminal Justice"?' (2015)

systemic ways of thinking about justice come with different approaches as to appropriate aims. Moreover, there has also been an increase in the expectations on international institutions, with original aims being modified or transcended.[7]

The aims of international criminal law also provide a narrative for this system of law and a way of explaining the value of international criminal law.[8] The system of international criminal law is reliant on the cooperation of states (notably for budgets, police, execution of warrants, and access to evidence and investigation sites). To convince these states, courts and tribunals must 'market' their own existence.[9] States need a reason to support international criminal law, and the aims of international criminal law provide such reasons.[10] There is, therefore, a clear overlap between the aims of international criminal law and the 'marketing' of international criminal law. A large and diverse number of aims will offer a greater range of reasons to support international criminal law.

Given the history, politics and structural characteristics of international criminal law, this abundance of aims – and a lack of consensus around which of them is to be emphasised – is perhaps unsurprising. However, these aims can compete and even diverge.[11] There is a lack of certainty around how these aims interact, which should be preeminent and whether any should be rejected or marginalised. Similar critiques have been made before. Mirjan Damaška argues that there is an overabundance of goals,

---

13(1) *JICJ* 77; Darryl Robinson, 'International Criminal Law as Justice' (2013) 11(2) *JICJ* 699; Sarah Nouwen and Wouter Werner, 'Monopolising Global Justice: International Criminal Law as Challenge to Human Diversity' (2015) 13 *JICJ* 157.

[7] Albin Eser, 'Procedural Structure and Features of International Criminal Justice: Lessons from the ICTY', in Bert Swart, Alexander Zahar and Göran Sluiter (eds), *The Legacy of the International Criminal Tribunal for the Former Yugoslavia* (OUP, 2011) 108, 113.

[8] Sophie Rigney, 'Postcard from the ICTY: Examining International Criminal Law's Narratives', in Daniel Joyce and Jessie Hohmann (eds) *International Law's Objects* (OUP, 2018).

[9] See Christine Schwöbel-Patel, *Marketing Global Justice: The Political Economy of International Criminal Law* (CUP, 2021); Christine Schwöbel, 'The Market and Marketing Culture of International Criminal Law' in Christine Schwöbel (ed), *Critical Approaches to International Criminal Law* (Routledge, 2014) 279; see also Rigney (n8); Sophie Rigney, 'You Start to Feel Really Alone: Defence Lawyers and Narratives of International Criminal Law in Film' (2018) 6(1) *LRIL* 97; Christine Schwöbel-Patel, 'The "Ideal" Victim of International Criminal Law' (2018) 29(3) *EJIL* 703.

[10] Rigney (n 8) 369.

[11] See e.g. Carsten Stahn, *A Critical Introduction to International Criminal Justice* (CUP, 2018) 173–182. Robinson has noted that the discourse surrounding the ICC suffers from a pattern where 'many of the arguments reflect underlying inescapable dyads. For any position the Court can possibly take, perfectly plausible and powerful criticisms can inevitably be made' (Robinson (n 2) 323–4). Yet Phil Clark argues that this framing, far from meaning the court 'can't win', rather means that the court 'can't lose' (Phil Clark, *Distant Justice: The Impact of the International Criminal Court on African Politics* (CUP, 2018) 23–5).

internal tensions between the goals, and an absence of a ranking order.[12] Such issues may result in 'disparities between aspiration and achievement', which may damage the reputation of international criminal justice.[13] Moreover, because aims influence processes, such ambiguity will affect the operation of the international criminal legal system, its institutions and its trials. While a variety of aims does not necessarily suggest a lack of certainty, there must be a shared appreciation of how this multiplicity of aims interact. If there is a variety of aims but no taxonomy, ranking order, or other organisational structure to understand the relationship between these aims, there is likely to be uncertainty in how the system, institutions and trials operate. As Damaška points out, 'until greater clarity is achieved about the proper mission of international criminal courts, a secure foothold will be missing for the legal-technical analysis of many aspects of their procedures'.[14] In addition, I argue that there is also a lack of nuanced thinking about how the aims of the system of law, the institutions of that system, and the processes of that system (namely trials) can be different and operate in different ways. I now turn to that argument.

B. THE AIMS OF THE LEGAL SYSTEM; THE AIMS OF THE INSTITUTIONS; THE AIMS OF THE TRIAL PROCESS

There is a need for greater clarity around how the aims of the system of international criminal law may differ from those of the specific institutions and of the trials themselves. While it is both possible and necessary to differentiate the aims of the three levels of analysis, the literature on international criminal law's aims tends to conflate them. In the discourses of international criminal law, institutions and trials, there are slippages between law and institutions, law and trial, and trial and courts. I argue that the discourses surrounding international criminal law, and its aims, can be improved by an understanding of the system of law, the institutions of law, and the processes of law (trials) as being distinct levels of analysis. By separating out the three levels, we can examine the various aims of these levels with more clarity, and we can analyse how those aims operate at the particular level of system, institution or process. This permits an improved understanding of what international criminal law should aspire to and is capable of achieving.

---

[12] Mirjan Damaška, 'What is the Point of International Criminal Justice?' (2008) 83 *CKLR* 329. See also Schrag (n 3); Jackson (n 3) 22. Alexander Heinze reconceptualises some of these as 'goals' and some as 'purposes': Alexander Heinze, 'Bridge over Troubled Water – a Semantic Approach to Purposes and Goals in International Criminal Justice' (2018) 18 *ICLR* 929.

[13] Mirjan Damaška, 'The International Criminal Court between Aspiration and Achievement' (2009) 14 *JILFA* 19.

[14] Mirjan Damaška, 'Problematic Features of International Criminal Procedure', Antonio Cassese (ed), *The Oxford Companion to International Criminal Justice* (OUP, 2009) 175, 175.

Because the system of law, the institutions of law (the courts and tribunals), and the processes of law (trials) undertake different functions and operate in different ways, it is important to conceive of them as separate levels of analysis. Trials are just one function of the system of law, and an international criminal trial is properly construed to be located *within* the system of international criminal law and is *implemented* by the institution of the court or tribunal. Indeed, the system of international criminal law, and the institutions of international criminal law, both operate in ways other than just undertaking trials. The system of law has functions that include improving domestic criminal legal systems (through the recognition of international criminal law in these domestic jurisdictions) and creating the law and institutions of the system (such as the drafting of the *Rome Statute*). Among other functions, the institutions of international criminal law investigate situations and individuals (and perhaps decide not to proceed with prosecution), create law, engage in didactic functions through outreach programs, and sometimes provide reparations to victims. Therefore, the trial is only part of the whole, and as such, should not be expected to meet all the aims of the system. Under this model, there is no cascade of aims from the system level to the trial level. However, this does not suggest that the system is fractured or malfunctioning: rather, I would argue that this is evidence that there should be greater clarity around the differences between the existence of the system and how it operates.

An example of this slippage in the discourse between system, institution and process, is found in Damaška's 'What is the Point of International Criminal Justice?' The title of this article suggests an examination of the system of law, but Damaška repeatedly refers to the aims of 'international criminal courts'. This blurring between system and institution level can be seen in this quote:

> Unlike Atlas, international criminal *courts* are not bodies of titanic strength, capable of carrying on their shoulders the burden of so many tasks. Even national *systems of criminal justice*, with their far greater enforcement powers and institutional support, would stagger under this load.[15]

Damaška then continues, discussing the objectives of courts but in fact, referring to court processes – that is, trials. Yet Damaška does not differentiate between the system of law, the institutions and the processes; rather, he deals with them all under the rubric of 'courts'.

There are some notable exceptions to the general conflation of these levels in the literature. Bert Swart differentiates between the aims of the macro and micro levels of international criminal justice. At the macro level, Swart argues, 'the ability of a system of criminal justice to reach its proffered goals depends on such factors as its general ability to investigate and

---

[15] Damaška (n 12) 331 (emphasis added).

adjudicate cases effectively'.[16] At the micro-level, the question is 'whether, and to what extent, the proffered goals are being pursued in each individual case'.[17] This analysis helps us understand the system of international criminal law, and the trial itself, as being different levels of analysis. Yet Swart sees the goals at these two levels as being the same. I argue that this can be refined further – to acknowledge that the different levels of system and trial (and also, in my argument, institutions) may have different aims.

Albin Eser advances Swart's analysis, noting that certain aims might be appropriate 'at the macro level of international criminal justice as an institution, whereas others have to be pursued on the micro level of the individual proceeding'.[18] However, Eser – in adopting Swart's macro and micro approach and in referring to 'international criminal justice as an institution' – conflates what I see as separate levels of analysis: the system of law, and its institutions.

Eser continues, distinguishing the aims, means ('the measures and instruments by which these goals are reached') and modes ('the ways in which it is to be done') of international criminal justice.[19] In this way, Eser articulates that 'what might be a direct aim of the individual trial, such as to punish an accused who has been found guilty, is an aim that can at the same time be a means of enforcing international law and paving the way for the reconciliation and lasting peace which the tribunal is for'.[20] Thus, Eser sees the aims of the trial as having an instrumental purpose towards achieving the aims of the institution/system.

Eser's conflation of institution and system is further seen in his sorting between aims, means and modes.[21] He describes eighteen aims as being vested with both the 'macro' level of institution/system and the 'micro' level of proceedings (suggesting a slippage between different levels of analysis).[22] He argues that the 'search for truth' and 'giving the victim a voice' are key 'means' to achieve these eighteen aims of international criminal justice: they are therefore not themselves aims of international criminal law or institutions, but rather ways of achieving the aims of international criminal justice.[23] Eser ultimately advocates for the adjustment of trial procedures to meet the preeminent aims of 'international criminal justice'. In his view, while each and every individual trial may not be able to 'render victim

---

[16] Bert Swart, 'International Criminal Justice and Models of Traditional Process' in Göran Sluiter and Sergey Vasiliev (eds), *International Criminal Procedure: Towards a Coherent Body of Law* (Cameron May, 2009) 93, 103. See also Swart (n 3) 101.

[17] Ibid.

[18] Eser (n 7) 115. See also Klamberg (n 3).

[19] Eser (n 7) 115.

[20] Ibid.

[21] Ibid. 115–16.

[22] Ibid.

[23] Ibid. 116.

satisfaction or contribute to the restoration of peace, the pursuit of such aims should be kept alive by the procedure or, at least, not obstructed by it'.[24] As discussed further below, I disagree with Eser on this conclusion and rather advocate that the aim *of the trial* should be recalibrated to focus on the determination of the guilt of the accused, which need not necessarily 'keep alive' (and therefore be subservient to) these other aims.

It is therefore possible – and necessary – to refine Swart and Eser's arguments. I argue that the three levels of system of law, institutions (namely the courts and tribunals themselves) and processes (trials) can have different aims, and that aims common to two or three of those levels may nevertheless operate differently at the different levels. If we accept this argument, it becomes possible to analyse international criminal law's aims in a more nuanced manner. Aims are liberated from the assumption that they must operate on all three levels in much the same way. Similarly, the different levels of analysis are liberated from the expectation that they must strive to meet all these aims.

To contextualise this argument, it is important to examine some of the aims of international criminal law, and how they may operate in different ways at the levels of the system of law, institutions and (trial) process. Many of the aims of international criminal law can be readily critiqued: for example, there is no hard evidence that deterrence actually works,[25] and nor is it established that these trials, in fact, advance reconciliation.[26] However, here I offer an analysis of three of the major aims of international criminal law: ending impunity, offering a meaningful voice for victims, and establishing the truth. These three aims are regularly invoked as being the most important or 'guiding' aims of international criminal law and have also been described as aims of the institutions of the courts and tribunals and of international criminal trials. In relation to each of these aims, my critique focuses on their role *as aims of the trial*. While ending impunity, providing a meaningful voice for victims, and ascertaining the truth, may all be galvanizing aims for the system of international criminal law, I argue

---

[24] Ibid. 120.

[25] See Mark Drumbl, 'Collective Violence and Individual Punishment: The Criminality of Mass Atrocity' (2005) 99 *NULR* 539, 548; Danilo Zolo, 'Peace through Criminal Law?' (2004) 2 *JICJ* 727; Immi Tallgren, 'Sensibility and Sense of International Criminal Law' (2002) 13 *EJIL* 561; Kate Cronin-Furman and Amanda Taub, 'Lions and Tigers and Deterrence, Oh My: Evaluating Expectations of International Criminal Justice' in William A Schabas, Yvonne McDermott and Niamh Hayes (eds), *The Ashgate Research Companion to International Criminal Law* (Ashgate, 2013) 435; Kate Cronin-Furman 'Managing Expectations: International Criminal Trials and the Prospects for Deterrence of Mass Atrocity' (2013) 7(3) *IJTJ* 434; Jennifer Schense and Linda Carter (eds), *Two Steps Forward, One Step Back: The Deterrent Effect of International Criminal Tribunals* (International Nuremberg Principles Academy, 2016).

[26] See Janine Natalya Clark, *International Trials and Reconciliation: Assessing the Impact of the International Criminal Tribunal for the Former Yugoslavia* (Routledge, 2014).

that they need not – and should not – be the aims of what that system and its institutions do: namely, the trials themselves.

(1) Ending impunity

The aim of ending impunity is writ large in international criminal justice. The Statutes of the different courts and tribunals mandate these institutions with a *raison d'être* of ending impunity.[27] Despite the prominence of the ending impunity aim in international criminal justice, definitions of the term are scarce.[28] However, impunity can be understood as 'the impossibility . . . of bringing the perpetrators of violence to account . . . since they are not subject to any inquiry that might lead to their being accused, arrested, tried and, if found guilty, sentenced to appropriate penalties, and to making reparations to their victims'.[29] Thus, the aim to end impunity can be explained as the desire to ensure that perpetrators are held to account for their actions through investigation, trial and punishment. However, the rationale of ending impunity poses a particular challenge for international criminal law: while ending impunity may be a worthwhile aim for the international criminal law system, using trials to achieve this – and vesting the ending impunity aim in the trial itself – is problematic. The ending impunity aim, if placed upon the trial process, leads to an impetus to prosecute and convict: something which is challenging when considered against the presumption of innocence, a central principle governing the trial.

The aim of ending impunity emphasises criminalisation, and criminal law, as the most appropriate mechanisms to address atrocities. There is no real acknowledgement of the limitations and problems associated with systems of punishment. As any failure to prosecute – either passive (for example, neglecting to investigate) or active (such as the use of amnesties) – signals impunity, the focus on ending impunity pushes the atrocities into the realm of criminal law. At the ICC, this emphasis on prosecution is linked to the principle of complementarity, where a case is inadmissible before the ICC if 'the case is being investigated or prosecuted by a State which has jurisdiction over it, unless the State is unwilling or unable genuinely to carry out the investigation or prosecution'.[30] To determine 'willing-

---

[27] *Rome Statute*, preamble; *ICTY Statute*, preamble. See also Koskenniemi (n 3); Jackson (n 3) 20; Mirjan Damaška, 'Reflections on Fairness in International Criminal Justice' (2012) 10 *JICJ* 611, 613.

[28] Lionel Nichols, *The International Criminal Court and The End of Impunity in Kenya* (Springer, 2015) 12.

[29] United Nations Economic and Social Commission on Human Rights, *Report of the Independent Expert to Update the Set of Principles to Combat Impunity*, E/CN.4/2005/102/Add.1 (8 February 2005).

[30] *Rome Statute* Art 17. For a comprehensive examination of the principle of complementarity at the ICC, and its unintended consequences, see Clark (n 11).

ness', the Court may also examine whether any prosecution or decision was undertaken 'for the purposes of shielding the person' from criminal responsibility.[31] Thus, a lack of prosecution (or a 'toothless' prosecution) at a national level may permit the admissibility of the case before the ICC. It is unclear whether other processes (such as Truth Commissions) would be sufficient to render the case inadmissible at the ICC, given the emphasis on prosecution.[32]

Once a prosecution is undertaken, ending impunity is inherently linked to securing a conviction. As impunity connotes an exemption from punishment – which only comes after a finding of guilt – ending impunity is tied to conviction. Indeed, international criminal law is a system that 'thrives on conviction'.[33] In this way, *conviction* becomes integral to the aims of international criminal law. As Damaška notes, given the central position of ending impunity in international criminal law, 'high acquittal rates could easily augur failure of [the courts'] mission'.[34] He instead advocates an 'abandonment, or relaxation, of some cherished domestic procedural arrangements', because international criminal justice must be 'responsive to the more challenging international environment' and 'international criminal courts cannot successfully pursue their manifold objectives by strictly abiding by most demanding domestic rules of procedure'.[35]

Furthermore, the ICC has a system of reparations, where the institution can order for payments to be made by the convicted person to the victims of the case – but these reparations proceedings only occur after a criminal conviction of the accused.[36] There is, therefore, an additional impetus to convict: victims can only receive reparations if the threshold condition of a 'guilty' verdict is reached. In theory, this satisfies the notion that an accused cannot be punished (in the form of paying in reparation) unless they are guilty; moreover, reparations proceedings also align with the aim of providing justice for victims. Holding reparations proceedings as a separate process after the trial also theoretically separates reparations from the aims of the trial itself. Nonetheless, this system also shows a structural incentive

---

[31] Ibid.
[32] See Diba Majzub, 'Peace or Justice?: Amnesties and the International Criminal Court' (2002) 3(2) *MJIL* 247; see also Clark (n 11), particularly Chapter 6.
[33] William A Schabas, 'Balancing the Rights of the Accused with the Imperatives of Accountability' in Ramesh Thakur and Peter Malcontent (eds), *From Sovereign Impunity to International Accountability: The Search for Justice in a World of States* (United Nations University Press, 2004) 154, 165.
[34] Damaška (n 27) 613; see also Douglas Guilfoyle, 'Lacking Conviction: Is the International Criminal Court Broken?' (2019) 20(2) *MJIL* 401.
[35] Damaška (n 27) 612; see also Damaška (n 3) 376.
[36] See *Rome Statute* Art 75. On reparations generally, see Luke Moffett and Clara Sandoval, 'Tilting at windmills: Reparations and the International Criminal Court' (2021) *LJIL* 1; Luke Moffett, 'Reparations for victims at the International Criminal Court: a new way forward?' (2017) 21(9) *IJHR* 1204.

towards conviction at trial, further bolstering the aim of 'ending impunity'. If victims cannot receive meaningful reparations without a guilty verdict, this strengthens the motivation for convictions.

Despite these motivations towards conviction apparently embedded in the structure of international criminal law, there is nonetheless a tension between an emphasis on conviction and the reality of criminal trials. While the call to end impunity has come to be equated with conviction, trials can result in acquittals. Indeed, sometimes acquittals may be the only appropriate outcome. Unless they are 'more show than trial', the accused retains the presumption of innocence,[37] and the standard that necessitates proof of guilt 'beyond a reasonable doubt' means that guilt must be established to a high standard.[38] If this cannot be discharged, the presumption of innocence remains, and an acquittal must follow. While ending impunity forces a resort to criminal law to address mass atrocities, criminal law necessarily involves the potential for acquittals. The emphasis on conviction at the level of the system of international criminal law, and the potential for acquittal at the trial level of international criminal law, form a tense relationship.

This tension between the desire to convict and the possibility of acquittal can be seen in the use of Regulation 55 at the ICC to 'recharacterise' the charges against the accused during, or even after, the trial. Pursuant to Regulation 55, judges may 'change the legal characterisation of facts to accord with the crimes under Articles 6, 7 or 8, or to accord with the form of participation of the accused under Articles 25 and 28, without exceeding the facts and circumstances described in the charges and any amendments to the charges'.[39] Regulation 55 was adopted by the ICC judges in 2004 and was designed to promote judicial efficiency.[40] It was also intended to avoid acquittals due to technicalities, or in a situation where 'the prosecution's

---

[37] ICTY *Statute* Art 21(3); *Rome Statute* Art 66.

[38] However, see concerns voiced by Simon De Smet (that there is a lack of certainty about what the standard 'beyond reasonable doubt' means) and Nancy Combs (that the judgments of international criminal trials rest on unsatisfactory epistemological grounds): Simon De Smet, 'The International Criminal Standard of Proof at the ICC – Beyond Reasonable Doubt or Beyond Reason?' in Carsten Stahn (ed), *The Law and Practice of the International Criminal Court: A Critical Account of Challenges and Achievements* (OUP, 2015) 861; Nancy Combs, *Fact Finding Without Facts: The Uncertain Evidentiary Foundations of International Criminal Convictions* (CUP, 2010); Nancy Combs, 'Deconstructing the Epistemic Challenges to Mass Atrocity Prosecutions' (2018) 75 *WLLR* 223.

[39] International Criminal Court, *Regulations of the Court*, Doc No ICC-BD/01-01-04 (adopted 26 May 2004) r 55(1) ('*ICC Regulations*').

[40] Jennifer Easterday, 'A Closer Look at Regulation 55 at the ICC' on *International Justice Monitor* (28 May 2013) <http://www.ijmonitor.org/2013/05/a-closer-look-at-regulation-55 -at-the-icc/> (last accessed 9 December 2021). See also *Prosecutor v Katanga, Jugement rendu en application de l'article 74 du Statut* (ICC-01/04-01/07, 7 March 2014) [10] (Judge Van den Wyngaert) ('*Katanga Judgment*'); *Prosecutor v Lubanga, Judgment on the Appeals of Mr Lubanga Dyilo and the Prosecutor Against the Decision of Trial Chamber I of 14 July 2009* (ICC-01/04-01/06 OA 15 OA 16, 8 December 2009) [71].

charges do not match the facts heard at trial'[41] and where there is proof beyond a reasonable doubt that the accused has committed a crime within the ICC's jurisdiction, although the prosecution has failed to charge the accused with that particular crime.[42] Thus, Regulation 55 allows the trial chamber to 'fill' such an undesirable impunity gap.

Regulation 55 was used to recharacterise the mode of liability of the charges against Germain Katanga.[43] Here, the use of Regulation 55 resulted in the conviction of the accused where, otherwise, it is likely that he would have been acquitted alongside his co-accused.[44] The prosecutor had failed to prove any of the charges against Katanga as they had been initially formulated,[45] and Katanga was convicted only of charges that were never laid by the prosecution. If ending impunity was the aim imposed on the trial, this case could be measured as a success. However, as I show in Chapter Three, there are significant concerns around the rights of the accused in this case and how those rights relate to the fairness of the trial. In closing the 'impunity gap' through the use of Regulation 55, the Court has prioritised ending impunity as a key goal of the trial process. Nevertheless, the criticisms of this majority judgment (in the dissent of Judge Christine Van den Wyngaert and by academics)[46] show the strain between the ending impunity goal and the criminal process and demonstrate that ending impunity cannot properly be a goal of the trial itself.

The conflict between the possibility of acquittal and the aim of ending impunity leads to a further source of tension. While human rights advocates have traditionally been critical of deficiencies in criminal legal processes in the domestic context, in the international realm, the call for ending impunity is so seductive that many human rights advocates consider conviction a noble aim. As William Schabas correctly articulates, there has been a shift in human rights law and advocacy 'from a defence-based to a

---

[41] Easterday (n 40).

[42] The regulation was also intended to avoid any overburdening that might occur from cumulative or alternative charging: Easterday (n 40); Carsten Stahn, 'Modification of the Legal Characterisation of Facts in the ICC System: A Portrayal of Regulation 55' (2005) 16 CLF 1,3.

[43] *Prosecutor v Katanga, Decision on the Implementation of Regulation 55 of the Regulations of the Court and Severing the Charges against the Accused Persons* (ICC-01/04-01/07, 21 November 2012); *Katanga Judgment*; Sophie Rigney, '"The Words Don't Fit You": Recharacterisation of the Charges, Trial Fairness, and Katanga' (2014) 15 *MJIL* 515.

[44] *Prosecutor v Ngudjolo, Judgment pursuant to Article 74 of the Statute* (ICC-01/04-02/12, 18 December 2012).

[45] See Kevin Heller, 'Another Terrible Day for the OTP' on *Opinio Juris* (8 March 2014) <http://opiniojuris.org/2014/03/08/another-terrible-day-otp/> (last accessed 9 December 2021); *Katanga Judgment* ([1] (Judge Van den Wyngaert).

[46] *Katanga Judgment* (Judge Van den Wyngaert); Dov Jacobs, 'The ICC Katanga Judgment: A Commentary (Part 3)', *Spreading the Jam* (12 March 2014) <http://dovjacobs.com/2014/03/12/the-icc-katanga-judgment-a-commentary-part-3-some-final-thoughts-on-its-legacy/> (last accessed 9 December 2021); Heller (n 45).

prosecution-based perspective',[47] and 'whereas in the past human rights law sought to protect the rights of the accused without real regard to guilt or innocence, it is now torn by another extreme, one that is orientated towards the victim and that thrives upon conviction'.[48] Indeed, the rhetoric of ending impunity has risen, particularly since the 1990s, when 'much human rights advocacy moved from naming, shaming, and sometimes judicially trying states for their violations of human rights to finding ways to hold individuals criminally responsible for them'.[49] We can see this shift in the fact that many civil society actors welcomed the conviction of Katanga,[50] despite the concerns that his rights had been violated.

Another example is the way that some human rights organisations heralded[51] the ICC's decision that Libya is both able and willing to try the case of Abdullah Al-Senussi, despite the fact that it is unlikely that Al-Senussi will receive a fair trial, with full respect afforded to his rights, in Libya.[52] Indeed, the issue of complementarity – whether the ICC determines that a national jurisdiction is willing and able to investigate and prosecute an

---

[47] Schabas (n 33) 155.

[48] Ibid. 165.

[49] Karen Engle, 'Anti-Impunity and the Turn to Criminal Law in Human Rights Law and Advocacy' (2015) 100 *CLR* 1070, 1071.

[50] See, e.g., Amnesty International, 'DRC/ICC: Katanga Found Guilty of War Crimes and Crimes Against Humanity' (7 March 2014) <http://amnesty.org/en/news/drcicc-katanga-f ound-guilty-war-crimes-and-crimes-against-humanity-2014-03-07> (last accessed 20 March 2020) and Coalition for the ICC, 'Qualified welcome for ICC's Katanga conviction' (20 March 2014), <https://www.coalitionfortheicc.org/news/20140320/qualified-welcome-iccs -katanga-conviction> (last accessed 9 December 2021). There were also organisations who criticised the judgment on the basis of Katanga's acquittal for crimes of sexual violence; see, e.g., Women's Initiatives for Gender Justice, 'Partial Conviction of Katanga by ICC, Acquittals for Sexual Violence and Use of Child Soldiers' (7 March 2014) <http://www.iccw omen.org/images/Katanga-Judgement-Statement-corr.pdf> (last accessed 9 December 2021).

[51] No Peace Without Justice, 'Libya: NPWJ and NRPTT Welcome ICC Ruling on the Al-Senussi Case, which Heralds New Potential for Justice and Strengthening Human Rights Protection' (24 July 2014), <http://www.npwj.org/ICC/Libya-NPWJ-and-NRPTT-welco me-ICC-ruling-Al-Senussi-case-which-heralds-new-potential-justice-and-> (last accessed 9 December 2021). Other organisations expressed concern at the decision, with Amnesty International going so far as to 'deplore' it: Amnesty International, 'Public Statement: ICC Decision to Allow Abdullah al-Senussi to Stand Trial in Libya "Deeply Alarming" Amidst Overwhelming Security Vacuum' (24 July 2014) <https://www.refworld.org/docid/53d23b5 b4.html> (last accessed 9 December 2021). See also Human Rights Watch 'Libya: ICC Judges Reject Sanussi Appeal' (24 July 2014) <https://www.hrw.org/news/2014/07/24/libya-icc -judges-reject-sanussi-appeal> (last accessed 9 December 2021).

[52] Jonathan O'Donohue and Sophie Rigney, 'The ICC Must Consider Fair Trial Concerns in Determining Libya's Application to Prosecute Saif al-Islam Gaddafi Nationally' (8 June 2012) *EJIL Talk!* <http://www.ejiltalk.org/the-icc-must-consider-fair-trial-concerns-in-determining-libyas-application-to-prosecute-saif-al-islam-gaddafi-nationally/> (last accessed 9 December 2021). But see Frédéric Mégret and Marika Giles Samson, 'Holding the Line on Complementarity in Libya: The Case for Tolerating Flawed Domestic Trials' (2013) 11 *JICJ* 571.

accused – and fair trial rights is vexed for human rights advocates. This is what Kevin Heller has called the 'shadow side' of complementarity, where any deferrals to a national jurisdiction 'will expose perpetrators to national judicial systems that are far less likely than the ICC to provide them with due process, increasing the probability of wrongful convictions'.[53] Despite some calls for the rights of the accused to be taken into account when determining the willingness and ability of a state to try the accused,[54] the ICC has declined to do so. Indeed, in the Al-Senussi case, the Chamber found that although Al-Senussi had not benefitted from his right to legal assistance at the investigation stage, this was not enough to justify a finding of unwillingness of Libya to investigate or prosecute him (and thus not sufficient for the case to be admissible at the ICC).[55] Where the ending impunity aim is imposed at the level of the trial, there is a challenge in ensuring the rights of the accused are protected.

It may be argued that the ICC's patchy record of convictions is evidence that there is no 'ending impunity' aim at the ICC. Indeed, the ICC currently has a far greater number of cases that have resulted in the accused being free than cases where convictions have been secured. There have only been four individual convictions for 'core crimes'. Conversely, there have been acquittals of four individuals,[56] charges vacated or withdrawn against four individuals,[57] charges not confirmed against four individuals,[58] and the case

[53] Kevin Jon Heller, 'The Shadow Side of Complementarity: The Effect of Article 17 of the *Rome Statute* on National Due Process' (2006) CLF 255, 256. See also Kevin Heller, 'Radical Complementarity' (2016) 14(3) *JICJ* 637; Clark (n 11).

[54] See O'Donohue and Rigney (n 52).

[55] *Prosecutor v Gaddafi, Decision on the Admissibility of the Case against Abdullah Al-Senussi* (ICC-01/11-01/11, 11 October 2013) [292].

[56] These were in the cases of *Ngudjolo Judgment; Prosecutor v Bemba Gombo, Judgment on the appeal of Mr Jean-Pierre Bemba Gombo against Trial Chamber III's "Judgment pursuant to Article 74 of the Statute"* (ICC-01/05-01/08-3636-Red, 8 June 2018) ('*Bemba Appeals Judgment*'); *Prosecutor v Gbagbo, Delivery of Decision* (ICC-02/11-01/15, 16 January 2019); *Prosecutor v Gbagbo, Reasons for Oral Decision of 15 January 2019 on the Requête de la Défense de Laurent Gbagbo afin qu'un jugement d'acquittement portant sur toutes les charges soit prononcé en faveur de Laurent Gbagbo et que sa mise en liberté immédiate soit ordonnée, and on the Blé Goudé Defence No Case to Answer Motion* (ICC-02/11-01/15, 16 July 2019) ('*Gbagbo Decision*').

[57] *Prosecutor v Muthaura and Kenyatta, Decision on the withdrawal of charges against Mr Muthaura* (ICC-01/09-02/11-696, 18 March 2013); *Prosecutor v Kenyatta*, 'Notice of withdrawal of the charges against Uhuru Muigai Kenyatta' (ICC-01/09-02/11-983, 5 December 2014); *Prosecutor v Ruto and Sang, Decision on Defence Applications for Judgments of Acquittal* (ICC-01/09-01/11, 5 April 2016).

[58] *Prosecutor v Mbarushimana, Decision on the Confirmation of Charges* (ICC-01/04-01/10, 16 December 2011); *Prosecutor v Abu Garda, Decision on the Confirmation of Charges* (ICC-02/05-02/09, 8 February 2010); *Prosecutor v Ruto, Decision on the Confirmation of Charges Pursuant to Article 61(7)(a) and (b) of the Rome Statute* (ICC-001/09-01/11, 23 January 2012); *Prosecutor v Kenyatta, Decision on the Confirmation of Charges Pursuant to Article 61(7)(a) and (b) of the Rome Statute* (ICC-001/09-02/11, 23 January 2012).

against one individual held to be inadmissible.[59] Controversial acquittals have included that of Jean-Pierre Bemba Gombo, whose trial conviction was overturned by a majority of the Appeals Chamber on 8 June 2018.[60] These acquittals could be said to suggest that 'ending impunity' is not a primary goal of international criminal law.

But again, this would be to confuse the levels of system, institution and trial. Simply because some trials do not result in convictions, we cannot speculate on the goals at the level of the system of law. Structurally, the call for 'ending impunity' can – and does – remain. I have already outlined that this sits uneasily with the reality of trials, which can result in acquittals. And, of course, just because an aim is not fulfilled or achieved, it does not follow that the aim does not exist. It may simply be a failure to achieve that aim: certainly, it can be argued that these acquittals, unconfirmed cases and withdrawn charges are primarily because the prosecution has not been adequately undertaking its mandate.

Moreover, while some might see the Bemba acquittal as suggesting no 'ending impunity' bias in international criminal law, others could argue that the acquittal on Appeal, in fact, *shows* that the conviction at trial was emblematic of a rush to conviction at trial. As we will examine in greater detail in Chapter Three, the Trial Decision was problematic; and it is likely, for example, that the majority judges on appeal (notably Van den Wyngaert and Morrison) would see their decision as righting a wrong.[61] Similarly, while the Gbagbo decision of 'no case to answer' is excluded from this study,[62] it is worth briefly noting that the Pre-Trial decision in 2014 to confirm the case has been robustly criticised and can be read as the Pre-Trial Chamber providing the prosecution with 'a series of second chances' which ultimately permitted a case to continue for years where the crimes could not be linked to the defendant.[63] On this reading, then, there was an impetus to continue prosecution – arguably linked to a structural aim towards 'ending impunity' – despite what would ultimately prove an overwhelming lack of evidence.

---

[59] *Prosecutor v Gaddafi, Decision on the Admissibility of the Case against Abdullah Al-Senussi* (ICC-01/11-01/11, 11 October 2013).

[60] *Bemba Appeals Judgment.* See also Richard Goldstone, 'Acquittals by the International Criminal Court', *EJILTalk!* (18 January 2019), <https://www.ejiltalk.org/acquittals-by-the-international-criminal-court/> (last accessed 9 December 2021).

[61] *Bemba Appeals Judgment*, Separate Opinion of Judge Van den Wyngaert and Judge Morrison.

[62] *Gbagbo Decision.*

[63] Guilfoyle (n 34) 420 and 430. Others were unsurprised by the acquittal: see Thijs Bouwknegt, 'Gbagbo: An Acquittal Foretold', Justiceinfo.net (News Post, 31 January 2019), <https://www.justiceinfo.net/en/tribunals/icc/40156-gbagbo-an-acquittal-foretold.html> (last accessed 9 December 2021). See also *Gbagbo Reasons for Oral Decision* annex B [78], [87], [91] (Judge Henderson), annex A [15], [51] (Judge Tarfusser).

These challenges demonstrate the problems associated with vesting the goal of ending impunity on international criminal trials. Ending impunity may operate at the system level of international criminal law as a key *raison d'être* of the system. It may even operate at the level of the institution as a rationale for the existence of the particular court or tribunal. However, ending impunity should not be an aim of the court's activities – and particularly, the aim of the trial process. More than a normative claim, it is also true that – unless the trials are closer to show trials, where a finding of guilt is assured – it is not possible for ending impunity to be a galvanising aim at the trial level of international criminal law. If ending impunity is placed as a key aim of international criminal trial processes, then the rights of the accused may be placed in jeopardy and even 'balanced away' in the pressure to convict.[64]

(2) Meaningful voice for victims

The aim of providing a meaningful voice for victims in international criminal trials has become an 'ennobling ambition' of international criminal law.[65] The reasons supporting this aim are understandable and routinely articulated.[66] The ICC is the first institution to allow victims to participate formally in proceedings (rather than only appearing as witnesses, as in earlier institutions),[67] and this has placed victim participation at the heart of ICC trials.[68] As a result, a new procedural regime has emerged at the ICC, to address the 'how' of victim participation. However, significant critiques of this aim can be made. Here, I focus on two arguments: first, that the aim of providing a meaningful voice for victims is not presently being achieved in the trial process; and second, that the current structure of victim participation facilitates a hierarchy of victimisation that can be disempowering for victims. I argue that the aim of 'meaningful victim participation' is not being achieved, and in fact, there are significant challenges, even for the victims themselves.

In the ICC trial process, victims are not a party to the trial[69] and are

---

[64] For more on the 'balancing away' of the defence, see Dov Jacobs, 'Neither here nor there: the position of the defence in International Criminal Trials', in Kevin Heller et al. (eds), *The Oxford Handbook of International Criminal Law* (OUP, 2020) 67, 82.

[65] Damaška (n 3) 372.

[66] See Christine Van den Wyngaert, 'Victims before International Criminal Courts: Some Views and Concerns of an ICC Trial Judge' (2011) 44 *CWRJIL* 475; Mariana Pena and Gaelle Carayon, 'Is the ICC Making the Most of Victim Participation?' (2013) 7 *IJTJ* 518; Luke Moffet, *Justice for Victims Before the International Criminal Court* (Routledge, 2014).

[67] Salvatore Zappalà, 'The Rights of Victims v the Rights of the Accused' (2010) 8 *JICJ* 137, 137–8.

[68] *Rome Statute* Art 68(3).

[69] See *Situation in the Democratic Republic of the Congo, Decision on the Application for Participation in Proceedings of VPRS1, VPRS 2-3-4-5-6* (ICC-01/04, 17 January 2006) [51].

understood to be motivated by different aims than the prosecution.[70] However, victims may gain the status of participants at trial.[71] The modalities of how this participation will take place are left to each individual Trial Chamber,[72] but judges have generally provided quite a broad interpretation to this provision.[73] The court has interpreted the object and purpose of Article 68(3) and the relevant *Rules*[74] to be to 'provide victims with a meaningful role in criminal proceedings before the Court . . . so that they can have a substantial impact in the proceedings'.[75] The requirement of meaningfulness is thus central to the participation itself.[76]

Yet significant barriers have ensured that the aim of 'meaningful victim participation' is not presently being achieved. One critique has been made by Christine Van den Wyngaert, writing extra-judicially but drawing on observations from her time as a judge at both the ICTY and ICC.[77] She notes concerns regarding the relationship between victims and truth-finding, the potentially negative effects of victim participation on the rights of the accused, and the sustainability of the system of victim participation.[78] Importantly, Van den Wyngaert also remains unconvinced that victim participation is meaningful for victims.[79] Victim participants themselves rarely appear in the trial (unless they are also appearing as witnesses), with their participation instead mediated through legal representatives.[80] But these lawyers – often located thousands of kilometres away and representing potentially hundreds of victim participants – may never receive detailed

---

[70] See Peter Morrissey, 'Applied Rights in International Criminal Law: Defence Counsel and the Right to Disclosure' in Gideon Boas, William A Schabas and Michael P Scharf (eds), *International Criminal Justice: Legitimacy and Coherence* (Edward Elgar, 2012) 68, 83.

[71] *Rome Statute* Art 68(3).

[72] Claus Kress, 'The Procedural Law of the International Criminal Court in Outline: Anatomy of a Unique Compromise' (2003) 1 *JICJ* 603, 605–6; Van den Wyngaert (n 66) 478.

[73] Van den Wyngaert (n 66) 483.

[74] International Criminal Court, *Rules of Procedure and Evidence*, Doc No ICC-ASP/1/3 (adopted 9 September 2002) ('ICC Rules') rr 91 and 92.

[75] *Prosecutor v Katanga, Decision on the Set of Procedural Rights Attached to Procedural Status of Victims at the Pre-Trial Stage of a Case* (ICC-01/04-01/07-474, 13 May 2008) [157]. See generally at [153]–[164]. See also *Prosecutor v Lubanga, Judgment on the Appeals of the Prosecutor and the Defence against Trial Chamber I's Decision on Victims' Participation of 18 January 2008* (ICC-01/04-01/06-1432, 11 July 2008) [97]: 'To give effect to the spirit and intention of article 68 (3) of the Statute in the context of the trial proceedings it must be interpreted so as to make participation by victims meaningful'.

[76] See Mariana Pena, 'Victim Participation at the International Criminal Court: Achievements Made and Challenges Lying Ahead' (2010) 16 *ILSA JILCA* 497; Van den Wyngaert (n 66); Pena and Carayon (n 66) 527.

[77] Van den Wyngaert (n 66).

[78] Ibid.

[79] Ibid. 489–91.

[80] Ibid. 489; Sara Kendall and Sarah Nouwen, 'Representational Practices at the International Criminal Court: The Gap between Juridified and Abstract Victimhood' (2013) 76 *LCP* 235, 235.

instructions from these participants.[81] There are difficulties in the process of applying to be a victim participant, the limited ability afforded to victim participants to frame and contest the scope of the case, and inadequacies in consultations with victim participants.[82] Ultimately, there are merely 'statistical victims', where the views of victims participants are captured numerically from consultations with a sample of victims participants.[83] This may pose 'a challenge to a system of victim participation that purports to rest upon the meaningful representation'.[84]

Such practical problems are matched with existential ones: a criminal trial is not the correct setting for victims to express their emotions, and victims may be disappointed with the trial process as a forum to express grief.[85] These issues pose real challenges for the ability of victim participation to be anything more than symbolic – and hence, this participation is not meaningful.[86] As Kamari Clarke has noted, there is a chasm here between 'justice' and 'law'; and

> the new conception of victimhood is being propelled by various judicially driven institutions for victims – such as the Victim's Trust Fund – that, on one hand, claim to work on behalf of victims, but on the other hand are unable to provide victims with the basic necessities for addressing their suffering.[87]

The aim of meaningful participation is therefore not being achieved – but taking this even further, victim participation in trials is often disempowering for victims.[88] The effect of the ICC making a formal determination of whether a particular victim meets the threshold for participation in a trial is to sort victims into the categories of the 'deserving' and the 'undeserving'; those who have their suffering acknowledged by virtue of their participation, and those who do not.[89] Thus, the structure of victim participation

---

[81] Van den Wyngaert (n 66) 489.

[82] See Pena and Carayon (n 66) 527–35. See also Gaelle Carayon and Jonathan O'Donohue, 'The International Criminal Court's Strategies in Relation to Victims' (2017) 15 *JICJ* 567; Kendall and Nouwen (n 80).

[83] Emily Haslam and Rod Edmunds, 'Whose Number is it Anyway? Common Legal Representation, Consultations, and the 'Statistical Victim'' (2017) 15 *JICJ* 931.

[84] Ibid. 951–2. On the challenges of victim representation and the limited agency permitted to victims, see Rachel Killean and Luke Moffett, 'Victim Legal Representation before the ICC and the ECCC' (2017) 15(4) *JICJ* 713.

[85] Van den Wyngaert (n 66) 489.

[86] Ibid. See also Sergey Vasiliev, 'Victim Participation Revisited – What the ICC is Learning About Itself' in Carsten Stahn (ed) (n 38) 1133.

[87] Kamari Maxine Clarke, 'We ask for justice, you give us law: The rule of law, economic markets, and the reconfiguration of victimhood', in Christian De Vos, Sara Kendall and Carsten Stahn (eds), *Contested Justice: The Politics and Practice of International Criminal Court Interventions* (CUP, 2015) 272, 277.

[88] But see Anushka Sehmi, '"Now that we have no voice, what will happen to us?" Experiences of Victim Participation in the Kenyatta Case' (2018) 16 *JICJ* 571.

[89] Kendall and Nouwen (n 80). See also Stahn (n 4).

facilitates a hierarchy of victimisation that may prove problematic for both individuals and conflicted communities. Clarke, importantly, links this 'narrowing of a particular type of "victim" subjectivity' to 'the rise of the rule of law', and argues that there is a 'certain epistemology of victimhood [that] has formed at the juncture of a new economic and political order: contemporary neoliberalism and the rise of 'good governance' indicators.'[90] This divide between 'deserving' and 'underserving' victims is further exacerbated by the system of reparations, which are only possible for victims of crimes where the accused has been found guilty. If, for example, the prosecutor chooses to only charge some offences against an accused, or if the accused is only found guilty of some offences, the result is that only some victims can receive reparations.[91]

In addition, existing narratives around victims foster a potentially false (or exaggerated) dichotomy between perpetrator and victim. The accused may have been themselves a victim of some crimes, and victims may have also been perpetrators – the example of child soldiers is an obvious case in point, where the child victims are likely to have committed crimes under the ICC's jurisdiction; and the accused is likely to also have been a victim.[92] This is true of Dominic Ongwen, who is the first individual to be explicitly charged with crimes of which he was also a victim. While this 'is not surprising', given that 'the lines between victims and victimizers in atrocity often are porous',[93] the Ongwen trial has demonstrated that the trial process is not able to fully reckon with the complexity of the victim-perpetrator dynamic. Prosecutor Fatou Bensouda, in her opening address to the Court, argued that these questions of complex victimhood are outside the remit of the trial:

> the focus of the ICC's criminal process is not on the goodness or badness of the accused person, but on the criminal acts which he or she has committed. We are not here to deny that Mr. Ongwen was a victim in his youth ... This Court will not decide his goodness or badness, nor whether he deserves sympathy, but whether he is guilty of the serious crimes committed as an adult, with which he stands charged.[94]

---

90 Clarke (n 87) 276.
91 On reparations and victimhood, see Moffett and Sandoval (n 36).
92 See Mark Drumbl, *Reimagining Child Soldiers in International Law and Policy* (OUP, 2012). See also Clarke (n 5); Kamari Clarke, 'The Rule of Law Through its Economies of Appearances: The Making of the African Warlord' (2011) 18 *IJGLS* 7.
93 Mark Drumbl, 'The Ongwen Trial at the ICC: Tough Questions on Child Soldiers' (14 April 2015) *Open Democracy* <https://www.opendemocracy.net/openglobalrights/mark-drumbl/ongwen-trial-at-icc-tough-questions-on-child-soldiers> (last accessed 9 December 2021). See Mark Drumbl, 'Victims who Victimise' (2016) 4(2) *LRIL* 217; Clark (n 11), Chapter 4.
94 ICC, 'Statement of the Prosecutor of the International Criminal Court, Fatou Bensouda, at the opening of Trial in the case against Dominic Ongwen' (4 December 2016) <https://

Bensouda's comments demonstrate that, as a medium of narrative, a trial process cannot abide the complexity of the victim/perpetrator dynamic. Trials are necessarily focused on only one side of an individual's story: a determination of their guilt for the crimes charged. Larger, contextual, stories are not permitted. Indeed, there is also little willpower to distort the comfortable narrative of good versus evil. Mark Drumbl points out that criminal law focuses on

> finality, disjuncture and category: guilty or not-guilty, persecuted or persecutor, abused or abuser, right or wrong, powerful or powerless [. . .] Victims are to be pure and ideal; perpetrators are to be unadulterated and ugly. International criminal law hinges upon these antipodes which, in turn, come to fuel its existence. . . . these binaries nonetheless undermine international criminal law's ability to speak in other than a crude register.[95]

Moreover, there is a lack of appreciation that victims may be 'ambivalent or even against the prosecution of those who allegedly offended against them'.[96] Frédéric Mégret has shown that this 'reluctant victim' is quite common in international criminal law but that this reality is 'largely hidden from conventional discourses'.[97] Moreover, while there are many different conceptions of 'justice', these are frequently 'pushed to the margins' by the colonising move of international criminal law to claim and frame justice.[98] Again, then, international criminal law flattens the complexity of the victims, including in terms of what 'justice' might meaningfully be for them.

These various issues may result in the victims being 'disembodied, depersonified, and . . . depoliticised'.[99] The victims are also 'racialize[d], feminize[d], and infantilize[d]'.[100] Rather than being empowered by a process to which they are perceived as central, the victims become 'not concrete persons of flesh, blood and water, with individual names and individual

---

www.icc-cpi.int//Pages/item.aspx?name=2016-12-06-otp-stat-ongwen>   (last   accessed   9 December 2021).

[95] Drumbl 2016 (n 93) 218.

[96] Frédéric Mégret, 'The Strange Case of the Victim Who Did Not Want Justice' (2018) 12 *IJTJ* 444, 445.

[97] Ibid.

[98] Nouwen and Werner (n 6) 173.

[99] Sarah Nouwen, 'Justifying Justice' in James Crawford and Martti Koskenniemi (eds), *The Cambridge Companion to International Law* (CUP, 2012) 327, 340.

[100] Schwöbel (n 9). For more on the construction of the 'ideal' victim, see Schwöbel-Patel (n 9); Laurel Fletcher, 'Refracted Justice: The Imagined Victim and the International Criminal Court' in De Vos, Kendall and Stahn (eds) (n 87) 302. Moreover, as Kamari Maxine Clarke has pointed out, there is a particular 'perpetrator figure' invoked in international criminal trials – 'a figure of African tragedy and uncivilised violence' – yet international criminal law does not adequately deal with continuing violence, like that of colonisation: Kamari Maxine Clarke, 'Refiguring the Perpetrator: Culpability, History and International Criminal Law's Impunity Gap' (2015) 19 *IJHR* 592, 594.

opinions, but a deity-like abstraction'.[101] In some respects, this depersonification of victims is unsurprising. Because international criminal law is a system lacking a sovereign, victims are positioned as the primary reasons for the existence and the performance of the system – 'the one in whose name criminal justice is exercised'.[102] Moreover, Clarke points out that because the figure of the victim is connected to the justifications for international criminal law, 'the more spectacular the conjuring of the victim, the more urgent the call to support – morally, fiscally, legally – the rule of law'.[103] But when we consider, for example, that reluctant victims may be reticent to 'legitimize or cooperate with processes nominally undertaken in their name',[104] we see that there is an uncomfortable disconnection between the positioning of the victim as sovereign and the ambivalence of the victims with the system of international criminal law.

Yet while victims may be the rationale for the system of international criminal law, they need not be the central aim for trial processes. Maintaining the aim of meaningful victim participation at the broader levels of the legal system generally, and institution specifically, keeps the position of victims at the heart of the international criminal legal mission. For example, public outreach and the position of public counsel for victims may be retained as functions of each institution. However, given the problems I have outlined concerning the meaningful role for victims being implemented at the trial level, I argue that ensuring meaningful victim participation should not be an aim of the trial process. This is for at least three reasons. First, as the above demonstrates, this aim is not being realised in any event, and it cannot be. Second, it is not necessary to place this aim on the trial process because the limited rights of the victims can be realised through other mechanisms. As Van Den Wyngaert posits:

> Victims' participation in criminal trials is not the only possible avenue if one wants to empower victims ... I do not believe that victims' procedural rights (such as the right to the truth, the right to reparations, and the right to be informed), recognized by human rights courts, necessarily need to be exercised by introducing the victims into the *criminal* trial proceeding.[105]

And third, the trial's primary aim should correctly be the determination of the accused's guilt or otherwise (as I go on to develop below) – locating meaningful victim participation as an aim of the trial may conflict with this primary aim.[106]

---

[101] Nouwen (n 99).

[102] Kendall and Nouwen (n 80) 254.

[103] Clarke (n 92).

[104] Mégret (n 96) 445.

[105] Van den Wyngaert (n 66) 495 (emphasis in original).

[106] See also Anni Pues, 'A Victim's Right to a Fair Trial at the International Criminal Court? Reflections on Article 68(3)' (2015) 13 *JICJ* 951.

However, victim participation has been built into the trial process at the ICC and is now firmly, and explicitly, a part of the trial itself. Nevertheless, I argue that victim participation can be implemented in a way that defers to the determination of the accused's guilt or otherwise, as the trial's primary aim. Giving prominence to the determination of an accused's guilt will constrain the expectations surrounding victim participation – possibly ameliorating some of the challenges outlined above. Victim participation must be managed 'in a manner not prejudicial to or inconsistent with' the rights of the accused.[107] This must be given practical application at all stages of the trial process and in all judicial decisions. Recalibrating the aim of the trial, to be centrally concerned with the determination of the accused's culpability rather than providing a forum for the victims, bolsters the position of the rights of the accused in determining how victims are involved in the trial process.

(3) Truth: legal or historical?

The aim of international criminal law to establish the 'truth' is frequently examined and invoked in the discourse of international criminal law,[108] and it is often said that these trials are 'less about judging a person than about establishing the truth of the events'.[109] Fact-finding is a crucial element of a trial: the facts that are determined by the Trial Chamber will form the basis of the conviction or acquittal of the accused. Yet while truth-telling is an aim that is routinely vested in the trial, the ability of the trial to deliver the 'truth' of events depends partly on which truth – legal or historical – is being considered: which facts are being found by the Trial Chamber, and how they fit those facts into a broader story of their role regarding the determination of 'truth'. Legal and historical truths, after all, are not one and the same.[110]

Legal truth is the determination of facts regarding the events that are in question due to the nature and content of the charges against the accused. Legal truth is relatively contained and does not seek to uncover the 'whole' truth regarding greater historical events beyond any relevance such events have to the charges the accused faces. Historical truth, however, seeks to go beyond the culpability of the accused, to broader questions of historical context, and to determining 'what really happened'. Of course, the lines between historical events and individual culpability are, in the context of

---

[107] *Rome Statute* Art 68(3).

[108] Gerry Simpson, *Law, War, and Crime* (Polity Press, 2007) 5; Damaška (n 3); Koskenniemi (n 3); Jackson (n 3); Lawrence Douglas, *The Memory of Judgment: Making Law and History in the Trials of the Holocaust* (YUP, 2000).

[109] Koskenniemi (n 3) 3.

[110] Ibid. 10. See also Sergey Vasiliev, *International Criminal Trials: A Normative Framework* (PhD Thesis, University of Amsterdam, 2014) 311.

these trials, blurred: an accused is often a historical figure, and the events in question are of historical importance. Moreover, the institutions accumulate a large archive of documents that may be used in historical analyses.[111] Indeed, ultimately the overlap of historical and judicial findings of culpability is precisely what is at stake in international criminal trials. None of this, however, leads to the conclusion that an aim of the international criminal trial process should be to ascertain historical truth. I argue that a trial cannot be vested with the aim of determining historical truth but can and should be vested with the aim of determining legal truth as an important intended result of the trial process.[112] It is not asserted that trials do not undertake history at all, but rather, that trials are not the best way of undertaking historical analyses or coming to conclusions on matters of history – and they should not aim to do so.

A trial process is predicated on the basis that 'a true account of events underlying the criminal prosecution can be discovered with a degree of accuracy that legitimizes a verdict and, thus, the process as such'.[113] In international criminal law, truth-seeking has been expanded to play an instrumentalist role in other ways, and truth-finding has thus been said to be 'one of the fundamental objectives' of international criminal institutions.[114] For example, Martti Koskenniemi notes that the recording and broadcasting of the 'truth' through the criminal process is seen as important 'for reasons that have little to do with the punishment of the individual'[115] – instead, it is an enabling mechanism to assist the healing of the victims, through public recognition of injustice; allowing conditions for affected communities to recover from trauma, and restoring the dignity of the victims.[116]

Truth-telling in international criminal law is also valued for disallowing the space for denial: setting out a record of the events in question, and their pre-cursors, may protect against historical revisionism.[117] However, as trials only involve a limited set of facts that are relevant to legal questions at issue, there is the potential for the trial to decontextualise the conflict from

---

[111] Fergal Gaynor, 'Uneasy Partners – Evidence, Truth and History in International Trials' (2012) 10 *JICJ* 1257, 1262. See also Drumbl (n 5) 174–5.

[112] Masha Fedorova, *The Principle of Equality of Arms in International Criminal Proceedings* (Intersentia, 2012) 76.

[113] Ibid. 78.

[114] *Prosecutor v Sikirica, Sentencing Judgment* (IT-95-8, 13 November 2001) [149].

[115] Koskenniemi (n 3) 4.

[116] Ibid. See also Eser (n 7) 121.

[117] The ICTY promotes this as a key achievement of the Tribunal: 'The Tribunal has contributed to an indisputable historical record, combating denial and helping communities come to terms with their recent history. Crimes across the region can no longer be denied. For example, it has been proven beyond reasonable doubt that the mass murder at Srebrenica was genocide': ICTY, *About the ICTY* <https://www.icty.org/en/about> (last accessed 9 December 2021).

its political and economic causes.[118] Koskenniemi ties this limitation to the goal of ending impunity and individual criminal responsibility, noting that a criminal process may 'obstruct' the process of historical truth-telling 'by exonerating from responsibility those larger (political, economic, even legal) structures within which the conditions for individual criminality have been created'.[119]

There are real doubts as to whether trials can construct proper historical accounts of the events in question.[120] With their focus on the individual accused and their culpability, trials are ill-equipped to craft or uncover a broader historical truth. Historians and lawyers employ different methods to examine and assess facts, and there are several limitations on the ability of international criminal trials to create full historical records: jurisdictional constraints; legal relevance; prosecutorial discretion (not to investigate or prosecute, or to do so in a limited way); temporal, territorial and substantive range of the indictment; confidentiality restrictions, including limitations on information provided by states; plea agreements; and finally, the exclusion of relevant evidence.[121] Any aspiration of a trial to tell a historical truth will thus be curtailed to such a degree that this aim cannot be achieved.

One example can be given to highlight the inability of the trial process, and even the institution, to reveal an accurate historical truth. At the ICTY, the death of Milošević and the acquittal, on appeal, of Perišić[122] means that there has been, and will be, no judicial finding of culpability of Serbia for events in Bosnia. In effect, the historical record of the ICTY is that the Serbian state was not culpable for events in Bosnia. Conversely, the finding of the *Prlić* case was that there was Croatian culpability for events in Bosnia.[123] If taken as a record of historical truth, these trial findings would deem Croatia to be more responsible than Serbia for the conflicts in Bosnia. This is not an accurate record of historical truth, but it may be an appropriate legal truth. Drumbl identifies a similar example at the ICTR, where

---

[118] Koskenniemi (n 3); Tor Krever, 'International Criminal Law: An Ideology Critique' (2013) 26 *LJIL* 701, 720.

[119] Koskenniemi (n 3) 14.

[120] See Jackson (n 3) 21; Koskenniemi (n 3) 23. But see R. A. Wilson, 'Judging History: The Historical Record of the International Criminal Tribunal for the Former Yugoslavia' (2005) 27 *HRQ* 908, 909; Richard Ashby Wilson, *Writing History in International Criminal Trials* (CUP, 2011). For more on the historical narratives that international courts are able to construct, see Barrie Sander, 'The Method is the Message: Narrative Authority and Historical Contestation in International Criminal Courts' (2018) 10 *MJIL* 299; Barrie Sander, 'Unveiling the Historical Function of International Criminal Courts: Between Adjudicative and Sociopolitical Justice' (2018) 12(2) *IJTJ* 334; Sofia Stolk, 'The Victim, the International Criminal Court and the Search for Truth: On the Interdependence and Incompatibility of Truths about Mass Atrocity' (2015) 13 *JICJ* 973.

[121] Gaynor (n 111) 1263–70.

[122] *Prosecutor v Perišić, Judgement* (IT-04-18-A, 28 February 2013).

[123] *Prosecutor v Prlić, Judgement* (IT-04-74-T, 29 May 2013).

different Trial Chambers reached different conclusions on the criminal involvement of a particular individual.[124] Drumbl argued that 'from the perspective of historical purity and due process legalism, it is perhaps discomfiting that different Trial Chambers (of the same tribunal) arrive at divergent factual findings when addressing a similar event'.[125] He also notes that other observers may be less concerned: 'Criminal trials intrinsically may be awkward mechanisms to arrive at a singular truth. Divergent fact-finding may simply be unavoidable'.[126] Yet, again, we see the inability of trial processes to determine one single, accurate, historical 'truth'.

For all these reasons, uncovering or assembling historical truth should not be the aim of an international criminal trial; rather, international criminal trials can only aspire to establish legal truth. Trial Chambers themselves have stated that their purpose is not to aspire to historical truth,[127] and in interviews I conducted, judges also expressed a view that historical truth is not their aspiration when conducting the trial. For example, one judge was emphatic that

> aims such as ... providing a historical document, may happen as a by-product of the trial process but it is not the aim of the judges to do that. And it should not be the aim of the judges ... The judges are there to provide a discrete verdict on the evidence. How that evidence plays out in the bigger picture and how the verdict plays out in the bigger picture, that is a matter perhaps for the historians and legal commentators.[128]

It is, therefore, clear that the aim of the trial is to determine a legal truth, but any attempt to graft historical truth-seeking onto the trial process is misplaced. Historical truth may be served through a variety of different mechanisms, some of which may be supported by other institutions (such as Truth Commissions). Historical truth may, therefore, be an aim of the system of international criminal law. It may even be an aim of the institution (although it may or may not be adequately fulfilled, as we have seen from the examples above). But when 'truth' is vested at the level of the trial process, this must be conceived of as legal rather than historical truth.

---

[124] Mark Drumbl, 'The Curious Criminality of Mass Atrocity' in Elies van Sliedregt and Sergey Vasiliev (eds), *Pluralism in International Criminal Law* (OUP, 2014) 68.

[125] Ibid. 99.

[126] Ibid.

[127] *Prosecutor v Stanišić, Decision Pursuant to Rule 73 bis(D)* (IT-03-69-PT, 4 February 2008) [21]; *Prosecutor v Karadžić, Decision on the Accused's Holbrooke Agreement Motion* (IT-95-5/18-T, 8 July 2009) [46].

[128] Interview with Judge Howard Morrison (29 May 2013).

C. A FORENSIC DETERMINATION OF AN INDIVIDUAL'S GUILT OR INNOCENCE: CALLING FOR A RECALIBRATION OF THE AIMS OF INTERNATIONAL CRIMINAL TRIALS

Having recognised that the aims of the trial need not necessarily be the same as those of the institutions or of the system of law, and in light of the challenges of certain key aims (ending impunity, a meaningful voice for victims, and historical truth) imposed upon the trial process, what can we say about the 'why' of international criminal trials? A recalibration of the aims of international criminal trials is both possible and necessary. I argue that the aim of these trials should be a narrow focus on the forensic determination of an individual's guilt or innocence for the crimes with which they are charged.

A renewed focus on the place of the accused (and determination of their guilt or otherwise) in international criminal trials is, in fact, complementary to the emphasis of international criminal law on individualised responsibility for crimes. The system of international criminal law was established on the basis of punishing *individuals* for crimes: as the Nuremberg Tribunal declared, 'crimes against international law are committed by men, not by abstract entities, and only by punishing individuals who commit such crimes can the provisions of international law be enforced'.[129] This focus on the individual as the subject of international criminal law – through placing that individual on trial, determining their guilt or acquitting them, and (where appropriate) rendering punishment – is well-established as the 'bedrock' of international criminal law.[130] This focus is closely linked with the system's overarching aim of ending impunity: ensuring that office or rank cannot shield the individual from responsibility for their actions.[131] It is also rationalised by the argument that vesting guilt in one person, rather than with a whole community, should prevent cycles of retribution against that community or group.[132] In removing a 'bad apple', the entire barrel will not be ruined; having expelled the personified problem, communities can move towards reconciliation. And not only does international criminal law individualise guilt, but it also holds individuals responsible for collective wrongdoing and for crimes physically perpetrated by others. Those who planned, instigated, ordered, or aided and abetted a crime committed by another person may be held individually criminally responsible for that crime through extended modes of liability;[133] a superior may be held

---

[129] 'Judgement of the Nuremberg International Military Tribunal 1946' (1947) 41 *AJIL* 172, 221.

[130] Krever (n 118) 712, citing *Prosecutor v Tadić, Judgement* (IT-94-1-A, 15 July 1999) [186].

[131] Krever (n 118) 712.

[132] See Martha Minow, *Between Vengeance and Forgiveness: Facing History after Genocide and Mass Violence* (Beacon Press, 1998).

[133] ICTY *Statute* Art 7; *Rome Statute* Art 25; Elies van Sliedregt, 'The Curious Case of International Criminal Liability' (2012) 10 *JICJ* 1171.

responsible for the acts of a subordinate.[134] For all these reasons, the individual is at the heart of the international criminal legal system.

This individualisation of guilt in international criminal law can be criticised as permitting a decontexutalisation of the events surrounding those crimes, thereby allowing the structural realities of why atrocities occur to be ignored.[135] The emphasis on trials may be seen as another symptom of international law's obsession with crises rather than engaging in a systematic examination of the causes of conflict.[136] Emphasising the determination of an accused's guilt (or otherwise) as the primary aim of trial might, therefore, be criticised as being reductionist. However, this criticism assumes that the system, institutions and proceedings must have the same aims or that such aims must operate in the same way at each of these levels. My argument that the trial should focus on determining an accused's guilt does not mean that the system of law and its institutions cannot have other aims – which could include engagement in broader conversations about the complexity of conflict and its structural causes. I do not hope for international criminal law to be narrow in either its operations or discourse; indeed, I agree with the critiques that are made of international criminal law's tendency towards decontextualisation. Nonetheless, engaging in an examination of the causes and complexities of conflict is neither the aim, nor the role, of individual trials.[137] Yet seeing the aims of the trial process as separate from the system of law permits us to understand that, while these conversations cannot be allowed to happen at the level of the trial, they may – and should – occur at the level of the institutions or the system of law.

The call for a simplification of the aims of international criminal law is not unprecedented. One example is Damaška's suggestion of whether

---

[134] *ICTY Statute* Art 7(3); *Rome Statute* Art 28.

[135] Koskenniemi (n 3); Krever (n 118); Tallgren (n 25) 594; Engle (n 49) 1119.

[136] See Hilary Charlesworth, 'International Law: A Discipline of Crisis' (2002) 65 *MLR* 377. See also Joseph Powderly, 'International Criminal Justice in an Age of Perpetual Crisis' (2019) 32 *LJIL* 1.

[137] Some defence lawyers have invoked a trial strategy known as 'rupture', which deconstructs and critiques the structural flaws of international criminal law through courtroom strategy (Mikael Baaz, 'Review Essay: Dissident Voices in International Criminal Law' (2015) 28 *LJIL* 673, 688). Rupture seeks to locate and contextualise the individual's criminal responsibility in broader societal issues, and can bring into issue questions of power, colonialism, structural violence, or 'slow violence' (for more on 'slow violence' see Michelle Burgis-Kasthala, 'Scholarship as Dialogue? TWAIL and the Politics of Methodology' (2016) 14 *JICJ* 921). However, as important as this trial strategy may be, it remains precisely that: a strategy, rather than an aim of international criminal trials. A defence lawyer may invoke rupture to challenge any alleged culpability, but the aim of the trial remains the forensic determination of the individuals' guilt or innocence for the crimes charged. For more on rupture and international criminal law, see Mikael Baaz and Mona Lilja, 'Using International Criminal Law to Resist Transitional Justice: Legal Rupture in the Extraordinary Chambers in the Courts of Cambodia' (2016) 2 *CAS* 142; Koskenniemi (n 3); Rigney (n 9).

some goals should be 'abandoned, muted, or downplayed'.[138] However, I am not suggesting that these goals need to be abandoned or minimised – simply that they are sorted more clearly, against the three levels of system, institution and process. Elsewhere, Damaška's solution to the proliferation of international criminal law's aims is to 'relax' some limited fairness considerations, given the unique place and aims of international criminal justice.[139] Contrary to Damaška, I advocate that such procedural safeguards should actually be emphasised. As discussed further in the following chapters, given the centrality of the accused to the trial process, the individual's rights (as procedural safeguards) must be protected. Rather than ameliorating the proliferation of aims, a relaxation of procedural safeguards could prove problematic where trials are located within a system that emphasises conviction.

In interviews conducted with international criminal judges, there was an emphasis on the determination of the accused's guilt as a key aim of international criminal trials. For example, a judge from the ICTY articulated that, in his view, 'the aims of any criminal trial are to examine the evidence around the allegations laid against the individual accused, try them according to due process rights, and deliver a verdict in line with the persuasiveness or otherwise of the evidence'.[140] Another noted that the aim of international criminal trials is 'to hold to account those who are found to have committed egregious crimes in . . . international law'.[141] One judge noted that 'the aims of an international criminal trial [are] to basically subject an individual who has been indicted through the entire legal process to establish his guilt, or otherwise', which – notably – he saw as distinguishable from 'the purpose and the *raison d'être* of the institution itself'.[142]

Emphasising the individual accused in the trial process is not a new concept. The judgment in the case of *Attorney General v Eichmann* articulated clearly that, while there were people 'who sought to regard this trial as a forum for the clarification of questions' such as 'how could this happen?', it was not for the court to answer such questions.[143] Indeed, the court considered – rather poetically – that

> In this maze of insistent questions, the path of the Court was and remains clear. It cannot allow itself to be enticed into provinces which are outside its sphere . . .

---

[138] Damaška (n 12). Another recent call for modesty in the goals of international criminal law is from Caleb Wheeler, who points out a difference between 'legal' and 'political' aims of international criminal trials and argues that trials should focus on legal goals (Wheeler (n 2)).

[139] Damaška (n 3).

[140] Interview with Judge Howard Morrison (29 May 2013).

[141] Interview with Judge Justice Bakone Moloto (27 May 2013).

[142] Interview with Judge X (14 May 2013).

[143] *A-G (Israel) v Eichmann* (1961) 36 ILR 5 [1]–[2].

Otherwise, the processes of law and of court procedure are bound to be impaired [. . .] and the trial would [. . .] resemble a rudderless ship tossed about by the waves.[144]

In the opinion of that court, the purpose of 'every criminal trial' was to determine guilt and, if the accused is convicted, to deliver punishment: 'everything which is foreign to these purposes must be entirely eliminated from the court procedure'.[145] In her reportage on the *Eichmann* case, Hannah Arendt argued that

> the purpose of the trial is to render justice, and nothing else; even the noblest ulterior purposes – 'the making of a record of the Hitler regime . . .' can only detract from the law's main business: to weigh the charges brought against the accused, to render judgment and to mete out due punishment.[146]

More recently, others have agreed that a 'key goal' of 'international criminal tribunals' is 'the need to reach an accurate verdict so far as the guilt of the accused is concerned in a fair and expeditious manner'.[147] Some, such as Gideon Boas, accept that there may be a variety of views of the purposes of trials but see these as 'legitimate derivative outcomes' of trials rather than the core concern of a trial.[148]

Placing the forensic determination of the accused's culpability as the key aim of the trial enables us to focus on this as the core organising value for a trial's processes. If, for example, there is a conflict between the aims of the system (ending impunity or giving victims a meaningful voice) and the aim of the trial (a forensic determination of the accused's guilt or innocence), this conflict is to be managed by prioritising the aim of the trial. What must be protected against is any conflation of the aims of the system – such as ending impunity – with the trial. Such a conflation would only replicate the difficulties outlined above.

Moreover, appreciating the aims of the trial as different from those of the system and institution may actually allow those aims to be more fully under-taken by other means. If 'ending impunity', a 'meaningful voice for victims' and 'truth' are necessary in post-conflict settings, they may be achieved from a range of processes rather than merely relying on trials. As we have seen above, international criminal law can be a colonising force that frames

---

[144] Ibid. [2].

[145] Ibid.

[146] Hannah Arendt, *Eichmann in Jerusalem: A Report of the Banality of Evil* (Penguin, 1963) 251.

[147] John Jackson, 'Transnational Faces of Justice: Two Attempts to Build Common Standards Beyond National Boundaries' in John Jackson, Máximo Langer and Peter Tillers (eds), *Crime, Procedure and Evidence in a Comparative and International Context: Essays in Honour of Professor Mirjan Damaška* (Hart Publishing, 2008) 221, 239.

[148] Gideon Boas, *The Milošević Trial: Lessons for the Conduct of Complex International Criminal Proceedings* (CUP, 2007) 4; see also Wheeler (n 2) 179.

'justice' in particular (criminalised) ways rather than permitting a complex multitude of conceptions of justice.[149] Perhaps sorting the aims of international criminal law more carefully against the system of law, the institutions and the processes will, in turn, allow those aims to be satisfied by other processes rather than just trials; and perhaps a number of other understandings of justice – rather than just criminal justice – will also be given greater emphasis. Although it could be argued that 'show trials' may serve some purposes, even if legally problematic (as is intimated by Damaška's position, for example), it is also true that reducing an emphasis on trials, including show trials, may allow those important aims to be met by other mechanisms which would perhaps be more appropriate to such aims.

In clarifying the 'why' of international criminal trials and how this differs from other aspects of international criminal law more broadly, this chapter has advocated an emphasis on the forensic determination of the accused's guilt or otherwise as the central aim of the trial. This recalibration of the aims of the trial places the accused firmly at the heart of the trial process. The rights of the accused thus become a fundamental concern. This will be the focus of the next chapter, along with an examination of how and why the idea of fairness is also central to international criminal trials. The current chapter, plus the two that follow, all work together to build the framework for an understanding of how rights, fairness and procedure interact in contemporary international criminal trials.

---

[149] Nouwen and Werner (n 6) 173.

Chapter 2
The centrality of rights and fairness in international criminal trials

The measure is going to be the fairness of the proceedings
– Richard Goldstone, first ICTY prosecutor[1]

Rights and fairness are both widely considered to be central to international criminal trials. In this chapter, I examine this centrality and why it is that rights and fairness are so important in these trials. This centrality can be seen in both the stated law and in the potential uses of rights and fairness. In this way, I show the centrality of rights and fairness as something that is both accepted and important for international criminal proceedings.

This chapter starts with an analysis of the idea of 'rights' in international criminal trials – what they are, who they attach to, and why they matter. Placing the individual, and the determination of their forensic guilt (or otherwise), properly at the heart of the trial also has implications for how we view the rights of the accused. It is difficult to conceive of a trial process that emphasises the individual and a determination of their culpability, without affording them rights as part of that trial process. If the accused is to be the central subject of a trial, they must be ensured rights as a core element of that process. The rights of the accused are an important aspect of the trial, linked to both the central aim of the trial (determination of the accused's culpability) and the placement of that trial within a system that is galvanised by other aims (ending impunity and meaningful victim participation).

In this chapter, I examine the 'rights' of other trial parties and participants (the prosecution and the victims), arguing that these trial participants do not have rights in the same way the accused does. Rather, they have interests, competencies, some duties – and some limited rights. I also examine the question of how rights are positioned in relation to truth-seeking in international criminal procedure, particularly with regards to the hybrid, *sui generis* structure of the international criminal procedural model.

I then move on to the idea of 'fairness' in international criminal trials. Fairness is widely considered to be at the heart of these trials, but the multitude of different views regarding what fairness is and how it manifests in trial proceedings has led to the concept being incoherent and ultimately unstable. In this chapter and the chapter that follows, I undertake a conceptual

---

[1] Quoted in Mark Ellis, 'Achieving Justice before the International War Crimes Tribunal' (2000) 7 *DJCICL* 519, 526.

and normative analysis of fairness in international criminal trials, and in doing so, I show both the centrality of fairness (in this chapter) and its incoherence and instability (in the next chapter). I am solely concerned with fairness in relation to contemporary international criminal trials and do not intend to make a comprehensive statement on fairness generally; nor do I address fairness in broad historical or philosophical terms, or attempt to provide an overarching theory related to, for example, international law.[2]

In this chapter, I demonstrate that fairness is generally considered to be a crucial aspect of international criminal procedure, and this centrality of fairness is accepted and protected by a wide array of practitioners and scholars. I then analyse why this is the case. What is fairness considered to be capable of doing, and of ensuring, in the trial process? What is the promise of fairness? I argue that fairness holds several uses: it may be an interpretive tool for trial chambers, an epistemic enabler, a legitimating force, and a tool to assist the system of law to achieve its aims. I also argue that the accepted centrality of fairness offers a great possibility: it is a point of convergence between most scholars and practitioners of international criminal law in a field in which there are otherwise so many areas of divergence. Protection of fairness is regarded by many as a key – if not *the* key – issue in international criminal trials. This common ground offers an opportunity, but it also brings the potential for greater friction if conceptions of fairness are in conflict. A coherent appreciation of fairness is therefore important – although, as I show in the following chapter, there is currently no such coherent appreciation in international criminal law.

A. RIGHTS IN INTERNATIONAL CRIMINAL TRIALS

Vast amounts of jurisprudence and scholarship have already analysed the content of the rights of the accused in international criminal law,[3] but it is important to make some initial observations and arguments about

---

[2] See Thomas Franck, *Fairness in International Law and Institutions* (OUP, 1998).

[3] See Salvatore Zappalà, *Human Rights in International Criminal Proceedings* (OUP, 2003); Gideon Boas, *The Milošević Trial: Lessons for the Conduct of Complex International Criminal Proceedings* (CUP, 2007) 21–63; John Jackson, 'The Effect of Human Rights on Criminal Evidentiary Process: Towards Convergence, Divergence or Realignment?' (2005) 68 *MLR* 737; Pascal Chenivesse and Christopher Piranio, 'What Price Justice? On the Evolving Notion of "Right to a Fair Trial" from Nuremberg to The Hague' (2011) 24 *CRIA* 403; Scott Johnson, 'On the Road to Disaster: The Rights of the Accused and the International Criminal Tribunal for the Former Yugoslavia' (1998) 10 *ILP* 111; Stefan Trechsel, 'Rights in Criminal Proceedings Under the ECHR and the ICTY Statute – A Precarious Comparison' in Bert Swart, Alexander Zahar and Göran Sluiter (eds), *The Legacy of the International Criminal Tribunal for the Former Yugoslavia* (OUP, 2011) 149; Masha Fedorova, Sten Verhoeven and Jan Wouters, 'Safeguarding the Rights of Suspects and Accused Persons in International Criminal Proceedings' in Cedric Ryngaert (ed), *The Effectiveness of International Criminal Justice* (Intersentia, 2009) 55.

the accused's rights here. In particular, I want to briefly consider what is meant when we consider the rights of the accused and why these rights are important.

A Trial Chamber has a duty to ensure that a trial is conducted 'with full respect for the rights of the accused'.[4] The rights of the accused are stipulated in the statutes of the ICC and the ICTY.[5] As already set out, these rights are essentially a replica of Article 14 of the *International Covenant on Civil and Political Rights*[6] and are therefore also found in international, regional and domestic legal frameworks. At the ICC and ICTY, the accused has the following rights: to be informed promptly and in detail in a language the accused understands of the nature and cause of the charge against him;[7] to have adequate time and facilities for the preparation of his defence and to communicate with counsel of his own choosing;[8] to be tried without undue delay;[9] to be tried in his presence, and to defend himself in person or through legal assistance of his own choosing;[10] to be informed, if he does not have legal assistance, of this right;[11] and to have legal assistance assigned to him, in any case where the interests of justice so require, and without payment by him in any such case if he does not have sufficient means to pay for it;[12] to examine, or have examined, the witnesses against him and to obtain the attendance and examination of witnesses on his behalf under the same conditions as witnesses against him;[13] to have the free assistance of an interpreter if he cannot understand or speak the language used in the court

---

[4] SC Res 827, UN SCOR, 48th sess, 3217th mtg, UN Doc S/RES/827 (25 May 1993), as amended by SC Res 1877, UN SCOR, 64th sess, 6155th mtg, UN Doc S/RES/1877 (7 July 2009) ('*ICTY Statute*') Art 20; *Rome Statute of the International Criminal Court*, opened for signature 17 July 1998, 2187 UNTS 90 (entered into force 1 July 2002) ('*Rome Statute*') Art 64(2).

[5] *ICTY Statute* Art 21, *Rome Statute* Art 67.

[6] The importance of Article 14 of the *ICCPR* has been outlined in no uncertain terms by courts themselves: for example, the Appeals Chamber in *Tadić* considered that Article 14 *ICCPR* reflects 'an imperative norm of international law to which the Tribunal must adhere': *Prosecutor v Tadić, Appeal Judgement on Allegations of Contempt Against Prior Counsel, Milan Vujin* (IT-94-1-A-AR77, 27 February 2001).

[7] *ICTY Statute* Art 21(4)(a); *Rome Statute* Art 67(1)(a). The *Rome Statute* modifies this to 'in a language which the accused fully understands and speaks': *Rome Statute* Art 67(1)(a).

[8] *ICTY Statute* Art 21(4)(b); *Rome Statute* Art 67(1)(b). The *Rome Statute* is explicit that the right to communicate with counsel 'in confidence': *Rome Statute* Art 67(1)(b).

[9] *ICTY Statute* Art 21(4)(c); *Rome Statute* Art 67(1)(c).

[10] *ICTY Statute* Art 21(4)(d); *Rome Statute* Art 67(d). Under the *Rome Statute*, this is subject to Art 63(2).

[11] Ibid.

[12] Ibid.

[13] *ICTY Statute* Art 21(4)(e); *Rome Statute* Art 67(e). The *Rome Statute* adds 'The accused shall also be entitled to raise defences and to present other evidence admissible under this Statute'.

or tribunal;[14] and not to be compelled to testify against himself or to confess guilt.[15] These are 'minimum guarantees', and they must be provided to the accused 'in full equality'[16] with all persons considered to be equal before the court.[17] Some consider these rights to be *jus cogens*.[18]

The accused is also entitled to the presumption of innocence.[19] The ICTY adds that the accused is entitled to a 'fair and public' hearing, while at the ICC, the accused is entitled to a 'public hearing' and 'to a fair hearing conducted impartially'.[20] At the ICC, there are additional rights: to make an unsworn oral or written statement in his or her defence;[21] and not to have imposed on him or her any reversal of the burden of proof or any onus of rebuttal.[22] The ICC also places the right to potentially exculpatory material as an articulated right of the accused.[23] There are further rights that attach to a suspect in the investigation and pre-trial phases.[24] The ICC also requires that the interpretation of law 'must be consistent with internationally recognised human rights'.[25] The primacy of these rights should be implemented through three dimensions in international criminal trials: they should be 'recognised within the relevant *normative* instruments regulating the activities of each given court'; they should be 'ensured by the *judges* in the proceedings on a case by case basis'; and there 'should be some mechanism of *redress* in case of violations'.[26]

---

[14] *ICTY Statute* Art 21(4)(f); *Rome Statute* Art 67(f). The *Rome Statute* adds that the interpreter be 'competent', and that the accused has a right to 'such translations as are necessary to meet the requirements of fairness, if any of the proceedings of or documents presented to the Court are not in a language which the accused fully understands and speaks'.

[15] *ICTY Statute* Art 21(4)(g); *Rome Statute* Art 67(g).

[16] *ICTY Statute* Art 21(4); *Rome Statute* Art 67.

[17] *ICTY Statute* Art 21(1); *Rome Statute* Art 67.

[18] See Patrick Robinson, 'The Right to a Fair Trial in International Law, with Specific Reference to the Work of the ICTY' (2009) 3 *BJILP* 1, 7.

[19] *ICTY Statute* Art 21(3); *Rome Statute* Art 66.

[20] *ICTY Statute* Art 21(2); *Rome Statute* Art 67(1).

[21] *Rome Statute* Art 67(1)(h).

[22] *Rome Statute* Art 67(1)(i).

[23] *Rome Statute* Art 67(2).

[24] *ICTY Statute* Art 18; ICTY, *Rules of Procedure and Evidence*, Doc No IT/32/Rev.50 (adopted on 11 February 1994, amended 10 July 2015) ('*ICTY Rules*') r 42; *Rome Statute* Art 55.

[25] *Rome Statute* Art 21(3). See Brianne McGonigle Leyh, 'Pragmatism over Principles: The International Criminal Court and a Human Rights-Based Approach to Judicial Interpretation' (2018) 41(3) *FILJ* 697; Leena Grover, 'A Call to Arms: Fundamental Dilemmas Confronting the Interpretation of Crimes in the Rome Statute of the International Criminal Court' (2010) 21(3) *EJIL* 543; Rosemary Grey, *Prosecuting Sexual and Gender-Based Crimes at the International Criminal Court: Practice, Progress and Potential* (CUP, 2019) 308–310.

[26] Salvatore Zappalà, 'The Rights of Victims v the Rights of the Accused' (2010) 8 *JICJ* 137, 140 (emphasis in original).

B. EQUALITY OF ARMS

The rights outlined above are the constituent, specific elements of 'the right to a fair trial'.[27] As will be discussed in Chapter Three, what else is included as elements of a 'fair trial' is a matter of contention and lacks certainty. However, a fair trial is generally accepted as also including equality of arms,[28] which is correctly viewed as a principle that 'seeks to ensure the application of rights in a fair and balanced manner',[29] rather than being a rule or particular right itself.[30] The rights of the accused are to be enjoyed 'in full equality'.[31] The relationship between rights and equality of arms is therefore close. Equality of arms is both a mechanism to ensure that such rights are provided their full expression and is a principle to govern trial processes. Equality of arms also assists in pursuing accuracy by ensuring that the information presented to the Chamber is not overly skewed in favour of one party.[32]

Equality of arms 'implies that each party must be afforded a reasonable opportunity to present his case – including his evidence – under conditions that do not place him at a substantial disadvantage *vis-à-vis* his opponent'.[33] Because of the 'inherent inequality between an individual defendant and the machinery of the court system', certain procedural guarantees are designed to redress problems in the balance between the parties in international criminal trials.[34] Hence, parties in international criminal trials are to be granted equal opportunities in a multitude of areas:

> production of pleadings and pieces of evidence within the same terms, of submission of the same number of briefs and comments, of allowance of equal time and means for preparation of the defence, of entitlement to reply to and comment on the other party's allegations and supporting evidence, of equal access to judicial remedies.[35]

---

[27] Zappalà (n 3) 111.

[28] Ibid. 112; Masha Fedorova, *The Principle of Equality of Arms in International Criminal Proceedings* (Intersentia, 2012); Gabrielle McIntyre, 'Equality of Arms – Defining Human Rights in the Jurisprudence of the International Criminal Tribunal for the Former Yugoslavia' (2003) 16 *LJIL* 269; Stefania Negri, 'The Principle of "Equality of Arms" and the Evolving Law of International Criminal Procedure' (2005) 5 *ICLR* 513; Charles Chernor Jalloh and Amy DiBella, 'Equality of Arms in International Criminal Law: Continuing Challenges' in William A Schabas, Yvonne McDermott and Niamh Hayes (eds), *The Ashgate Research Companion to International Criminal Law* (Ashgate, 2013) 251.

[29] Fedorova (n 28) 46.

[30] Ibid. 7.

[31] *Rome Statute* Art 67; *ICTY Statute* Art 21.

[32] Ibid. 23.

[33] *Prosecutor v Tadić*, Judgement (IT-94-1-A, 15 July 1999) ('*Tadić Judgement*') [48]–[49]; Fedorova (n 28) 37.

[34] Fedorova (n 28) 3.

[35] Negri (n 28) 523.

Yet opportunities meted out in strictly equal measure cannot ensure actual equality if one party enjoys an advantage over the other – this would simply consolidate the disadvantage. There are thus two aspects of the equality of arms: formal equality and material equality.[36] Masha Fedorova explains formal equality as 'ensuring equality between two equally situated parties; this corresponds to "a level playing field" where the advantage of one party would lead to an unfair outcome'.[37] Material equality, meanwhile, is defined as 'the idea that a state should ensure some level of equality between the stronger and weaker party (through, for example, a legal aid system)'.[38] Because international courts and tribunals are dependent on state cooperation for assistance with investigations, warrants and logistical considerations, they are perhaps not as powerful as domestic prosecution bodies: equality of arms is therefore given a 'more liberal interpretation' in international trials than it is in domestic trials,[39] in order to recognise the challenges faced by the prosecution.[40] Nevertheless, it should equally be recalled that the defence in international criminal trials is often at a structural disadvantage because they are frequently 'unable to make effective investigations to combat the prosecution case',[41] for reasons including distance from the crime scene, finances, a lack of institutional memory, and other logistics.

C. 'RIGHTS' OR INTERESTS OF OTHERS

The examination of rights and the principle of equality of arms raises the question of the proper relationship between the parties and participants in the trial – and how rights regulate the roles of, and relationships between, these parties. Chapter Three will analyse in more detail how the 'rights' of victims and the 'rights' of the prosecution are related to concepts of fairness – particularly with reference to their relationship to the rights of the accused. However, at the outset, it is important to note that I conceive of these in very different ways than I do the rights of the accused. I take the approach advocated by Yvonne McDermott that

> the accused individual ought to be regarded as the *only* actor that holds enforceable rights related to their status at trial. Other actors such as the prosecutor,

---

[36] Fedorova (n 28) 11.

[37] Ibid.

[38] Ibid.

[39] *Tadić Judgement* [51]–[52].

[40] Mark Harmon and Fergal Gaynor, 'Prosecuting Massive Crimes with Primitive Tools: Three Difficulties Encountered by Prosecutors in International Criminal Proceedings' (2004) 2(2) *JICJ* 403, 407.

[41] John Jackson, 'Finding the Best Epistemic Fit for International Criminal Tribunals: Beyond the Adversarial–Inquisitorial Dichotomy' (2009) 7 *JICJ* 17, 28.

witnesses, victims and the international community might be regarded as interest-holders, and holders of personal rights as human rights but not as rights deriving from their status of actor at trial.[42]

Particularly in light of the ICC's novel regime for the participation of victims, there is rhetorical weight given to the notion of 'the rights of the victims'. However, there are clear and fundamental differences between the position of the accused and the victims in these trials. First, victims (at the ICC) have the procedural status in the trial process of *participants* and not *parties*.[43] It is therefore understandable that they do not have the same procedural 'rights' as those possessed by trial parties. This is particularly so, given that victims do not have *duties* in the same way that the parties have.[44]

Indeed, due to their position as the object of the trial process – a position that the victims are not in – the accused must have particular rights, which are applied to guarantee that the accused receives a fair trial.[45] These rights, therefore, attach specifically, and only, to the accused, and not to other trial parties or participants. As McDermott argues, the accused possesses these rights by virtue of their status as accused.[46] These rights are explicitly articulated in the statutes as attaching to the accused: as mentioned above, the relevant articles are entitled 'Rights of the Accused', and they commence by setting out that '[i]n the determination of any charge, *the accused* shall be entitled to . . . a fair hearing conducted impartially, and to the following minimum guarantees, in full equality', before stipulating the particularised rights that the accused is entitled to.[47] The statutes also reinforce that a fair trial must be ensured with 'full respect for the rights of the accused and due regard for the protection of victims and witnesses'.[48] These articles articulate a clear difference between the 'rights' of the accused and the 'protection' of victims and witnesses; and a clear difference between the level of importance attached to them ('full respect' as opposed to 'due regard').[49]

---

[42] Yvonne McDermott, 'Rights in Reverse: A Critical Analysis of Fair Trial Rights under International Criminal Law' in William A Schabas, Yvonne McDermott and Niamh Hayes (eds), *The Ashgate Research Companion to International Criminal Law* (Ashgate, 2013) 165, 166 (emphasis in original).

[43] See *Situation in the Democratic Republic of the Congo, Decision on the Application for Participation in Proceedings of VPRS1, VPRS 2-3-4-5-6* (ICC-01/04, 17 January 2006) [51].

[44] *Prosecutor v Katanga, Judgment on the Appeal of Mr Katanga against the Decision of the Trial Chamber II of 22 January 2010 entitled 'Decision on the Modalities of Victim Participation at Trial* (ICC-01/04-01/07 OA 11, 16 July 2010) ('*Katanga Appeals Decision on Victims Participation*') [85].

[45] Boas (n 3) 13. See also Zappalà, who notes that 'these rights and principles have been created for the benefit of the defendants': Zappalà (n 26) 143.

[46] McDermott (n 42) 166.

[47] *Rome Statute* Art 67 (emphasis added); *ICTY Statute* Art 21 (emphasis added).

[48] *ICTY Statute* Art 20; *Rome Statute* Art 64(2).

[49] Judge Ninian Stephen called this a 'marked contrast' between 'full respect' and 'due regard', and this contrast is further emphasised by 'the detailed and emphatic enumeration

McDermott notes that victims enjoy 'pure human rights', and recognising this does not challenge the 'status human rights' of an accused – but there is an 'inherent tension' present in attaching 'the status rights of [one] actor . . . to a person to whom the same status rights simply do not apply'.[50]

Yet despite the fact that these rights clearly only attach to the accused, the language of 'rights' has been affixed to victims in several ways.[51] Victims do possess certain rights under international law,[52] such as the right to the truth, the right to reparations, and the right to be informed.[53] However, these victims' rights need not be implemented as part of the trial proceedings,[54] and it is important to ensure that there is no confusion between 'the panoply of rights granted to victims under various branches of international law with their procedural rights in the international justice system'.[55] This again shows the importance of the arguments advanced in Chapter One, above.

As Zappalà argues, 'it is essential that the modes and the boundaries of *victim participation* in international criminal trials are properly identified *in the light of the rights of the defendants*'.[56] This theme is adopted and examined in this book. In Chapter Three, I examine the extent to which the increasing recognition extended to 'rights' of the victims is influencing the rights of the accused and how this relates to trial fairness. I also examine the 'rights' of the prosecution, and I demonstrate that such 'rights' are also increasingly emphasised in these trials. However, again I reiterate that it is the accused who primarily has rights in international criminal trials. While the victims, the prosecution and the international community have various interests in these trials (and some very limited rights), it is to be stressed in the strongest possible terms that rights attach particularly to the accused. The rationales for this position are now examined.

D. WHY RIGHTS?

The rights of the accused are so fundamental in international criminal trials that the United Nations Secretary-General once noted that 'it is

---

of distinct rights of the Accused in Article 21' and the less specific provisions of witness protection. See *Prosecutor v Tadić, Separate Opinion of Judge Stephen on the Prosecutor's Motion Requesting Protective Measures for Victims and Witnesses* (IT-94-1-T, 10 August 1995).
[50] McDermott (n 42) 166.
[51] Mariana Pena and Gaelle Carayon, 'Is the ICC Making the Most of Victim Participation?' (2013) 7 *IJTJ* 518, 519.
[52] Zappalà (n 26) 144.
[53] Christine Van den Wyngaert, 'Victims before International Criminal Courts: Some Views and Concerns of an ICC Trial Judge' (2011) 44 *CWRJIL* 475.
[54] Zappalà (n 26) 144; Van den Wyngaert (n 53).
[55] Zappalà (n 26) 144.
[56] Ibid. 139–40 (emphasis in original).

axiomatic that the International Tribunal must fully respect internationally recognised standards regarding the rights of the accused at all stages
of the proceedings'.[57] But beyond their status in the statutes of the various
international criminal institutions, why do rights matter? There are several
reasons why the protection of an accused's rights is important in international criminal trials. We are familiar with the rationales for rights from
traditional domestic analogies. Rights are designed to ensure the protection
of the individual against a system vested with the powers of a sovereign and
the ability to take liberty or property as a form of punishment. Thus, rights
protect an individual against the overreach of a zealous prosecutor or from
arbitrary, incorrect or vindictive or excessive punishment. Despite the lack
of a clear sovereign power in international criminal law, these rationales for
rights are no less true of the international realm than they are of national
criminal legal systems. As Damaška correctly notes, 'the ghost of the innocent men convicted must continue to hover over international criminal
justice just as it hovers over domestic criminal law enforcement'.[58]

Indeed, the principle of protecting an individual against a system arguably has an extra layer of complexity in international criminal law, where
trials are located within a system that holds onto an overarching aim to
'end impunity', as I have discussed in Chapter One. This system focuses on
individualised justice and holds a person responsible for atrocities committed in a widespread manner, often physically perpetrated by others. In such
a system, ensuring that the individual is not subject to arbitrary punishment
takes on an extra resonance. Although some argue that the system's aim of
ending impunity warrants a weakening of rights protection,[59] I argue that
such protection is, in fact, even more necessary and important.

Furthermore, in a legal system built on the basis of ending impunity,
rights at the trial stage not only act as a protector but also as an equaliser.
As high office is no longer a shield against prosecution, all individuals must
be seen to be equal before the law. This should be accompanied by an assurance that law cannot be used against any one individual in an arbitrary
manner. As Martha Minow notes, 'No one is above or outside the law,
and no one should be legally condemned or sanctioned outside legal procedures'.[60] Rights are thus integral to an international rule of law. In some
ways, the importance of the international rule of law is heightened, given
the subject matter of these trials: mass human rights abuses. It would be

---

[57] *Report of the United Nations Secretary-General, Submitted to the Security Council 3 May 1993, pursuant to Operative Paragraph 2 of Security Council Resolution 808*, UN SCOR, 48th sess, UN Doc
S/25704 (3 May 1993).

[58] Mirjan Damaška, 'Reflections on Fairness in International Criminal Justice' (2012) 10 *JICJ*
611, 615.

[59] Ibid. 612.

[60] Martha Minow, *Between Vengeance and Forgiveness: Facing History after Genocide and Mass
Violence* (Beacon Press, 1998) 25.

contradictory for a legal system established to ameliorate rights abuses (like trials without rights guarantees) to then undermine such rights.[61]

E. RIGHTS AND TRUTH

A further use of rights is to assist in achieving the ultimate aim of the trial: the forensic determination of the accused's guilt or otherwise. We have already considered this 'legal truth' and how legal truth-seeking is an aim that operates at the trial level to determine the accused's culpability. However, the question then arises as to how best to account for legal truth, within a *sui generis* and hybrid procedural model, such as international criminal procedure. In particular, should legal truth be construed as 'substantive truth', 'procedural truth', or some hybrid of these? How can (or how should) legal truth be realised under this procedural model?

The contention arises because while both typical adversarial and inquisitorial systems 'have an objective to search for the truth', there is no shared vision on 'what kind of truth and how it is best achieved'.[62] Procedural truth is the truth of facts as determined by following procedural rules, as well as the stipulated rights of the accused. Substantive truth is the 'real' truth of events, ascertainable via the trial process. As such, procedural truth may emphasise the rights of the accused and other procedural concerns over any desire to uncover the 'real' or whole truth. If the quest for truth conflicted with the rights of the accused, a system grounded in procedural truth would prioritise the rights of the accused over the truth, while a system grounded in substantive truth would value the determination of that truth more highly than the accused's rights. It is generally considered that the inquisitorial model of criminal procedure is aligned with 'substantive' truth, and the adversarial model is focused on the 'procedural truth'.[63] How is this accounted for in a system that is a hybrid, *sui generis* system? Which of these truths can – and should – be aspired to?

The ICC has accorded substantive truth a particular position, with the Court having 'the authority to request the submission of all evidence that it considers necessary for the determination of the truth'.[64] The judges, therefore, have significant 'truth-seeking' functions: it is not only for the parties to place evidence before the Court, but for the Court itself to seek evidence, if so required, for the determination of the truth. In the *Katanga* case, the Appeals Chamber emphasised its authority under Article 69(3) of

---

[61] Richard Vogler, 'Making International Criminal Procedure Work: From Theory to Practice' in Ralph Henham and Mark Findlay (eds), *Exploring the Boundaries of International Criminal Justice* (Ashgate, 2011) 105, 118.
[62] Fedorova (n 28) 81.
[63] See ibid. 79.
[64] *Rome Statute* Art 69(3).

the *Statute* to request the submission of evidence to assist it to determine the truth, in deciding that victims may testify on matters relating to the guilt of the accused.[65] Thus, because evidence pertaining to the guilt of the accused may be relevant to a Trial Chamber's determination of the truth, the Trial Chamber may request victims to testify on this subject. In considering that this did not make the victims a 'supplementary prosecutor', the Appeals Chamber did not address the question of equality of arms or the rights of the accused.[66] At both the ICTY and the ICC, judges also have the ability to call their own witnesses[67] or to question witnesses.[68] And (as already discussed) at the ICC, Regulation 55 permits the judges to 'recharacterise' the charges against the accused, to charges that more accurately represent culpability, and thereby avoid any 'technical acquittal'. This provision must be viewed against the backdrop of the aim to 'end impunity' but can also be seen as a desire for substantive truth rather than procedural truth.

However, the hybrid system of procedure might not be properly capable of uncovering the substantive truth. As John Jackson notes, 'the present hybrid of adversarial gathering and presentation of evidence combined with its liberal admission . . . falls short of providing the optimal epistemic conditions for ensuring that verdicts are based on a rigorous investigation and testing of the evidence'.[69] Thus, the hybridisation of the mechanisms for ascertaining the legal truth – utilising both typically procedural and typically substantive aspects – may not provide the best epistemic model. Indeed, Nancy Combs suggests that the verdicts of international criminal trials rest on unsafe epistemic grounds.[70] She argues that 'by using the Western trial form, international criminal proceedings cloak themselves in a garb of fact-finding competence, but it is only a cloak, for many of the key expectations and assumptions that underlie the Western trial form do not exist in the international context'.[71]

Moreover, this preference for substantive truth provides a particular challenge for the rights of the accused and whether those rights can be used as part of the epistemological framework of the trial. Under one view, a forensic determination of guilt can only occur after rigorous testing of properly admitted evidence, which is assisted by procedural safeguards in the form of rights. As Zappalà correctly asserts, the rights of the accused

---

[65] *Katanga Appeals Decision on Victims Participation*; see also *Prosecutor v Katanga, Decision on the Set of Procedural Rights Attached to Procedural Status of Victims at the Pre-Trial Stage of a Case* (ICC-01/04-01/07, 13 May 2008) [31]–[36].

[66] Ibid.

[67] *ICTY Rules* r 98; *Rome Statute* Art 69(3).

[68] *ICTY Rules* r 85(B); *Rome Statute* Art 69(3).

[69] Jackson (n 41) 19.

[70] Nancy Combs, *Fact Finding Without Facts: The Uncertain Evidentiary Foundations of International Criminal Convictions* (CUP, 2010).

[71] Ibid. 7.

'are not "just" human rights guarantees: they are part and parcel of the epistemological mechanism for fact finding in criminal proceedings'.[72] Zappalà goes on to note that '[r]especting the rules to establish the truth requires full consistency with the rights of the accused: these must be seen as an essential component of accurate and truthful fact finding on which punishment is premised'.[73] Yet this does not sit easily with the preference for substantive truth over procedural truth. In light of the divergence around how rights might assist truthful fact-finding, one of the challenges for the ICC – with its hybrid and *sui generis* procedural system – is how to ensure legal truth.

F. FAIRNESS IN INTERNATIONAL CRIMINAL TRIALS: CENTRALITY ACCEPTED

In this section of this chapter, I shift the object of analysis to the idea of fairness in international criminal trials and examine how and why fairness is considered to be central to these trials.

Trial Chambers are vested with a statutory responsibility to 'ensure that a trial is fair and expeditious and is conducted with full respect for the rights of the accused and due regard for the protection of victims and witnesses'.[74] Fairness is therefore integral to a Trial Chamber's role and to the proper proceeding of the trial, as stipulated under the relevant statutes. The importance of fairness has also been articulated in judicial decisions, as epitomised by the *Lubanga* Appeals Chamber, who noted that '[a] fair trial is the only means to do justice. If no fair trial can be held, the object of the judicial process is frustrated and the process must be stopped'.[75]

It is not surprising, then, that judges view fairness to be of central importance. When asked about fairness in international criminal trials, judges were unanimous in their support of the concept of fairness.[76] Fairness was described as 'absolutely crucial. It's the core concern';[77] and as the 'number one leading idea ... throughout the whole proceedings'.[78] One judge described fairness as 'fundamental. It's fundamental. I mean, it's the alpha and the omega of the whole process ... the beginning and the end. If

---

[72] Zappalà (n 26) 145.

[73] Ibid.

[74] *ICTY Statute* Art 20; *Rome Statute* Art 64(2).

[75] *Prosecutor v Lubanga, Judgment on the Appeal of Mr Thomas Lubanga Dyilo against the Decision on the Defence Challenge to the Jurisdiction of the Court pursuant to article 19(2)(a) of the Statute of 3 October 2006* (ICC-01/04-01/06, 14 December 2006) [37].

[76] Interview with Judge Howard Morrison (29 May 2013); Interview with Judge A (31 May 2013); Interview with Judge Justice Bakone Moloto (27 May 2013); Interview with Judge X (14 May 2013).

[77] Interview with Judge Howard Morrison (29 May 2013).

[78] Interview with Judge A (31 May 2013).

fairness is not the underlying governing principle relating criminal proceedings, then the whole purpose of criminal proceedings is defeated'.[79]

There appears to be a dedication to fairness among international legal practitioners, regardless of which role they play in the trial process. Prosecutors, defence teams and victims' representatives have all referenced fairness in litigation. Alex Whiting, a former prosecutor at the ICTY and now an international legal scholar, noted:

> there exists a deep and genuine concern for the fairness of trials that is shared among judges, prosecutors and defence counsel. There may be disagreements on what fairness requires, but no failure to understand the importance of fairness for the accused and the institution.[80]

In scholarship, the centrality of fairness to international criminal trials is reiterated time and again. It is described as 'the foundation of international criminal procedure'[81] and as 'perhaps the most important justification advanced in support of "International Criminal Justice"'.[82] Even where fairness is listed as only one of multiple factors associated with international criminal justice,[83] it is still expressed as being integral to trials.

Fairness is a core part of the identity of international criminal law. Contrary to many domestic criminal legal systems, where historically fairness has not always been a central concern,[84] the contemporary international criminal justice system has been established to satisfy the concept of fairness. The creation of the Nuremberg and Tokyo tribunals was grounded in a belief that '"justice" and "fairness" are too precious to be traded off against vengeance and effective sanction'.[85] To this day, international criminal justice has maintained a strong emphasis on rejecting 'show trials' and instead on conducting 'trials that are fair'. Indeed, international criminal law has built a conception of itself around its adherence to fair trial concerns. As a legal system established – at least nominally – on the premise of trials that are fair and conducted with full respect for the rights of the accused, international criminal law stands in contradistinction to national systems that permit show trials, arbitrary punishments and human rights

---

[79] Interview with Judge X (14 May 2013).

[80] Alex Whiting, 'Guest Post: The ICC's Last Days? Not So Fast' on *Spreading the Jam* (20 March 2014) <http://dovjacobs.com/2014/03/20/guest-post-the-iccs-end-days-not-so-fast/> (last accessed 9 December 2021).

[81] Gideon Boas et al. (eds), *International Criminal Law Practitioner Library: Volume III, International Criminal Procedure* (CUP, 2011) 4.

[82] Carsten Stahn, 'Between "Faith" and "Facts": By What Standards Should We Assess International Criminal Justice?' (2012) 25 *LJIL* 251, 267.

[83] Ibid. 270; Jackson (n 41); Mirjan Damaška, 'The Competing Visions of Fairness: The Basic Choice for International Criminal Tribunals' (2001) 36 *NCJILCR* 365.

[84] See Stefan Trechsel, 'Why Must Trials be Fair?' (1997) 31 *ILR* 94, 97.

[85] Stahn (n 82) 267.

violations. Fairness is something the system of international criminal law proudly adorns itself with. Fairness may also become part of its marketing toolkit.[86] Moreover, this is linked to the functions of fairness, outlined below and particularly the idea of fairness as a legitimating force: in legitimating the system of law, international criminal law turns to fairness for support; in doing so, it builds fairness into its identity and gains strength from it. As one defence lawyer noted, 'it is pointless to have a trial if it's not a fair trial because what's the alternative, an unfair trial? Why bother? Then just take the person out and shoot them behind the building and get it over with. No, obviously you want to have a fair trial'.[87] Fairness has been an explicit choice of international criminal law and its institutions and is tied intimately to their creation and maintenance.

G. WHY THE CENTRALITY OF FAIRNESS IS IMPORTANT (OR, WHAT DOES FAIRNESS DO?)

It is therefore clear that fairness is central to international criminal trials. This centrality is accepted by trial stakeholders (judges, parties and participants) and academics, and is consistent with the history and identity of international criminal law. In addition, this centrality of fairness matters because fairness has several important functions. I will examine some of these now: that fairness can act as an interpretive tool for Trial Chambers, as an epistemic enabler, as a legitimating force, and as a tool to assist institutions in meeting their aims.

(1) Fairness as a key interpretive tool of trial chambers

Fairness is a tool to assist international criminal Trial Chambers in interpreting, supplementing, or even constructing the law. This is consistent with the statutory responsibility of Trial Chambers to 'ensure a trial that is fair',[88] and with the 'requirement to interpret and apply the *Statute* in the light of its fundamental purpose, which is not merely to bring persons to trial, but to a trial that is fair'.[89] This appeal to fairness to interpret and apply the law is particularly important in a *sui generis* system of international

---

[86] See Christine Schwöbel, 'The Market and Marketing Culture of International Criminal Law' in Christine Schwöbel (ed), *Critical Approaches to International Criminal Law* (Routledge, 2014) 264; Sara Kendall, 'Commodifying Global Justice: Economics of Accountability at the International Criminal Court' (2015) 13 *JICJ* 113.

[87] Interview with Colleen Rohan and Gregor Guy-Smith (8 May 2013).

[88] *ICTY Statute* Art 20; *Rome Statute* Art 64(2).

[89] Patrick Robinson, 'Rough Edges in the Alignment of Legal Systems in the Proceedings at the ICTY' (2005) 3 *JICJ* 1037, 1055. See also Patrick Robinson, 'Fair but Expeditious Trials' in Hirad Abtahi and Gideon Boas (eds), *The Dynamics of International Criminal Justice* (Brill, 2006) 169, 174.

criminal procedure, where there is almost inevitably tension between traditional common law and civil law approaches to procedural questions.[90] In situations where there is a conflict between the approaches of traditional criminal legal systems, and no governing provision in the *Statute* or *Rules*, resolution of this conflict may occur by using fairness 'as the plane to smooth the edges in the alignment of the legal systems'.[91] Patrick Robinson, writing extra-judicially, has argued that unless fairness is used in this way, unfairness may result.[92]

Fairness may be used as an interpretative tool to assist Chambers where there are silences or ambiguities in the law. Indeed, there are significant gaps, or 'constructive ambiguities', in the procedural framework, particularly of the International Criminal Court.[93] In order to address these gaps, judges have a particular role in interpreting – and thus developing – the law.[94] Fairness may be the principle that assists judges to do this. In addition to judicial interpretation, the international criminal legal system also vests judges with roles in law-creation, with judges able to amend the rules or to create new rules and regulations.[95] This role of judges as law-makers is particularly important given the ambiguities in the law and in the absence of a global legislature.[96] Fairness is 'the principle most frequently invoked as the

---

[90] Robinson (n 89) 1040.

[91] Ibid. 1058.

[92] Ibid. 1040.

[93] Claus Kress, 'The Procedural Law of the International Criminal Court in Outline: Anatomy of a Unique Compromise' (2003) 1 *JICJ* 603, 605–6.

[94] See Elies van Sliedregt, 'The Curious Case of International Criminal Liability' (2012) 10 *JICJ* 1171, 1186.

[95] At the *ad hoc* tribunals, judges may amend the rules in plenary sessions (*in camera*), and thus their considerations in law-making are unknown. At the ICC, amendments to provisions are more complex. Amendments to the *Rome Statute* must be agreed to by the Assembly of States Parties (ASP) after proposal by a State Party (*Rome Statute* Art 121). Amendments to the *Rules* may be proposed by a State Party, the judges (by an absolute majority), or the Prosecutor; and amendments will enter force by a two-thirds majority of the members of the ASP (*Rome Statute* Art 51). Judges can also draw up provisional rules, 'in urgent cases where the Rules do not provide for a specific situation'. These provisional rules would be applied 'until adopted, amended or rejected at the next ordinary or special session' of the ASP (*Rome Statute* Art 51(3)). The regulations of the ICC are changed by the judges, acting by absolute majority (*Rome Statute* Art 52), and will take effect upon adoption (unless otherwise decided by the judges) and circulated to States Parties for comment. If there are no objections from a majority of States Parties within six months, the amendments will remain in force (*Rome Statute* Art 52). In amending the regulations, the judges will consult the prosecution and registry, but there is no explicit mention of seeking the input of the Office for the Public Counsel for Defence (*Rome Statute* Art 52 (1)).

[96] Although in the case of the ICC, the ASP does have some 'legislative' roles. For more on the topic of judicial creativity in international criminal trials, see Joseph Powderly and Shane Darcy (eds), *Judicial Creativity at the International Criminal Tribunals* (OUP, 2010); see also Hannah Woolaver and Emma Palmer, 'Challenges to the Independence of the International Criminal Court from the Assembly of States Parties' (2017) 15(4) *JICJ* 641.

basis for a new rule or the rationale for a decision',[97] and it would certainly be possible to use fairness as a key consideration in determining how to make new provisions.

The use of fairness as a key interpretive tool is supported by judges.[98] As one judge noted, when asked whether 'fairness' is used to resolve tensions or ambiguities:

> definitely, definitely, and that's what we do ... many a time we have had instances ... where we had absolutely no help from either the *Statute* or the *Rules*, and we had to devise or find a solution ... In doing so we are guided by the basic principles of a fair trial, namely the presumption of innocence of the accused, the right to remain silent, and other principles ... Most of the time we also keep in mind the principle of when in doubt ... the advantage [or] benefit [must go to] the accused.[99]

This judge reiterated that:

> we are always guided by this fairness – it's an obsession ... you may not find it written in the decision itself, but you can rest assured that the end product [of the decision] ... is the result of considerations made by the trial judges, guided by the knowledge that they need to be fair to the parties.[100]

Another judge noted that 'as a judge fulfilling a judicial function, obviously fairness is something that is built into our DNA'.[101] One judge held the view that the interpretive tool used by Trial Chambers to resolve silence in the *Rules* or *Statute* would be the 'interests of justice', which applies to 'both sides'[102] and involves fairness to the accused. It can therefore be seen that judges do use fairness in their decision-making and interpretation, and this will be a key focus of my analysis in Chapters Four, Five and Six, where I examine how fairness is invoked in procedural decision-making in contemporary international criminal trials.

(2) Fairness as an epistemic enabler

A trial's main aim should be to make a forensic determination of the guilt or innocence of the accused.[103] Such a forensic determination is made by a process of fact-finding to ascertain the 'legal truth', determined by the admission and evaluation of evidence. To ascertain this legal truth, fairness may

---

[97] Robinson (n 89) 1055.
[98] Interview with Judge X (14 May 2013); Interview with Stefan Trechsel (28 May 2013); Interview with Judge Adrian Fulford (5 June 2014).
[99] Interview with Judge X (14 May 2013).
[100] Ibid.
[101] Interview with Judge Adrian Fulford (5 June 2014).
[102] Interview with Judge Justice Bakone Moloto (27 May 2013).
[103] See above, Chapter One.

assist the Trial Chamber, by ensuring that evidence is properly admitted, rigorously tested and of high quality. In making decisions on how to admit evidence, and what evidence to admit, judges will appeal to the relevant rules and, where necessary (for example, where the rules do not cover a particular set of circumstances), to fairness. In this way, fairness links procedure (process) to outcome (verdict) in a way that is consistent with the aim of the trial. Fairness hence becomes an epistemic enabler: a tool to assist the Trial Chamber to reach an appropriate verdict on the charges faced by the accused.

As outlined above, the pursuit of this legal truth has traditionally been conceived of as either 'procedural' or 'substantive' in nature. As we have already seen, the complexities of the hybrid system, and the melding of typically procedural and typically substantive mechanisms for ascertaining legal truth, mean that international criminal trials may not possess the optimal epistemic model. In this context, fairness may provide a 'mediating discourse' between the different conceptions of truth and the mechanisms to ascertain it: in particular, which evidence to admit and how to test it. In this way, fairness can be an epistemic enabler. Indeed, the requirements on the admissibility of evidence refer to fairness. At the ICTY, in cases that are not covered by the general rule on admissibility,[104] the Chamber 'shall apply rules of evidence which will best favour a fair determination of the matter before it and are consonant with the spirit of the *Statute* and the general principles of law'.[105] While generally 'a Chamber may admit any relevant evidence which it deems to have probative value',[106] a Chamber may also 'exclude evidence if its probative value is substantially outweighed by the need to ensure a fair trial'.[107] Similarly, at the ICC, the Court

> may rule on the relevance or admissibility of any evidence, taking into account, *inter alia*, the probative value of the evidence and any prejudice that such evidence may cause to a fair trial or to a fair evaluation of the testimony of a witness, in accordance with the *Rules of Procedure and Evidence*.[108]

Relevant evidence may be excluded if it 'may prejudice the fairness of the trial, including the rights of the accused or the fair evaluation of testimony or other evidence'.[109] Evidence may be excluded if its prejudice is great and its probative value relatively slim.[110] Hence, while admissibility of evidence is relatively free at both the ICTY and ICC, it is closely related to, and constrained by, considerations of fairness.

---

[104] *ICTY Rules* r 89.

[105] Ibid. r 89(B).

[106] Ibid. r 89(C).

[107] Ibid. r 89(D).

[108] *Rome Statute* Art 69(4).

[109] *Prosecutor v Ruto, Decision on the Prosecution's Request for Admission of Documentary Evidence* (ICC-01/09-01/11, 10 June 2014) [16].

[110] Ibid.

In line with what we will see in the next chapter – namely that fairness is incoherent and can be used to support a variety of arguments – fairness can be used as a basis to support either lax or tight admissibility requirements for evidence. Indeed, as set out above, evidence can be excluded on the basis of fairness concerns. Initially, this might appear to be contrary to the Chamber's mission to determine the 'truth', but in fact, it may be that more limited evidence presented to the Court is of greater utility in the Court's role to determine the legal truth of the accused's culpability. Fairness considerations may operate to restrict information that is of questionable provenance or credibility or that otherwise should not be relied upon. Fairness may therefore ensure that only the most accurate evidence is submitted as a means to establish the outcome of the trial.

Fairness can also act as an epistemic enabler through ensuring a fact-finding process that admits high-quality evidence, promotes equality between the parties and is rigorous in its evaluation of evidence. The current difficulties associated with a hybrid approach to truth and the processes to ensure it may be addressed by using fairness in this manner. For example, John Jackson highlights the principles of equality of arms and of adversarial procedure to ensure accuracy. This happens through making sure that 'the sources of information brought to the attention of the tribunal are not overly skewed by one party' (equality of arms)[111] and by creating 'epistemic assurance that the sources of evidence brought before the court can be tested' (adversarial procedure).[112] Jackson argues that these 'can be regarded as part and parcel of the right to a fair criminal procedure but it can also be argued that they point in the direction of better epistemic procedures'.[113] Thus, there is a close relationship between fairness and legal truth.

(3) Fairness as a legitimating force

If trials are considered to be unfair, the verdict is unlikely to be seen as legitimate; and if verdicts are perceived to be invalid, the institution is unlikely to be seen favourably. Unless fairness is present, the legitimacy of the outcome may be questionable, and this may then cast the authority of the institution into disrepute. Fairness is therefore important to protect and promote the legitimacy of the trial, the institution and the system of law. This is achieved through verdicts that are considered reasonable after a trial that is seen as fair. The use of rights as protective agents was outlined above, and advancing this further, fairness is also a protective agent: rights protect the individual accused, and fairness protects the process of the trial. They are connected, with rights of the accused being necessary for the fairness of the

---

[111] Jackson (n 41) 23.
[112] Ibid. 23–4.
[113] Ibid. 23.

trial. Thus, without rights, the trial will lack fairness as a protecting – and ultimately legitimating – force. The close relationship between legitimacy and fairness has also been theorised in relation to international law more broadly.[114]

The link between fairness and legitimacy in international criminal trials was made as early as the Nuremberg trial, where Robert Jackson intoned that 'the record on which we judge these defendants is the record on which history will judge us tomorrow. To pass these defendants a poisoned chalice is to put it to our own lips as well'.[115] More recently, Judge Christine Van den Wyngaert articulated the link between the 'moral authority' of an international criminal institution and the fairness of its trials:

> In order for a court of law to have the legal and moral authority to pass legal and moral judgment on someone, especially when it relates to such serious allegations as international crimes, it is essential . . . to scrupulously observe the fairness of the proceedings and to apply the standard of proof consistently and rigorously. It is not good enough that most of the trial has been fair. All of it must be fair.[116]

Hence, courts gain moral authority through fairness – and fairness is especially important in these trials, given the seriousness of the crimes examined. David Luban argues that the legitimacy of international criminal institutions comes from the fairness of their procedures and punishments rather than the authority that creates them.[117] In his view, '[t]ribunals bootstrap themselves into legitimacy by the quality of the justice they deliver; their rightness depends on their fairness'.[118] This, then, reinforces international criminal courts and tribunals: these institutions gain legitimacy through the fairness of their processes, and this bolsters their identity. Sergey Vasiliev correctly points out that international criminal institutions have

> conceptualized their own legality as institutions and the legitimacy of their proceedings in terms of compliance with the international rule of law, which in

---

[114] Thomas Franck argues that legitimacy is 'a key factor in fairness, for it accommodates a deeply felt popular belief that for a system of rules to be fair, it must be firmly rooted in a framework of formal requirements about how rules are made, interpreted, and applied' (Franck (n 2) 7–8). Franck links fairness, rights, legitimacy, and community, arguing that rights are 'defined, acquired, and protected through the legitimate and legitimating processes of the community' (Ibid. 27).

[115] International Military Tribunal, *The Trial of the Major War Criminals Before the International Military Tribunal* (International Military Tribunal, 1947) 2, 101.

[116] *Prosecutor v Katanga, Jugement rendu en application de l'article 74 du Statut* (ICC-01/04-01/07, 7 March 2014) ('*Katanga Judgment*'), [311] (Judge Van den Wyngaert).

[117] David Luban, 'Fairness to Rightness: Jurisdiction, Legality, and the Legitimacy of International Criminal Law' in Samantha Besson and John Tasioulas (eds), *Philosophy of International Law* (OUP, 2010) 569, 579.

[118] Ibid.

turn was interpreted principally as the duty to fully respect some objective and external . . . international standards of fair trial.[119]

Joanna Nicholson has also emphasised the relationship between trial fairness and the legitimacy of international criminal institutions, arguing that fairness is 'a key element in enhancing the process of international criminal courts and tribunals'.[120] While fairness as a legitimating force may be true of traditional domestic trials and institutions, Nicholson points out that international courts and tribunals are 'newcomers to the criminal justice system' and as such, they must build 'legitimacy capital' and 'persuade their constituencies of their effectiveness'.[121] As such, the drive for legitimacy – through fairness – is given 'additional piquancy'.[122]

One defence lawyer voiced his view that trial fairness and institutional legitimacy are interlinked, saying:

> without a fair trial these courts are not legitimate, won't be perceived as legitimate. Therefore international justice won't work. It will just be viewed as another political tool . . . In order for [these tribunals] to succeed the trials have to be fair . . . if the trial is not perceived as fair then the whole process is really illegitimate and they shouldn't even begin to undertake such a thing if they're not going to guarantee that the trial will be fair.[123]

The defence lawyer here ties the ability of international justice to 'work' with the legitimacy of the courts, which is drawn from whether or not they are perceived as running trials that are fair.

Without being perceived as legitimate, it is unlikely that an international trial, institution, or system of law will have the moral authority to achieve its respective aims. Fairness's legitimating function, therefore, also affects its ability to act as a tool to assist the trial, institution and system, to meet their aims. I now examine this point.

---

[119] Sergey Vasiliev, *International Criminal Trials: A Normative Framework* (PhD Thesis, University of Amsterdam, 2014) 96.

[120] Joanna Nicholson, '"Too High", "Too Low", or "Just Fair Enough"? Finding Legitimacy Through the Accused's Right to a Fair Trial' (2019) 17(2) JICJ 351, 353. See also Caleb Wheeler, who notes that 'without fairness international . . . criminal courts and tribunals lack legitimacy and without legitimacy they lack effectiveness'. Caleb H Wheeler, 'The Scales of Justice: Balancing the Goals of International Criminal Trials' (2019) 30 CLF 145, 146. For more on trial legitimacy and fairness, see Jonathan Hafetz, *Punishing Atrocities Through a Fair Trial* (CUP, 2018) 145–7.

[121] Nicholson (n 120) 354.

[122] Ibid.

[123] Interview with Peter Robinson (2 May 2013).

(4) Fairness as a tool to assist the trial, institution and legal system to meet their aims

As outlined in Chapter One, the purported aims of international criminal law are both legion and complex. I have made the argument that the aims of the system of law, the institutions of the courts and tribunals, and the trials themselves, may differ. At the level of the trial, the primary aim of international criminal trials must be to determine the guilt or innocence of the accused after rigorous testing of admissible evidence and, as I have set out above, the concept of fairness can be used to assist this, through its use as an epistemic enabler. Fairness is, therefore, crucial to the primary aim of the trial.

Fairness is also relevant to the purported aims at the level of the institution of the courts and tribunals. One such aim might be to enact a socio-pedagogic function.[124] Reminiscent of the earlier point linking legitimacy and fairness, Damaška argues that fairness is crucial to the socio-pedagogic function of international criminal judges, who are 'moral teachers'.[125] However, in order to be successful in such a role, judges must be 'perceived by their constituencies as having a legitimate authority. Lacking coercive power, their legitimacy hangs almost entirely on the quality of their decisions and their procedures'.[126] Elsewhere, Damaška explicitly links this to fairness: the ability of judges to be moral teachers necessitates them being 'perceived by their audiences as fair. Fairness is thus of crucial importance for the attainment of a goal which is – or should be – at the heart of international criminal justice'.[127] Hence, fairness is a tool to assist international criminal judges to have authority as moral teachers and thus to help further the socio-pedagogic aim of these institutions. Fairness assists both the trial and the institution to reach their aims.

The above 'uses' of fairness – as an interpretive tool, an epistemic enabler, a legitimating force, and to assist the institution to meet its aims – demonstrate the reasons why fairness is central. It is not simply true that the centrality of fairness is written in the statutes of Courts and Tribunals or that the centrality of fairness is widely accepted by all stakeholders. It is also accepted because fairness operates in a number of ways, which are important for international criminal trials, institutions and ultimately the system of law as a whole. Fairness is therefore perceived to be important for what it can be used to do, and to achieve, in international criminal trials. Fairness is not only important for its own sake but also to ensure a trial process where rules are interpreted and constructed appropriately; which can undertake

---

[124] Damaška (n 58) 614; Mirjan Damaška, 'What is the Point of International Criminal Justice?' (2008) 83 *CKLR* 329, 345. See also Nicholson (n 120) 364–5.

[125] Damaška (n 58) 614.

[126] Damaška (n 124) 345.

[127] Damaška (n 58) 614.

fact-finding; that is legitimate; and that can assist the trial, institution and system of law, to fulfil its aims. One of the questions that then arises is how this is linked to the operationalisation of trials – namely, trial procedure – and this is considered in the case studies in this book.

Understanding the significance of fairness allows us to appreciate the potential ramifications of any incoherence. But conversely, fairness offers a significant hope. Fairness represents a shared expectation and aspiration between all the stakeholders in the international criminal justice mission; and therefore, fairness offers a possibility of acting to bind stakeholders who may otherwise be adversaries. Yet where conceptions of fairness differ, this can provide an additional source of animosity and distrust between various stakeholders. A coherent vision of fairness is therefore worthy of examination and ultimately of pursuit. However, as I go on to examine in the next chapter, the concept of fairness in contemporary international criminal trials is fundamentally incoherent and unstable; and – as I demonstrate in later chapters of the book – is separated from the rights of the accused in procedural decisions.

Chapter 3
The incoherence of fairness in international criminal trials

Maybe it's like pornography; you can't define it but you know it when you see it
– Defence lawyer, when asked about fairness
in international criminal trials[1]

Despite its centrality to international criminal trials, there is no coherent understanding of fairness. In some respects, this is unsurprising – fairness is a normative question, and so any attempt to measure or assess fairness is 'a normative judgement'[2] which will probably be contested. Fairness seems to lack the ability to be quantified, and 'there are no clear indicators' of levels of fairness.[3] Nonetheless, this chapter attempts to set out a taxonomy of the factors contributing to the conceptual incoherence of fairness. As Yvonne McDermott notes, fairness questions have been answered in a 'piecemeal fashion', and there is a 'lack of an overarching theory guiding the procedural fairness of trials', which has resulted in a failure of international criminal law to set the standard for fairness.[4] The present chapter intends to lay out the various perspectives on, and challenges to, fairness in an attempt to provide greater conceptual clarity.

I argue that there is a conceptual incoherence surrounding the concept of fairness, for three main reasons: a conflict over what principles are constitutive of fairness; a conflict over who should be the key beneficiary of fairness in trials; and a conflict around how to ensure fairness in a *sui generis* procedural system (where there is a lack of agreement around translating the traditional inquisitorial and adversarial approaches to a hybrid system). In other words, there is a lack of shared understanding around *what* fairness includes, *whom* fairness is owed to, and *how* fairness can be assured. In relation to each of these three points, a diversity of opinions shows that there is little coherence regarding what fairness requires. The different approaches on these questions are all related to the links between fairness and rights in the trial setting. I argue that there is a growing disconnect between fairness

---

[1] Interview with Colleen Rohan and Gregor Guy-Smith (8 May 2013).
[2] Carsten Stahn, 'Between "Faith" and "Facts": By What Standards Should We Assess International Criminal Justice?' (2012) 25 *LJIL* 251, 268–9.
[3] Ibid.
[4] Yvonne McDermott, 'Rights in Reverse: A Critical Analysis of Fair Trial Rights under International Criminal Law' in William A Schabas, Yvonne McDermott and Niamh Hayes (eds), *The Ashgate Research Companion to International Criminal Law* (Ashgate, 2013) 165.

and the rights of the accused in international criminal trials, which emerges from, and adds further to, the conceptual incoherence of fairness.

A. WHAT PRINCIPLES ARE REQUIRED TO ENSURE FAIRNESS?

Beyond the rights of the accused (which we have already seen to be closely linked to fairness), *what else* does fairness entail? Fairness is not perfection or infallibility: a trial must be fair, but it need not be perfect.[5] However, the question of what is needed to ensure fairness does not have a clear answer. As Damaška argues, while there are certain 'minimal requirements of fairness', identifying these requirements is 'highly controversial'.[6] A survey of what different authors outline in their discussions of fairness shows that there is a lack of a shared understanding about which principles are constitutive of fairness.

Some authors prioritise the rights of the accused as being central to fairness, with little examination on what else – if anything – fairness might include. For example, Christoph Safferling has referred to a 'kaleidoscope of rights', which are constitutive of fairness.[7] These include 'moral principles' such as the equality of arms, and particular rights.[8] This suggests that 'fairness' *is* rights, with little else to be considered when examining fairness.

However, generally, it is understood that fairness includes more than the rights of the accused. The *Milošević* Trial Chamber set out the relationship between fairness and rights:

> Within the ambit of fairness fall a number of rights, all intended to achieve for the accused a fair trial . . . The concept of fairness not only includes these specific rights but also has a much wider ambit, requiring that in all aspects the conduct of the trial must be fair to the accused. Hence, the specific rights are described as 'minimum guarantees'. Fairness is thus the overarching requirement of criminal proceedings.[9]

It could thus be said that the rights of the accused are thus necessary, but not sufficient, to ensure fairness. As I have argued above, fairness – as an 'overarching requirement' of the trial – is given content by the rights of the accused. If rights are violated, a trial cannot be said to be fair. But if these

---

[5] Patrick Robinson, 'Fair but Expeditious Trials' in Hirad Abtahi and Gideon Boas (eds), *The Dynamics of International Criminal Justice* (Brill, 2006) 169, 171.

[6] Mirjan Damaška, 'Reflections on Fairness in International Criminal Justice' (2012) 10 *JICJ* 611, 616.

[7] Christoph Safferling, *Towards an International Criminal Procedure* (OUP, 2001) 30. See also Salvatore Zappalà, *Human Rights in International Criminal Proceedings* (OUP, 2003) as another early text which emphasises the rights of the accused as being central to fairness.

[8] Safferling (n 7) 30–1.

[9] *Prosecutor v Milošević, Reasons for Decision on Assignment of Defence Counsel* (IT-02-54-T, 22 September 2004) [29].

rights are upheld, is anything further required in order for a trial to be considered fair? There is little agreement in the literature on the question of 'what else', in addition to rights, is integral to the concept of fairness.

Elements that may be constitutive of fairness include the safety of victims and witnesses; the interests of other stakeholders, including the prosecution; expeditiousness; equality of arms; the presumption of innocence; the ability to present one's case; a 'public trial'; and 'the interests of justice'. Patrick Robinson has stated that fairness is 'to be just and equitable',[10] and the question 'is whether the accused has had a fair chance of dealing with the allegations against him'.[11] At the ICC, the Chambers emphasised the connection between fairness and equality, when they noted – relying on jurisprudence from the International Court of Justice (ICJ) – that:

> The term "fairness" (equité), from the Latin "equus", means equilibrium, or balance. As a legal concept, equity, or fairness, "is a direct emanation of the idea of justice". Equity of the proceedings entails equilibrium between the two parties, which assumes both respect for the principle of equality and the principle of adversarial proceedings.[12]

Yet as Anni Pues points out, this reliance on ICJ jurisprudence is flawed, as that institution deals with proceedings between two theoretically equal states as opposed to criminal cases with an 'inherent disparity' between an individual accused and an Office of the Prosecutor.[13] Pues argues that it would be more helpful to conceive of fairness as containing 'two concepts entailed in important human rights provisions: (i) a general component of fairness applicable to various types of legal proceedings; and (ii) a specific one, applicable to the rights of the defendant in criminal proceedings'.[14] She, therefore, argues that the 'right to a fair trial' should apply 'first and foremost to a defendant while the general component of fairness is preserved to the benefit of all participants in the proceedings'.[15] In this way, Pues correctly conceptualises a difference between fairness and rights.

Some authors reiterate the importance of rights to fairness but also suggest additional principles that are integral to fairness. For example,

---

[10] Patrick Robinson, 'The Right to a Fair Trial in International Law, with Specific Reference to the Work of the ICTY' (2009) 3 *BJILP* 1.

[11] Ibid. 5.

[12] *Situation in the Democratic Republic of the Congo, Decision on the Prosecutor's application for leave to appeal the Chamber's Decision of 17 January 2006 on the Applications for Participation in the Proceedings of VPRS 1, VPRS 2, VPRS 3, VPRS 4, VPRS 5 and VPRS 6* (ICC-01/04-135-tEN, 31 March 2006) ('*Congo Decision on Leave to Appeal Decision on Participation*') [38] and the sources there cited.

[13] Anni Pues, 'A Victim's Right to a Fair Trial at the International Criminal Court? Reflections on Article 68(3)' (2015) 13 *JICJ* 951, 956.

[14] Ibid.

[15] Ibid.

McDermott describes 'a number of key principles of fairness' which 'include transparency, consistency, equality and impartiality'.[16] The 'highest standards of fairness' requires that the rights of the accused are fully implemented in a way that is 'consistent with the principles of fairness, such as neutrality, equality, and consistency'.[17] McDermott argues that 'adjudicators should be neutral and impartial; the law must be applied equally and consistently; the accused should have an effective defence . . .; the process should be as open and transparent as possible; and the law and procedure should be clear and fully articulated in advance of the trial'.[18] Stahn emphasises the 'perception of independence (ie freedom from external interference) and impartiality (ie lack of bias and investigation of all sides to a conflict)' as 'a key prerequisite of "fairness"'.[19] Issues with selectivity of cases pose a challenge for the perception of impartiality and independence of international criminal institutions.[20] Jackson reinforces the 'international fair trial norms of the right to equality of arms and the right to adversarial procedure', which he argues 'can be accommodated across the common law and civil law traditions'.[21]

Some principles are, at least in theory, reasonably uncontroversial. The presumption of innocence and the principle of equality of arms are two that would see widespread support as being inherent in fairness. However, there is even some divergence in this regard. For example, the presumption of innocence has a different resonance in the inquisitorial system than in the adversarial system; there may, therefore, be a lack of agreement about its place in international criminal trials and what, precisely, it means. Such disagreement may also be linked to the multiplicity of views on what standard of proof is required to establish guilt.[22] As discussed above, the principle of equality of arms also has two very different approaches (formal or material), which may result in very different consequences for the relative position of the parties.

The relationship between fairness and expeditiousness is also an important consideration in terms of what principles are necessary for a trial to be fair. The two issues of fairness and expedition 'intersect' in the trial context,[23] with statutes requiring Trial Chambers to ensure that trials are

[16] Yvonne McDermott, *Fairness in International Criminal Trials* (OUP, 2016) 6.

[17] Ibid. 34.

[18] Ibid. 31.

[19] Stahn (n 2) 269.

[20] Ibid.

[21] John Jackson, 'Finding the Best Epistemic Fit for International Criminal Tribunals: Beyond the Adversarial–Inquisitorial Dichotomy' (2009) 7 *JICJ* 17, 19.

[22] See Simon De Smet, 'The International Criminal Standard of Proof at the ICC – Beyond Reasonable Doubt or Beyond Reason?' in Carsten Stahn (ed), *The Law and Practice of the International Criminal Court: A Critical Account of Challenges and Achievements* (OUP, 2015) 861.

[23] Gideon Boas, *The Milošević Trial: Lessons for the Conduct of Complex International Criminal Proceedings* (CUP, 2007) 63.

both 'fair *and* expeditious'.[24] As Gideon Boas notes, 'achieving a balance between fairness and expedition is crucial to achieving best practice' in these trials.[25] More particularly, expedition is also a right of the accused: there is a right to be tried without undue delay,[26] and in this sense, the accused has a right to a trial that is expeditious. However, this does not mean that the relationship between fairness and expedition is necessarily mutually enforcing. Indeed, an emphasis on expeditiousness may lead to fairness being curtailed or sacrificed.[27] Expeditiousness is related to trial fairness, but properly considered, it is not an element of fairness: it is, indeed, a value that may operate to enhance or constrain the fairness of the trial.

There is also divergence in the literature between authors that favour a 'fair enough' approach to trial fairness and those that emphasise a 'highest standard of fairness' approach. Some scholars, like McDermott, advocate that international criminal procedure ought to set the highest possible standards of fairness.[28] Others argue that it may not be appropriate to apply fairness norms that have developed at a domestic level in international criminal trials when the international arena deals with so many competing objectives in imperfect circumstances.[29] Damaška, for example, lists 'aspects of international criminal justice that might be regarded as fair enough'[30] and is of the view that some fairness considerations should be 'relaxed'.[31] Vasiliev refers to these scholars as 'realists' and notes that what unites these scholars is 'the recognition that the operational context may have

---

[24] SC Res 827, UN SCOR, 48th sess, 3217th mtg, UN Doc S/RES/827 (25 May 1993), as amended by SC Res 1877, UN SCOR, 64th sess, 6155th mtg, UN Doc S/RES/1877 (7 July 2009) ('*ICTY Statute*') Art 20 (emphasis added); *Rome Statute of the International Criminal Court*, opened for signature 17 July 1998, 2187 UNTS 90 (entered into force 1 July 2002) ('*Rome Statute*') Art 64(2) (emphasis added).

[25] Boas (n 23) 69.

[26] *ICTY Statute* Art 21(4)(c); *Rome Statute* Art 67(1)(c).

[27] See Boas (n 23) 53; Patrick Robinson, 'Rough Edges in the Alignment of Legal Systems in the Proceedings at the ICTY' (2005) 3 *JICJ* 1037. However, others argue that 'Fairness and expediency do not contradict, but *complement each other*' (Kai Ambos, 'Fairness and Expediency in International Criminal Procedure', in John Jackson and Sarah Summers, *Obstacles to Fairness in Criminal Proceedings: Individual Rights and Institutional Forms* (Hart, 2018) 179–189, 182, emphasis in original).

[28] McDermott (n 16), particularly Chapter 5.

[29] Jackson (n 21) 23; Mirjan Damaška, 'The Competing Visions of Fairness: The Basic Choice for International Criminal Tribunals' (2001) 36 *NCJILCR* 365; Damaška (n 6). See also Colin Warbrick, 'International Criminal Courts and Fair Trial' (1998) 3 *JACL* 45, 54; Frédéric Mégret, 'Beyond "Fairness": Understanding the Determinants of International Criminal Procedure' (2009) 14 *UCLA JILFA* 37. For a useful critique of Colin Warbrick's view that international trials should be 'fair enough', see Caleb H Wheeler, 'The Scales of Justice: Balancing the Goals of International Criminal Trials' (2019) 30 *CLF* 145, 150.

[30] Damaška (n 6) 616.

[31] Damaška (n 29); Damaška (n 6) 616.

a reductive effect on the scope of rights protection'.[32] Recently, Joanna Nicholson has advocated for a standard that is 'just fair enough' – as she puts it, neither 'too high' (which she defines as interpreting the right to a fair trial 'as strongly as possible') nor 'too low' (which she defines as allowing the courts 'to adopt weaker human rights standards than those set by international human rights law on occasion').[33] In her view, although fair trial 'should lie at the heart of any international criminal proceedings, there is also a need for an injection of realism and modesty as to what this means in practice.'[34] For Nicholson, a 'just fair enough' standard will bring increased legitimacy to the courts and tribunals. We, therefore, see multiple approaches to the position of fairness in these trials.

We can therefore see that there is a wide variety of opinions on what else (beyond the rights of the accused) is constitutive of fairness in international criminal trials and what legal principles are needed for fairness to operate properly in the trial context. This lack of shared understanding shows a lack of coherence regarding what fairness requires or entails. Although there are some early views of fairness and rights being essentially the same, there is a difference between fairness and rights – fairness is an 'overarching' concept or requirement of trials, and that rights are an important constitutive part of this. However, there is no shared agreement about what *else*, in addition to rights, constitutes fairness – and this adds to the conceptual incoherence of fairness.

B. TO WHOM IS FAIRNESS OWED? THE ASCENDANCY OF THE 'SHARED PROCESS-CENTRED APPROACH'

A second particular issue for our understanding of fairness is the question of to whom fairness is owed. In the trial process, who should be the beneficiary of fairness decisions and discussions – the accused, the prosecutor, or others? Here, I outline two views, which I term the 'rights-centred approach' and the 'shared process-centred approach'. The 'rights-centred approach' emphasises the rights of the accused as being central to fairness, while the 'shared process-centred approach' views fairness as owed to all parties and participants in proceedings.

These two approaches are, perhaps, a matter of degree: many would argue that fairness is due to all parties in a trial but that the accused has particular rights – a middle ground between these two positions. The two

---

[32] Sergey Vasiliev, *International Criminal Trials: A Normative Framework* (PhD Thesis, University of Amsterdam, 2014) 147.

[33] Joanna Nicholson, '"Too High", "Too Low", or "Just Fair Enough"? Finding Legitimacy Through the Accused's Right to a Fair Trial' (2019) 17(2) *JICJ* 351, and particularly at 352.

[34] Ibid. 368.

approaches offer different emphases on either on the rights of the accused or on the other parties and participants. Nonetheless, these differences are significant, as is clear when we examine how this question has been addressed and resolved in trials. I demonstrate that there has been a shift away from placing the procedural rights of the accused at the heart of the concept of fairness (the rights-centred approach) towards a greater emphasis on the procedural rights of other stakeholders (the shared process-centred approach), including the prosecution, the victims and even states. I argue that the extension of 'fairness' considerations to parties and participants other than the accused shows a lack of coherence about whom fairness is owed to and how the rights of the accused affect trial fairness.[35]

(1) Rights-centred approach

The rights-centred approach emphasises the procedural rights of the accused in any conception of trial fairness. The rights of the accused will be paramount, even in cases where the interests of other stakeholders are considered. The accused is the key subject of the trial proceeding, and therefore also the key beneficiary of trial fairness considerations. This will be manifested through a protection of the accused's procedural rights. As discussed in Chapter Two, the accused's status as a rights-bearer is fundamentally different from the prosecution and the victims, who are viewed as 'interest holders, and holders of personal rights such as human rights but not as rights deriving from their status as an actor at trial'.[36] Because the other trial stakeholders have interests but not rights (or very limited rights), this approach attaches rights primarily to the accused.

This approach gains support from the *Statutes*. In particular, the provision that a Trial Chamber will 'ensure that a trial is fair and expeditious and conducted with full respect for the rights of the accused and due regard for the protection of victims and witnesses'[37] shows a difference between the 'full respect' afforded to the rights of the accused, and the 'due regard' for the protection of victims and witnesses. This reinforces a rights-centred approach.[38] The structure of the provision that articulates the trial rights – where three of the four rights attach specifically to the accused – also supports the rights-centred approach.[39]

This rights-centred approach is grounded in a 'retributive' conception of justice, based on rules, procedures and punishment.[40] Because the accused

---

[35] See also McDermott (n 16), particularly Chapter 4.
[36] McDermott (n 4) 166.
[37] ICTY *Statute* Art 20; *Rome Statute* Art 64(2).
[38] See *Prosecutor v Tadić, Separate Opinion of Judge Stephen on the Prosecutor's Motion Requesting Protective Measures for Victims and Witnesses* (IT-94-1-T, 10 August 1995).
[39] McDermott (n 4) 167.
[40] See Stahn (n 2) 267.

may be punished (losing their liberty and/or property), they must benefit from the key protective measures against any unfairness. The accused is, therefore, fundamentally different from the prosecution, who has duties rather than rights.[41] As one defence lawyer noted,

> everyone has the right to a fair day in court but . . . it's very different between the prosecution and the defence. The defence is, by definition, fighting an uphill battle and needs various kinds of protections that the prosecution just doesn't need. The defence doesn't owe anything to anyone. They don't carry the burden of proof . . . (but) the prosecution has a lot of other obligations.[42]

Under the rights-centred approach, then, fairness will ensure that the rights of the accused are indeed granted 'full respect', and these rights will be emphasised in the case of any conflict with the interests of the prosecution or victim participants.

(2) Shared process-centred approach

The 'shared process-centred approach' to fairness emphasises the need to balance the rights and interests of the multiple participants in the trial process. Fairness is seen to be owed to all stakeholders. The rights of the accused are not placed at the centre of the concept of fairness. In fact, under this approach, some curtailment of the rights of the accused may be permitted in order to protect the interests of stakeholders like the prosecution or victims.

The shared process-centred approach gains support from the fact that where the *Statute* stipulates that a Trial Chamber will 'ensure that a trial is fair and expeditious and is conducted with full respect for the rights of the accused and due regard for the protection of victims and witnesses',[43] the fairness requirement is not limited to one participant but rather describes the character of the trial process, which must include 'the protection of victims and witnesses' as part of a 'fair trial'. Further, while three of the four subsections of the provisions that deal with trial rights explicitly attach to the accused, the fourth stipulates that 'all persons shall be equal'. McDermott argues that this 'has been used as a gateway through which the rights of the accused have come to be bestowed upon the prosecution, the argument being that "equality" in this sense cannot see one party favoured at the expense of another'.[44] McDermott criticises this approach as ignoring a contextual approach to interpretation: in this case, the reference to equality

---

[41] *Prosecutor v Haradinaj (Judgement)* (IT-04-84-A, 19 July 2010) ('*Haradinaj Appeals Judgement*') (Judge Robinson); Interview with Colleen Rohan and Gregor Guy-Smith (8 May 2013).

[42] Interview with Colleen Rohan and Gregor Guy-Smith (8 May 2013).

[43] *ICTY Statute* Art 20; *Rome Statute* Art 64(2).

[44] McDermott (n 4) 167.

is 'under the chapeau of "rights of the accused", indicating that this equality was intended as being between accused persons, as opposed to ensuring that the prosecutor should be treated "as equally" as the defendants'.[45]

Representing this view of parity of the parties being paramount, one judge indicated that the approach the Trial Chambers took was to treat the parties as equal, with neither the defence nor the prosecution being entitled to more fairness than the other. In their view, 'I don't really think that we ever distinguished much between the prosecution and the defence. I mean, fairness is applicable to both, not to one rather than the other, or to one more than the other . . . It all depends on the issues involved in each and every case . . . I think everyone gets a fair deal'.[46]

Similarly, one defence lawyer noted that every party is entitled to fairness:

> I cringe when I hear the judges say that the prosecution is entitled to a fair trial, but they are, I have to admit. So I think that all parties are entitled to a fair trial and that's really a fundamental part of the courts being legitimate and being perceived as legitimate.[47]

Nonetheless, the same defence lawyer still voiced a belief that the rights of the accused are paramount.[48]

The shared process-centred approach is reflected in jurisprudence which states that fairness is owed to all parties to proceedings.[49] The ICC has defined fairness as being either 'general' or 'specific', with flow-on implications for the rights of the participants.[50] Although the 'specific' fairness relates to the rights of the accused, the more broad 'general fairness' is for the benefit of all participants in the trial process, including the prosecution.[51] Fairness necessitates respect for 'the procedural rights of the prosecutor, the defence, and the victims'.[52] Fairness has been described as 'a shared rather than exclusive right'.[53] Under this approach, some diminution of the rights of the accused may be justified.

---

[45] Ibid.
[46] Interview with Judge X (14 May 2013).
[47] Interview with Peter Robinson (2 May 2013).
[48] Ibid.
[49] *Situation in Uganda, Decision on the Prosecutor's Applications for Leave to Appeal dated the 15th of March 2006 and to suspend or stay consideration of leave to appeal dated the 11th day of March 2006* (ICC-02/04-01/05, 10 July 2006) ('*Uganda Decision on Prosecutor's Applications for Leave to Appeal*') [24]; *Decision on the Prosecution's Application for Leave to Appeal the Decision on Victims' Applications for Participation a/001/06, a/0064/06 to a/0070/06, a/0104/06 and a/0111/06 to a/0127/06* (19 December 2007) [27].
[50] *Uganda Decision on the Prosecutor's Applications for Leave to Appeal* [24].
[51] Ibid.
[52] *Congo Decision on Leave to Appeal Decision on Participation* [38].
[53] International Bar Association, 'Fairness at the International Criminal Court' (Report, International Bar Association, August 2011) 19.

(3) The ascendancy of the 'shared process-centred approach'

McDermott has described an 'irony', where the rights of the accused – initially the object of protection – have been detrimentally affected by the extension of 'rights' to other actors in the trial.[54] I argue that the ascendancy of the 'shared process-centred approach' can be seen in recent trends that have used the concept of fairness in order to emphasise the 'rights' of victims, the prosecution and even states. This is the case even where the rights of the accused are adversely affected. In determining who should be the core focus of fairness, we see a wedge that is increasingly driven between fairness and the rights of the accused.

(a) The role and rise of victim participants

The placement of victims at the heart of international criminal law presents the 'greatest stress on considerations of fairness towards the defendant'.[55] While increased victim participation need not necessarily be prejudicial to the rights of the accused,[56] there is nonetheless a 'rocky relationship' between the two,[57] and victim participation poses clear challenges for the rights of the accused. It is also important to manage the tension between the rights of the accused and the interests of the victims because the procedural framework provides little guidance for how best to regulate victim participation. With the ICC's innovative system of victim participation,[58] the question of the correct balance between the rights of the accused and the interests of the victims has become acute. Pues has described victims participation under Rule 68(3) at the ICC as 'celebrated as a great achievement in the sense that the fair trial guarantee in the ICC Statute differs from the 'traditional' approach – focussed on due process for the defendant – instead entailing a component of fairness for victims'.[59] The novel approach of victim participation suggests that when determining who should be the beneficiary of fairness in international criminal trials, the balance may have been altered towards a 'shared process-centred approach'. As Pues points out, since the emergence of academic literature 'celebrating' the notion that fairness has been extended to victims, ICC victims representatives 'have repeatedly claimed their clients' 'right to a fair trial'' and 'a considerable body of case law has also developed on the issue'.[60] In this way, 'fairness' to victims has slipped into 'rights' discourse.

[54] McDermott (n 4) 166.
[55] Damaška (n 29) 372.
[56] Salvatore Zappalà, 'The Rights of Victims v the Rights of the Accused' (2010) 8 *JICJ* 137, 139.
[57] Mirjan Damaška, 'What is the Point of International Criminal Justice?' (2008) 83 *CKLR* 329, 333.
[58] Zappalà (n 56) 137–8.
[59] Pues (n 13) 951.
[60] Ibid. 952.

If well-managed, with the 'fundamental principles of due process and fair trial ... respected and granted primacy over any other potentially conflicting interest',[61] the rights of the accused and the interests of the victims may be able to co-exist. Fairness is thus the regulator between these potentially divergent agendas, and fairness should be the core consideration when resolving conflicts between them. However, if not well-managed, there may come a point where 'the desire to satisfy the victims' interests begins to impinge on considerations of fairness toward the defendants'.[62] Damaška points out several conflicts between the rights of the accused and the interests of the victims: delays to the trial, interfering with the accused's right to an expeditious trial; victims' stories could 'induce judges to attribute to the accused a larger role in the atrocities than the accused really played';[63] and there may be pressures to lower the standard of proof 'and the temptation ... to program proceedings for easy conviction'.[64] At the ICC, the system of reparations for victims – which are only triggered upon conviction of an accused – adds a further incentive for the victims to support a guilty verdict. Ultimately, the interests of the accused and the victims tend to be in opposition: acquittal and conviction are a zero-sum game.

Due to constructive ambiguities in the *Rome Statute*,[65] there is uncertainty around how Trial Chambers reconcile the interests of victims with the rights of the accused and considerations of fairness. I would argue that victim participation should be undertaken in a way that defers to the determination of the accused's guilt or otherwise, as the trial's primary aim; and in a way that respects the rights of the accused. Where the rights of the accused are affected by the interests of victims, the rights of the accused must be prioritised to ensure fairness.[66] Indeed, the *Rome Statute* is explicit that victim participation must be done in a manner 'not prejudicial to or inconsistent with the rights of the accused and a fair and impartial trial'.[67] This has been reiterated in jurisprudence.[68]

However, despite this, jurisprudence also shows an emphasis on the interests of victims by providing them with far-ranging modalities of participation. While there is no specific right for victims to present evidence,

---

[61] Zappalà (n 56) 139.
[62] Damaška (n 57) 334.
[63] Ibid.
[64] Ibid.
[65] Christine Van den Wyngaert, 'Victims before International Criminal Courts: Some Views and Concerns of an ICC Trial Judge' (2011) 44 *CWRJIL* 475, 478; Zappalà (n 56) 138.
[66] See Zappalà (n 56).
[67] Rome Statute Art 68(3).
[68] See *Prosecutor v Katanga, Decision on the Modalities of Victim Participation at Trial* (ICC-01/04-01/07-1788, 22 January 2010) ('*Katanga Decision on Victim Participation*') [53]–[54]; *Prosecutor v Lubanga, Judgment on Appeals of the Prosecutor and the Defence against Trial Chamber I's Decision on Victims' Participation of 18 January 2008* (ICC-01/04-01/06, 11 July 2008).

they may apply to the Trial Chamber to do so.[69] Victims may introduce evidence pertaining to the guilt or innocence of the accused;[70] challenge the admissibility and relevance of evidence tendered by the parties;[71] and while victims are not entitled to conduct investigations in order to establish the guilt of the accused, they are able to undertake investigations 'in order to collect information with a view to establishing the existence, nature and extent of the harm suffered'.[72] Victims have requested the Chamber to consider recharacterising the facts (under Regulation 55) to include sexual slavery; if this request had been successful, the accused would have faced five additional charges involving sexual violence.[73] These are significant participatory roles for victims, which may adversely affect the rights of the accused, and the fairness of the trial.

An example from the ICTY also demonstrates the invocation of the interests of the victims, in a situation that would conflict with the interests – and potentially the rights – of the accused. This is despite the fact that victims do not have a participation role at the ICTY and thus their place is more limited than at the ICC. Not long after Momčilo Perišić was acquitted on appeal at the ICTY, a differently composed Appeals Chamber bench in the *Šainović* case voiced their view that the *Perišić* Appeals Chamber bench had erred when they considered that specific direction was an element of aiding and abetting liability.[74] As a result, the prosecution filed a motion requesting reconsideration of the acquittal of Perišić.[75] The prosecution did not offer a 'new fact' which was not known at the time of trial and had been subsequently discovered, as is required for such a motion.[76] Instead, the prosecution based its motion on the argument that 'the interests of justice for the tens of thousands of victims, substantially outweighs Perišić's interest in finality of proceedings. Justice must be restored to the victims'.[77] The prosecution was invoking the interests of the victims in an attempt to

---

[69] *Katanga Decision on Victim Participation* [105].

[70] *Prosecutor v Lubanga, Decision on the Defence and Prosecution Requests for Leave to Appeal the Decision on Victims' Participation of 18 January 2008* (26 February 2008).

[71] Ibid.

[72] *Katanga Decision on Victim Participation* [102]–[103].

[73] *Prosecutor v Lubanga, Decision Giving Notice to the Parties and Participants That the Legal Characterisation of the Facts May be Subject to Change in Accordance with Regulation 55(2) of the Regulations of the Court* (14 July 2009). See also Kevin Jon Heller, '"A Stick to Hit the Accused With": The Legal Recharacterization of Facts under Regulation 55' in Carsten Stahn (ed), *The Law and Practice of the International Criminal Court: A Critical Account of Challenges and Achievements* (OUP, 2015) 981.

[74] *Prosecutor v Šainović, Judgement* (IT-05-87-A, 23 January 2014) [1649]–[1650].

[75] *Prosecutor v Perišić*, 'Motion for Reconsideration' (IT-04-81-A, 3 February 2014) ('*Perišić* Motion for Reconsideration').

[76] ICTY, *Rules of Procedure and Evidence*, Doc No IT/32/Rev.50 (adopted on 11 February 1994, amended 10 July 2015) ('*ICTY Rules*'), r 119.

[77] *Perišić* Motion for Reconsideration [5].

re-open a case, to the detriment of the accused – where it had no legal basis in the *Rules* to do so.

This motion was denied, with the Appeals Chamber considering that the 'victims' interest in the success of the Motion does not constitute a legal basis which would justify granting the Motion'.[78] Thus, the Appeals Chamber at the ICTY clearly and appropriately confined the place of the victims' interests in this case. However, this example demonstrates the rhetoric of the interests of the victims being used to the detriment of the accused.

Increased victim participation, the emphasis provided to victims interests, and the wide-ranging modalities of participation at the ICC all suggest that there is an ascendancy of the 'shared process-centred approach' to fairness, where the interests of the victims are given a significant stand. While fairness could be the mediating discourse to ensure the interests of the victims do not conflict with the rights of the accused, we are, in fact, witnessing an extension of fairness concerns to the victims: potentially at the expense of the rights of the accused.

(b) The role and rise of the prosecutor

Jurisprudence from both the ICTY and the ICC demonstrates the ascendancy of the interests of the prosecutor, even in situations where this will affect the rights of the accused. For example, in both *Haradinaj* (Appeals Chamber at the ICTY) and *Katanga* (Trial Chamber at the ICC), the majority decisions represent the view that fairness is generalised, with the prosecution's interests requiring protection. In both cases, the dissenting opinions represent the view that fairness requires a particular emphasis on the rights of the accused. These cases suggest the ascendancy of a shared process-centred approach, but the strong dissenting opinions also demonstrate the power of the rights-centred approach. These cases also show the vehemence with which both approaches are advanced and the deep divide between these two approaches.

The ICTY Appeals Chamber decision to order a partial retrial in the *Haradinaj* case focused on questions of fairness and to whom such fairness is owed.[79] The prosecution argued that 'the Trial Chamber committed an error of law by violating its right to a fair trial under Article 20(1) of the *Statute*'.[80] The Prosecution contended that the Trial Chamber erred in refusing prosecution requests for additional time to secure the testimony of two witnesses.[81] The majority upheld this ground of appeal and ordered a partial

---

[78] *Prosecutor v Perišić, Decision on Motion for Reconsideration* (20 March 2014).

[79] *Haradinaj Appeals Judgement; Prosecutor v Haradinaj, Corrigendum to Judgement of 19 July 2010* (23 July 2010) ('*Haradinaj Corrigendum to Judgement*'). For analysis of the Haradinaj retrial, see McDermott (n 16); McDermott (n 4).

[80] *Prosecutor v Haradinaj*, 'Prosecution Appeal Brief' (16 July 2008) [5].

[81] Ibid.

retrial.[82] Ultimately the accused were acquitted again, four-and-a-half years after their original acquittal on those charges.[83]

The Appeals Chamber decision stated that the Trial Chamber had placed 'logistical considerations over the *Prosecution's right to a fair* trial'.[84] A corrigendum issued four days later changed this to 'over the Trial Chamber's *duty to safeguard the fairness* of the proceedings'.[85] The change was said to be due to a 'clerical error'.[86] This change in the wording of the judgment – several days after its issuance – is curious and perhaps revealing. The initial wording suggests that the Chamber was of the view that the prosecution has a 'right' to a fair trial. In issuing the corrigendum, the Chamber did not take the opportunity to clarify the difference between 'the prosecution's right to a fair trial' and 'the fairness of the proceedings', which may have been useful. To be clear, the Chamber *changed its rationale for its decision* and did not explain this change. McDermott suggests that the corrigendum 'may well have been issued in the knowledge that the original explicit reference to the prosecution's right to a fair trial, and the clear consequences for the accused in this instance, would be highly controversial'.[87] Regardless of their motivation, the majority effectively granted the prosecution's ground of appeal, that its 'right to a fair trial' had been undermined. When permitting the appeal, the Appeals Chamber did not articulate the grounds on which it was doing so – and did not reject the prosecutor's appeal to fairness as its justification.[88] This decision shows the move towards a shared process-centred approach, with the prosecution provided rights and considered in questions of fairness.

Judge Robinson dissented in strong terms.[89] He noted that the responsibility of a Trial Chamber to 'ensure a trial that is fair' applies to both the defence and prosecution and that the interests of the prosecution should be provided protection.[90] However, this is qualified by the fact that it is 'to be enjoyed "with full respect for the rights of the accused"'.[91] Robinson argued that the prosecution and defence are dissimilar and exist in an asymmetrical relationship, with the prosecution bearing the burden of proof and therefore having 'duties, which the defence does not have, and the defence

---

[82] *Haradinaj Appeals Judgement* [50].
[83] *Prosecutor v Haradinaj (Public Judgement with Confidential Annexes)* (IT-04-84*bis*-T, 29 November 2012).
[84] *Haradinaj Appeals Judgement* [46] (emphasis added).
[85] *Haradinaj Corrigendum to Judgement* (emphasis added).
[86] Ibid.
[87] McDermott (n 16) 114.
[88] Dov Jacobs, 'Partial Retrial Ordered in Haradinaj' on *Spreading the Jam* (21 July 2010) <http://dovjacobs.com/2010/07/21/partial-retrial-ordered-in-haradinaj/> (last accessed 9 December 2021).
[89] *Haradinaj Appeals Judgement* (Judge Robinson).
[90] Ibid. [15].
[91] Ibid. [16].

has rights, which the prosecution does not have'.[92] The correct relationship between Articles 20 and 21 of the *ICTY Statute* ensures that 'any fairness rights of the prosecution . . . are to be applied "with full respect for the rights of the accused"',[93] and the majority's decision incorrectly arranged fair trial rights 'into a hierarchical structure that finds no support in a proper interpretation and application of the *Statute*'.[94] As will be discussed further below, Robinson's dissent is evidence of a rights-centred approach to the question of to whom fairness is owed.

Particularly illustrative of the tension between the interests of the prosecution and the rights of the accused is the ICC judgment in the *Katanga* case. In this case, the judges used Regulation 55 to 'recharacterise' the charges against Germain Katanga. This 'recharacterisation' occurred in the final judgment, issued more than a year after a majority of the Trial Chamber judges announced that they were severing the cases against Katanga and his then co-accused, and indicated that they were considering recharacterising the charges against Katanga.[95] Judge Van den Wyngaert dissented 'in the strongest possible terms'.[96] In its final judgment, a majority of the Trial Chamber did recharacterise the mode of liability with which Katanga was charged: while the prosecution had charged Katanga under Article 25(3)(a) of the *Rome Statute* with liability for indirect co-perpetration, the Trial Chamber convicted him on the basis of common-purpose liability pursuant to Article 25(3)(d)(ii) of the *Statute*. Katanga was convicted of one charge of crimes against humanity and four charges of war crimes,[97] under a mode of liability that was never the subject of the trial. He was subsequently sentenced to twelve years in gaol.[98]

It is difficult to see how the recharacterisation of charges in this case aligns with ensuring 'a fair trial that is conducted with full respect for the rights of the accused'. Regulation 55 is not meant to be invoked in instances where it would violate the rights of the accused,[99] but in this case, the rights of the accused to know the case against him, to time and facilities to prepare a defence, to be tried without undue delay, and the right against self-incrimination, were all affected.[100] The prosecution and a conviction

---

[92] Ibid. [17].

[93] Ibid. [18].

[94] Ibid. [15].

[95] *Prosecutor v Katanga, Decision on the Implementation of Regulation 55 of the Regulations of the Court and Severing the Charges against the Accused Persons* (ICC-01/04-01/07, 21 November 2012) (*'Katanga Decision on the Implementation of Regulation 55'*).

[96] Ibid.

[97] *Katanga Judgment*.

[98] *Prosecutor v Katanga (Décision relative à la peine (article 76 du Statut))* (23 May 2014).

[99] International Criminal Court, *Regulations of the Court*, Doc No ICC-BD/01-01-04 (adopted 26 May 2004) r 55.

[100] For more detail, see Sophie Rigney, '"The Words Don't Fit You": Recharacterisation of The Charges, Trial Fairness, and *Katanga*' (2014) 15 MJIL 515.

were favoured at the expense of the rights of the accused. In her minority opinion, Judge Van den Wyngaert examined the standard by which fairness should be evaluated and argued that 'the trial must be first and foremost fair towards the accused. Considerations about procedural fairness for the Prosecutor and the victims and their Legal Representatives, while certainly relevant, cannot trump the rights of the accused'.[101] The majority did acknowledge fairness and the rights of the accused,[102] but despite this rhetorical respect, the recharacterisation of the charges had a significant and deleterious effect on Katanga's trial rights. We see a separation between 'fairness' and the rights of the accused, and we also see a clear gap between the language used by the majority and the implications of their decision.

Both Judges Van den Wyngaert (in *Katanga*) and Robinson (in *Haradinaj*) represent a rights-centred approach to fairness. They argue that where the rights of an accused are affected, these must be given pre-eminence over the interests of other stakeholders for fairness to be ensured. However, these are minority opinions, and the majority in each case favoured a shared process-centred approach to fairness. The majority decisions in both *Haradinaj* and *Katanga* saw the Chambers intervening to 'correct' the proceedings, and in so doing, they bolstered the prosecution's position. These two cases demonstrate judicial intervention placing one interpretation of fairness – that is, one closely linked to the parties other than the accused, and 'ending impunity', or securing a conviction – above another interpretation, namely the fairness of the proceedings with full respect for the rights of an accused.[103] This is particularly problematic in a system of law animated by the aim of 'ending impunity', as I examined in Chapter One. These examples are further evidence of what McDermott calls a recent trend

> to extend the fair trial rights regime to the prosecution, and to elevate the interests of the prosecution to the status of rights. This elevation, in turn, permits the Chamber to place the rights of the accused in a 'balance' with the prosecution's interests, while the rights of the accused properly belong at the apex of any hierarchy of considerations.[104]

---

[101] *Katanga Judgment* (Judge Van den Wyngaert) [311].

[102] *Katanga Judgment* [1590]–[1592].

[103] There are other examples of the language of 'a right to fair trial' being extended to the prosecution. For example, in *Prlić*, the prosecution made submissions to the Appeals Chamber that the Trial Chamber had violated 'the fundamental right of the victims, the Prosecution and the international community to a fair trial': *Prosecutor v Prlić* ('Prosecution Appeal Concerning the Trial Chamber's Ruling Dated 13 November 2006 Reducing Time for the Prosecution Case') (IT-04-74, 30 November 2006). The appeal was granted: *Prosecutor v Prlić, Decision on Prosecution Appeal Concerning the Trial Chamber's Ruling Reducing Time for the Prosecution Case* (IT-04-74-AR73.4, 6 February 2007).

[104] McDermott (n 4) 172.

A further example can be seen in the case of Katanga's original co-accused, Mathieu Ngudjolo, where the prosecution appealed the accused's acquittal. In the Appeals Chamber judgement, the issue of the 'rights' of the prosecution again arose under the guise of trial fairness.[105] The Prosecutor had submitted that the Trial Chamber failed to 'ensure the fairness of the trial proceedings'[106] and 'violated [the prosecution's] right to a fair trial under article 64(2)' of the *Rome Statute*.[107] It was further submitted that the prosecution's 'right to a fair trial' includes, in particular, the right to 'exercise the powers and fulfil the duties listed in Article 54' to have 'the genuine opportunity to present [its] case' and to tender evidence.[108]

The majority held that it did not 'consider it necessary to determine whether and to what extent the Prosecutor has a "right to a fair trial" in the abstract' because it considered that the 'overall trial fairness vis-à-vis the Prosecutor' was not at issue.[109] They also noted that 'it is commonly understood that the right to a fair trial/fair hearing in criminal proceedings, first and foremost, inures to the benefit of the accused'.[110] The Appeals Chamber found no errors and therefore dismissed the grounds of appeal – without offering further guidance on the prosecution's alleged 'right to a fair trial'.

However, Judges Ekaterina Trendafilova and Cuno Tarfusser offered a dissent in which they expressed the view that the prosecutor does have a right to fairness and that 'this right was not guaranteed for the Prosecutor in the case at hand'.[111] Thus, while the majority refused to characterise the issue as one of fairness and did not comment on whether the prosecution has a 'right to fairness', the minority argued that the prosecutor does, indeed, have a right to fairness. The minority adopted a shared process-centred approach to fairness, while the majority did not offer any considered opinion on how to characterise rights and fairness. This case leaves open the question of how fairness and rights are being approached in international criminal trials.

(c) The role and rise of states

States are not parties to international criminal trials, but the system of international criminal law and its institutions must interact with states and

---

[105] *Prosecutor v Ngudjolo (Judgment on the Prosecutor's Appeal against the Decision of Trial Chamber II entitled 'Judgment Pursuant to Article 74 of the Statute')* (ICC-01/04-02/12A, 27 February 2015) ('*Ngudjolo Appeal Judgment*').

[106] *Prosecutor v Ngudjolo*, 'Second Public Redacted Version of "Prosecution's Document in Support of Appeal against the 'Jugement rendu en application de l'article 74 du Statut'" (ICC-01/04-02/12 A, 19 March 2013) [142].

[107] Ibid.

[108] Ibid. [205].

[109] *Ngudjolo Appeal Judgment* [256].

[110] Ibid. [255].

[111] Ibid. [6] (Judges Trendafilova and Tarfusser).

are affected by state behaviour. The question arises: how does the role of states affect the fairness of the trial? Perhaps the stage at which states have most involvement and influence is in determining a case's admissibility at the ICC, and particularly in determining whether the principle of complementarity is triggered. A state can challenge the admissibility of a case it may have jurisdiction over and make submissions on its willingness and ability to prosecute.[112] The litigation in the Libya situation demonstrates the potential for states to invoke fairness – potentially to the detriment of the accused – in order to bolster their own role in proceedings.

The Government of Libya challenged the admissibility of the cases against Saif Al-Islam Gaddafi and Abdullah Al-Senussi at the ICC.[113] Libya claimed it was both able and willing to try the cases under domestic law in Libya.[114] There has been significant concern around Libya's ability to grant a fair trial, with full respect to the rights of the accused.[115] In relation to the case against Gaddafi, the admissibility challenge was unsuccessful,[116] and Libya appealed the decision.[117] In doing so, they claimed that

> the Chamber erred procedurally, or *acted unfairly*, by failing to 'take appropriate measures for the proper conduct of the procedure', thereby depriving Libya of the ability to rely upon highly relevant evidence in support of its admissibility challenge. It is submitted that the *unfairness* and the errors, 'materially affected the impugned decision' occasioning a decision that was so *unfair* and unreasonable as to constitute an abuse of discretion. The decision would have been 'substantially different' *but for the unfairness* and the errors.[118]

Libya also argued that the Pre-Trial Chamber 'was obliged to promulgate a procedure that provided Libya with fairness and certainty'.[119] A further submission was that the Chamber's 'procedural unfairness with regards to

---

[112] *Rome Statute* Art 19.

[113] *Prosecutor v Gaddafi* ('Application on behalf of the Government of Libya pursuant to Article 19 of the ICC Statute') (ICC-01/11-01/11, 1 May 2012).

[114] Ibid.

[115] See, e.g., Jonathan O'Donohue and Sophie Rigney, 'The ICC Must Consider Fair Trial Concerns in Determining Libya's Application to Prosecute Saif al-Islam Gaddafi Nationally', *EJIL Talk!* (8 June 2012) <http://www.ejiltalk.org/the-icc-must-consider-fair-tr ial-concerns-in-determining-libyas-application-to-prosecute-saif-al-islam-gaddafi-nationally/> (last accessed 9 December 2021).

[116] *Prosecutor v Gaddafi, Decision on the Admissibility of the Case against Saif Al-Islam Gaddafi* (31 May 2013).

[117] *Prosecutor v Gaddafi*, 'The Government of Libya's Appeal against Pre-Trial Chamber I's *Decision on the Admissibility of the Case against Saif Al-Islam Gaddafi*' (7 June 2013).

[118] *Prosecutor v Gaddafi*, 'Document in Support of the Government of Libya's Appeal against the *Decision on the Admissibility of the Case against Saif Al-Islam Gaddafi*' (24 June 2013) [47] (emphasis added).

[119] Ibid. [121].

this additional evidence unfairly deprived Libya of due process and highly probative evidence in support of its challenge'.[120]

The Appeals Chamber did not accept this argument, and ruled that the Pre-Trial Chamber 'provided Libya with ample opportunity to substantiate its challenge to the admissibility of the case against Mr Gaddafi'.[121] However, in making this decision, the Appeals Chamber stated that its guiding question for review would be 'whether the procedure the Pre-Trial Chamber adopted was so unfair and unreasonable as to constitute an abuse of discretion'.[122] The Appeals Chamber thus confirmed that the state of Libya has an expectation of fairness in decision-making. This is further indication of the ascendancy of a shared process-centred approach to fairness, where even states can invoke fairness in international criminal trials.

Fairness is therefore influenced away from the accused in three separate directions, with the victims, the prosecution and states all benefitting from the ascendancy of a shared-process approach. Some may dispute this and instead argue that jurisprudence shows a willingness of the Trial Chambers to emphasise the rights of the accused over the interests of the prosecution. For example, the acquittal of Ngudjolo[123] may be seen as an example of the rights of the accused being given precedence over the interests of other parties. In that case, the prosecution claimed that the Trial Chamber misapplied the standard of proof and acquitted the accused on the basis of 'hypothetically possible contrary inferences, however unrealistic or unsupported'.[124] This was rejected by the Appeals Chamber,[125] but it shows the view of the prosecution that the balance of the trial was in support of the defence.

Other acquittals, and cases rejected by the judges at the confirmation stage of proceedings at the ICC, may again suggest that there is not a general trend to prioritise the prosecution's case over that of the defence. For example, it could be argued that the Appeals Chamber judgement in the *Bemba* case was a rejection of the shared-process approach, with the rights of the accused given prominence in the Majority decision. Again, however, this must be approached with some caution for two reasons. First, the Bemba Appeal decision was deeply divided, decided 3:2, and with two

---

[120] Ibid. [123].
[121] *Prosecutor v Gaddafi, Judgment on the Appeal of Libya against the Decision of Pre-Trial Chamber I of 31 May 2013 entitled 'Decision on the Admissibility of the Case against Saif Al-Islam Gaddafi'* (ICC-01/11-01/11/OA4, 21 May 2014) [168].
[122] Ibid. [162].
[123] *Prosecutor v Ngudjolo, Judgment pursuant to Article 74 of the Statute* (ICC-01/04-02/12, 18 December 2012).
[124] *Prosecutor v Ngudjolo, 'Prosecution's Appeal of Judgment'* (ICC-01/04-02/12A, 3 April 2013).
[125] *Prosecutor v Ngudjolo, Judgment on the Prosecutor's Appeal against the Decision of Trial Chamber II entitled 'Judgment Pursuant to Article 74 of the Statute'* (ICC-01/04-02/12 A, 27 February 2015).

divergent opinions within the majority: this is hardly a clear and unequivocal rejection of the shared-process approach, and the minority and majority
were fundamentally at odds on issues of fairness and rights.

Secondly, in his separate (majority) opinion, Judge Eboe-Osuji makes
some interesting comments about the fairness of the trial, the rights of the
accused, and the new standard of appellate review applied in the Bemba
Appeals majority decision – in which he reiterates the 'neutrality' of 'the
right to a fair trial'. He notes that while the *Rome Statute* does not provide
for any notion of 'appellate deference', it does provide the right to a fair
trial; and this means that 'the notion of appellate deference becomes a difficult one where an appeal is lodged on the ground that the trial has been
so unfair as to engage the risk of a miscarriage of justice, because the Trial
Chamber made serious mistakes in the admission, appreciation and evaluation of the evidence'.[126] For the Judge, it is 'wholly unsatisfactory' for the
Appeals Chamber to defer to the Trial Chamber, whose findings were the
result of an unfair trial.[127] But the Judge then goes on to extend this to all
parties and participants in the trial:

> it is also to be kept in mind, in this connection, that *the right of fair trial is a neutral
> right enjoyed at the ICC by the defendants, the Prosecution and the victims.* The notion
> of appellate deference can prove just as inconvenient for the Prosecution and the
> victims, given *the real possibility of a case in which they may complain that the Trial
> Chamber's acquittal of an accused resulted from an erroneous factual finding.*[128]

Here, there is a clear preference for understanding fairness as shared; and
the acceptance that this may result in the prosecution appealing a Trial
Chamber decision based on their 'right to a fair trial'. It cannot, therefore, be argued that the Bemba acquittal suggests any move away from the
shared-process approach. Rather, it shows that there is significant contemporary acceptance of a shared-process approach to fairness.

C. WHAT LEGAL PROTECTIONS ARE REQUIRED TO ENSURE FAIRNESS? TRANSLATING FAIRNESS TO A *SUI GENERIS* SYSTEM

The conceptual incoherence of fairness is due, in part, to the lack of agreement around how to conceive of fairness in a *sui generis* system of international criminal procedure. What does the hybrid nature of international

---

[126] *Prosecutor v Bemba Gombo, Judgment on the appeal of Mr Jean-Pierre Bemba Gombo against Trial Chamber III's "Judgment pursuant to Article 74 of the Statute"* (ICC-01/05-01/08-3636-Red, 8 June 2018) ('*Bemba Appeal Judgement*') (Separate Concurring Opinion of Judge Eboe-Osuji) [48].

[127] Ibid.

[128] Ibid. [51] (emphasis added).

criminal procedure mean for understanding fairness in that legal system? How do we translate conceptions of fairness – relatively settled in national systems – to the evolving international criminal procedure? How do the differences in approach affect the conceptual understanding of fairness internationally? The development of international criminal procedure from national approaches and understandings poses an obvious threat to the concept of fairness: what is considered fair in one system may not be emphasised in the other system; the adversarial and inquisitorial approaches may differ regarding what legal protections are required to ensure fairness; and in resolving such issues, there may be uncertainty about which 'version' of fairness should be prioritised. The outcome of this, I argue, is an approach that takes elements from both adversarial and inquisitorial systems, with no care to create a cohesive system. In seeking the best of both systems, fairness is left untethered. The dangers of merging the two systems include the possibility that this may produce a less satisfactory process – and fact-finding result – than either the adversarial or inquisitorial system may offer.[129]

In order to build a *sui generis* international criminal procedure, the shared elements of inquisitorial and adversarial systems should be emphasised. Chief among these, in addition to their shared dedication to rights, is a shared dedication to fairness. As such, fairness should be a core element of any hybrid *sui generis* model. In addition, as noted above, fairness is a key tool for interpreting or constructing the law in cases of ambiguities or gaps. This is particularly true for a *sui generis* system,[130] where fairness becomes integral as a mediator between the different national approaches.

However, there has been a disaggregation of elements from various systems, and a melding together of these elements into a new system, risking international criminal procedure being a messy amalgamation of approaches and elements rather than a cohesive system. This approach has been described as a 'Frankenstein's monster', lacking the 'checks and balances' of national systems.[131] In Chapter Five, I will examine the use of adjudicated facts as an example of this move from an adversarial approach to a more inquisitorial approach, adopted without sufficient safeguards to protect the system or the accused.

This is not to say, of course, that there is no fairness in international criminal trials. As one defence lawyer noted:

---

[129] Jackson (n 21) 33, citing Mirjan Damaška, 'The Uncertain Fate of Evidentiary Transplants: Anglo-American and Continental Experiments' (1997) 45 *AJCL* 839, 852.

[130] See Robinson (n 27).

[131] Rupert Skilbeck, 'Frankenstein's Monster: Creating a New International Procedure' (2010) 8 *JICJ* 451, 452. See also Jackson (n 21) 33; Richard Vogler, 'Making International Criminal Procedure Work: From Theory to Practice' in Ralph Henham and Mark Findlay (eds), *Exploring the Boundaries of International Criminal Justice* (Ashgate, 2011) 105.

the whole use of the term 'fair' . . . presupposes a shared system of what's fair. If you mean fair from the standpoint of procedural due process as [it] is understood in the United States, then these trials are not fair. But I don't think that you could say that there's no procedural form of due process that exists. I think there most definitely is.[132]

Similarly, it is not that the inquisitorial system is less fair than the adversarial system. Rather, the question is how to ensure fairness where aspects of the inquisitorial system are integrated into a model with strong adversarial elements, where the corresponding safeguards or limits may not also be adopted.

This haphazard adoption of some elements from each domestic system is further complicated by structural issues regarding how to approach evidence and law. First, there is a lack of certainty within institutions – and even within Chambers – due to different judges having divergent approaches to procedural questions. International criminal procedure has been developed by judges and practitioners educated and socialised in domestic systems, often wedded to their own understandings, values and traditions.[133] This leads to a 'lack of coherence and consistency between the procedural practices', both of the various tribunals, and even 'occasionally between chambers of the same tribunal'.[134] As Frédéric Mégret points out, it must be 'perplexing' to the accused (and lawyers) 'that the type of procedure and courtroom style they are entitled to may hinge on something as arbitrary as the allocation of [one] chamber rather than another'.[135] Even worse, some trials have seen the Directions on the Conduct of Proceedings amended part-way through the trial, 'leading to divergence in practice by the same Chamber within the same trial'.[136]

In particular, there appears to be a real issue with different judicial views on how to assess evidence and how this links to fairness. McDermott has set out that there are 'two broad schools of thought' on how to evaluate evidence

---

[132] Interview with Colleen Rohan and Gregor Guy-Smith (8 May 2013).

[133] Elies van Sliedregt, 'Introduction: Common Civility – International Criminal Law as Cultural Hybrid' (2011) 24 *LJIL* 389, 389; James Crawford, 'The ILC Adopts a Statute for an International Criminal Court' (1995) 89 *AJIL* 404, 408; Frédéric Mégret, 'International Criminal Law: A New Legal Hybrid?' (2003) <http://papers.ssrn.com/sol3/papers.cfm?abstract_id=1269382> (last accessed 9 December 2021) 15.

[134] McDermott (n 16) 103. See also John Jackson, 'Transnational Faces of Justice: Two Attempts to Build Common Standards Beyond National Boundaries' in John Jackson, Máximo Langer and Peter Tillers (eds), *Crime, Procedure and Evidence in a Comparative and International Context: Essays in Honour of Professor Mirjan Damaška* (Hart Publishing, 2008) 221, 238; Elies van Sliedregt and Sergey Vasiliev 'Pluralism: A New Framework for International Criminal Justice' in Elies van Sliedregt and Sergey Vasiliev (eds), *Pluralism in International Criminal Law* (OUP, 2014) 3, 28–9.

[135] Mégret (n 133) 17.

[136] Yvonne McDermott, 'International Criminal Procedure and the False Promise of an Ideal Model of Fairness' in Jackson and Summers (eds) (n 27) 191, 200.

in international criminal trials: the 'atomists' and the 'holists'.[137] 'Atomists' adopt an approach that 'examines each piece of evidence in the context of the evidential record, before forming an opinion on whether the totality of the evidence as a whole supports a conclusion'. 'Holists', meanwhile, view the evidence more in its totality, rather than carefully weighing the probative value of each piece of evidence – but McDermott warns that this risks 'papering over the cracks' of a prosecution case and is incompatible with a system of proof beyond a reasonable doubt. We see, then, that there are hugely different views within the judiciary (not infrequently, on the same bench) about this fundamental question of evidence, closely related to trial fairness.[138]

Complicating this further, there is a lack of a hierarchy of sources of law in international criminal trials, resulting in uncertainty about how law will be applied. Even at the ICC, where the sources of applicable law are stated, there is a lack of clarity around the application of 'general principles of law derived by the Court from national laws of legal systems' (which may be appealed to in the absence of other relevant laws).[139] There is no guidance on which national jurisdictions, or how to manage a conflict of approaches from different legal systems. Taken together, the lack of certainty around courtroom behaviour from Chamber to Chamber, different judicial approaches to evidence and proof, and the lack of certainty around sources of law, leads to an unregulated legal pluralism which ultimately challenges any cohesion that fairness might seek to claim.

Integral to the trial process is the role of the judge as the finder of fact. However, the threat of a hybridised system is that the role of the judge may be unclear. Is the judge meant to be an office independent from the parties (as in the traditional adversarial typology), or are they to take a more

---

[137] Yvonne McDermott, 'Strengthening the Evaluation of Evidence in International Criminal Trials' (2017) 17(4) *ICLR* 682. See also Mark Klamberg, 'Epistemological Controversies and Evaluation of Evidence in International Criminal Trials', in Kevin Heller et al. (eds), *The Oxford Handbook of International Criminal Law* (OUP, 2020) 450; Hemi Mistry, 'The Significance of Institutional Culture in Enhancing the Validity of International Criminal Tribunals' (2017) 17(4) *ICLR* 703.

[138] See particularly *Bemba Appeal Judgement* (n 126), annex 2 [14]–[15], [76]–[78] (Judges Van den Wyngaert and Morrison); *Katanga Judgment* annex II [4]–[5] (Judges Diarra and Cotte). Another striking example is the 'Partially Dissenting Opinion of Judge Flavia Lattanzi' in *Prosecutor v Šešelj* (IT-03-67-T, 31 March 2016). On how this relates to the issue of judicial collegiality, see Douglas Guilfoyle, 'Lacking Conviction: Is the International Criminal Court Broken?' (2019) 20(2) *MJIL* 401, 32–6. However, similar patterns could be seen at the ICTY at least as early as 2013: see Sophie Rigney, 'The Deep Fractures in International Justice', *New Matilda*, (4 June 2013) <https://newmatilda.com/2013/06/04/deep-fractures-international-justice/> (last accessed 9 December 2021). In particular, see Judge Picard's dissent in the case of *Stanišić and Simatović* (IT-03-69, 30 May 2013), where she disagrees with the majority's interpretation of the evidence and concludes that 'I would say we have come to a dark place in international law indeed'. On dissents, judicial culture, and institutional legitimacy, see Mistry (n 137).

[139] *Rome Statute* Art 21.

investigatory and active role (as in the inquisitorial approach)? Blending the two systems could lead to a lack of certainty or agreement on this role, and particularly whether the judge is meant to engage in any activities that could be considered 'prosecutorial'. Again, the use of Regulation 55 at the ICC and the *Katanga* case is illustrative. In recharacterising the charges to ensure conviction, the majority in *Katanga* adopted an active, and even prosecutorial, role. The majority determined that

> it is for the chambers, guided by the sole concern of determining the truth of the charges referred to them, having considered the evidence admitted into the record of the case, to reach a decision on the *guilt* of the accused, without necessarily restricting themselves to the characterisation employed by the Pre-Trial Chamber and on which the Prosecutor has elaborated during the trial.[140]

In finding this, the majority exercised its power to call any evidence it deems necessary for the determination of the truth,[141] and a decision of the Appeals Chamber that the 'fact that the onus lies on the Prosecutor cannot be read to exclude the statutory powers of the court, as it is the court that "must be convinced of the guilt of the accused beyond reasonable doubt"'.[142] While it is true that Trial Chambers must reach a conclusion on the guilt – or otherwise – of the accused, this is in relation to the guilt of the accused *as charged*. In this case, the majority obviously perceived its role as being related to the conviction of the accused, if necessary, on charges that were never the subject of the trial.

Moreover, the conviction was based in significant part on testimony from Katanga himself – which he provided in response to the questioning *of the bench* rather than of the prosecutor or other trial participants.[143] The judges, therefore both laid the (new) charges and adduced the evidence that led to the conviction: effectively the work of the prosecution. It appears they had their own 'case', and reflective of this view, Judge Van den Wyngaert's minority opinion repeatedly refers to 'the majority's case'.[144] In response, the majority issued a separate opinion 'concurring' with their own majority Judgment,[145] in which they asserted that

---

[140] *Katanga Decision on the Implementation of Regulation 55* [8] (emphasis in original).

[141] Ibid. [21].

[142] *Prosecutor v Lubanga, Judgment on the Appeals of the Prosecutor and the Defence against Trial Chamber I's Decision on Victims' Participation of 18 January 2008* (ICC-01/04-01/06-1432, 11 July 2008) [95].

[143] Katanga's testimony is cited 354 times in the 711-page judgment. See, e.g., *Katanga Judgment* [314], [360]. Katanga was questioned by the bench on 18 and 19 October 2011: see *Prosecutor v Katanga*, 'Transcript of Proceedings of 18 October 2011'; 'Transcript of Proceedings of 19 October 2011'.

[144] *Katanga Judgment* (Judge Van den Wyngaert).

[145] *Katanga Judgment* (Judges Diarra and Cotte).

we in no wise [sic] sought to appropriate a 'case', and even less, to take the place of the Prosecution. Indeed, we are fully aware of its role and prerogatives and have no intention of encroaching on its authority. We understand, and have understood for a long time, our own role and the limits in which we must operate. As is the duty of any judge, we merely conducted, with objectivity and without preconceived ideas, as careful and thorough an examination of the evidence in the record as possible.[146]

Although both Judge Van den Wyngaert and the majority agree that the role of the judge is distinct from that of the prosecutor, they differ about whether the majority here overstepped their role and took on a 'case'. This division demonstrates that there is significant uncertainty about what is appropriate for a judge in a *sui generis* system of procedure. When the judges take on a more prosecutorial role, their ability to regulate the trial process and the relationships between the trial participants (as envisaged by the *Rome Statute*) is not clear; and under Regulation 55, there are also real questions about the proper role of other trial participants, such as the independence of the prosecutor.[147] Kevin Heller points out that a use of Regulation 55 by the Trial Chamber of its own volition is inconsistent with the guarantee of 'a fair trial conducted impartially'[148] as '[a] Trial Chamber does not act impartially when it intervenes during or after a trial to save the prosecution from itself'.[149] In Heller's view, a Trial Chamber that wishes to take a more inquisitorial role should explicitly adopt such a system.[150] In the absence of such an adoption, it is unacceptable that a Trial Chamber adopts a prosecutorial role after the completion of the trial, leading to a conviction.

The role of the judge is clearly linked to the question of fairness. The perception of judicial independence and impartiality is integral to trial fairness.[151] Moreover, judges – as the managers of the trial process – are the

---

146 Ibid. [2].
147 Heller (n 73).
148 *Rome Statute* Art 67(1), cited in Heller (n 73) 1005.
149 Heller (n 73) 1005.
150 See ibid.
151 Stahn (n 2) 269. This issue also significantly arose in the case of Šešelj, where Judge Harhoff was disqualified: *Prosecutor v Šešelj, Decision on Defence Motion for Disqualification of Judge Frederick Harhoff and Report to the Vice-President* (IT-03-67-T, 28 August 2013). This followed Judge Harhoff sending a letter to friends, in which he alleges 'tenacious pressure' by President Meron and suggests he was 'determined to achieve an acquittal' in recent cases. He suggests there are rushed judgments, uncertain law and process, and a pressure to acquit in certain cases. This letter shows significant issues around judicial independence and impartiality at the ICTY. Judge Harhoff's dismissal occurred after the completion of trial, and close to when judgment was scheduled to be delivered. Instead, Judge Niang was appointed to the bench and given six months to familiarise himself with the case: *Prosecutor v Šešelj (Order Assigning a Judge pursuant to Rule 15)* (31 October 2013). It is unlikely that a judge who had not attended any of the court proceedings or the judicial deliberations would be able to adequately reach a determination on the accused's guilt: see Kevin Jon

guardians of the trial's fairness.[152] If the position of the judge is unclear, there will be significant implications for how fairness is conceptualised. And yet *Katanga* demonstrates that there is uncertainty about how best to ensure this judicial function. There are thus several concerns regarding how to conceive of fairness in a *sui generis* procedural system, and this plurality of views and uncertainty contributes to the incoherence of fairness.

D. WHAT IS THE OUTCOME OF FAIRNESS'S INCOHERENCE?

I have demonstrated that fairness is conceptually incoherent due to divergence in three main respects: first, *what* constitutes fairness, and what legal principles are needed for fairness to operate; second, *whom* fairness is owed to, and which actor should be the key beneficiary of fairness; and third, *how* to ensure fairness in a *sui generis* system of procedure. In each of these respects, there is a lack of coherence around what fairness requires or entails in respect of international criminal trials.

Such incoherence allows fairness to be malleable and readily manipulated. It could be argued that its incoherence provides fairness with a certain flexibility and is therefore useful. In particular, fairness can be invoked in argument by all sides in a trial: prosecution, defence, victim participants and even states are all able to use fairness in their arguments. Further, fairness is then able to be used as the rationale for a decision by decision-makers – the judges. To borrow Martti Koskenniemi's language, fairness can be understood as an 'argumentative architecture' which allows '*any* decision, and thus also the critique of any decision'.[153]

However, I rather argue that such malleability leaves the concept of fairness without a strong basis. Without a shared understanding of fairness, it cannot be invoked to set the standards for trials,[154] and cannot fulfil its promise of being a binding quality between otherwise divided communities of international criminal justice stakeholders. The centrality of fairness suggests that fairness may either be a binding agent or alternatively – where conceptions of fairness differ – the lack of shared understanding of fairness

---

Heller, 'The Final Nail in the ICTY's Coffin' on *Opinio Juris* (16 December 2013) <http://opiniojuris.org/2013/12/16/final-nail-ictys-coffin/> (last accessed 9 December 2021); Sophie Rigney, 'Yugoslav Tribunal's Reputation under Threat', *New Matilda*, 23 September 2013 <https://newmatilda.com/2013/09/23/yugoslav-tribunals-reputation-under-threat> (last accessed 9 December 2021); Marko Milanovic, 'Breaking: Judge Harhoff Disqualified from the Seselj Case' on *EJIL Talk!* (28 August 2013) <http://www.ejiltalk.org/breaking-judge-harhoff-disqualified-from-the-seselj-case/> (last accessed 9 December 2021). Again, this raises live issues regarding the independence and impartiality of judges.

[152] *Rome Statute* Art 64(2).

[153] Martti Koskenniemi, *From Apology to Utopia: The Structure of International Legal Argument* (CUP, 2005) 589 (emphasis in original).

[154] McDermott (n 16) 165.

could be a source of distrust between stakeholders. The incoherence of fairness does not provide strength to the concept: it makes it vulnerable. In particular, the incoherence of fairness means that fairness can be invoked in ways contrary to the constituent elements of fairness – the rights of the accused. This can be witnessed in the way that fairness and rights are able to be disconnected from each other.

E. FAIRNESS AND RIGHTS: CENTRAL AND RELATED, BUT ALSO SEPARABLE AND SEPARATED

While fairness is central in international criminal trials, there is no coherent understanding of what it is. Fairness is conceptually hollow. It operates as a normative ideal to strive for, but without any real content or agreed meaning. The hope of fairness is that it might be something to bring together and bind various parties to a trial, as it is an aim that is shared by all. However, the incoherence of fairness means that it, in fact, divides scholars and practitioners into different tribes: those that emphasise certain principles, and those who emphasise other principles; those who favour a rights-centred approach versus those who favour a shared process-centred approach; those from adversarial backgrounds versus those from inquisitorial backgrounds. Fairness is vague and variable, increasingly without a strong tether or foundation. The only foundation fairness really enjoys – a close relationship with the rights of the accused – is challenged.

Fairness and rights are separate concepts, and although fairness cannot exist without adherence to rights, we see from all the foregoing that the two are different. Because fairness and rights are separable, it is, therefore, conceivable that there could be attempts to separate each from the other. In particular, can 'fairness' be invoked to limit or curtail rights? Such an approach is perhaps best exemplified by Damaška's view that some fairness considerations should be 'relaxed', given the unique place and aims of international criminal justice.[155] Similarly, the ICTY Appeals Chamber has noted that

> there are various provisions that, by balancing the rights of the accused against other relevant interests, safeguard the overall fairness of the proceedings … under the cloak of 'fairness', a court may be led to construe troublesome curtailments of the rights of the accused in specific instances, which in turn might impact on fundamental rights of the accused.[156]

We witness the divergence between fairness and rights in several key examples outlined in this chapter. The above discussion on the ascendancy

---

[155] Damaška (n 29).
[156] *Prosecutor v Prlić, Decision on Appeals Against Decision Admitting Transcript of Jadranko Prlić's Questioning into Evidence* (IT-04-74-AR73.6, 23 November 2007) [41].

of the shared process-centred approach to fairness gives a particularly strong example of the rights of the accused being distanced from the concept of fairness. Indeed, the concept of fairness has been invoked specifically to limit the rights of the accused. In both the *Haradinaj* and *Katanga* cases, we see the interests of the prosecution being advanced, even though the rights of the accused are adversely affected (by a long retrial in *Haradinaj* and by a conviction on new charges in *Katanga*).

However, the statutory responsibility of a Trial Chamber to ensure that a trial 'is fair . . . and conducted with full respect for the rights of an accused and due regard for the protection of victims and witnesses' is challenged by the extension of 'rights' to parties other than the accused. As Damaška has argued, the approach of abandoning

> the traditional emphasis of fairness on defensive safeguards and [the placement of] all procedural participants under the same protective umbrella of fairness . . . is likely to provoke a comprehensive balancing process – a 'mediating discourse' – in the course of which some precious defensive safeguards might be attributed less weight than they deserve. Some could even be 'balanced away'.[157]

Similarly, Pascal Chenivesse and Christopher Piranio have described 'the right to a fair trial' as 'an evolving seesaw', trying to balance the rights and protections of the different stakeholders.[158] They ask whether 'reaching an optimum distribution of rights and protections [is] either desirable or possible'.[159] That this 'balancing act' has been undertaken through the language of fairness shows the incoherence and ultimate instability of the concept of fairness. In the absence of a strong and shared understanding of how fairness and rights interlink, what each is, whom they are owed to, and how the rights of one party affect the fairness owed to another party, it is easy to undermine either fairness or rights, or both.

If international criminal justice is 'still partly in search of its "identity"' and there are real questions about how to measure its success or failure,[160] coming to a coherent acceptance of 'fairness' will assist the international criminal legal project. Without a coherent understanding of fairness, the questions of what international criminal law is trying to achieve, and how it will do so, remain similarly uncertain. This chapter has set out a taxonomy of the various perspectives of and challenges to fairness. The incoherence of fairness at the conceptual level aligns with fairness being poorly invoked in procedural decisions by Trial Chambers in international criminal trials. In particular, the disconnection between fairness and rights can be seen

---

[157] Damaška (n 6) 615.
[158] Pascal Chenivesse and Christopher Piranio, 'What Price Justice? On the Evolving Notion of "Right to a Fair Trial" from Nuremberg to The Hague' (2011) 24 *CRIA* 403, 421.
[159] Ibid. 422.
[160] Stahn (n 2) 254.

when examining procedural practice. Chapters Four, Five and Six of this book demonstrate the incoherence of fairness in its application in matters of disclosure, the use of adjudicated facts, and the protection of witnesses. I now turn to these case studies to provide an examination of fairness and rights in procedural decision-making.

Chapter 4
Fairness, the rights of the accused and disclosure

As we have seen in previous chapters, the relationships between fairness, rights and procedure are theoretically complex. In this chapter and those that follow, we see how these issues are addressed within trials, through procedural decisions – revealing how fairness, rights and procedure interact in practice, as well as theory. This chapter examines the links between fairness, the rights of the accused, and procedural rules, in relation to a particular case study: the disclosure of information from the prosecution to the defence. The rights of the accused that are particularly affected by disclosure are the right to time and facilities to prepare a defence, and the right to know the case alleged by the prosecution, as well as the principle of equality of arms. In examining the relationships between these rights, trial fairness, and the way that disclosure is undertaken in international criminal trials, I ask: how has fairness been considered by Chambers when making decisions on issues of disclosure? What have been some of the outcomes of these procedural decisions? And how do these outcomes reconcile with the rights of the accused? These questions allow an examination of how fairness and the rights of the accused are connected – or separated – in procedural decisions in international criminal trials.

In the first part of this chapter, I outline the significance of disclosure in examinations of fairness and rights, and how disclosure interacts with both the rights of the accused, and the fairness of the trials. I then analyse how the concept of fairness has been used by the parties and the Trial Chambers when reaching determinations on disclosure. This analysis focuses on three issues regarding the way that disclosure is undertaken in international criminal trials. First, I briefly outline the challenges posed by the electronic nature of disclosure. Secondly, I demonstrate that Trial Chambers may be unable to adequately manage large volumes of disclosure provided in violation of the prescribed time limits and that this inability has a detrimental effect on the rights of an accused. Thirdly, I argue that at the ICC, there is an emerging environment that permits non-disclosure of material (including, particularly, exculpatory material) that is in the possession of both victims and the prosecution. In examining these issues, I argue that while Trial Chambers often reiterate the importance of disclosure as fundamental to ensuring a fair trial, the way Chambers regulate disclosure creates a trial environment where the rights of the accused are not upheld. Trial Chambers are unable to control the informational relationship between the parties. Ultimately, the way that disclosure is given effect in these trials demonstrates a separation between fairness and the rights of the accused.

Disclosure is 'at the heart' of international criminal trials,[1] and 'compliance with disclosure obligations is essential to a fair trial'.[2] Both the ICTY and the ICC prescribe what disclosure must occur within what time limits.[3] At both institutions, exculpatory material must be provided to the defence 'as soon as practicable',[4] and the ICC has emphasised the accused's right to exculpatory material as a particular right of the accused.[5] In addition to being closely linked to the rights of an accused, disclosure is closely linked to the presumption of innocence and to the ability of an accused to challenge the prosecution's case, as it is essential to understanding what evidence might exist to support the prosecution's case. Disclosure is also important for ensuring the relationship between the parties is levelled through requiring a party with an informational advantage to provide that information to the other party, thereby ensuring that the trial is not an 'ambush'.[6] This regulation of the informational relationship between the parties (particularly when viewed with reference to the presumption of innocence) should assist in achieving the trial's key aim – to determine the accused's guilt or innocence for the crimes with which they are charged – as well as the key responsibility of the Trial Chamber, to ensure a fair trial, with full respect to the rights of the accused.[7]

---

[1] Kate Gibson and Cainnech Lussiaà-Berdou, 'Disclosure of Evidence' in Karim Khan, Caroline Buisman, and Christopher Gosnell (eds), *Principles of Evidence in International Criminal Justice* (OUP, 2010) 306, 306. For more on disclosure generally, see Alexander Heinze, *International Criminal Procedure and Disclosure* (Dunker & Humblodt, 2014); Elmar Widdar, *A Fair Trial at the International Criminal Court? Human Rights Standards and Legitimacy* (Peter Lang, 2016); Brando Fiori, *International Criminal Procedural Systems and Human Rights Law* (Wolf Legal, 2015).

[2] *Prosecutor v Kordić, Judgement* (IT-95-14/2-A, 17 December 2004) ('*Kordić Judgement*') [183]; *Prosecutor v Karadžić*, 'Motion for New Trial for Disclosure Violations' (IT-95-5/18-T, 13 August 2012 ('Karadžić Motion for New Trial') [8].

[3] ICTY, *Rules of Procedure and Evidence*, Doc No IT/32/Rev.50 (adopted on 11 February 1994, amended 10 July 2015) ('ICTY Rules'), rr 65 *ter*, 66, and 68; ICC, *Rules of Procedure and Evidence*, Doc No ICC-ASP/1/3 (adopted 9 September 2002) ('ICC Rules') rr 76–84; *Rome Statute of the International Criminal Court*, opened for signature 17 July 1998, 2187 UNTS 90 (entered into force 1 July 2002) ('*Rome Statute*') Arts 61, 64, and 67.

[4] *ICTY Rules* r 68; *Rome Statute* Art 67.

[5] *Rome Statute* Art 67(2); *Prosecutor v Bemba, Decision on the Evidence Disclosure System and Setting a Timetable for Disclosure between the Parties* (ICC-01/05-01/08–55, 31 July 2008 [67]). For useful overviews of the ICC disclosure regime, see Xavier-Jean Keïta, 'Disclosure of Evidence in the Law and Practice of the ICC' (2016) 16 *ICLR* 1018; Karim Khan and Caroline Buisman, 'Sitting on Evidence? Systemic Failings in the ICC Disclosure Regime – Time for Reform' in Carsten Stahn (ed) *The Law and Practice of the International Criminal Court* (OUP, 2015) 1029.

[6] Masha Fedorova, *The Principle of Equality of Arms in International Criminal Proceedings* (Intersentia, 2012) 233.

[7] ICTY *Statute*, Art 20; *Rome Statute* Art 64(2).

However, as this chapter demonstrates, there are significant problems with the provision of disclosure from the prosecution to the defence. Disclosure may be provided in violation of prescribed time limits, and exculpatory material may not ever be provided to the defence. Given the centrality of disclosure to the trial, defence teams are likely to challenge these violations, and thus, disclosure has emerged as a key battleground between the parties. It is highly litigated at all international courts and tribunals, and has proved to be 'one of the most intriguing, complex, and time-consuming procedural issues'[8] in international trials. Certainly, defence counsel tend to believe there is a problem with how Chambers manage disclosure: a 2016 survey of ICC defence lawyers showed that 'limits on the ability to adequately review evidence disclosed by the prosecution' was the most commonly experienced 'procedural action that unduly limited defence rights or interests'; sixty-five per cent of respondents indicated they had experienced this.[9]

A. THE RELATIONSHIP BETWEEN DISCLOSURE AND FAIRNESS

Disclosure is 'arguably the most important mechanism for ensuring that the accused receives a fair trial'.[10] Given its centrality to the trial and its integral relationship to the rights of the accused, this link between fairness and disclosure is not surprising. However, while Chambers often explicitly acknowledge the importance of disclosure to trial fairness, these same Chambers also frequently fail to enforce disclosure obligations in these trials.[11]

The particular relationship between trial fairness and the disclosure of exculpatory material has been made explicit at both the ICTY and the ICC. Exculpatory material includes that which – in the prosecution's view – 'shows or tends to show the innocence of the accused, or to mitigate the guilt of the accused, or which may affect the credibility of prosecution evidence'.[12]

---

8 Lars Büngener, 'Disclosure of Evidence' in Christoph Safferling (ed), *International Criminal Procedure* (OUP, 2012) 374.

9 Jenia Iontcheva Turner, 'Defence Perspectives on Fairness and Efficiency at the International Criminal Court', in Kevin Heller et al. (eds), *Oxford Handbook of International Criminal Law* (OUP, 2020).

10 Gibson and Lussiàà-Berdou (n 1) 306.

11 See e.g. Wayne Jordash, 'Fairness of Karadzic Trial in Question' (4 October 2010) *International Justice Tribune* <http://www.rnw.nl/international-justice/article/fairness-karadzic-trial-question> (last accessed 19 July 2013); Gibson and Lussiàà-Berdou (n 1) 313.

12 *Rome Statute* Art 67(2). See also *ICTY Rules* r 68; *Prosecutor v Lubanga, Decision on the Consequences of Non-Disclosure of Exculpatory Materials Covered by Article 54(3)(e) Agreements and the Application to Stay the Prosecution of the Accused, Together with Certain other Issues Raised at the Status Conference on 10 June 2008* (ICC-01/04-01/06, 13 June 2008) ('*Lubanga Decision on the Consequences of Non-Disclosure of Exculpatory Materials*') [59].

The ICTY Appeals Chamber has stipulated that '[t]he disclosure of exculpatory material is fundamental to the fairness of proceedings . . . and considerations of fairness are the overriding factor in any determination of whether the governing Rule has been breached'.[13] At the ICC, Trial Chambers have concluded that the right to a fair trial includes an entitlement to disclosure of exculpatory material.[14]

One defence lawyer, however, identified the complexity of the relationship between fairness and disclosure. In their view,

> it's very easy to say, well, 'the disclosure regimes are bad therefore everything's unfair' . . . but it's not entirely accurate. The disclosure regimes are bad, there is no doubt about that. They do not take into account the idea of allowing the parties, specifically the defence, to properly and adequately prepare their cases. [But] ultimately, would a different result be achieved [if the disclosure regimes were better]? There's no way of knowing that.[15]

While there may be no way of knowing whether there would be a different result for trial fairness if disclosure regimes were improved, it is nonetheless important to understand the relationship between fairness and rights in the context of disclosure procedures. Disclosure is a practical example to assess and describe the ways in which procedural rules and decisions affect fairness and rights in these trials.

B. THE RELATIONSHIP BETWEEN DISCLOSURE AND THE RIGHTS OF THE ACCUSED

Disclosure is one of the main procedural mechanisms to ensure the rights of the accused are upheld in international trials. The rights of an accused that are affected by disclosure are, in particular, the right to time and facilities to prepare a defence[16] and the right to know the case against them.[17] While some will emphasise one or the other of these rights, they are, in fact, interrelated: preparing a defence is not possible without knowing the case.[18] Rather than characterising the disclosure provisions as 'rights' themselves, I argue that it is more appropriate to frame the disclosure regime as procedural 'rules' whose application, non-application and misapplication must be examined in light of their relationship to the rights of the accused articulated in the statutes of the Courts and Tribunals (as well as to the fairness of the trial).[19]

---

[13] *Prosecutor v Krstić, Judgement* (IT-98-33-A, 19 April 2004) [180].
[14] *Lubanga Decision on the Consequences of Non-Disclosure of Exculpatory Materials* [34].
[15] Interview with Colleen Rohan and Gregor Guy-Smith (8 May 2013).
[16] *Rome Statute* Art 67(1)(b); *ICTY Statute* Art 21(4)(b).
[17] *Rome Statute* Art 67(1)(a); *ICTY Statute* Art 21(4)(a).
[18] Büngener (n 8) 346–8.
[19] This can be compared to the position taken by Peter Morrissey, who frames disclosure itself

(1) The right to know the case

The right 'to be informed promptly and in detail of the nature, cause and content of the charge'[20] is intrinsically related to disclosure because, to be so informed, the accused must receive material that outlines the nature, cause and content of the charge. Without this material, the accused cannot know what the prosecution's case is, and therefore what case they must meet (and how to raise reasonable doubt). As Lars Büngener correctly points out, however, the information on the charges generally refers to the indictment or charges; disclosure is broader than this and refers to 'pieces of evidence and factual information which go beyond the contents of an indictment'.[21] Both the charges themselves and the broader category of disclosable material (including witness materials, documents sought to be tendered, and potentially exculpatory materials) are important for the rights of the accused. The broader category of material will affect the accused's ability to meet the prosecution case in its entirety and will also have implications for the accused's right to time and facilities to prepare a defence.

(2) The right to time and facilities to prepare a defence

Disclosure is intimately linked with being able to prepare a case effectively and the particular right to time and facilities to prepare a defence.[22] Without disclosure of the evidentiary basis for the prosecution case, an accused will not know what they are expected to address and thus will not be able to adequately prepare their defence. Prosecution disclosure is, therefore, 'the sole means for affording the accused adequate time and facilities in which to investigate that evidence and prepare to meet it at trial'.[23] For Jordash, 'the importance of prompt disclosure cannot be overstated', particularly in complex cases concerning years of armed conflict and involving allegations of joint criminal enterprise;[24] and he points out that:

as a package of rights of the accused: Peter Morrissey, 'Applied Rights in International Criminal Law: Defence Counsel and the Right to Disclosure' in Gideon Boas, William A Schabas and Michael P Scharf (eds), *International Criminal Justice: Legitimacy and Coherence* (Edward Elgar, 2012) 68, 68.

[20] *ICTY Statute* Art 21(4)(a); *Rome Statute* Art 67(1)(a).

[21] Büngener (n 8) 347.

[22] *ICTY Statute* Art 21(4)(b); *Rome Statute* Art 67(1)(b).

[23] Colleen Rohan, 'Protecting the Rights of the Accused in International Criminal Proceedings: Lip Service or Affirmative Action?' in William A Schabas, Yvonne McDermott and Niamh Hayes (eds), *The Ashgate Research Companion to International Criminal Law* (Ashgate, 2013) 289, 291. See also Jordash (n 11); Gregor Guy-Smith, 'Developing a Case Theory and a Defence Strategy', in Gentian Zyberi and Colleen Rohan (eds), *Defense Perspectives on International Criminal Justice* (CUP, 2018) 385; Jens Dieckmann and Marie O'Leary, 'The Role of Defense Counsel in Pre-Trial' in Zyberi and Rohan (eds) 237.

[24] Ibid.

The devil of a prosecution and defence case is in the detail provided by this disclosure. The smallest of details may prove important and the more that are available at an early stage the better. This aids the taking of instructions, detailed investigations, the planning of overall strategy, and trial management, including efficient and focussed court sessions.[25]

Disclosure must be provided in a manner that allows time for the disclosed material to be integrated into a defence case. If disclosure is not timely, the utility of the information may be limited, and there may be a negative consequence for the accused's 'adequate time and facilities' to prepare – both in relation to the examination of particular witnesses and to the overall case. As one defence lawyer noted, if a defence team receives disclosure 'three days before the witness comes . . . you can't investigate it, you can't integrate it into any theory of the case that you have'.[26]

Because the accused enjoys the presumption of innocence and need not run an affirmative defence case (but can simply put the prosecution's case to proof), time and facilities to prepare a defence include the ability to run investigations and the ability to address the prosecution's evidence and case theory from the commencement of trial, rather than from the start of the defence phase of trial.[27] Disclosure must be provided in a manner that allows it to be integrated into a defence case from the outset. If disclosure is not provided in this manner, the utility of the information could be limited, and there may be a negative consequence for the accused's time and facilities to prepare.

(3) The principle of equality of arms

The principle of equality of arms incorporates the notion that neither party is to be placed at a material disadvantage vis-à-vis the other party with regards to information. Disclosure of information is therefore integral to the principle of equality of arms between the parties and without access to necessary information, there cannot be meaningful equality of arms.[28] While disclosure obligations exist for both the prosecution and the defence,[29] obligations tend to be more onerous for the prosecution. This is for two main reasons: first, as the burden of proof rests with the prosecution, they

---

[25] Ibid.

[26] Interview with Colleen Rohan and Gregor Guy-Smith (8 May 2013).

[27] Rohan (n 23) 290–1. On the relationship between disclosure and defence investigations in particular, see Caroline Buisman and David Hooper, 'Defence Investigations and the Collection of Evidence' in Zyberi and Rohan (eds) (n 23) 519.

[28] Fedorova (n 6) 233–4. See also Büngener (n 8) 347–8; see also *Prosecutor v Banda & Jerbo, Judgment on the Defence Appeal for the Disclosure of Documents* (ICC-02/05-03/09-501 OA4, 28 August 2013 [34]).

[29] *ICTY Rules* r 67(A)(ii); *ICC Rules* r 79. For more information, see Gibson and Lussiaà-Berdou (n 1) 338–44.

bear primary responsibility for gathering the evidence (and then disclosing it to the defence); and second, the prosecutor 'enjoys massive advantages in the facilities for the gathering of evidence'.[30] The facilities available to the prosecution (but not the defence) for gathering material may include investigators, search warrants, and wiretaps,[31] as well as the ability to initiate investigations and certain powers that accompany the status of being a prosecutorial office.[32] These resources grant the prosecution 'superior, and sometimes even sole access to this material'.[33] All this necessitates a degree of 'equalising' of arms between the parties, which prosecution disclosure obligations attempt to ensure.[34]

The ICC has taken further steps to ensure equality of arms by placing a burden on the prosecutor to investigate incriminating and exonerating circumstances alike and to disclose all evidence to the defence that appears relevant to both the defence and the prosecution cases.[35] This provision recognises the advantages the Office of the Prosecutor enjoys compared to the defence. It has been said that this 'demonstrates a strong case of the drafters of the ICC for both fairness and truth-finding'.[36] However, the prosecutor's duty to investigate exonerating material is only effective if the potentially exculpatory material is disclosed to the defence, and as I show below, this is far from certain.

The appropriate application of disclosure rules will therefore assist in ensuring the 'full respect' of the rights of the accused to know the case and to time and facilities to prepare their defence, as well as to the principle of equality of arms. Given the close relationship between these rights and trial fairness, the expression of these rights (through appropriate disclosure procedure) is integral to the 'overarching requirement' that the trial is fair. The connection between disclosure and trial fairness is made explicit in the jurisprudence, and Trial Chambers 'regularly recall'[37] the importance of disclosure to trial fairness. However, I will now demonstrate that, despite this rhetorical nod to the importance of disclosure to fairness and the clear connection between disclosure and both fairness and rights, Trial Chambers permit the violation of disclosure rules and facilitate an environment where such violations are tolerated. Thus, the theoretical relationships between disclosure and fairness, and disclosure and rights, are not given practical

[30] Büngener (n 8) 350.

[31] Ibid.

[32] Fedorova (n 6) 234.

[33] *Prosecutor v Kordić, Decision on Appellant's Notice and Supplemental Notice of Prosecution's Non-Compliance with Its Disclosure Obligations under Rule 68 of the Rules* (IT-95-14/2, 11 February 2004) [17].

[34] Gibson and Lussiaà-Berdou (n 1) 306; see also Fedorova (n 6) 234.

[35] *Rome Statute* Arts 54(1)(a) and 54(1)(f).

[36] Büngener (n 8) 353.

[37] Gibson and Lussiaà-Berdou (n 1) 313.

expression through the full adherence to disclosure rules. We can then examine how the misapplication, or the violations, of procedural rules, allows dislocations between fairness, rights and procedure in contemporary international criminal trials.

C. THREE WAYS IN WHICH DISCLOSURE, RIGHTS AND FAIRNESS ARE SEPARATED IN INTERNATIONAL CRIMINAL TRIALS

In this section, I outline three issues in the practice of disclosure at international criminal trials. These issues are: first, the electronic nature of disclosure; second, the provision of large volumes of late disclosure; and third, the non-disclosure of material (particularly exculpatory material) by both prosecutors and victims' representatives at the ICC. I argue that Chambers, while routinely invoking the concept of fairness in their decision-making on disclosure issues, are actually facilitating the creation of a system that permits such violations and thus challenges the rights of the accused.

(1) Issue one: the electronic nature of disclosure

A preliminary challenge to briefly note is the way in which disclosure is undertaken, namely the electronic nature of disclosure. For example, at the ICTY, the 'Electronic Disclosure Suite' ('the EDS') is used by the prosecution to allow the defence to access investigative material (apart from confidential or privileged materials)[38] and is one of the main ways that disclosure is provided.[39] ICTY jurisprudence reiterates that the 'crucial question is whether the principle of fairness is breached by providing material in electronic format'.[40] As long as 'such assistance as is reasonable and

---

[38] Gideon Boas et al.(eds), *International Criminal Law Practitioner Library: Volume III, International Criminal Procedure* (CUP, 2011) 233.

[39] At the ICC, disclosure is often provided via CD-ROM, and 'Ringtail' software is used to organise the material. This software appears not to have caused any major difficulties, 'as the parties have praised it as being the "most convenient" format for disclosure' (Büngener (n 8) 374). However, the Ringtail system cannot be used for analysis, and although it allows for some searches it does not work for searches of handwritten documents. The defence in the *Lubanga* case also had 'practical difficulties in coping with the enormous masses of evidence disclosed to it via data CD-Rom' (Sabine Swoboda, 'The ICC Disclosure Regime – A Defence Perspective' (2008) 19 *CLF* 449, 459). The defence could not effectively search the material due to redactions and a lack of electronic search mechanisms to examine the 15,000 documents (ibid.). Further challenges for the defence of the ICC's 'E-Court' practices and disclosure are set out in Karim Khan and Anand Shah, 'Defensive practices: Representing Clients Before the International Criminal Court' (2014) 76 *LCP* 191, 215–218.

[40] *Prosecutor v Šešelj, Decision on Form of Disclosure* (IT-03-67-PT, 4 July 2006) ('*Šešelj Decision*'); *Prosecutor v Karadžić, Decision on Motion on Modalities of Rule 66(A)(ii) Disclosure* (27 April 2009).

necessary in the circumstances is given to the accused for the purpose of accessing, retrieving, and . . . effectively utilising material disclosed in electronic format, no unfairness results'.[41] Nonetheless, defence resources are significantly affected by the electronic provision of disclosure, as the EDS system is 'cumbersome and difficult to both access and use'.[42] In particular, documents can be stored across a multitude of folders but it is not possible to search across folders.[43] This means that the search has to be replicated multiple times within each folder.[44] Documents may also be duplicated across the EDS,[45] meaning that any search will return multiple copies of the same document. As an example, in the *Karadžić* case, for each witness, the defence team will first search through their disclosure logs 'to see if what we are looking for has actually been disclosed' and then they use EDS to locate the document.[46] However, on other occasions, a defence team will need to search by 'witness name or topic just broadly through the EDS' in order to find any relevant information.[47] This process is 'unwieldy . . . very time consuming and not that comprehensive'[48] and, as a result, is highly resource-intensive. Indeed, Counsel Assisting Karadžić, Peter Robinson, noted that on the *Karadžić* case, 'almost our entire intern team is devoted to that. We . . . have six to eight people doing that on a full time basis'.[49] This equates to between 240 and 360 hours every week, devoted just to the process of searching electronic systems for disclosure. This is in addition to the hours spent on document and disclosure management by paid Case Managers and Legal Assistants.[50] Thus, the electronic provision of disclosure poses challenges for a defence team to retrieve and use the material, and this then may affect the accused's right to time and facilities to prepare a defence.

The electronic system also poses challenges for prosecutors in discharging their disclosure obligations. Electronic management assists the prosecution to know what documents are under their possession or control (and which should be disclosed), and difficulties with these systems will have profound implications for the ability of the prosecution to undertake disclosure. The prosecution will have millions of pages of documents, which have been scanned using Optical Character Recognition ('OCR') to make them

---

[41] *Šešelj Decision* [12].
[42] Gibson and Lussiaà-Berdou (n 1) 314.
[43] Interview with Peter Robinson (2 May 2013).
[44] Ibid.
[45] Ibid.
[46] Ibid.
[47] Ibid.
[48] Ibid.
[49] Ibid.
[50] Karadžić attempted to challenge this system: *Prosecutor v Karadžić*, 'Motion on Modalities of Rule 66(A)(ii) Disclosure' (14 April 2009); 'Accused's Motion for Disclosure of Rule 68 Material' (6 February 2009) [8]. However, this was unsuccessful: *Decision on Motion on Modalities of Rule 66(A)(ii) Disclosure* (27 April 2009).

searchable. However, these documents may have gone through an imperfect OCR process and so prosecutors cannot always search documents properly.[51] As an example, a search for 'Srebrenica' will not return results for a document that has incorrectly registered the word as 'Slebrenica' or 'Srebnenica'. Unless the OCR process has been done perfectly, searching electronically for documents cannot be undertaken in a way that excludes every possible error – and subsequently, disclosure cannot be said to be exhaustive.[52] Former prosecution Senior Trial Attorney Joanna Korner argues that disclosure violations usually occur because the prosecutor, in all good faith, did not know about the documents due to these issues with the electronic systems.[53] There is, she notes, 'no foolproof method of knowing what is in the possession of the prosecutor'.[54] Thus, many disclosure violations may occur due to problems the prosecution faces in managing or retrieving its documents and not from any malicious intent.[55]

(2) Issue two: large volumes of material provided late

Disclosure that is provided in breach of the prescribed time limits, in a large volume and in a piecemeal fashion, may affect an accused's rights to time and facilities to prepare a defence and to know the case, as well as challenge the principle of equality of arms. If disclosure is provided late, an accused will not be properly able to organise and prepare their case. One defence lawyer articulated that problems with late disclosure included not being able to investigate the information, not being able to use it, or receiving it so late that the lawyer's approach to cross-examination or presentation of a witness is 'dramatically changed based upon information handed to you five minutes before you walk into court'.[56]

Late disclosure also affects how defence teams use and organise their limited team resources – therefore affecting the accused's time and facilities to prepare their case. The same defence lawyer said that they might spend 'hours and hours writing emails [requesting information] and getting responses that say, "no, we don't have anything"', only to then be provided with the information.[57] Disclosure that is provided late, therefore,

---

[51] Interview with Joanna Korner (21 May 2013).

[52] Ibid.

[53] Ibid.

[54] Ibid. See also Morrissey (n 19) 90.

[55] For more on the challenges for both parties, and particularly the accused, of the EDS, see *Prosecutor v Mladić, Decision on Submissions Relative to the Proposed "EDS" Method of Disclosure* (IT-09-92-T, 26 June 2012); *Decision on Defence Interlocutory Appeal Against the Trial Chamber's Decision on EDS Disclosure Methods* (IT-09-92-AR73.2, 28 November 2013).

[56] Interview with Colleen Rohan and Gregor Guy-Smith (8 May 2013).

[57] Ibid.

also affects the ability of the accused to know the case they are expected to meet. Finally, until disclosure occurs, the accused is placed at an informational disadvantage vis-à-vis the prosecution and, therefore, the principle of equality of arms is also affected. In many cases, the prosecution will have had possession of the material for years (perhaps even decades) before the pre-trial processes commence and disclosure obligations are triggered. Even if the prosecution had not recently reviewed the information, it still rests in the possession and under the control of the prosecution and may not be available to the defence. The prosecution has access to the material and can discover its contents at any time, but the defence does not have this access or ability.

The *Karadžić* case demonstrates the difficulties for the rights of the accused posed by large volumes of late disclosure. The scale of the *Karadžić* case – one of the largest in the history of international criminal law – has proved challenging for both parties. The Trial Chamber set a deadline of May 2009 for all disclosure of witness statements under Rule 66(A)(ii) and all exhibits under Rule 65 *ter*(E).[58] In September 2009, the accused filed a motion to set deadlines for disclosure as, at that stage, over 1,500 pages of disclosure had been provided after the May deadline.[59] The Trial Chamber denied this motion.[60] Subsequently, between this time and Judgment being delivered in March 2016, Karadžić filed 108 motions for disclosure violations by the prosecution.[61] In his Appeal of conviction, Karadžić claimed that there were eighty-two separate occasions when the Trial Chamber found the prosecution to be in violation of its disclosure obligations.[62] It is difficult to quantify exactly how much information this relates to. In 2012 (at a point when there were 58 violations), it was clear that the violations related to over 335,126 pages of exculpatory material.[63] This was a 150 per cent increase in the volume of exculpatory material disclosed prior to the commencement of trial, 'the vast majority of which was not disclosed as soon as practicable'.[64] In 2016, in his final Appeal Brief, Karadžić claimed that the material amounted to 552,828 pages of exculpatory material, or seventy-eight per cent of the total exculpatory material.[65] Such a figure is

---

[58] *Prosecutor v Karadžić, Order Following on Status Conference and Appended Work Plan* (6 April 2009)

[59] *Prosecutor v Karadžić,* 'Motion to Set Deadlines for Disclosure' (9 September 2009).

[60] *Prosecutor v Karadžić, Decision on Accused's Motion to Set Deadlines for Disclosure* (1 October 2009) ('*Karadžić Decision to Set Deadlines for Disclosure*').

[61] *Prosecutor v Karadžić,* 'Second Motion for Finding Disclosure Violation and for Remedial Measures' (14 May 2010) to '108th Motion for Finding of Disclosure Violation and for Remedial Measures' (14 March 2016).

[62] *Prosecutor v Karadžić,* 'Radovan Karadžić's Appeal Brief' (MICT-13-55-A, 23 December 2016) ('Karadžić Appeal Brief') [73].

[63] 'Karadžić Motion for New Trial'.

[64] 'Karadžić Motion for New Trial' [4].

[65] 'Karadžić Appeal Brief' [93].

staggering. The material ranges from single-page documents of limited value to exculpatory material of potentially significant importance. It appears that all prosecution disclosure violations have been made by accident or omission, and both the accused and the Trial Chamber have consistently acknowledged that the prosecution has acted in good faith in relation to discharging its disclosure obligations.

Disclosure violations in this case fall into two main categories. The first is prosecution witness statements or transcripts of testimony that were in the prosecution's possession prior to the May 2009 disclosure deadline and which should have been disclosed by this deadline under Rule 66(A)(ii).[66] Karadžić has noted that the prosecution failed to disclose 406 of these statements and transcripts, which, he submitted, represented twenty-five per cent of the prosecution's witness statements and testimony.[67] Counsel Assisting Karadžić, Peter Robinson, has noted the effect of this non-disclosure on the ability of the accused and his defence team to prepare their case:

> as a result of not having all of that we basically were on the wrong foot because we . . . tried to look at the case as a whole at the beginning and find out what our strategies should be. But we never really had the whole picture because of not having so many statements.[68]

Robinson shows the challenge for defence teams in preparing to meet the prosecution case if they are not on proper notice of that case to be met. The lack of timely disclosure of a quarter of the statements in support of the prosecution case is a large part of the case. It appears that the prosecution must have known about these documents in order to compile the prosecution witness list, to know which witnesses it was to call and what documents it would tender through those witnesses. This suggests a large discrepancy of knowledge and access to documents – and thus a significant inequality of arms – between the prosecution, who must have been aware of these documents, and the accused. Moreover, it is hard to imagine that the accused's right to know the case against them can be afforded 'full respect' in the absence of such a large body of material.

When that material is eventually provided, the issue then arises as to how a defence team will allocate resources to managing a large volume of late disclosure. This has implications for the accused's right to time and facilities to prepare a defence: time and facilities will need to be allocated to this large body of material provided in violation of the proscribed time limits, diverting resources from other activities.

The second area of disclosure violations is non-disclosure of exculpatory material under Rule 68. Because disclosure of exculpatory material is

---

[66] 'Karadžić Motion for New Trial' [3].
[67] Ibid.
[68] Interview with Peter Robinson (2 May 2013).

an ongoing obligation, the Trial Chamber refused to impose a deadline on the prosecution to complete its disclosure of this information, but the Trial Chamber considered that it was essential that such material was disclosed as soon as practicable.[69] As Robinson explained, this meant that

> the prosecution had the idea that they could disclose [exculpatory material] on a rolling basis throughout the trial . . . we ended up getting a lot of material after the trial started or in the late stages of the trial that would have, if we had seen it all before, changed the way we actually defended the case.[70]

The prosecution's belief it could disclose the exculpatory material 'on a rolling basis' represents a fundamental misunderstanding of the importance of exculpatory material. Such material will either 'suggest the innocence or mitigate the guilt of the accused or affect the credibility of prosecution evidence' and, therefore, will be of crucial significance to a defence case. It is for this reason that it must be disclosed 'as soon as practicable'. The *Karadžić* Trial Chamber explicitly stated that the ongoing obligation to disclose exculpatory material 'relates only to the fact that as new material comes into the possession of the Prosecution it should be assessed as to its potentially exculpatory nature and disclosed accordingly'.[71] The Trial Chamber was clear that the continuing obligation on the prosecution to disclose exculpatory material does not allow the prosecution to delay disclosing potentially exculpatory material or to 'identify and disclose potentially exculpatory material on a "rolling basis"'.[72] Such an approach 'demonstrates a failure to comply with the Chamber's repeated instructions'.[73] The Chamber expressed its 'deep concern at the lack of organisation and the unsystematic manner in which the Rule 68 searches are being conducted'.[74]

Robinson is of the opinion that the combination of these two issues – the non-disclosure of witness statements and transcripts, and the non-disclosure of exculpatory material – meant that the *Karadžić* defence team 'never really had the whole picture in front of us like we were supposed to have when the trial started. The volume of the late disclosure was so great that . . . we've never had enough time to read it'.[75] Thus, without this disclosure provided in a timely manner, the accused was not, in his argument, able to adequately prepare the case and integrate this material into the

---

[69] *Karadžić Decision to Set Deadlines for Disclosure* [19]–[20].

[70] Interview with Peter Robinson (2 May 2013). *Prosecutor v Karadžić, Decision on Prosecution's Request for Reconsideration of Trial Chamber's 11 November 2010 Decision* (10 December 2010) (*'Karadžić Decision on Reconsideration'*) [6].

[71] *Karadžić Decision on Reconsideration* [11].

[72] Ibid.

[73] *Prosecutor v Karadžić, Decision on Accused's Forty-Seventh Motion for Finding of Disclosure Violation and for Further Suspension of Proceedings* (10 May 2011) [11].

[74] *Karadžić Decision on Reconsideration* [12].

[75] Interview with Peter Robinson (2 May 2013).

overarching defence strategy – affecting his right to know the case against him. His right to time and facilities to prepare a defence was adversely affected by the volume of late disclosure, which had implications for defence team resources as they attempted to review and manage the incoming material while simultaneously maintaining other trial preparation and attendance.

The Trial Chamber decisions on these defence motions for disclosure violations can be examined to provide an understanding of how a Trial Chamber attempts to regulate the disclosure relationship between the parties in a trial with a significant number of disclosure violations. An analysis of these decisions reveals, first, how the Trial Chambers address fairness and rights in their decision-making; and, second, how they address the cumulative nature of these violations. In both respects, I argue, we can see a clear separation between fairness and rights in the procedural decision-making on disclosure: where rights are adversely affected, nonetheless fairness is determined to have remained untouched.

(3) Fairness, rights and prejudice in decision-making

The Trial Chamber rarely mentioned fairness, a fair trial, or the rights of the accused in their decisions on the accused's motions for disclosure violations. Indeed, of the thirty-five written decisions issued before the end of 2013, 'fairness' or 'rights' were only mentioned in fourteen of these decisions (and once in a Dissenting Opinion).[76] Of these, however, five decisions mentioned 'fairness' or 'rights' only in relation to summarising the submissions of the parties on this point,[77] and four decisions mentioned

---

[76] *Prosecutor v Karadžić, Decision on Accused's Second Motion for Finding Disclosure Violation and for Remedial Measures* (17 June 2010) [7]; *Decision on Accused's Eighteenth to Twenty-First Disclosure Violation Motions* (2 November 2010) [42]; *Decision on Accused's Twenty-Second, Twenty-Fourth and Twenty-Sixth Disclosure Violation Motions* (11 November 2010) [9], [14], [24], [28], [39]; *Decision on Accused's Twenty-Seventh Disclosure Violation Motion* (17 November 2010) [14]; *Decision on Accused's Twenty-Ninth Disclosure Violation Motions* (11 January 2011) [13], [15], [16]; *Decision on Accused's Thirtieth and Thirty-First Disclosure Violation Motions* (3 February 2011) [14]; *Decision on Accused's Thirty-Seventh to Forty-Second Disclosure Violation Motions with Partially Dissenting Opinion of Judge Kwon* (29 March 2011) [3] (Judge Kwon); *Decision on Accused's Forty-Third to Forty-Fifth Disclosure Violation Motion* (8 April 2011) [23], [28]; *Decision on Accused's Forty-Seventh Motion for Finding of Disclosure Violation and for Further Suspension of Proceedings* (10 May 2011) [13], [21]; *Decision on Accused's Forty-Ninth and Fiftieth Disclosure Violation Motion)* (30 June 2011) [28], [29], [32], [53]; *Decision on Accused's Fifty-First and Fifty-Second Disclosure Violation Motions* (7 July 2011) [7]; *Decision on Accused's Fifty-Third and Fifty-Fourth Disclosure Violation Motions* (22 July 2011) [8]; *Decision on Accused's Sixty-Fifth Disclosure Violation Motion* (12 January 2012) [11]; *Decision on Accused's Sixty-Sixth Disclosure Violation Motion* (8 February 2012) [6]; *Public Redacted Version of 'Decision on Accused's Sixty-Seventh and Sixty-Eight Disclosure Violation Motions' Issued on 1 March 2012* (1 March 2012) [11].

[77] *Prosecutor v Karadžić, Decision on Accused's Eighteenth to Twenty-First Disclosure Violation Motions* (2 November 2010); *Decision on Accused's Forty-Third to Forty-Fifth Disclosure Violation*

'fairness' or 'rights' only in relation to summarising the applicable law.[78] It is only in relation to five decisions that 'fairness' or 'rights' are considered in the Trial Chamber's determination of whether there was a disclosure violation. The Trial Chamber, therefore, did not routinely examine the effect of disclosure violations on either the rights of the accused or the fairness of the trials. This lack of association between disclosure and either rights or fairness is illuminating in itself. Here, the Trial Chamber refused, as a matter of routine, to consider fairness or rights – in spite of the clear implications of disclosure violations for trial fairness and the rights of the accused.

Yet rather than addressing fairness or rights concerns arising from the disclosure violations, the Trial Chamber focused on whether the accused suffered prejudice from the breach of the disclosure rule and repeatedly emphasised the necessity of prejudice in order to make a finding of disclosure violations. Prejudice became the standard used for the Trial Chamber's decision. However, there are several problems with this. First, the Trial Chamber uses the prejudice standard inappropriately. In the jurisprudence of the ICTY, in order to determine the appropriate remedy for a breach of Rule 68 (non-disclosure of exculpatory materials), the Trial Chamber must consider what prejudice the accused suffered.[79] However, the *Karadžić* Trial Chamber's use of prejudice as a standard for a disclosure breach extends beyond this jurisprudence because it uses prejudice as the standard to determine the fact of the breach as well as the appropriate remedy. In fact, in multiple cases where the Trial Chamber found that there was no prejudice suffered by the accused, the Trial Chamber 'noted' the disclosure violation but denied the motion.[80] Thus, prejudice was not only used to determine remedy – but also was used to deny the finding of a violation at all.

Motion (8 April 2011); *Decision on Accused's Fifty-First and Fifty-Second Disclosure Violation Motions* (7 July 2011); *Decision on Accused's Fifty-Third and Fifty-Fourth Disclosure Violation Motions* (22 July 2011); *Decision on Accused's Sixty-Fifth Disclosure Violation Motion* (12 January 2012).

[78] *Prosecutor v Karadžić, Decision on Accused's Second Motion for Finding Disclosure Violation and for Remedial Measures* (17 June 2010); *Decision on Accused's Twenty-Seventh Disclosure Violation Motion* (17 November 2010); *Decision on Accused's Thirtieth and Thirty-First Disclosure Violation Motions* (3 February 2011); *Decision on Accused's Sixty-Sixth Disclosure Violation Motion* (8 February 2012).

[79] *Kordić Judgement* [179].

[80] *Prosecutor v Karadžić, Decision on Accused's Second Motion for Finding Disclosure Violation and for Remedial Measures* (17 June 2010); *Decision on Accused's Third, Fourth, Fifth and Sixth Motions for Finding Disclosure Violation and for Remedial Measures* (20 July 2010); *Decision on Accused's Seventh and Eighth Motions for Finding Disclosure Violation and for Remedial Measures* (18 August 2010); *Decision on Accused's Ninth and Tenth Motions for Finding Disclosure Violation and for Remedial Measure* (26 August 2010); *Decision on Accused's Eleventh to Fifteenth Motions for Finding of Disclosure Violation and for Remedial Measures* (24 September 2010); *Decision on Accused's Seventeenth Motion for Finding Disclosure Violation and for Remedial Measure* (29 September 2010); *Decision on Accused's Eighteenth to Twenty-First Disclosure*

The *Karadžić* Trial Chamber is also flawed in its use of prejudice as a standard because it has failed to explain what this standard is, how it is violated, or how prejudice relates to the rights of the accused. Two examples from one decision are illustrative. In that decision, the Trial Chamber noted that the prosecution was in violation of the disclosure rules in relation to multiple documents and occasions, but nonetheless held that

> having considered the number, length and subject matter of these documents, and the time available to the accused to consider them before the relevant witnesses will be called to testify, the Trial Chamber is not satisfied that the accused has demonstrated that he has been prejudiced by their late disclosure.[81]

Given the lack of prejudice found by the Trial Chamber, the Chamber 'noted' the disclosure violation but denied the motion.

The first example of the reasoning in this case is compelling: a one-page document disclosed after the proscribed disclosure time limits but in advance of the witness's planned testimony.[82] It is unlikely that such a disclosure violation would prejudice the accused or impede his rights. But a second example is problematic: a record of a conversation with a former United Nations Military Observer who expressed that he 'did not believe the number of casualties associated with one of ... attacks'. The Trial Chamber acknowledged that this material, in the prosecution's possession since 1995, 'could potentially affect the credibility of Prosecution evidence relating to this incident and therefore should have been disclosed to the Accused "as soon as practicable" pursuant to Rule 68' – but again, found that it was 'not satisfied that the Accused has demonstrated that he has been prejudiced by their late disclosure'.[83] The Trial Chamber provided no further justification or explanation for its opinion that the accused suffered no prejudice by receiving this piece of exculpatory material in a time that was certainly not 'as soon as practicable'. Further, there is not an

---

Violation Motions (2 November 2010); *Decision on Accused's Twenty-Second, Twenty-Fourth and Twenty-Sixth Disclosure Violation Motions* (11 November 2010); *Decision on Accused's Twenty-Seventh Disclosure Violation Motion* (17 November 2010); *Decision on Accused's Seventeenth Bis and Twenty-Eighth Disclosure Violation Motions* (16 December 2010); *Decision on Accused's Twenty-Ninth Disclosure Violation Motion* (11 January 2011); *Decision on Accused's Thirtieth and Thirty-First Disclosure Violation Motion* (3 February 2011); *Decision on Accused's Thirty-Second, Thirty-Third, Thirty-Fifth and Thirty-Sixth Disclosure Violation Motion* (24 February 2011).

[81] *Prosecutor v Karadžić, Decision on the Accused's Eleventh to Fifteenth Motions for Finding of Disclosure Violation and for Remedial Measures* (24 September 2010).

[82] Ibid. [29].

[83] Ibid. [37].

examination of, nor an explanation of, how prejudice is linked to the rights of the accused in the case of disclosure violations.

Regarding this second document, it is difficult to understand how such late disclosure of a potentially significant piece of exculpatory material, in such a clear breach of the rules related to disclosure of exculpatory material, could not cause some prejudice to the accused – or impede his rights to know the case against them and to time and facilities to prepare a defence. Yet, the Trial Chamber did not explain why this breach, with adverse implications for rights, caused no prejudice. Where a breach of a rule clearly has negative implications on the rights of the accused, it is confounding that 'prejudice' is the rationale for decision-making, and yet prejudice is not considered with reference to either these rights or to trial fairness. While considering prejudice as a basis for decisions is understand-able, where prejudice does not adequately take into account the implica-tions of the procedural breach for the accused's rights, we see again that the rights of the accused are not given adequate consideration – even in cases where the implications for rights are potentially significant and clearly deleterious.

The approach of the Trial Chamber, to 'note' the disclosure violation but – due to a finding of a lack of prejudice – to deny the motion, changed in a March 2011 decision.[84] In this decision, a majority of the Trial Chamber found that there had been disclosure violations but that no prejudice was suffered by the accused – and yet despite this lack of prejudice, partially granted the motions. The prosecution's request to appeal this decision was denied.[85] The Chamber has adopted this position in its subsequent deci-sions and has granted or partially granted motions for disclosure violations, regardless of there being no finding of prejudice to the accused. There was no explanation for the change of approach.

Judge Kwon offered a dissent to this decision, and he would continue to hold this dissenting position in future decisions on disclosure violations.[86] While Judge Kwon agreed with the majority that disclosure violations had occurred,[87] he emphasised the lack of prejudice to the accused from these violations. In the absence of any prejudice to the accused, Judge Kwon was of the opinion that it was 'unnecessary, moot, or even frivolous to issue a declaratory finding that the Prosecution has violated Rule 68 of the *Rules*. It serves no purpose'.[88] For Judge Kwon, in light of jurisprudence that the

---

[84] *Prosecutor v Karadžić, Decision on Accused's Thirty-Seventh to Forty-Second Disclosure Violation Motions with Partially Dissenting Opinion of Judge Kwon* (29 March 2011).

[85] *Prosecutor v Karadžić, Decision on Prosecution Request for Certification to Appeal Decision on Accused's Thirty-Seventh to Forty-Second Disclosure Violation Motions* (7 April 2011).

[86] *Prosecutor v Karadžić, Decision on Accused's Thirty-Seventh to Forty-Second Disclosure Violation Motions* (29 March 2011) (Judge Kwon).

[87] Ibid. [2].

[88] Ibid.

Tribunal will consider prejudice before considering whether a remedy is appropriate, 'in the absence of prejudice the accused will not be given any remedy, including a declaration that the Prosecution has violated Rule 68'.[89] He concluded that

> it is unwarranted to seek a declaratory finding of disclosure violation every time that a potentially exculpatory document is belatedly disclosed in violation of Rule 68 without demonstrating any prejudice on the part of the accused. Otherwise, it would only encourage the accused to continue filing unnecessary motions.[90]

Judge Kwon's position that a finding of disclosure violations is 'frivolous', 'unnecessary', and 'would only encourage the accused to continue filing unnecessary motions' is problematic. These motions are not vexatious: the findings of disclosure violations demonstrate the merit of these motions. The findings also demonstrate that there was a recurring problem of prosecution non-disclosure, of which the Trial Chamber must be made aware, and which should be placed on the public trial record. These motions serve, at a minimum, to notify the Trial Chamber (and the general public) of the issues with prosecution disclosure practices, which may be affecting the rights of the accused. Given the centrality of disclosure, and the number of violations in this case, to place the blame on the accused for drawing the Trial Chambers' attention to the issue – rather than with the prosecution, for causing the problem in the first place – is concerning. It is also in contrast to the Trial Chamber's stated position, that the accused has a 'legitimate interest in documenting disclosure violations'.[91] It is not accurate that granting declaratory relief is without merit. The alternative would be for the Trial Chamber to not even acknowledge their own findings of disclosure violations. This would be tantamount to allowing – perhaps even encouraging – an environment of persistent disclosure violations without any attempt to address the situation.[92] Trial Chambers are limited in their enforcement powers relating to breaches of disclosure rules, but they are able to offer declaratory relief, and in doing so, they can acknowledge the repeated disclosure violations. Any reduction in the ability of Trial Chambers to do even this would be inappropriate and would further limit the powers of the Chambers.

Although the above decisions focus on prejudice rather than rights or fairness, there are some decisions on disclosure issues where the Trial Chamber does explicitly examine fairness and rights. One example is in

---

[89] Ibid.

[90] Ibid. [7].

[91] *Prosecutor v Karadžić, Decision on Accused's Thirty-Second, Thirty-Third, Thirty-Fifth and Thirty-Sixth Disclosure Violation Motion* (24 February 2011).

[92] A similar argument is made in Masha Fedorova, 'The Principle of Equality of Arms in International Criminal Proceedings' in Zyberi and Rohan (eds) (n 23) 204, 229.

the *Decision on the Accused's Eighteenth to Twenty-First Disclosure Violations Motions*.[93] There, the Trial Chamber was unequivocal that it had 'actively taken steps to protect the accused's fair trial rights when necessary'; in particular 'by ordering the Prosecution to take measures to ensure that the pattern of disclosure violations was brought to an end by 1 October 2010'.[94] The Trial Chamber further acknowledged that 'the cumulative effect of this stream of disclosure violations by the prosecution is likely to have placed a strain on the resources of the accused in the preparation of his defence'.[95] As a remedy, and to ensure the accused did not suffer any prejudice, the Chamber ordered that none of the witnesses affected by late disclosure could be called before 31 January 2011.[96] This would, in the Trial Chamber's view, allow the accused sufficient time to review the material and incorporate it into his defence strategy.[97] In taking steps to ameliorate the effects of the disclosure violations on the rights of the accused, the Trial Chamber made clear the fact that late disclosure has adverse implications on these rights and that the relationship between procedure and rights must be managed in order to ensure trial fairness.[98]

However, the violations persisted throughout the trial. The continued violations undermine the Trial Chamber's assertion that it had taken sufficient steps to prevent the accused's fair trial rights by ordering an end to disclosure violations. This reveals the inadequacy of such an order absent any substantial penalties for failure to comply. Moreover, it demonstrates a gap between, on the one hand, an order that is meant to ensure the rights of the accused are protected through halting disclosure violations, and on the other hand, the reality of continued violations that may challenge these rights. Even where Trial Chambers attempt to regulate and manage the disclosure relationship between the parties, they may be limited in their ability to ensure this, and there may be an environment of consistent violations.

---

[93] *Prosecutor v Karadžić, Decision on the Accused's Eighteenth to Twenty-First Disclosure Violations Motions* (2 November 2010).

[94] Ibid. [42].

[95] Ibid. [43].

[96] Ibid.

[97] Ibid.

[98] Similar comments were made in the Trial Chamber's *Decision on the Accused's Twenty-Ninth Disclosure Violation Motion* (11 January 2011). There, the Trial Chamber noted that it had 'consistently recognised the additional burden placed on the accused and his team as a consequence of the failure by the prosecution to maintain an efficient and effective system for the timely . . . disclosure of materials in accordance with the *Rules*' [13]. The Trial Chamber reiterated that it had 'taken steps to ensure that this does not impact on the accused's right to a fair trial', through ordering the prosecution 'to take concrete measures to ensure that the pattern of disclosure violations is brought to an end', as well as suspensions of the trial to allow the accused to review disclosed material [ibid]. The Trial Chamber therefore claimed it had taken action to stop the disclosure violations, mindful of the need for fairness and the protection of the rights of the accused.

(4) The effect of cumulative violations

Although the Trial Chamber found no prejudice in individual instances, the repeated disclosure violations in the *Karadžić* case raises the issue of the cumulative effect of these violations. What was the effect of the repeated violations, and the large amount of material they concern, on the rights of the accused and the fairness of the trial?

Defence lawyers have articulated the relationship between repeated disclosure violations and the rights of the accused. For Jordash, 'the scale of the problem and the effect on the fairness and progress of the trial ought now to be crystallising into a major cause for concern'.[99] He argues that the question of disclosure in the *Karadžić* case can no longer be assessed 'on a document by document basis' but rather 'must be viewed in its totality'.[100] This affects the right of the accused to time and facilities to prepare a defence, as 'there is an almost incalculable loss of overview and strategy arising from the drip-feeding of evidential material', and Jordash argues that an accused should not be 'constantly thrown off-balance by having to review and incorporate thousands of pages of new evidence throughout the trial'.[101] Similarly, Counsel Assisting Karadžić, Peter Robinson, argues that there is a difference between the prejudice arising from individual violations and the cumulative effect of the ongoing nature of the violations. As he articulated:

> I have to say that we don't have very much prejudice from individual violations because we can ask that the witness be called back if there's something new from the prosecution's witness statements, or if there's exculpatory evidence disclosed to us, but the trial is still ongoing ... But not knowing the case in advance, I think, was very prejudicial to the right of a fair trial. You shouldn't have to defend a trial in this way. That's why the disclosure rules are there in the first place.[102]

Karadžić raised this cumulative effect of disclosure violations on the fairness of the trial in August 2012.[103] Karadžić noted the fifty-eight occasions that the Trial Chamber had (at that time) found the prosecution to be in violation of its disclosure obligations and submitted that the extent of disclosure violations was 'unprecedented in international criminal justice'.[104] While the individual decisions of the Trial Chamber were that the accused had not been prejudiced by each separate prosecution disclosure violation, Karadžić submitted that the Trial Chamber should consider the cumulative

---

[99] Ibid.
[100] Jordash (n 11).
[101] Ibid.
[102] Interview with Peter Robinson (2 May 2013).
[103] 'Karadžić Motion for New Trial'.
[104] Ibid. [5]–[6].

effect of these violations.[105] He further argued that the continuing nature of the disclosure violations meant that his defence 'never recovered',[106] and that 'the idea that favourable material within the possession of the prosecution would not be available to the accused before the trial so that he can plan and prepare a coherent defence is antithetic to the very notion of a fair trial'.[107] In conclusion, he requested that the Trial Chamber, pursuant to its role as 'the guardian of the right of the accused to a fair trial' and given the fact that 'when disclosure is a failure, the trial is a failure,' must order 'a new, and fair, trial'.[108]

In its response, the prosecution reiterated the primacy of a fair trial when it argued as its first sentence that '[t]his trial is fair and should continue'.[109] The prosecution submitted that because the accused had failed to establish any prejudice, 'he also fails to demonstrate the necessity of a new trial to ensure the fairness of the proceedings'.[110] The prosecution relied on the fact that the Trial Chamber had declined to find that the accused suffered any prejudice in any individual case,[111] and submitted that the accused 'cannot claim to have been prejudiced by the aggregation of such instances'.[112] The prosecution further submitted that the Trial Chamber had taken 'active management' of the proceedings, including temporarily suspending proceedings; postponing the testimony of witnesses; imposing disclosure deadlines; and requiring explanations from the prosecution as to difficulties experienced in relation to disclosure.[113] These measures were, in the prosecution's view, sufficient to safeguard the fairness of the proceedings.[114]

The Trial Chamber dismissed the defence motion. In contrast to the lack of discussion of fairness in the previous Trial Chamber decisions on disclosure violations, in this decision, the Chamber repeatedly invoked the fairness of the trial and ultimately held that the trial was fair. In this decision, the question of prejudice re-emerged, despite the fact that it had been explicitly abandoned as a standard for the determination of individual violations. Here, the Trial Chamber stated that it had been 'cognisant of the cumulative effect of those violations and had taken measures throughout the case to ensure that the accused's preparations for trial have not been prejudiced and that the disclosure violations have not compromised his

---

105 Ibid. [13], [21].
106 Ibid. [5]–[6].
107 Ibid.
108 Ibid. [1].
109 *Prosecutor v Karadžić*, 'Prosecution Response to Motion for New Trial for Disclosure Violations' (7 August 2012) [1].
110 Ibid.
111 Ibid. [2], [5]–[7].
112 Ibid.
113 Ibid. [7]–[8].
114 Ibid.

right to a fair trial'.[115] The Chamber noted that it had suspended proceedings 'on multiple occasions' to allow the accused to review and incorporate newly disclosed material into his trial preparations 'in order to protect his fair trial rights'.[116] Further, The Trial Chamber did note that 'in assessing the potential prejudice to the accused from each disclosure violation', the Chamber 'had regard to the specific documents concerned as well as the cumulative effect of these violations on the accused's fair trial rights'.[117] However, the Chamber did not provide any explanation of how cumulative violations relate to prejudice and rights. The Chamber again focused on the lack of prejudice, and given the findings of no prejudice to the accused, the Trial Chamber ruled that 'there is no basis for the accused's renewed claim that the prosecution's disclosure violations, even in a cumulative sense, have caused him prejudice'.[118]

However, the Chamber did not properly examine any of the accused's particular rights: while it noted the right to have time and facilities to prepare his defence,[119] there was no specific consideration of any of the rights of the accused. In particular, there was no examination of how the cumulative violations might affect defence resources, the ability of the accused to know the case, or the equality of arms. Thus, while the Trial Chamber ruled that the case was fair, it did not examine the effect of these violations on the rights of the accused and the links between these rights and the fairness of the trial.

In this way, there is a divide shown between rules, rights and fairness: rules can be repeatedly violated, but in deciding that there is no unfairness as a result, a Trial Chamber may not enquire as to the effect of those violations on the accused's rights. The Trial Chamber can use fairness as a rationale for its decision without any examination of the rights of the accused. This is incorrect, because as I have argued, the concept of fairness is given content by rights, and rights are operationalised through procedural rules. The three levels of rules, rights and fairness must be understood as separate but as concomitant. In this case, the Trial Chamber should have examined whether these violations were adversely affecting the rights of the accused, rather than simply appealing to fairness in the abstract.

In the *Karadžić* trial, disclosure issues have proved challenging for both prosecution and defence parties, as well as for the Trial Chamber. The case demonstrates the challenges for large volumes of material, provided late and in a piecemeal fashion to the defence, in violation of disclosure rules. This

---

[115] *Prosecutor v Karadžić, Decision on Accused's Motion for New Trial for Disclosure Violations* (3 September 2012) [14].
[116] Ibid.
[117] Ibid. [19].
[118] Ibid. [17].
[119] Ibid. [13].

proves problematic for the accused's ability to prepare their case, to manage their limited resources, and to know the prosecution case. Here, the rights of the accused to time and facilitates to prepare their defence and to know the case, as well as the principle of equality of arms, were all challenged.

In this case, procedural rules related to disclosure were violated flagrantly and continuously – over seventy-seven individual violations, including more than 300,000 pages of potentially exculpatory material – and there was little consideration given by the Trial Chamber to how these violations affect the rights of the accused, yet the Chamber nonetheless stated that the trial was fair. The Trial Chamber did not properly examine the links between the rules, the rights of the accused, and the implications for trial fairness. We, therefore, see the separation between fairness and rights in judicial procedural decision-making. In the *Karadžić* case, even where there were extensive violations of disclosure rules, the trial was deemed to be fair.

D. ISSUE THREE: NON-DISCLOSURE AT THE ICC: THE ROLE OF VICTIMS, AND THE USE OF CONFIDENTIALITY AGREEMENTS BY PROSECUTORS

Another key example of disclosure issues is that at the ICC, the ICC's *Rules* – and their implementation by Trial Chambers – permit an environment of non-disclosure.[120] Here, I examine two particular concerns: first, the lack of clarity around the disclosure responsibilities of victims' representatives, and possible non-disclosure of material (including potentially exculpatory material) in the possession of the victims; and second, the non-disclosure of exculpatory material in the possession of the prosecution. This environment of non-disclosure has significant consequences for the accused's rights to time and facilities to prepare a defence, to know the case, and to equality of arms. Moreover, the rules permitting non-disclosure curtail the ability of Trial Chambers to manage the informational disparity between the parties. There is, therefore, a separation between the way disclosure is undertaken at the ICC and the rights of the accused. Rather than being mutually reinforcing, the ability of prosecutors and victims to withhold evidence means that disclosure rules permit an environment where the rights of the accused are restricted.

(1) Potential non-disclosure by victims

The ICC's provision for an increased role for victim participation in trial raises novel questions about the management of information and disclosure, as well as the regulation of the disclosure relationship between

---

[120] For more on how the ICC results in 'systemic failings' of disclosure, see Khan and Buisman (n 5).

the parties and participants. As outlined in Chapter One, victims' representatives are not a party to the trial,[121] and they have different aims than the prosecution.[122] However, under Rule 68(3), where the 'personal interests' of the victims are affected, the Court shall permit the views and concerns of victims to be presented and considered.[123] This will be done in a manner 'not prejudicial to or inconsistent with the rights of the accused and a fair and impartial trial'.[124] The modalities of victim participation are to be determined by the relevant Trial Chamber on a case-by-case basis.[125] Victims may apply to a Trial Chamber to present evidence,[126] and it is likely that victims would have standing on disclosure matters.[127]

Despite holding these abilities and powers, victims' representatives do not have the same duties or responsibilities of disclosure as do prosecutors.[128] Indeed, the ICC's procedural framework does not include any duty of victims' representatives to undertake disclosure.[129] The disclosure regime thus applies only to prosecutors: as the *Lubanga* Trial Chamber noted, there is 'no positive obligation . . . on the other organs of the Court, the defence or the participants to disclose exculpatory material to the defence under Article 67(2) of the *Statute*, Rule 76 or Rule 77 of the *Rules*'.[130] The *Katanga* Trial Chamber further noted that given the lack of a specific right for victims to present evidence, there could be no duty on the victims to disclose evidence – regardless of whether that evidence is incriminating or exculpatory.[131] This approach was approved by the Appeals Chamber.[132]

While this approach has been accepted by both Trial and Appeals Chambers, such non-disclosure is problematic. As Christine Van den

---

[121] See *Situation in the Democratic Republic of the Congo, Decision on the Application for Participation in Proceedings of VPRS1, VPRS 2-3-4-5-6* (ICC-01/04-101-tEN_Corr, 17 January 2006) [51].

[122] See Morrissey (n 19) 83.

[123] *Rome Statute* Art 68(3).

[124] Ibid.

[125] Christine Van den Wyngaert, 'Victims before International Criminal Courts: Some Views and Concerns of an ICC Trial Judge' (2011) 44 *CWRJIL* 475, 478.

[126] *Prosecutor v Katanga, Decision on the Modalities of Victim Participation at Trial* (ICC-01/04-01/07, 22 January 2010) [105] ('*Katanga Decision on Victims Participation*').

[127] Morrissey (n 19) 95.

[128] *Prosecutor v Katanga, Judgment on the Appeal of Mr Katanga against the Decision of the Trial Chamber II of 22 January 2010 entitled 'Decision on the Modalities of Victim Participation at Trial'* (ICC-01/04-01/07 OA 11, 16 July 2010) [85] ('*Katanga Appeals Judgment on Victims Participation*').

[129] Büngener notes that 'the procedural framework of the ICC does not foresee [a duty to disclose material], which is also the main reason why the Chambers of the Court have answered this question in the negative' (Büngener (n 8) 372–3).

[130] *Prosecutor v Lubanga, Decision on the Defence Application for Disclosure of Victims Applications* (ICC-01/04-01/06-1637, 21 January 2009) [10].

[131] *Katanga Decision on Victims Participation* [105].

[132] *Katanga Appeals Judgment on Victims Participation*.

Wyngaert, writing extra-judicially, has noted, '[t]his might strike some as odd: how can victims have a right to tender incriminating evidence without a corresponding duty to disclose exculpatory material?'[133] As a result of there being no disclosure obligations, information which comes under the possession or control of victims' representatives may never be provided to the parties – and in particular, it may never be provided to the defence. Although victims are not able to conduct investigations in order to establish the guilt of the accused – as this would effectively make them second prosecutors and would 'be prejudicial to the rights of the defence, the principle of equality of arms and the requirements of a fair trial' – they are able to undertake investigations 'in order to collect information with a view to establishing the existence, nature and extent of the harm suffered'.[134] This could then result in important or exculpatory material coming under their control.[135] Victims' representatives may even have even greater access to such material, given their role representing victims. If this occurred, the accused would not then have any access to the material, and there would be no requirement or obligation for the victims to disclose the material to the defence.[136] The problematic nature of this is further reinforced by the fact that, while the prosecution has an obligation to be independent, victims are not under any such obligation.[137]

Because the prosecutor has a responsibility to investigate exonerating and incriminating circumstances equally,[138] the prosecutor's investigation can extend to discovering any exculpatory evidence in the possession of the victims.[139] This information would then have to be disclosed to the accused under Article 67(2) of the *Statute* and Rule 77.[140] However, this approach is predicated on the assumption that the prosecutor will become aware of the existence of this information. There is no guarantee that this will occur: the information could remain entirely under the control of the victims without the prosecution having any knowledge of it. There is no legal obligation on the victims to inform the prosecution of the existence of such material. Indeed, it may be in the interests of victims to withhold such information, particularly considering the reparations system, which only operates in the case of a conviction of an accused. It is therefore entirely conceivable that victims' representatives who have control over exculpatory material would not make this known to the prosecutor.

As a result, victims' representatives may hold exculpatory material which

---

[133] Van den Wyngaert (n 125) 488.
[134] *Katanga Decision on Victims Participation* [102]–[103].
[135] Ibid.
[136] *Katanga Appeals Judgment on Victims Participation* [85].
[137] See also Büngener (n 8) 373.
[138] *Rome Statute* Art 54(1)(a).
[139] *Katanga Appeals Judgment on Victims Participation* [85].
[140] Ibid.

the defence cannot access and which the victims are under no obligation to provide to the defence (or to notify the prosecutor of, for subsequent investigation and disclosure). If the defence cannot access material that suggests their innocence or undermines the credibility of prosecution evidence, their ability to mount an effective defence is curtailed, and thus their right to time and facilities to prepare their case is adversely affected. As an example, there may be exculpatory material that undermines the credibility of a prosecution witness, and if the defence had access to this material, they could have cross-examined the witness on it and challenged the prosecution's evidence and case – but without access to this material, the prosecution's evidence goes untested. Without a legal obligation on victims' representatives to disclose any exculpatory material in their possession or under their control, a Trial Chamber cannot readily ensure the defence has this material. The Trial Chamber cannot manage this aspect of the disclosure regime, and the informational relationship between the parties – and the ability of a Trial Chamber to ensure a fair and expeditious trial with full respect for the rights of the accused – will thus be restricted.

Any responsibility of victims' representatives to disclose incriminating documents they themselves seek to rely upon in the proceedings is also not clear. In the *Katanga* case, the Trial Chamber rejected arguments made by the Ngudjolo defence team that allowing victims to lead incriminating evidence would effectively render the victims as a second prosecutor.[141] It is therefore clear that some defence teams hold concerns about the ability of victims to lead this evidence and its effect on the equality of arms. In the *Lubanga* case, it was held that victims 'may be permitted to tender and examine evidence if in the view of the Chamber it will assist in the determination of the truth',[142] but there was no guidance provided as to whether victims would need to disclose documents to the defence before seeking to tender them. On appeal, the Appeals Chamber also failed to provide a decision on this point. Instead, the Appeals Chamber remitted the issue to the Trial Chamber to decide on a case-by-case basis, noting that the Trial Chamber 'could rule on the modalities for the proper disclosure of such evidence before allowing it to be introduced'.[143]

The Appeals Chamber in the *Katanga* case determined that the Trial Chamber may request victims to submit evidence that was not previously

---

[141] *Prosecutor v Katanga* ('Application to Determine the Modalities of the Participation of Victims at the Trial Stage') (ICC-01/04-01/07, 13 January 2009) [47]; *Katanga Decision on Victims Participation* [102].

[142] *Prosecutor v Lubanga, Decision on Victim's Participation* (ICC-01/04-01/06, 18 January 2008) [108]. See also *Prosecutor v Lubanga, Judgment on the Appeals of the Prosecutor and the Defence against Trial Chamber I's Decision on Victims' Participation of 18 January 2008* (ICC-01/04-01/06, 11 July 2008) ('*Lubanga Judgment of Appeal*'); *Katanga Decision on Victims Participation* [81].

[143] *Lubanga Judgment of Appeal* [100].

disclosed to the accused,[144] and moreover, that this was not incompatible with the accused's right to a fair trial.[145] If victims are authorised to present evidence, it is for the Trial Chamber to set the modalities of disclosure 'and to decide on the measures required to safeguard the fairness of the trial, given the need to respect the rights of the accused, but also the inter-ests of the victims'.[146] The *Katanga* Trial Chamber specified a procedure for victims' representatives to tender documentary evidence: they would need to make a written application to the Trial Chamber regarding the documents they intended to present, showing its relevance and how it might 'contribute to the determination of the truth'.[147] The application, and the documents, must also 'be notified to the parties . . . for their obser-vations'.[148] However, this procedure does not require the disclosure of the actual document to the parties, simply the 'notification' of the document's existence. Non-disclosure of the actual material is therefore still permitted. The Chamber will only authorise the presentation of evidence 'provided that it is not prejudicial to the defence or to the fairness or impartiality of the trial'.[149]

The Appeals Chamber also ruled that, in the case where a Trial Chamber requests the victims to submit evidence that was not previously disclosed to the accused, the Trial Chamber must order disclosure of this material to the accused 'sufficiently in advance of its presentation at the trial, and take any other measures necessary to ensure the accused's right to a fair trial, in particular the right to "have adequate time and facilities for the prepa-ration of the defence"'.[150] This is the correct approach and acknowledges the link between disclosure processes, material held by victims and defence resources.

A further issue is the ability of victims to make submissions on disclosure issues. While victims are not intended to act as a second prosecutor, defence teams face two opponents with the capacity to make submissions on dis-closure issues. In responding to such submissions from victims as well as prosecutors, 'defence resources are stretched, time is wasted and disclosure is compromised'.[151] This also poses significant issues for the equality of arms in the proceedings, as well as the accused's time and facilities to prepare their defence.[152]

These issues – the ability of victims' representatives to hold (and not to

---

144 *Katanga Appeals Judgment on Victims Participation* [55].
145 Ibid.
146 *Katanga Decision on Victims Participation* [107].
147 Ibid. [99].
148 Ibid. [99].
149 Ibid. [101].
150 *Katanga Appeals Judgment on Victims Participation* [55].
151 Morrissey (n 19) 95.
152 See Swoboda (n 39) 462.

disclose) potentially exculpatory material, and to intervene in matters of disclosure, matched with their ability to speak to the innocence or guilt of the accused – raise particular challenges for equality of arms.[153] These issues may also be cumulative: it may be that victims hold exculpatory material which they do not disclose, seek to rely on incriminating documents which they have not previously disclosed, and can intervene in disclosure matters while speaking to the guilt of the accused. While the *Rome Statute* clearly states that the accused has a particularised right to the disclosure of exculpatory material, there is no obligation on victims' participants to disclose exculpatory material in their possession. The ICC disclosure regime, and the way it is being enforced by Trial Chambers, is therefore allowing an environment of non-disclosure of exculpatory material to the defence – which is matched with potentially expansive abilities of the victims to intervene in disclosure matters. These possibilities are clearly at odds with the accused's right at the ICC to exculpatory material and are likely to have significant consequences for the rights of the accused to time and facilities to prepare a defence and to know the case, as well as to the principle of equality of arms.

(2) Non-disclosure of exculpatory material held by the Prosecutor

The second major issue is the non-disclosure of potentially exculpatory material in the prosecution's control. Given the importance of disclosure, restrictions on disclosure must be strictly limited, and non-disclosure must be an exception rather than the rule.[154] However, the ICC's procedural regime includes several provisions that allow for non-disclosure of material.[155] Non-disclosure may occur due to the material being an 'internal document';[156] because disclosure of the information 'may prejudice further or ongoing' prosecution investigations;[157] to ensure the confidentiality of the material;[158] to 'protect the safety of witnesses and victims and members of their families';[159] or because the material in question relates to the 'steps that have been taken' by the Prosecution to either ensure the confidentiality of the information, or the protection of the witnesses, victims and members of their families.[160]

The obligation on the prosecutor to disclose potentially exculpatory

---

[153] Interview with Danya Chaikal (23 May 2013).

[154] Bernhard Kuschnik, 'International Criminal Due Process in the Making: New Tendencies in the Proceedings before the ICC' (2009) 9 *ICLR* 157, 166; Büngener (n 8) 361.

[155] Ibid. 166. See also Michelle Ahronovitz, 'Guilty Until Proven Innocent: International Prosecutorial Failure to Disclose Exculpatory Evidence' (2017) 48 *UPLR* 343.

[156] *ICC Rules* r 81(1).

[157] Ibid. r 81(2).

[158] Ibid. r 81(3).

[159] Ibid. r 81(4).

[160] Ibid. rr 81(2), 81(4) and 81(3); see also Kuschnik (n 154); Büngener (n 8) 361–7.

material in its possession to the defence as soon as practicable is set out in the *Rome Statute*,[161] is formulated as constitutive of the rights of the accused, and is understood as being necessary for a fair trial.[162] However, the ICC's procedural regime also allows such materials to be withheld. Article 54(3)(e) of the *Rome Statute* (read conjunctively with Rule 82 of the ICC *Rules*) provides for non-disclosure of material that the prosecution has obtained under confidentiality arrangements with sources, and that is to be used solely as 'springboard' information to generate new evidence.[163] This material can only be introduced into evidence after the consent of the provider has been given, and there has been 'adequate prior disclosure to the accused'.[164] These provisions – both necessitating disclosure of exculpatory material but also permitting its non-disclosure – have been described as a 'collision course' present in the *Rome Statute* itself[165] and has been the subject of significant litigation.

In the *Lubanga* case,[166] the use of information from intermediaries gathered under Article 54(3)(e) and the non-disclosure of exculpatory evidence led to a stay in proceedings. This was a measure that was closely linked to the rights of the accused and the fairness of the trial.[167] Some argue that this shows that Trial Chambers put 'weight on fairness and impartiality, rather than speediness when conducting the trials'.[168] Some may further argue that the Trial Chamber was prepared to do 'anything it takes' to ensure the defence receives the material it requires, that the rights of the accused are upheld, and that the fairness of the proceedings is not compromised.[169] Without disclosure being undertaken in a way that reinforces the rights of the accused and trial fairness, the trial cannot be permitted to continue.

However, while ultimately the defence gained the initially undisclosed material, this was 'at the cost of resources, time and extended custody

---

[161] *Rome Statute* Art 67(2).

[162] *Lubanga Decision on the Consequences of Non-Disclosure of Exculpatory Materials* [34]. In case of any doubt as to the application of this provision, the Court will decide: *Rome Statute* Art 67(2).

[163] *ICC Rules* r 82 (which regulates non-disclosure pursuant to Art 54(3)(e)).

[164] Ibid.

[165] Christian M De Vos, '*Prosecutor v Lubanga*: "Someone Who Comes between One Person and Another": *Lubanga*, Local Cooperation and the Right to a Fair Trial' (2011) 12 *MJIL* 217, 231.

[166] The details of the decisions in the *Lubanga* case have been thoroughly addressed by other authors; see, e.g. ibid.; Swoboda (n 39) 459; Rachel Katzman, 'The Non-Disclosure of Confidential Exculpatory Evidence and the *Lubanga* Proceedings: How the ICC Defence System Affects the Accused's Right to a Fair Trial' (2009) 8 *NJIHR* 77; Sara Anoushirvani, 'The Future of the International Criminal Court: The Long Road to Legitimacy Begins with the Trial of Thomas Lubanga Dyilo' (2010) 22 *PILR* 213.

[167] *Lubanga Decision on the Consequences of Non-Disclosure of Exculpatory Materials*.

[168] Kuschnik (n 154) 185; Anoushirvani (n 166) 224.

[169] Anoushvirani argues that 'By imposing a stay on the proceedings, the ICC is emphasizing the importance of a fair trial' (n 166, 222).

for Mr Lubanga'.[170] Moreover, the stay in proceedings demonstrates that the Trial Chamber was unable to regulate the informational relationship between the parties, uphold procedure, and ensure the rights of the accused and the fairness of the trial by any less radical means. A stay in proceedings is a significant step and prima facie incompatible with a Chamber's statutory responsibility to ensure an expeditious trial. Trial Chambers will therefore not lightly undertake this step. It is not satisfactory that, to ensure trial fairness, the Chamber must stop proceedings. Indeed, this shows the flaws in the present system again.[171] Non-disclosure of material due to confidentiality agreements under Article 54(3)(e) has continued to be problematic in the case of *Katanga*,[172] which shows that the internal inconsistencies in the *Statute* remain challenging.

Lubanga clarified that a prosecutor cannot use Article 54(3)(e) to gather materials in a widespread manner and not disclose them,[173] but it is nonetheless still possible, under this provision, for a prosecutor to gather exculpatory material and not disclose it to the defence. Despite the accepted importance of disclosure of exculpatory material, there is an environment of non-disclosure permitted by the *Rules*. While the *Lubanga* stay of proceedings shows how seriously Trial Chambers view the right of the accused to disclosure of exculpatory material, it also demonstrates how difficult it is for Chambers to manage the tension in the *Rome Statute* between the provisions to gather material under confidentiality agreements, and to disclose exculpatory material to the defence. There are, therefore, significant challenges for providing the rights of the accused 'full respect' within a procedural framework that explicitly allows exculpatory materials to be withheld. In turn, we again see a fracturing between the procedural rules of disclosure and the accused's rights.

These two issues of non-disclosure of information by victims and prosecution pose challenges for the rights of the accused to time and facilities to prepare their case, to know the case against them, and for the principle of equality of arms. If an accused cannot access potentially exculpatory

---

[170] Morrissey (n 19) 90.

[171] See also Colleen Rohan, who argues that this case showed the problems of an absence of professional rules of conduct for prosecutors; the newer Code of Conduct for ICC Prosecutors may change this and be 'the kind of enforcement provision which will, it is hoped, motivate prosecutors to comply in a timely fashion with disclosure obligations, particularly disclosure of exculpatory evidence': Colleen Rohan, 'Ethical Standards in the practice of international criminal law', in Zyberi and Rohan (eds) (n 23) 41, 61.

[172] *Prosecutor v Katanga, Decision on Article 54(3)(e) Documents Identified as Potentially Exculpatory or Otherwise Material to the Defence's Preparation for the Confirmation Hearing* (ICC-01/04-01/07-621, 20 June 2008) [3]–[6].

[173] In that case, the prosecutor received over fifty per cent of its documentary evidence on condition of confidentiality: Swoboda (n 39) 463. The Trial Chamber deemed this broad use of Article 54(3)(e) to be unacceptable: *Lubanga Decision on the Consequences of Non-Disclosure of Exculpatory Materials*.

material in the possession of either the victims' representatives or the prosecution, they are at an informational disadvantage; and are at a disadvantage in terms of preparing their defence. These rules contribute to an environment where the rights of an accused are limited rather than given 'full respect', and the implementation by Trial Chambers of these rules ensure that they facilitate the maintenance of such an environment. These two issues also demonstrate the difficulties for Trial Chambers in attempting to regulate the relationships between the parties. The rules permitting non-disclosure curtail the ability of Trial Chambers to manage the informational parity between the parties. It has been shown that in this case, there was a separation between the way the disclosure was undertaken – namely, that it may be withheld – and the rights of the accused, which are limited by this, rather than reinforced.

E. THE FRACTURED RELATIONSHIP BETWEEN DISCLOSURE, RIGHTS AND FAIRNESS

Disclosure gives practical expression to the rights of the accused to time and facilities to prepare their case, to know the case against them, and to equality of arms. Without disclosure, these rights cannot be fully realised. Disclosure is also integral to trial fairness. However, this close relationship in principle between disclosure, rights and fairness is not reflected in the context of contemporary international criminal trials. Indeed, as this chapter has demonstrated, there are several problems with how disclosure is provided in international criminal trials, each of which contributes to an environment of non-disclosure of information to the defence. The problems with how disclosure is provided – or, more accurately, the ways in which disclosure is withheld – in international criminal trials demonstrates the fractures in the relationships between fairness and rights in procedural decision-making in these trials. Inherent in the duty of a Trial Chamber to 'ensure a fair and expeditious trial, with full respect for the rights of the accused and due regard to the other parties', is the need to ensure the rights of the accused are given full expression; and the need to regulate the roles of, power of and relationships between, the parties to the trial. Yet this chapter has shown that the procedural rules concerning disclosure are regularly violated in international criminal trials and that Trial Chambers are ill-equipped to enforce disclosure rules. In addition, there are rules which themselves permit non-disclosure. As a result, the rights of the accused are not given full protection or expression, and indeed, are threatened by the ways in which Trial Chambers allow disclosure rules to be violated.

First, voluminous disclosure provided in violation of proscribed time limits, and in a piecemeal fashion, is problematic for the accused to be able to prepare their case, to manage their resources, and to know the prosecution case they must meet. The series of decisions in the *Karadžić* case reveals that, although Trial Chambers may be concerned about disclosure violations, they are not able to adequately regulate the relationship between the parties. Here, disclosure violations have continued in spite of multiple Trial Chamber findings concluding that violations occurred and in spite of Trial Chamber orders for disclosure to be finalised. Ultimately, the Trial Chamber decided that the trial was fair in spite of these continued violations, with no examination of the effect of the violations on the rights of the accused. Rules, rights and fairness were divorced in the Trial Chamber's reasoning. As outlined in Chapter Two, fairness may be an 'argumentative architecture'[174] that permits any decision to be rationalised; here, we see clearly a situation when fairness is used to justify continuous rules violations that appear to have deleterious effects on the rights of the accused.

Second, the disclosure regime at the ICC permits non-disclosure – in particular, of exculpatory material – by both the prosecutors and the victims. The ability of the victims' representatives and the prosecution to withhold exculpatory material is problematic, particularly in light of the specific right of the accused under the *Rome Statute* to exculpatory material. The rules which permit non-disclosure facilitate an environment where the rights of the accused are jeopardised, and the implementation of these rules by the Trial Chambers maintain this environment. Ultimately the ability of the Trial Chambers to protect and promote the rights of the accused, and to regulate the relationships between the parties and participants, is curtailed.

In these ways, Trial Chambers are unable to ensure a situation where rules, rights and fairness operate together. Fairness is invoked in ways that challenge rights. Procedure allows rights to be jeopardised. Trial Chambers use fairness to justify an environment where rights are not provided 'full respect' without accounting for the fact that their statutory responsibility is to ensure a trial is both fair *and* conducted with full respect for the accused's rights. Fairness and rights are separated through decisions on procedural rules. In the next chapter, the relationships between fairness, rights and procedural rules will be examined in relation to the use of adjudicated facts in international criminal trials.

---

[174] Martti Koskenniemi, *From Apology to Utopia: The Structure of International Legal Argument* (CUP, 2005) 589.

Chapter 5
Fairness, the rights of the accused and the use of adjudicated facts

This chapter analyses the relationships between fairness, the rights of the accused, and procedure, in the case of the use of adjudicated facts at the ICTY – that is, where Trial Chambers take judicial notice of facts which were previously adjudicated in other proceedings at the Tribunal, as permitted under Rule 94(B).[1] Facts may be entered into the trial record without actual evidence on that contested fact being brought in the proceedings at hand. The evidentiary foundation for the fact – the document or testimonial evidence that was used to establish the fact in the first trial – is not necessarily admitted to the evidential record of the second trial. Thus, adjudicated facts are admitted to the trial record, potentially without the accused being able to contest the reliability of the document or to cross-examine the witness whose testimony formed the basis of that fact.[2] The use of adjudicated facts is, therefore, 'an exception to the general rule that all facts in issue or relevant to the issue must be proved by evidence – testimony, statements, documents or other material'.[3] In this way, the use of adjudicated facts is one example of an 'inquisitorial drift' in the procedural regime governing international criminal trials, which has increasingly seen written evidence admitted instead of oral testimony.

Adjudicated facts are particularly helpful for crime-base evidence, where they will theoretically help to narrow the scope of the litigation to issues that are particularly in dispute, such as issues of linkage (connecting the accused to events alleged to have been physically perpetrated by subordinates) and authority (establishing the responsibility of the accused for events allegedly perpetrated by others). At the ICTY, where repeated cases have examined the same incidents, adjudicated facts are meant to take

---

[1] ICTY, *Rules of Procedure and Evidence*, Doc No IT/32/Rev.50 (adopted on 11 February 1994, amended 10 July 2015) ('ICTY Rules'), r 94(B).

[2] Unlike agreed facts (*ICTY Rules*, r 65 *ter*(F)), which are points on which the parties agree, adjudicated facts are points which have been accepted by the Trial Chamber but which are still possibly in contention between the parties. Useful summaries of the law on adjudicated facts (and judicial notice) can be found in Nina Jørgensen, 'Judicial Notice', Karim Khan, Caroline Buisman, Christopher Gosnell (eds) *Principles of Evidence in International Criminal Justice* (OUP, 2010) 695, and in Koen Vriend, *Avoiding a Full Criminal Trial: Fair Trial Rights, Diversions and Shortcuts in Dutch and International Criminal Proceedings* (Springer, 2016).

[3] Eugene O'Sullivan and Deidre Montgomery, 'The Erosion of the Right to Confrontation under the Cloak of Fairness at the ICTY' (2010) 8 *JICJ* 511, 520.

advantage of evidence that has already been admitted at the Tribunal. The use of adjudicated facts is also designed to ensure that successive Chambers are consistent in their rulings. Despite these theoretical benefits, as I will outline below, there are significant concerns about the use of adjudicated facts on both the fairness of the trial and the rights of the accused.

An understanding of the issues raised by adjudicated facts at the ICTY is important, in part to understand the potential for similar issues at the ICC. At present, the ICC does not have the same provisions as the ICTY for the use of adjudicated facts. However, it remains possible for such a provision to be inserted into the ICC procedural regime, and recent amendments to the *ICC Rules* demonstrate an increase in the use of written evidence in trials.[4] This may result in future calls to permit the use of adjudicated facts, as indeed occurred at the ICTY.

In this chapter, I examine procedural decisions made by Chambers to analyse how fairness has been used by the Chambers when reaching determinations on adjudicated facts. To examine the connections between fairness, rights and the use of adjudicated facts, I also analyse the outcomes of these decisions and how they reconcile with the rights of the accused. There are four major issues I examine. First, I demonstrate that concerns around fairness and the rights of the accused have, perhaps counter-intuitively, been used to expand the use of adjudicated facts. I then examine the *Karadžić* case and how the shifting evidential burden permitted by this rule may affect the equality of arms. The third issue I examine is the judicial reformulation of facts to ensure they meet admissibility requirements, as happened in the *Mladić* case. Finally, in the *Stanišić* case fairness has been used to disallow the use of adjudicated facts, but I argue that, in this case, the lateness and inconsistency of these adjudicated facts decisions adversely affected the rights of the accused (as well as the interests of the prosecution). Ultimately, I show that while there is a claimed connection between rights, fairness and procedure, a closer examination of institutional practices exposes a disconnection between fairness and rights in procedural decision-making, to the detriment of the rights of the accused. Although Chambers invoke fairness in their decisions on adjudicated facts, the implications of these decisions have often undermined the rights of the accused. Chambers have difficulty reconciling fairness, rights and procedure around the use of adjudicated facts.

---

[4] International Criminal Court, *Rules of Procedure and Evidence*, Doc No ICC-ASP/1/3 (adopted 9 September 2002) r 68 ('*ICC Rules*').

A. ADJUDICATED FACTS IN CONTEXT: GREATER USE OF WRITTEN EVIDENCE

The use of adjudicated facts in international criminal trials is a relatively recent procedural innovation. At the ICTY, adjudicated facts are admitted through Rule 94(B), which simply provides:

> At the request of a party or *proprio motu*, a Trial Chamber, after hearing the parties, may decide to take judicial notice of adjudicated facts or documentary evidence from other proceedings of the Tribunal relating to matters at issue in the current proceedings.

Rule 94 was originally adopted on 11 February 1994 to allow for the judicial notice of 'facts of common knowledge',[5] and was amended on 10 July 1998 to incorporate Rule 94(B).[6] However, the rule lay dormant for five years: until 2003, Rule 94(B) had never been used to admit a fact to which the accused objected or where the fact was seen as being capable of reasonable dispute.[7] In contrast, the rule is now routinely invoked in trial proceedings.

The increased use of Rule 94(B) must be seen against the backdrop of an 'inquisitorial drift' that has occurred at the ICTY. Initially, the tribunal adopted a more typically adversarial approach. Rule 90(A) originally stated that '[w]itnesses shall, in principle, be heard directly by the Chambers'.[8] However, the difficulties associated with an oral trial – that it can be slow, repetitive, wasteful of resources, and may result in the re-traumatisation of the witnesses – became increasingly apparent. Antonio Cassese has argued that the length of international criminal trials has primarily been the result of 'the adoption of the adversarial system' and its requirement of oral examination and cross-examination.[9] Adducing evidence in this way may take many hours with one witness.[10] Moreover, because various cases consider the same events, similar or identical evidence is often adduced in consecutive trials.[11] One witness might be brought to the tribunal repeatedly over many years in order to give essentially the same evidence.[12] The need to establish the same points time and again, in case after case, by adducing the same evidence from the same witnesses is inherently inconsistent with

---

[5] *ICTY Rules* r 94(B).

[6] ICTY, *Rules of Procedure and Evidence*, Doc No IT/32/Rev.13 (adopted on 11 February 1994, amended 10 July 1998).

[7] O'Sullivan and Montgomery (n 3) 521; Gideon Boas, *The Milošević Trial: Lessons for the Conduct of Complex International Criminal Proceedings* (CUP, 2007) 50.

[8] *ICTY Rules* r 90(A).

[9] Antonio Cassese, *International Criminal Law* (OUP, 2003) 442.

[10] Iain Bonomy, 'The Reality of Conducting a War Crimes Trial' (2007) 5 *JICJ* 348, 349. See also O-Gon Kwon, 'The Challenge of an International Criminal Trial as Seen from the Bench' (2007) 5 *JICJ* 360, 364.

[11] Kwon (n 10) 369 and 363.

[12] Ibid. 363.

judicial economy and preserving limited court resources. This process has also 'subjected witnesses to the wear and tear of repeated testimony, and, in the case of victim-witnesses, to considerable emotional toil and psychological pressures'.[13] It also potentially conflicts with the accused's rights right to an expeditious trial.[14]

There are other issues that bring into question the use of oral evidence. Adversarial cross-examination may result in the counsel or witness selecting passages from documents and thereby distorting the overall effect of the document, which can be 'counter-productive' and 'not the best way of getting at the truth'.[15] Witnesses may be unfamiliar with the nature of cross-examination and its emphasis on challenging witness testimony.[16] This can 'antagonise witnesses' and revive conflict.[17] Witnesses may also understandably view the giving of testimony as an opportunity to tell their story, and it may prove difficult to limit the witness's testimony to what is relevant to the indictment.[18]

These are all significant problems, and cause real concern for all involved in the trial process. In attempting to rectify these issues, there has been a move to graft 'inquisitorial features' onto the adversarial procedural framework.[19] This has particularly involved a greater emphasis on the admission of written testimony in place of oral testimony. Rule 90(A), with its emphasis on oral trials, was deleted from the ICTY *Rules* in 2001.[20] Several new rules were inserted, largely in response to jurisprudential shifts,[21] to permit and govern the admission of evidence in ways other than through oral testimony. A Trial Chamber may now admit the evidence of a witness through a written statement or a transcript of evidence given by the witness in proceedings before the Tribunal (rather than requiring a witness

---

[13] David Tolbert and Fergal Gaynor, 'International Tribunals and the Right to a Speedy Trial: Problems and Possible Remedies' (2009) 27 *LIC* 33, 52.

[14] See Boas (n 7) 48–9.

[15] Bonomy (n 10) 350.

[16] Kwon (n 10) 364; Bonomy (n 10) 350.

[17] Bonomy (n 10) 350.

[18] Ibid.

[19] John Jackson, 'Finding the Best Epistemic Fit for International Criminal Tribunals: Beyond the Inquisitorial–Adversarial Dichotomy' (2009) 7 *JICJ* 17, 33; see also Richard Vogler, 'Making International Criminal Procedure Work: From Theory to Practice', in Ralph Henham and Mark Findlay (eds), *Exploring the Boundaries of International Criminal Justice* (Ashgate, 2011) 105, 108.

[20] This followed two Appeals Chamber decisions of *Prosecutor v Kordić, Decision on Appeal Regarding Statement of a Deceased Witness* (IT-95-14/2-AR73.5, 21 July 2000) and *Decision on Appeal Regarding the Admission into Evidence of Seven Affidavits and One Formal Statement* (18 September 2000). See, amendments to ICTY *Rules* r 90(A), amended by ICTY, *Rules of Procedure and Evidence*, Doc No IT/32/Rev.19 (adopted on 11 February 1994, amended 19 January 2001).

[21] Yvonne McDermott, 'The Admissibility and Weight of Written Witness Testimony in International Criminal Law: A Socio-Legal Analysis' (2013) 26 *LJIL* 971.

appear in person).[22] Certain evidence can be admitted from a deceased or unavailable person.[23] As will be examined in more detail in the next chapter, evidence can be admitted in the form of a written statement or transcript, where the Trial Chamber is satisfied that the witness has failed to give material evidence as a result of 'improper interference, including threats, intimidation, injury, bribery, or coercion'.[24] While these provisions are available to be used by both the prosecution and the defence, they are more often utilised by the prosecution,[25] perhaps because defence teams have difficulty 'availing themselves of these forms of evidence'.[26]

Some commentators have voiced concerns about these rules and, in particular, their effect on the rights of the accused.[27] Proponents of these measures, however, emphasise their benefits.[28] For Judge O-Gon Kwon, the increased use of written evidence has enhanced 'the ability of chambers to manage trials of a vast scale',[29] and he notes that the use of adjudicated facts may reduce the repetition of testimony and exhibits in successive cases, thereby speeding up trials.[30] However, as we will see in the below case studies, this is not always so clear.

Just as the ICTY moved from favouring orality to emphasising document-driven trials, a similar inquisitorial drift is evident at the ICC. Article 69(2) of the *Rome Statute* provides that:

> The testimony of a witness at trial shall be given in person, except to the extent provided by the measures set forth in article 68 or in the *Rules of Procedure and Evidence*. The Court may also permit the giving of *viva voce* (oral) or recorded testimony of a witness by means of video or audio technology, as well as the introduction of documents or written transcripts, subject to this *Statute* and in accordance with the *Rules of Procedure and Evidence*. These measures shall not be prejudicial to or inconsistent with the rights of the accused.[31]

---

[22] *ICTY Rules* rules 92 *bis*, 92 *ter*, 92 *quarter* and 92 *quinquies*.

[23] *ICTY Rules* r 92 *quater*.

[24] *ICTY Rules* r 92 *quinquies*.

[25] McDermott (n 21) 976; Patrick Robinson, 'Rough Edges in the Alignment of Legal Systems in the Proceedings at the ICTY' (2005) 3 *JICJ* 1037, 1041. See also Stephen Kay, 'The Move from Oral to Written Evidence' (2004) 2 *JICJ* 495, 496.

[26] *Prosecutor v Milošević, Decision in Relation to Severance, Extension of Time and Rest* (IT-02-54-T, 12 December 2005) [20].

[27] See O'Sullivan and Montgomery (n 3); McDermott (n 21); Stéphane Bourgon, 'Procedural Problems Hindering Expeditious and Fair Justice' (2004) 2 *JICJ* 526; Patricia Wald, 'The International Criminal Tribunal for the Former Yugoslavia Comes of Age: Some Observations on Day-to-Day Dilemmas of an International Court' (2001) 5 *WUJLP* 87.

[28] See Kwon (n 10); see also Bonomy (n 10); Geoffrey Nice and Philippe Vallières-Roland, 'Procedural Innovations in War Crimes Trials' (2005) 3 *JICJ* 354; Theodor Meron, 'Procedural Evolution in the ICTY' (2004) 2 *JICJ* 520.

[29] Kwon (n 10) 365.

[30] Ibid. 369.

[31] *Rome Statute* Art 69(2).

Thus, the ICC continues to favour the oral presentation of evidence, but there is also provision for the introduction of transcripts or documents. The introduction of previously recorded audio or visual testimony of a witness, or other documented evidence of this testimony, is explicitly permitted by Rule 68.[32] The use of this material has been further reinforced by significant amendments to Rule 68, adopted by the Assembly of States Parties in 2013. These amendments were designed to promote the efficiency of the trial 'by increasing the instances in which prior recorded testimony could be introduced instead of hearing the witness in person, while paying due regard to the principles of fairness and the rights of the accused'.[33] Prior recorded testimony can now be admitted, in the absence of the witness, if either: both the prosecution and defence had the opportunity to examine the witness during the recording; or, alternatively, the prior recorded testimony goes to proof of a matter other than the acts and conduct of the accused.[34] In addition, two new provisions allow the admission of prior recorded testimony even in cases where such testimony does go to the acts or conduct of the accused. These are Rule 68(c), which permits prior recorded testimony to be admitted if the witness had 'died, must be presumed dead, or is, due to obstacles that cannot be overcome with reasonable diligence, unable to testify orally', and Rule 68(d) which permits the admission of prior recorded testimony in cases where the witness has been subjected to 'interference' (and which will be examined in more detail, in the next chapter). Moreover, the amendments to Rule 68 also provided for a limited introduction of adjudicated facts in cases where a witness has been subjected to interference, and there are proceedings concerning offences against the administration of justice.[35]

There are concerns about the amended Rule 68 and the rights of the accused, particularly to examine witnesses against them. First, the amended rule allows the admission of untested material that goes to the acts and conduct of the accused in limited circumstances.[36] The International Bar Association noted that it is 'difficult to conceive of a case in which such evidence could be used as the (unique) basis for conviction (or indeed to establish an instrumental adverse fact) without resulting in an unsafe verdict'.[37] Moreover, Amnesty International noted that this amendment

> could result in evidence being introduced which tends to inculpate the accused, without an opportunity for cross-examination, from a witness despite the fact

---

[32] *ICC Rules* r 68.

[33] Assembly of States Parties to the Rome Statute of the International Criminal Court, *Report of the Working Group on Amendments*, Doc No ICC-ASP/12/44 (24 October 2013) [8].

[34] *ICC Rules* r 68.

[35] *ICC Rules* r 68(2)(d)(iii).

[36] *ICC Rules* r 68(2)(c) and (d).

[37] International Bar Association, 'IBA ICC Programme Legal Opinion: Rule 68 Proposal' (Report, International Bar Association, 12 November 2013) 4.

their credibility has been undermined as a result of them accepting a bribe or withdrawing their cooperation due to an inducement or threat.[38]

Even if the testimony went to material other than the acts and conduct of the accused, the removal of the requirement for cross-examination of prior recorded testimony could result in material being admitted which could be used to corroborate other evidence – even where the accused does not have the opportunity to cross-examine the maker of the statement.[39] These concerns show that the changes to Rule 68 pose challenges for the rights of the accused. Nonetheless, the amended Rule 68 has been used extensively.[40]

Thus, although the ICC does not currently have the same provision for the use of adjudicated facts, the use of written evidence is evolving, and the use of adjudicated facts may expand. The fact that Rule 94(B) was inserted, amended and effectively activated during the ICTY's operations shows that a similar change is possible for the ICC. The increased desire to rely on written evidence at the ICC – evidenced in part by a limited introduction of the use of adjudicated facts in Rule 68 – could eventually lead to the insertion of general provisions for adjudicated facts. A full understanding of the use of adjudicated facts at the ICTY is therefore important for appreciating how these facts could be used in future trials.

B. FAIRNESS AND THE USE OF WRITTEN EVIDENCE AND ADJUDICATED FACTS

The ability to cross-examine witnesses 'has become an issue of fundamental importance to the question of fairness in international criminal trials'.[41] In particular, the inquisitorial drift can challenge the coherence of a procedural system that was originally conceived of as being essentially adversarial in nature. As outlined in Chapter Three, the *sui generis* system of international criminal procedure has involved a disaggregation and melding together of elements from various systems. The result is a potentially messy patchwork of approaches and legal protections. Combining an adversarial presentation of the case with the admission of written statements and adjudicated facts shows a merging of adversarial and inquisitorial elements in a

---

[38] Amnesty International, 'Recommendations to the Twelfth Session of the Assembly of States Parties (20 to 28 November 2013)' (Report, Amnesty International, November 2013) 10–11.

[39] Ibid. 10.

[40] See Simon de Smet, 'All Roads Lead to Rome – Lifting the Veil on the ICC's Procedural Pluriformity' in Pavel Šturma (ed), *The Rome Statute of the ICC at Its Twentieth Anniversary: Achievements and Perspectives* (Brill Nijhoff, 2019) 193; see also Hirad Abtahi and Shehzad Charania, 'Expediting the ICC Criminal Process: Striking the Right Balance between the ICC and States Parties' (2018) *ICLR* 18 383

[41] Boas (n 7) 46.

way that may jeopardise the ability of the defence to access information and to challenge evidence.[42] The increased use of written evidence has occurred, although 'many of the safeguards appropriate for such a procedure have not been put in place'.[43] In particular, there is difficulty reconciling the ICTY's emphasis on an impartial judiciary with the use of written evidence – which, in an inquisitorial system, will be vetted by a more active investigating judge.[44] Megan Fairlie thus argues that the ICTY engages 'in "cafeteria inquisitorialism", drawing upon aspects of the process that will enable [the Tribunal] to save time, yet passing over the inherent procedural safeguards' that were part of the procedural system originally adopted.[45]

The use of written evidence in place of oral testimony is one of the key areas where there is a tension between traditional common and civil law approaches, and this 'may lead to unfairness'.[46] However, fairness is also the solution, as we have seen in earlier chapters: where there is a conflict between the traditional approaches and no governing provision in the relevant international *Statute* or *Rules*, resolution 'must take place using the principle of fairness as the plane to smooth the edges in the alignment of the legal systems'.[47] Typifying the fairness concerns surrounding the move to greater amounts of written testimonial evidence, Eugene O'Sullivan and Deidre Montgomery are strongly critical of the effect of the changes to the relevant *Rules* on the fairness of ICTY trials. They argue that this shift

> brings the administration of justice into disrepute ... [it casts] doubt upon the legitimacy of the trial process for those with the greatest interest in a fair trial: the accused. In addition, any neutral interested bystander would be bound to view as unfair a trial conducted in this way.[48]

The concerns about the use of written evidence on the fairness of the trial relate in large part to the importance of the physical presence of the witness in the courtroom. As outlined in Chapter One, the aim of the trial should be a forensic determination of an individual's guilt or innocence for the crimes with which they are charged. The presence of a witness is 'intended to ensure confrontation between the witness and the accused and to enable the judges to observe the demeanour of the witness when giving evidence',[49] which

---

[42] Jackson (n 19) 33; Rupert Skilbeck, 'Frankenstein's Monster: Creating a New International Procedure' (2010) 8 *JICJ* 451, 452.

[43] Vogler (n 19) 109.

[44] Megan A Fairlie, 'Due Process Erosion: The Diminution of Live Testimony at the ICTY' (2003) 34 *CWILJ* 47, 82.

[45] Ibid.

[46] Robinson (n 25) 1040.

[47] Ibid. 1058.

[48] O'Sullivan and Montgomery (n 3) 538.

[49] *Prosecutor v Delalić, Decision on the Motion to Allow Witnesses K, L and M to Give Their Testimony by Means of Video-Conference* (IT-96-21, 28 May 1997) ('*Delalić Decision*') [15].

allows the judges to evaluate the credibility of the witness. Cross-examination of an honest witness may expose the weaknesses of the evidence, and it is for this reason that O'Sullivan and Montgomery call cross-examination 'the ultimate means of demonstrating truth and of testing veracity and credibility'.[50] Cross-examination, then, tests the veracity of the evidence and allows the Chamber to reach a conclusion on the ultimate question before them: whether the prosecution has established the guilt of the accused beyond a reasonable doubt.

C. THE RELATIONSHIP BETWEEN THE USE OF ADJUDICATED FACTS AND THE RIGHTS OF THE ACCUSED

There is a particular concern surrounding the use of adjudicated facts. In theory, adjudicated facts have been garnered from a process of testing in the previous proceedings, where they were established after cross-examination of witnesses and challenging of evidence. However, there are serious concerns over the admission of these facts in subsequent proceedings *against entirely different accused*. It cannot be safely concluded that these facts have been rigorously tested with regard to the second trial they are admitted into. The lack of cross-examination (in the secondary proceedings) of the maker of the statement means that the latter proceedings do not gain the forensic benefit of cross-examination. This is exacerbated because these facts are admitted without the underlying evidential basis for the fact – the document or testimonial evidence of the witness – being admitted. Moreover, the testimony and cross-examination of the witness in the first trial is not admitted into the subsequent proceedings. As a result, the fairness of the proceedings, the ability of the proceedings to reach a forensic determination of the accused's guilt, and the rights of the accused may all be adversely affected. The use of adjudicated facts may affect the rights of the accused to examine and cross-examine witnesses,[51] to time and facilities to prepare a defence[52] and the principle of equality of arms.[53]

(1) The right to examine witnesses

The accused is entitled to a 'minimum guarantee' of being able 'to examine, or have examined, the witnesses against him and to obtain the attendance and examination of witnesses on his behalf under the same conditions as

---

[50] O'Sullivan and Montgomery (n 3) 513. See also Kweku Vanderpuye, 'Traditions in Conflict: The Internationalization of Confrontation' (2010) 43 *CILJ* 513, 564.

[51] *Rome Statute* Art 67(1); *ICTY Statute* Art 21(4).

[52] *Rome Statute* Art 67(1)(b); *ICTY Statute* Art 21(4)(b).

[53] *Rome Statute* Art 67(1); *ICTY Statute* Art 21(4).

witnesses against him'.[54] This has been interpreted as an affirmation of the right of an accused to confront the witnesses against him or her.[55] The admission of evidence without cross-examination may 'interfere with an accused person's capacity to challenge an aspect of the case against them'.[56] This has been recognised as a fundamental right[57] but is not absolute.[58] Some argue that the changes to the *Rules* outlined above have eroded the accused's right to confrontation. O'Sullivan and Montgomery conclude that

> it has proven dangerously easy for the judges to seriously infringe into the right of an accused to effectively challenge evidence against him through cross-examination. There has been a lack of judicial robustness in ensuring that the right to fair trial is not compromised.[59]

In particular, even though the Appeals Chamber proclaimed that the right to confrontation is not violated by the admission of adjudicated facts,[60] the use of adjudicated facts does pose a 'profound challenge to the right of an accused to confront witnesses and the evidence against him'.[61] The accused is not able to cross-examine the witness whose testimony provided the basis of a particular adjudicated fact. Instead, the accused will attempt to rebut the fact through adducing evidence by other means – for example, cross-examination of another witness on the same point, or the introduction of a new witness to counter the previous evidence, in order to adduce evidence to 'disprove' the already admitted fact.

Nevertheless, the situation is concerning. The defendant in the previous proceedings may have no reason to challenge the evidence, which leads to the finding of fact, which later becomes an adjudicated fact in subsequent proceedings. Indeed, they may even be motivated 'to allow blame to fall to others'[62] – including the person who would later be accused in a subsequent trial. Further, the evidence on which adjudicated facts are based may be unreliable,[63] but the accused in the subsequent proceedings is not able to challenge it. Hence, without cross-examination *by the accused being tried in the immediate proceedings*, the evidence has not been properly tested as against

---

[54] *Rome Statute* Art 67(1)(e); *ICTY Statute* Art 21(4)(e).

[55] Boas (n 7) 43. See also O'Sullivan and Montgomery (n 3); Vanderpuye (n 50); Fairlie (n 44).

[56] Boas (n 7) 48.

[57] *Prosecutor v Prlić, Decision on Joint Defence Interlocutory Appeal against the Trial Chamber's Oral Decision of 8 May 2006 Relating to Cross Examination by Defence and Association of Defence Counsel's Request for Leave to File an Amicus Curiae Brief* (IT-04-74, 4 July 2006) [2].

[58] *Delalić Decision* [14].

[59] O'Sullivan and Montgomery (n 3) 535.

[60] See Boas (n 7) 50–3.

[61] Boas (n 7) 50.

[62] O'Sullivan and Montgomery (n 3) 526; Kwon (n 10) 370.

[63] Ibid.

that accused. The use of adjudicated facts certainly impedes the right of the accused to examine and cross-examine witnesses.

(2) The right to time and facilities to prepare a defence

The way in which a case is presented and evidence is adduced will affect the way a defence team organises their resources and, therefore, the accused's right to time and facilities to prepare a defence. In particular, once an adjudicated fact has been admitted to the record, there is a rebuttable presumption of the truth of that fact. The evidential burden then shifts to the non-moving party (frequently the accused) to bring evidence to attempt to rebut the adjudicated fact.[64] The moving party (usually the prosecution) no longer needs to bring evidence on the fact or witnesses to testify to such events, conditions, or facts. Thus, the use of adjudicated facts will simultaneously lower the burden on the prosecution and increase the burden on the accused. The accused will need to expend resources on reviewing, considering and perhaps rebutting these facts. This will include both the defence team's time and resources in the preparation of their case and also the expenditure of allocated court hours of examination and cross-examination of witnesses. Further, while the use of adjudicated facts may in principle be a way to expedite trials and thereby protect resources, it is not clear that this occurs: all that is demonstrable is that admitting adjudicated facts shifts the burden of expending resources and time to the non-moving party – generally the accused – with potentially significant implications for the time and facilities to prepare a defence.

(3) The principle of equality of arms

The only way to address the increased burden on the accused and protect their time and facilities to prepare a defence, is to allocate the accused greater resources with which to rebut the adjudicated facts. However, Trial Chambers have been reluctant to do this – in part, raising the principle of equality of arms to justify not providing the accused any extra 'benefit'. Equality of arms theoretically ensures that neither party is placed at a disadvantage vis-à-vis the opposing party regarding the presentation of their case. Masha Fedorova points out that Chambers have 'generally followed a rather arithmetical approach for delineating the time for case

---

[64] *Prosecutor v Krajišnik, Decision on Prosecution Motions of Judicial Notices of Adjudicated Facts and for Admission of Written Statements of Witnesses pursuant to Rule 92 bis* (IT-00-39-PT, 28 February 2003) ('Krajišnik Decision'); *Prosecutor v Milošević, Decision on the Prosecution's Interlocutory Appeal against the Trial Chamber's 10 April 2003 Decision on Prosecution Motion for Judicial Notice of Adjudicated Facts* (IT-02-54, 28 October 2003) ('Milošević Decision').

presentation'.[65] In other words, Trial Chambers often view formal equality as an allocation of the same amount of time to both the prosecution and defence to present their case. There might be no examination of whether an inequality of hours is justified 'on the basis of the difference in the respective roles of the parties'.[66]

The admission of adjudicated facts and testimonial evidence in written form is designed to reduce the number of hours in case presentation and, as the prosecution tends to make more use of these provisions than does the defence,[67] this may affect such a strict arithmetical approach to equality of arms in case presentation. In addition, the reversal of the onus to the accused may mean that the defence must spend a significant amount of their limited hours on attempting to adduce information to rebut these facts. If equality is formally construed by Trial Chambers, the admission of greater amounts of prosecution testimonial evidence in written form and the use of adjudicated facts may have implications for the material equality between the parties.

To summarise, there are particular concerns with how the use of adjudicated facts aligns with trial fairness, with the rights of the accused (particularly to examine witnesses and to time and facilities to prepare a defence), and with the principle of equality of arms. Indeed, defence lawyers have articulated the admission of adjudicated facts as one of 'the most challenging aspects of standing up for the rights of the accused'.[68] In the next part of this chapter, I examine four issues related to the use of adjudicated facts and demonstrate that Trial Chambers face significant challenges in ensuring fairness, rights and procedure are aligned in the use of adjudicated facts at the ICTY by examining how Trial Chambers have invoked the concept of fairness in judicial decision-making regarding adjudicated facts.

D. FOUR ISSUES RELATED TO THE USE OF ADJUDICATED FACTS

Through a rhetorical appeal to fairness and rights, ICTY judges have expanded the use of adjudicated facts. However, this has had a negative effect on the rights of the accused – in particular, the right to time and facilities to prepare a defence, as well as the principle of equality of arms. I examine the effect of this separation between fairness and rights

---

[65] Masha Fedorova, *The Principle of Equality of Arms in International Criminal Proceedings* (Intersentia, 2012) 433, more generally at 386–400.

[66] Ibid.

[67] McDermott (n 21) 976; Robinson (n 25) 1041; Kay (n 25) 496.

[68] Frédéric Mégret, 'The Legacy of the ICTY as Seen Through Some of Its Actors and Observers' (2011) 3 *GJIL* 1011, 1023.

in procedural decision-making, in the *Karadžić, Mladić,* and *Stanišić and Župljanin* trials.

(1) Issue one: the use of fairness and rights to extend the application of adjudicated facts

Despite the apparent benefits of using adjudicated facts, Trial Chambers initially had concerns about the ways adjudicated facts may affect the rights of the accused and possessed 'a great deal of reluctance' to use such facts.[69] However, judicial interpretation of Rule 94(B) has addressed these 'rights concerns' and has allowed Trial Chambers to admit adjudicated facts more frequently and liberally. As mentioned, Rule 94(B) simply provides that a Trial Chamber may take notice of adjudicated facts. Judicial construction has expanded the application of Rule 94(B) beyond this literal reading in two main ways: the admissibility requirements and the shifting evidential onus of proof. With regard to the admissibility requirements, in order to admit an adjudicated fact under Rule 94(B), the Chamber must examine, first, whether each fact satisfies the various admissibility requirements in the Tribunal's jurisprudence, including that the fact cannot be essentially legal in character or go to the acts, conduct, or mental state of the accused.[70] Secondly, the Chamber must consider whether a fact, despite having satisfied such requirements, should be excluded on the basis that its judicial notice would not be in the interests of justice.[71]

   As discussed above, the admission of an adjudicated fact results in the evidential onus shifting to the non-moving party to disprove the fact. This implication does not 'appear to have been intended by the terms of the rule'[72] but was established by a decision of the ICTY Appeals Chamber.[73] There, the judges overturned a decision of the *Milošević* Trial Chamber and effectively approved an earlier decision of the *Krajišnik* Trial Chamber, adopting a position that taking judicial notice of an adjudicated fact establishes a 'well-founded presumption for the accuracy of this fact, which

---

[69] Kwon (n 10) 370.

[70] These are that the fact (a) must be relevant to the current proceedings; (b) must be distinct, concrete and identifiable; (c) must not differ in any substantial way from the formulation of the original judgment; (d) must not be unclear or misleading in the context in which it is placed in the moving party's motion; (e) must be identified with adequate precision by the moving party; (f) must not contain characterisations or findings of an essentially legal nature; (g) must not be based on an agreement between the parties to the original proceedings; (h) must not relate to the acts, conduct, or mental state of the accused; and (i) must clearly not be subject to pending appeal or review. See *Prosecutor v Popović, Decision on Prosecution Motion for Judicial Notice of Adjudicated Facts with Annex* (IT-05-88-T, 26 September 2006) ('*Popović Decision*').

[71] Ibid. [4].

[72] Bonomy (n 10) 359.

[73] *Milošević Decision.*

therefore does not need to be proven again at trial – *unless* the other party brings out new evidence and successfully challenges and disproves the fact at trial'.[74] This was reaffirmed by the Appeals Chamber in *Karemera*,[75] which stated that the only effect of taking judicial notice of adjudicated facts was 'to relieve the prosecution of its initial burden to produce evidence on the point: the defence may then put the point into question by introducing reliable and credible evidence to the contrary'.[76] This does not reverse the presumption of innocence or reverse the onus of ultimate proof: the standard remains that the prosecution must establish their case beyond a reasonable doubt.[77]

Building particular admissibility requirements into the rule, and allowing the accused to rebut any admitted facts, have assuaged the 'rights concerns' that judges previously held regarding the use of adjudicated facts. The requirement that the Chamber address 'the interest of justice' ensures that a Chamber can enquire as to the effect of the proposed facts on the rights of the accused or on the fairness of the trial. This is an example of using fairness and rights as interpretive tools to construe the relevant rule. Although a concern about rights originally precluded Trial Chambers from invoking Rule 94(B), reading rights protections into the rule has allowed it to be used more readily. As a result, a more widespread use of these facts has occurred.[78]

Yet despite the prima facie protection of the rights of the accused in both limbs of the admissibility requirements, and the fact that this addressed the original 'rights concerns' of judges, this expanded use of adjudicated facts at the ICTY may have implications that are inconsistent with fairness and rights. Rhetorical protection of fairness and rights has allowed a procedural rule to operate in ways that may actually challenge the rights of the accused. In the next section of this chapter, I examine three particular aspects of the use of adjudicated facts that challenge the rights of the accused. First, an examination of the *Karadžić* case demonstrates that the widespread admission of adjudicated facts poses a challenge to the principle of equality of arms, and the rights to examine witnesses and to time and facilities to prepare a defence. Second, in the *Mladić* case, we see judges inappropriately intervening to 'fix' prosecution proposed facts to

---

[74] *Krajišnik Decision* [16] (emphasis in original).

[75] *Prosecutor v Karemera, Decision on Prosecutor's Interlocutory Appeal of Decision on Judicial Notice* (ICTR-98-44, 16 June 2006) ('*Karemera Decision*').

[76] *Karemera Decision* [42]. See also *Prosecutor v Tolimir, Decision on Prosecution Motion for Judicial Notice of Adjudicated Facts Pursuant to Rule 94(B)* (IT-05-88/2-PT, 17 December 2009) [9] ('*Tolimir Decision*'); *Krajišnik Decision* [16]–[17].

[77] *Karemera Decision* [42].

[78] Kwon (n 10) 371. Two other reasons exist for the increase in the use of adjudicated facts: a greater number of cases where there has been final judgement; and the more pressing need to complete trials, given the ICTY completion strategy.

meet admissibility requirements, even where the rights of the accused are adversely affected. Third, even the denial of adjudicated facts can challenge the right to time and facilities to prepare a defence when such a decision is given late in the trial proceedings – as occurred in the *Stanišić and Župljanin* trial. While the decisions in these cases were made with reference to fairness, they reveal a disconnection between the invocation of fairness in decision-making and the adverse effects of those decisions on the accused's rights.

(2) Issue two: time and facilities to prepare a defence, and the shifting of the evidential burden

Because the ICTY's particular interpretation of the use of adjudicated facts has placed the onus of rebuttal on the non-moving party, the consequence has been a shift in the evidential onus to the accused (where facts have been submitted by the prosecution). Trial Chambers can reject a fact under the second limb of admissibility, exercising their discretion to withhold judicial notice 'in the interests of justice' if the admission of the facts would place too high a burden on the party who holds the onus of rebutting the fact.[79] Thus, Trial Chambers have explicitly attempted to avoid a situation where the use of adjudicated facts creates a heavy burden on the accused. Kwon writes that, subsequent to the Appeals Chamber decision in *Milošević*, the main concern for Trial Chambers has been how to 'strike the right balance between the need for an expeditious trial and the need to guarantee the rights of the accused'.[80] The *Milošević* Trial Chamber articulated that, in exercising its discretion to admit an adjudicated fact, Chambers will be mindful of the potential detrimental effect on judicial economy of widespread admission of facts.[81] Due to the rebuttable presumption that is raised by the admission of facts, 'the admission of adjudicated facts on a wholesale basis would raise the probability of placing a heavy burden upon the accused in the preparation and conduct of his case', and moreover, 'attempts by the accused to rebut these facts may absorb considerable time and resources during the course of the proceedings, thereby not promoting judicial economy or expeditiousness'.[82] Furthermore, Trial Chambers have ruled that the prosecution is not precluded from 'bringing witnesses to give evidence that overlaps with the content of adjudicated facts'[83] – in other words, the adjudicated facts can be admitted *and* the prosecution can still

---

[79] *Tolimir Decision* [32].

[80] Kwon (n 10) 371.

[81] *Prosecutor v Milošević, Final Decision on Prosecution Motion for Judicial Notice of Adjudicated Facts* (IT-02-54-T, 16 December 2003) [11].

[82] Ibid.

[83] *Prosecutor v Karadžić, Decision on Accused's Motion to Preclude Evidence or to Withdraw Adjudicated Facts* (IT-95-5/18-T, 31 March 2010) [18].

bring the witness to testify to the facts. Thus, the shifting of the evidential burden to the accused may not actually promote judicial economy. It is also crucial that judicial notice is not taken of irrelevant facts with the danger of overburdening the trial record[84], particularly in light of the reversal of the evidential onus. The rule ought not to be applied 'to circumvent the ordinary requirement of relevance and thereby clutter the record with matters that would not otherwise be admitted'.[85]

These issues have been raised in the *Karadžić* case. In an attempt to expedite and streamline the proceedings in the large, complicated case, the prosecution applied for judicial notice to be taken of prior adjudicated facts. Five motions were filed between 27 October 2008 and 14 December 2009, proposing that the Trial Chamber take judicial notice of 2,607 adjudicated facts.[86] In each motion, the prosecution submitted that the admission of the adjudicated facts would achieve judicial economy while also ensuring the accused's right to a fair, public and expeditious trial.[87] The Trial Chamber granted judicial notice of the majority of the proposed facts, and approximately 2,300 prior adjudicated facts were entered into the trial record before the case began.[88]

Some of these facts were, individually, reasonably unproblematic for the rights of the accused, such as the admission of an adjudicated fact which stated that 'The town of Srebrenica is nestled in a valley in Eastern Bosnia'.[89] However, other facts are more contentious. In the same decision, the Trial Chamber agreed to take judicial notice of a proposed adjudicated fact, which read that:

> In November 1992, General Ratko Mladić issued Operational Directive 4, which outlined further operations of the Bosnian Serb Army ('VRS'). Included in the Directive are orders to the Drina Corps to defend 'Zvornik and the corridor, while the rest of its forces in the wider Podrinje region shall exhaust the enemy, inflict the heaviest possible losses on him and force him to leave the Birač, Žepa

---

84 *Tolimir Decision* [11].
85 Ibid.
86 *Prosecutor v Karadžić*, 'First Prosecution Motion for Judicial Notice of Adjudicated Facts' (IT-95-5/18-PT, 27 October 2008); 'Second Prosecution Motion for Judicial Notice of Adjudicated Facts and Corrigendum to First Prosecution Motion of Judicial Notice of Adjudicated Facts' (16 March 2009); 'Third Prosecution Motion for Judicial Notice of Adjudicated Facts' (6 April 2009); 'Fourth Prosecution Motion for Judicial Notice of Adjudicated Facts' (25 August 2009); 'Fifth Prosecution Motion for Judicial Notice of Adjudicated Facts' (14 December 2009).
87 Ibid.
88 *Assessment and Report of Judge Patrick Robinson*, UN Doc S/2010/588 (19 November 2010) [33].
89 *Prosecutor v Karadžić, Decision on Third Prosecution Motion for Judicial Notice of Adjudicated Facts* (9 July 2009).

and Goražde areas together with the Muslim population. First offer the able-bodied and armed men to surrender, and if they refuse, destroy them'.[90]

This fact asserts actions undertaken by Mladić – originally co-indicted with Karadžić, and listed as one of the members of the joint criminal enterprise (JCE) pursuant to which Karadžić's alleged liability is charged. A finding of fact about the actions of a member of the JCE, before the trial commences and without the underlying evidentiary source for that finding being admitted to the trial record, may have significant implications for the construction of the culpability of all members of that alleged JCE – including the accused. Indeed, admitting a fact regarding the acts and conduct of others, whose acts and conduct are integral to the culpability of the present accused, goes to the heart of the prosecution's case. This is problematic for the rights of this accused, in particular to examine witnesses against them, as the witness testimony underlying this adjudicated fact will not necessarily be tendered. Shifting the evidentiary burden to the accused to disprove this fact heightens these concerns.

In addition, this adjudicated fact also excerpts sections from a document that appear to be particularly inflammatory, which uses language of destruction and the infliction of harm. Yet if the actual document were tendered rather than simply admitting this adjudicated fact to the trial record, the Trial Chamber would be able to view these excerpts in context, including the overarching context of military action, which may explain the language used. Indeed, in its next sentence, the document continues: 'After that, unblock and repair the Konjevic Polje–Zvornik road, make it fit for traffic, and stand by for intensive combat against infiltrated sabotage, terrorist, surprise and ambush attacks and paramilitary groups.'[91] Reading this suggests that the language of destruction could be viewed as a possibly legitimate military objective, to 'destroy' the enemy. Given that one of the criticisms of oral trials is that counsel may distort the true nature of documents by selecting passages from them during witness examination,[92] it is difficult to see how the use of the adjudicated facts in this way improves on that aspect of oral trials. Indeed, the decontextualisation of parts of documents, rather than tendering the documents as a whole for the consideration of the Trial Chamber, may allow the prosecution to frame or present documents in a particular way to the Trial Chamber, which may not be easy for the accused to challenge.

Furthermore, the prosecution will submit these adjudicated facts well in advance of the trial commencing, and the Trial Chamber will usually

---

[90] Ibid.

[91] Cited in Richard Butler, 'Srebrenica Military Narrative (Revised) Operation "Krivaja 95"' (1 November 2002) <http://s3.documentcloud.org/documents/274491/srebrenica-military-narrative-operation-krivaja-95.pdf> (last accessed 9 December 2021) [1.22].

[92] Bonomy (n 10) 350.

review the facts and decide on them before the trial starts. In this way, the prosecution can construct a narrative of events – which fits the prosecution case theory and strategy – through the submission of particular adjudicated facts. The example above is demonstrative of the power of this. An account that includes aspects of destruction and the infliction of harm, presented without the broader context or potential alternative explanation, is provided to the Trial Chamber as an initial step before the trial even starts, without the accused being able to present their own version, or being able to rebut the story the prosecution is able to weave for the Chamber. This is further complicated when the accused may be constrained during the trial in his ability to cross-examine or lead evidence to rebut the adjudicated facts. A Trial Chamber may place limits on an accused's time in leading evidence in order to comply with formal equality of arms, but as Judge Patrick Robinson has noted, 'the Defence will have its narrative to tell and must be afforded the fullest opportunity to do so'.[93] Any restriction on the accused's time to tell their narrative – when the prosecution has been able to take advantage of adjudicated facts to tell their narrative before the trial even commences – may result in a one-sided story reaching the Trial Chamber before its determination of the accused's culpability. This cannot be squared with the trial's aim of a forensic determination of the accused's guilt or with the principle of equality of arms.

It is not merely individual facts that may or may not be problematic. How does the widespread admission of adjudicated facts reconcile with the rights of the accused and the principle of equality of arms? Counsel Assisting Karadžić, Peter Robinson, outlined the concerns of the defence team regarding the magnitude of the adjudicated facts admitted into evidence when he said:

> we [had] a huge mountain to climb when the trial started; 2300 adjudicated facts already in evidence including that the Serbs who were under the command of Karadžić were responsible for shellings – specific shellings which he was charged with [. . .] we were starting off the trial way, way behind. Instead of having a presumption of innocence we had this mountain of adjudicated facts to climb just to be able to get to the same place as the prosecution . . . it's had a really monumental effect on Karadžić's case.[94]

On 1 April 2010, Karadžić filed a motion articulating some of these concerns. This motion was filed before all the prosecution motions for adjudicated facts had been ruled on, and at that stage, judicial notice had been

---

[93] *Prosecutor v Karadžić, Decision on Appeal from Decision on Duration of Defence Case* (IT-95-05/18-AR73.10, 29 January 2013) ('*Karadžić Appeal Decision on Case Duration*') (Patrick Robinson) [9].

[94] Interview with Peter Robinson (2 May 2013).

taken of 1,500 facts.[95] Karadžić submitted that the cumulative effect of the large number of adjudicated facts, in addition to the admission of 144 prior statements from witnesses, would require the accused to 'mount a massive case to rebut the adjudicated facts and assertions of facts in prior statements and testimony'.[96] In his submission, this violates the right of the accused to a presumption of innocence and reverses the burden of proof resting on the prosecution.[97] Karadžić submitted that the 'massive use' of the devices of judicial notice and admission of prior statements and testimony 'has tipped the scales to where a fair trial is no longer possible'.[98] The Trial Chamber denied the motion.[99] The Chamber noted that, in admitting the adjudicated facts, it had 'made every effort to ensure that the fair trial rights of the accused are protected',[100] and emphasised that the accused would have the opportunity to attempt to rebut the admitted adjudicated facts.[101]

Yet despite this ruling, the admission of 2,379 adjudicated facts (an additional 800 facts after this Trial Chamber decision)[102] and the reversal of the evidential burden regarding this large number of facts is a significant onus to place on an accused. While the ultimate legal burden rests with the prosecution, the aim of adjudicated facts is clearly, in part, to lighten their evidential burden – and make it easier for them to discharge their overall legal burden of proof. In one sense, this may be unproblematic: the prosecution has already established these facts, albeit in other cases against different accused. Yet this lightening of the load for the prosecution is matched by a corresponding heavier burden placed upon the accused, who must now invest resources into reviewing and investigating the facts, deciding on a strategy regarding each fact, and attempting to adduce evidence to rebut certain facts. In the *Karadžić* case, the Trial Chamber was correct that the accused will be able to bring evidence to rebut adjudicated facts – but the scale of such a task will result in a large evidential burden on the accused and a significant effect on the right to time and facilities to prepare a defence and the principle of equality of arms. Peter Robinson articulated these concerns when he argued that the admission of adjudicated facts 'benefitted the prosecution without a corresponding benefit to us because we didn't get to contest it and didn't get enough time really, or resources, to investigate [the facts] and to properly rebut [them]'.[103]

---

95 Ibid. [2].

96 Ibid. [17].

97 Ibid.

98 Ibid. [19].

99 *Prosecutor v Karadžić, Decision on Motion for Stay of Proceedings* (8 April 2010).

100 Ibid. [5].

101 Ibid. [6].

102 This was the total number eventually admitted: see *Prosecutor v Karadžić, Judgement* (MICT-13-55-A, 20 March 2019) ('*Karadžić Appeal Judgement*') [109].

103 Interview with Peter Robinson (2 May 2013).

The use of adjudicated facts interacts with evidence admitted in written form through other rules, and concern about the burden of this on the accused is heightened where the accused is self-represented, as in the *Karadžić* case. In this case, the vast majority of prosecution testimonial evidence was adduced in written form under rules 92 *bis* or *ter*. When an accused is self-represented, he will have the onus of cross-examining the witnesses for lengthy periods of time, while the prosecutor will often spend a limited amount of time with each witness to clarify their statement. The prosecution team of several people will be able to rotate prosecutors for the witnesses. Each separate prosecutor, then, may only spend an hour or two in court every month and might only have responsibility for a limited number of witnesses, while the self-represented accused will have the responsibility for the bulk of the court time. When the accused also needs to spend significant amounts of time cross-examining in order to adduce evidence to be led in rebuttal of the adjudicated facts, this further adds to their burden. This is particularly challenging given the fact that Trial Chambers often insist on parity of actual time spent by both prosecution and defence in the presentation of their cases as a demonstration of 'equality of arms'. While Karadžić chose to be self-represented and therefore accepted the difficulties of this, it is nonetheless important to understand that the rules which permit the admission of evidence in written form interact and together may result in a heavy onus being placed on the accused to conduct the bulk of the trial proceedings. As O'Sullivan and Montgomery have pointed out,

> a combination of denying the accused his right to confront the evidence and shifting the burden of rebutting the evidence on which his criminal liability can be established may make it practically impossible for him to provide full answer and defence to the allegations and charges against him.[104]

The *Karadžić* Trial Chamber explicitly rejected the argument that 'the cumulative effect of taking judicial notice of a large number of adjudicated facts and the admission of a large number of written evidence [sic] violates the presumption of innocence and denies him the right to a fair trial'.[105] Elsewhere, the Trial Chamber held that

> Whether the admission of evidence of persons who are unavailable for cross-examination, combined with a large number of judicially accepted facts, *would* affect the fairness of the trial or the outcome of the case can only be determined in

---

[104] O'Sullivan and Montgomery (n 3) 524–5.
[105] *Prosecutor v Karadžić, Decision on Second Prosecution Motion for Judicial Notice of Adjudicated Facts* (9 October 2009) ('*Karadžić Decision on Second Prosecution Motion*') [53].

light of the weight given to that evidence in the overall context of the assessment of all the evidence in the case, including *viva voce* evidence.[106]

In other words, in order to know whether adjudicated facts affected the fairness of the trial, one has to wait until after the case has closed and the judgment has been issued. This may be accurate in terms of understanding the effect of adjudicated facts on the overall fairness of the trial, but this says nothing about the effect of adjudicated facts on the rights of the accused. The approach of the Trial Chamber, to simply ignore the question of the effect of the cumulative burden of written evidence and adjudicated facts on the right to time and facilities to prepare a defence and the principle of equality of arms, is flawed.

Frustratingly, the accused has not made such submissions to the Trial Chamber. His submissions that the burden of proof was reversed[107] did not have any basis in law, given the jurisprudence has been clear that the ultimate burden of proof remains with the prosecution. Even in his later appeal of conviction, Karadžić framed his argument in terms of the 'presumption of innocence and the burden of proof'.[108] It is unfortunate that the accused did not make more nuanced submissions, requiring the Trial Chamber to examine the issues of time and facilities to prepare a defence, and equality of arms, in this respect. The Trial Chamber (and later, the Appeals Chamber) was correct to reject Karadžić's argument that 'the cumulative effect of taking judicial notice of a large number of adjudicated facts . . . violates the presumption of innocence'.[109] But the question of whether the cumulative effect of taking judicial notice of 2,300 adjudicated facts – shifting the burden to the accused in relation to these facts – together with a large amount of written evidence violates the accused's time and facilities to prepare a defence, as well as the principle of equality of arms, is important. This is particularly true, given the Trial Chamber's assertion that the accused's 'right to a fair trial' was not violated by the large admission of adjudicated facts. This conclusion cannot be sustained without an examination of how the admission of these facts will affect the rights of the accused. In reaching that conclusion, without an examination of the effect of procedural decisions on the rights of the accused, the Chamber again demonstrated a distance between an adjudication on the trial's fairness and a lack of inquiry into the rights of the accused.

Furthermore, despite the Trial Chamber's repeated assertions that taking notice of this number of adjudicated facts would ensure the expeditiousness

---

[106] *Prosecutor v Karadžić, Decision on Accused's Application for Certification to Appeal Decision on Rule 92 Quater (Witness KDZ198)* (31 August 2009) [12] (emphasis in original).

[107] *Prosecutor v Karadžić* 'Motion For Stay of Proceedings: Violation of Burden of Proof and Presumption of Innocence' (1 April 2010) [17].

[108] *Prosecutor v Karadžić*, 'Radovan Karadžić's Appeal Brief' (MICT-13-55-A, 23 December 2016) ('Karadžić Appeal Brief') [134].

[109] *Karadžić Decision on Second Prosecution Motion* [54].

of the *Karadžić* trial, there is no way of ascertaining this. Karadžić argued that 'taking judicial notice of all the facts proposed ... would place an unreasonable and unfair burden on him and that, as the process of rebutting the evidence takes excessive time and resources, it would frustrate, rather than promote, judicial economy'.[110] Boas has argued that the prosecution should be required to file lists of witnesses or time saved to justify its requests for adjudicated facts, to assist a Trial Chamber to determine the genuine effect on the expeditiousness of the trial – which they could then balance against the effect on the fairness of the trial.[111] However, such an identification has not occurred here. In addition, if the accused adduces evidence to rebut the 2,379 adjudicated facts, it is difficult to see how using Rule 94(B) will expedite the trial – it will simply shift the responsibility of adducing evidence from the prosecution to the accused. As Boas argues, the admission of adjudicated facts 'reduces marginally – if at all – the number of witnesses or scope of evidence led in [prosecution] cases. On the other hand, the defence is in a position where it must rebut any evidence that it considers harmful to an accused'.[112] In the *Karadžić* trial, the Trial Chamber was 'not persuaded' that the accused would need more time and facilities to rebut the adjudicated facts than they would require to counter the prosecution's evidence if the Chamber did not take notice of the facts.[113]

Subsequent to this, and after the Trial Chamber's acceptance of two more motions for adjudicated facts, Karadžić filed for an additional 300 hours to be added to his defence case, in order to rebut the adjudicated facts that have been judicially noticed.[114] This was denied by the Trial Chamber.[115] The Trial Chamber noted Appeals Chamber jurisprudence which states that 'the time allotted to the Defence should be reasonably proportional to the Prosecution's allocation and sufficient to permit a fair opportunity for the accused to present his case, in a manner which is consistent with the accused's rights'.[116]

The Appeals Chamber – by majority, with Judge Patrick Robinson dissenting – upheld the Trial Chamber's decision. The Appeals Chamber noted (as the Trial Chamber had also noted) that Karadžić had already

---

[110] *Prosecutor v Karadžić*, 'Response to Third Prosecution Motion for Judicial Notice of Adjudicated Facts and Motion for List of Witnesses to be Eliminated' (29 May 2009) [4].

[111] Boas (n 7) 52–3.

[112] Ibid. 52.

[113] *Prosecutor v Karadžić*, *Decision on Third Prosecution Motion for Judicial Notice of Adjudicated Facts* (9 July 2009) [61].

[114] *Prosecutor v Karadžić*, 'Defence Submission Pursuant to Rule 65 *ter* and Related Motions' (27 August 2012).

[115] *Prosecutor v Karadžić*, *Decision on Time Allocated to the Accused for the Presentation of His Case* (19 September 2012) ('*Karadžić Trial Chamber Decision on Case Duration*'); and *Karadžić Appeal Decision on Case Duration*.

[116] *Karadžić Appeal Decision on Case Duration* [8].

spent 'more than twice as much time as the Prosecution during the presentation of the Prosecution case'.[117] Both Chambers failed to note that the prosecution was utilising methods of the admission of evidence which limit the time required for examination-in-chief, and so the fact that Karadžić had spent significantly more time than the prosecution might be readily explicable. Rather, the Appeals Chamber noted that Karadžić was able to elicit information relevant to his defence in cross-examination, and that this was relevant to the time allocated to the defence for the presentation of his case.[118] The Appeals Chamber did not mention the fairness of the trial or the rights of the accused.

Judge Robinson provided a strong dissent – a dissent that focused on the rights of the accused, in sharp contrast to the majority judgments. In doing so, Robinson pointed out many of the difficulties with the use of adjudicated facts for the rights of the accused, and argued that, in focusing on the fact that the prosecution retains the burden of proof, 'the Trial Chamber has undervalued the need for the Defence to rebut the adjudicated facts'.[119] Robinson correctly calls this 'a deficiency in the Trial Chamber's analysis, and it is one that is significant'.[120]

Robinson then noted that the Trial Chamber had used Karadžić's 'customary and statutory right to cross-examine as a basis for reducing the time allocated to the Defence case'.[121] The accused has two separate rights: to be given sufficient time and resources to present his case, and separately, to cross-examine a prosecution witness.[122] In Robinson's view,

> what is done by way of cross-examination ... should not be used as a basis for effectively reducing the time to be allocated to the Defence to present its case. To do so would be unfair to the Defence, since it would have no assurance from the trial chamber as to the effectiveness of its cross-examination.[123]

Robinson's dissent demonstrates that a different conclusion can be reached if the rights of the accused are given prominence in decision-making. In particular, his understanding that two rights – to time and facilities to prepare a defence, and to cross-examine a witness – should not be played off against each other is a sophisticated analysis of how rights are operationalised in international criminal procedure. Robinson's approach is far preferable to the simple disregard shown by the Trial Chamber and the majority of the

---

[117] *Karadžić Appeal Decision on Case Duration* [16]; *Karadžić Trial Chamber Decision on Case Duration* [9].
[118] *Karadžić Appeal Decision on Case Duration* [22].
[119] Ibid. [6] (Judge Robinson).
[120] Ibid.
[121] Ibid. [7].
[122] Ibid.
[123] Ibid.

Appeals Chamber to the question of how to provide multiple rights of the accused with full respect.

Because the Appeals Chamber upheld the decision not to provide the accused with further time to present his case, the defence team had relatively limited time to attempt to adduce evidence to rebut the previously admitted adjudicated facts. Peter Robinson is of the view that Karadžić did not have enough time to rebut the adjudicated facts.[124] In his opinion, the Trial Chamber provided the prosecution with a 'short cut . . . to prove a lot of things without calling witnesses, but [did not provide the defence] the corresponding time to be able to rebut them'.[125] The Karadžić defence team began a strategy that involved their defence witnesses stating in their written statements that particular adjudicated facts were incorrect.[126] Yet, due to a lack of clarity around what standard is required to rebut adjudicated facts, it was not clear whether this would be sufficient.[127] On Robinson's estimation, they were still only able to address 'maybe 10 or 20 per cent of the adjudicated facts because [there are] so many of them'.[128] While not every adjudicated fact may need to be rebutted, it is confounding that a measure like the use of adjudicated facts will be adopted with the explicit intent of lightening the load for the prosecution, and with the explicit consequence that the burden of disproving those facts moves to the defence, without any corresponding adjustment of time allocated to the accused – and no inquiry as to how to adequately ensure his right to time and facilities to prepare a defence.[129]

---

124 Interview with Peter Robinson (2 May 2013).

125 Ibid.

126 Ibid.

127 It was clarified in the *Karadžić Appeal Judgement* that 'the mere presentation of evidence seeking to rebut an adjudicated fact does not deprive a trial chamber of its discretion to assess the credibility or probative value of such evidence or prevent it from drawing conclusions from the relevant adjudicated fact' ([131]). In other words, it is not sufficient for an accused just to adduce evidence that the adjudicated fact is incorrect: this will not automatically place the fact back into contention. The Appeals Chamber confirmed the Trial Chamber's position, relying on *Karemera Decision* [42] that the accused would need to introduce 'reliable and credible' evidence to 'put the point into question'. Nonetheless, Karadžić, at least, felt that this was unclear: Karadžić Appeal Brief [136]-[141]. It would certainly be useful to have greater clarity as to the standard needed to dispel an adjudicated fact – whether it is necessary to merely raise a reasonable doubt as to the fact's accuracy, or whether it is necessary to disprove the fact beyond a reasonable doubt. The difference in these two standards of proof has profound implications for how much evidence an accused must adduce in rebuttal of a fact and, therefore, for the accused's time and facilities to prepare their defence.

128 Interview with Peter Robinson (2 May 2013).

129 In his appeal of conviction, Karadžić raised adjudicated facts in two grounds of appeal. He argued that there had been errors in taking judicial notice of adjudicated facts (Ground 7) and that there had been errors concerning the admission of adjudicated facts and written evidence under Rules 92 *bis* and *quater* (Ground 16). He argued that the Chamber relied on

This analysis of the *Karadžić* case demonstrates the considerable implications for the rights of the accused and the principle of equality of arms, of the widespread admission of adjudicated facts and the corresponding shift in the burden of proof to the accused. While considerations of fairness and rights were used as the rationale for the expanded use of Rule 94(B), the use of the rule – in particular, to admit large numbers of adjudicated facts to the record before the trial even starts – has shifted a significant burden of proof to the accused. In a trial where the prosecutor had benefitted from adducing evidence in written form and having their narrative of events presented to the Trial Chamber in the form of adjudicated facts before the trial even commenced, the accused has had to expend a great number of trial hours merely attempting to rebut the adjudicated facts. And yet, there has been no attempt to equalise the resources between the parties through, for example, increased court hours allocated to the accused – rather, his utilisation of his right to cross-examine has been invoked to limit his right to time and facilities to prepare a defence. Thus, we again see a situation where fairness and rights have been invoked, to the ultimate detriment of the rights of the accused – demonstrative, again, of the fissure between fairness and rights in procedural decision-making.

(3) Issue three: judicial reformulation of adjudicated facts

In the *Mladić* case, the issue of adjudicated facts and its relationship to fairness and rights particularly arose with regards to the ability of judges to 'fix' the prosecution's submission of adjudicated facts. Here, Trial Chamber took judicial notice of over 2,000 facts before the commencement of trial.[130] The accused had disputed the vast majority of these. During the process of taking judicial notice, the Trial Chamber 'reformulated' certain proposed prosecution adjudicated facts. This 'reformulation' applied to a total of 473 adjudicated facts that were proposed by the Prosecution and then reformulated in order to be accepted by the Trial Chamber and admitted to the record.[131]

---

adjudicated facts to make adverse findings and put too much weight on the facts, which 'violated the presumption of innocence and shifted the burden of proof', rendering the trial 'unfair by requiring the defence to divert resources to rebut adjudicated facts' (Karadžić Appeal Brief, Ground 7), and he argued that the 'cumulative effect' of admitting evidence by way of adjudicated facts plus through rules 92 *bis* and *quater* shifted the burden of proof 'and resulted in an unfair trial', again linked to a 'required diversion of defence resources to rebutting this mountain of untested evidence' (Ibid. Ground 16). Both these grounds of appeal were rejected by the Appeals Chamber (*Karadžić Appeal Judgement*).

[130] *Prosecutor v Mladić, Judgement* (IT-09-92-T, 22 November 2017) [16].

[131] The Accused submitted that there were 274 facts reformulated and then judicially noticed in the First Decision, 71 such facts in the Second Decision, and 128 in the Third Decision: *Prosecutor v Mladić, Decision on Ratko Mladić's Appeal Against the Trial Chamber's Decisions on*

Mladić appealed three decisions of the Trial Chamber to admit adjudicated facts.[132] It was not until almost eighteen months later, on 12 November 2013, that the Appeals Chamber provided their decision.[133] Ultimately, the Appeals Chamber removed forty previously judicially noticed facts on the basis that 'the Trial Chamber exceeded its discretion in reformulating them'; as well as an additional eighteen facts that were from the *Popović* Trial Judgement, 'on the basis that the Trial Chamber exceeded its discretion in finding that they are not subject to appeal'; and a further three facts that were removed after notification from the Prosecution. The Appeals Chamber noted that the fact that adjudicated facts create a reversible presumption that can be rebutted by the non-moving party meant that 'chambers ought to take a cautious approach' in admitting adjudicated facts 'in order to ensure the right of the accused to a fair trial'.[134]

On the issue of reformulation of adjudicated facts, the Appeals Chamber noted jurisprudence where Trial Chambers had held it was within their discretion 'to make minor corrections to proposed facts to render their formulation consistent with the meaning intended by the original judgement, as long as the corrections do not introduce any substantive changes',[135] but that Chambers 'must decline to take judicial notice of facts if it considers that the way they are formulated – abstracted from the context in the judgement from whence they came – is misleading or inconsistent with the facts actually adjudicated'.[136] The Appeals Chamber, therefore, held (Judge Robinson dissenting) that such an approach to reformulation was permissible, as long as it was only to make minor amendments or additions that do not 'alter the meaning of the original judgement from which the proposedadjudicated fact originates'.[137] It was not permissible for a Trial Chamber to reformulate a fact in a manner that 'introduces new information, which is extraneous to the proposed fact as submitted by the moving party'.[138]

The Appeals Chamber then examined the impugned adjudicated facts. Some of the additions made by the Trial Chamber were significant. As an example:

> 45. The Trial Chamber reformulated Proposed Fact No. 397 on the basis that it was not clear, distinct, or identifiable:

the *Prosecution Motion for Judicial Notice of Adjudicated Facts* (IT-09-92-AR73.l, 12 November 2013) ('*Mladić Adjudicated Facts Appeal Decision*') [6].

[132] *Prosecutor v Mladić*, 'Defense Interlocutory Appeal Brief Against the Trial Chamber Decisions on the Prosecution Motion for Judicial Notice of Adjudicated Facts' (IT-09-92-AR73.1, 4 July 2012).

[133] *Mladić Adjudicated Facts Appeal Decision*.

[134] Ibid. [24].

[135] Ibid. [26].

[136] Ibid. [27], quoting *Karemera Decision*.

[137] Ibid. [28].

[138] Ibid. [33].

~~Accordingly,~~ On 10 June 1992, ~~it~~ **the Bosnian-Serb Presidency** issued an official decision establishing war commissions **to further tighten the central grip over the municipalities.**

The Appeals Chamber is of the view that indicating that 'it' refers to 'the Bosnian-Serb Presidency' was within the Trial Chamber's discretion. However, the addition of 'to further tighten the central grip over the municipalities' amounts to a substantive change.[139]

The Appeals Chamber was correct in rejecting this significant, subjective addition. Yet it is concerning that Trial Chamber considered these amendments to be acceptable, as it suggests a level of pre-determination of the type of actions of the accused and the motivations of the JCE. That they then proceeded for more than two years of trial with this as their stated understanding is additionally concerning. Moreover, the accused (incorrectly) bore the responsibility to rebut this new level of information, for two years. These are all worrying aspects of the Trial Chamber's use of adjudicated facts in this case. Again, this was just one of forty changes that the Appeals Chamber held to be unacceptable.

The Appeals Chamber decision was, however, not unanimous. Again, Judge Robinson provided a partial dissent; and here, he offers a blistering commentary on the issue of fairness as going to the heart of the constitutionality of the very use of adjudicated facts. He noted that he has 'always' had 'concerns' about the validity of Rule 94(B).[140] He reiterated the argument that he advanced in the *Karadžić* case: that 'the accused's failure to rebut the proposed fact will inevitably strengthen the Prosecution's case'.[141] He went even further and stated that Rule 94(B) is 'unusual and dangerous' and that there is a 'consequential need for caution to ensure that in its application it does not produce any unfairness to the accused'.[142] Robinson was particularly concerned in this case with the measures that the Trial Chamber took to make a proposed fact admissible, namely '(a) adding additional information from the original judgement; (b) deleting information which it found infringed one or more criteria for judicial notice; and (c) merging information from proposed facts and/or from findings from more than one original judgement.'[143]

Robinson continued to question the validity of the rule. He stated that if Rule 94(B) can allow 'perfecting of the evidence presented by the Prosecution' by the Trial Chamber reformulating the facts, then the constitutionality of the rule itself is 'must be questioned'.[144] Any rule that permits

[139] Ibid. [45].
[140] 'Partial Dissenting Opinion of Judge Patrick Robinson' [101].
[141] Ibid.
[142] Ibid.
[143] Ibid. [100].
[144] Ibid. [103].

a Trial Chamber to 'assume a protagonist-party role in a trial' may be *ultra vires* of the Statute and customary international law. He summarises this by asking,

> is it a part of the function of a Trial Chamber to make substantive changes to evidence presented by the Prosecution in the form of an adjudicated fact so as to make admissible that evidence which is otherwise inadmissible for failing to meet one of the nine criteria that the Tribunal's case-law has set for the judicial notice of adjudicated facts?[145]

He continues, linking this to the concept of fairness and the rights of the accused:

> The overriding, overarching requirement of fairness to the accused called for by both the Statute and customary international law may be compromised by a system that not only enables the Trial Chamber to adduce evidence that strengthens the case of one party (in this case, the Prosecution) but also to pare, prune, tailor, amend and perfect evidence presented by the Prosecution so as to make it admissible.[146]

Robinson then makes the point that there is no other rule at the ICTY which permits a Trial Chamber to not only engage in evidence-gathering but 'also allows it to mould and bring evidence adduced by one party to a level where it can convert inadmissible evidence into admissible evidence'.[147] It is therefore arguable, in Robinson's view, that the power of a Trial Chamber to take notice of adjudicated facts 'infringes on its basic duty under Article 20(1) to ensure that a trial is fair'.[148] The minimum standard of the rights of the accused and the fairness of the trial 'may be breached by the evidence-gathering function under Rule 94(B)'.[149] In this case, then, the issue may not be whether the Trial Chamber abused its discretion in reformulating the proposed adjudicated facts, but rather whether the law of the Tribunal actually permits a Trial Chamber to undertake such a reformulation at all.[150]

Robinson noted that he would not have to address the constitutionality issue if, in this case, the Appeals Chamber decided that the moving party – and not the Trial Chamber – would be responsible for making any amendments to adjudicated facts. As he noted, the advantage of a Trial Chamber making the amendment 'is that it promotes expeditiousness; the question, however, is whether it also promotes fairness.'[151] Here, Robinson is clearly linking fairness to the constitutionality of a procedural provision, but also

---

[145] Ibid. [103].
[146] Ibid. [103].
[147] Ibid. [104].
[148] Ibid. [105].
[149] Ibid.
[150] Ibid.
[151] Ibid. [106]. Robinson's arguments on the 'constitutionality' of Rule 94(B) were raised

to the exercise of power by a Trial Chamber and their role as either active trial participant or more reserved adjudicator.

In this case, the Trial Chamber reformulated adjudicated facts in order to remedy deficiencies with how the prosecution had formulated them. In the case of several of the proposed facts, the fact as formulated by the prosecution would have fallen foul of the admissibility requirements. By reformulating them, and thereby making them admissible (and admitted), the Trial Chamber 'fixed' the problems with the prosecution evidence. Much like the recharacterisation of the charges at the ICC, examined above, the reformulation of proposed adjudicated facts allows the Trial Chambers to have a more active role in the shaping of the trial. Robinson makes the argument that this more active role is fundamentally at odds with the role of the Trial Chamber to ensure trial fairness.[152]

Several other points are worth mentioning when it comes to the reformulation of adjudicated facts and the rights of the accused. In this case, the number of facts affected – 473 facts reformulated by the Trial Chamber, with ten per cent of them subsequently found to have been impermissibly reformulated – only adds to the significance of this issue. When we consider the accused's right to time and facilities to prepare a defence, substantial resources would have been spent in simultaneously litigating this appeal while also addressing the adjudicated facts as they had been (wrongly) admitted. In particular, the accused may be attempting to adduce evidence to rebut the adjudicated facts while also challenging their admission. Meanwhile, in 'fixing' the adjudicated facts – rather than sending them back to the prosecution to reformulate and seek readmission – the Trial Chamber is assisting the prosecution and minimising the time and facilities the prosecution would need to expend on the drafting of adjudicated facts. Here, then, we see a double-whammy hit on the equality of arms and the accused's right to time and facilities for their defence: simultaneously, the Trial Chamber undertakes the job properly conceived of as the prosecution's, while the accused bears the uncertain evidentiary burden of rebuttal.

It should also be noted that the significant time lag while waiting for the decision of the Appeals Chamber is problematic. A lack of clarity about the scope and content of adjudicated facts can be deeply challenging for both parties (as we will see in more detail in the case of *Stanišić and Župljanin* below). It is also clear that the litigation of this issue would have been a significant issue for both parties as well as the Trial and Appeals Chambers. Again, it is therefore very unclear as to whether the admission of adjudicated facts (and their subsequent litigation) in fact served the purpose it is meant to, namely, to assist trial expeditiousness. In this case, the rights

---

by Karadžić in his Appeal: *Karadžić Appeal Brief* [116]. However, these arguments were rejected by the Appeals Chamber in that case: *Karadžić Appeal Judgement* [124].
[152] Ibid. [102].

of the accused appear to have been deleteriously affected for a significant portion of trial; the role of the Trial Chamber has been questionable; the effect on trial fairness is also at stake – and there has been little clear gain.

(4) Issue four: fairness and rights in late and inconsistent decisions

In the case against Mićo Stanišić and Stojan Župljanin, the Trial Chamber relied upon fairness considerations when making decisions on the use of adjudicated facts – here, to deny the admission of certain facts. However, as I will show, the process of decision-making was undertaken in a way that was significantly delayed and inconsistent with previous decisions on the use of adjudicated facts. As such, the contours of the trial were not clear, and the rights of the accused, in particular to time and facilities to prepare a defence, were adversely affected – as were the interests of the prosecution.

In preparation for the commencement of trial, the prosecution filed numerous motions for judicial notice of adjudicated facts.[153] Initially, on 14 December 2007, the Trial Chamber took notice of 752 adjudicated facts that had been proposed by the prosecution.[154] At this stage, proceedings were only against Stanišić, as Župljanin was not yet in the custody of the Tribunal. When Župljanin was arrested, and the case against him was joined to that against Stanišić in September 2008, the prosecution filed a request to admit the adjudicated facts granted in the December 2007 decision against Župljanin,[155] and for the adjudicated facts which had not yet been ruled upon to relate to both Stanišić and Župljanin.[156] Between January 2008 and February 2010, the prosecution filed a further four motions requesting the Chamber take judicial notice of prior adjudicated facts.[157] In reliance on these pending motions and the facts proposed in them, the prosecution filed its witness list with reduced numbers of witnesses, assuming that they

---

[153] *Prosecutor v Stanišić*, 'Prosecution's Motion for Judicial Notice of Facts of Common Knowledge and Adjudicated Facts, with Annex', (IT-04-79-PT, 31 August 2006); 'Prosecution's Second Motion for Judicial Notice of Adjudicated Facts, with Revised and Consolidated Annex' (10 May 2007); 'Prosecution's Third Motion for Judicial Notice of Adjudicated Facts, with Annex' (25 January 2008) ('Stanišić Third Motion'); 'Prosecution's Fourth Motion for Judicial Notice of Adjudicated Facts, with Annex' (24 April 2008) ('Stanišić Fourth Motion'); 'Prosecution's Fifth Motion for Judicial Notice of Adjudicated Facts, with Annex' (IT-08-91-PT, 21 August 2009) ('Stanišić Fifth Motion'); and 'Prosecution's Sixth Motion for Judicial Notice of Adjudicated Facts, with Annex' (2 February 2010) ('Stanišić Sixth Motion').

[154] *Prosecutor v Stanišić, Decision on Judicial Notice* (IT-04-79-PT, 14 December 2007) (*'First Stanišić Decision on Judicial Notice'*).

[155] *Prosecutor v Stanišić*, 'Prosecution's Request and Notice Regarding Application of Adjudicated Facts to Stojan Župljanin, with Annex' (IT-08-91-PT, 23 February 2009) [8].

[156] Ibid.

[157] Stanišić Third Motion; Stanišić Fourth Motion; Stanišić Fifth Motion; and Stanišić Sixth Motion.

would not be put to proof on the facts proposed.[158] The trial commenced on 14 September 2009.

However, the Trial Chamber did not hand down its decision until 1 April 2010 – nearing what was meant to be the end of the prosecution case.[159] Here, the Trial Chamber took judicial notice of 1,086 adjudicated facts but declined to take judicial notice of 239 facts. Of these, 233 of the declined facts had been previously accepted under the Trial Chamber's decision in the case against Stanišić.[160] The Trial Chamber had determined that where a proposed fact failed to meet the admissibility requirements in relation to either accused, it would not be admissible at all. As a result, they had come to a different determination on those facts than they had reached in the first decision.[161]

In making this decision, the Trial Chamber emphasised its 'paramount duty to ensure that the trial proceedings are fair and expeditious and that the rights of the accused are fully respected'.[162] The Chamber was mindful of 'whether the volume or type of evidence which either of the accused would have to produce in rebuttal could place such a significant burden on him that it would jeopardise his right to a fair trial'.[163] This is particularly so 'where the proposed fact goes to the core of the prosecution case',[164] for example, if it pertains to an objective of the JCE or relates to the acts and conduct of persons for whose conduct the accused is allegedly responsible.[165] Although the Trial Chamber found that such facts were not inadmissible, it exercised its discretion to withhold judicial notice to such facts, as taking judicial notice would not serve the interests of justice and a fair trial.[166] Fairness and the rights of the accused were therefore articulated as an integral part of the process of decision-making.

The decision to deny previously granted adjudicated facts opened areas to litigation which the parties had, for the first seven months of trial, viewed as being the responsibility of the accused to rebut if they chose to do so. The very aim of adjudicated facts is to streamline the case for trial, reduce the scope of the case, and delineate the boundaries of what

---

[158] *Prosecutor v Stanišić*, 'Prosecution's Motion to Amend its Rule 65 *ter* Witness List as a Result of the Trial Chamber's 1 April 2010 Granting in Part Prosecution's Motions for Judicial Notice of Adjudicated Facts Pursuant to Rule 94(B), with Confidential Annex' (26 May 2010) ('Stanišić Prosecution's Motion to Amend Its 65 *ter* List') [19].

[159] *Prosecutor v Stanišić, Decision Granting in Part the Prosecution's Motions for Judicial Notice of Adjudicated Facts Pursuant to Rule 94(B)* (1 April 2010) ('Second Stanišić Decision on Judicial Notice').

[160] Ibid; *First Stanišić Decision on Judicial Notice*.

[161] *Second Stanišić Decision on Judicial Notice* [26].

[162] Ibid. [45].

[163] Ibid.

[164] Ibid.

[165] Ibid. [46].

[166] Ibid.

is contested; as such, decisions on adjudicated facts should be made 'well before the Pre-Trial Conference in order to permit the parties and the pre-trial Judge to determine the scale of the case and to allow the parties to take appropriate witness-related decisions'.[167] In contrast, due to the Chamber's late and inconsistent ruling, the scope of the case and the responsibilities of the parties were confused and placed back into contention at a late stage. The prosecution was not able to set out its case in a structured and sequential way from the beginning of the trial – and nor could the defence adequately respond to such a case, potentially affecting their time and facilities to prepare a defence. As the onus had shifted to the accused in relation to these facts, the requirement on the accused to raise evidence to rebut these facts may have also affected their time and facilities to prepare a defence.

Moreover, as the Trial Chamber made this decision in large part due to concerns about the fairness of the trial and the rights of the accused (particularly the concern about the burden of rebuttal),[168] the suggestion arises that these rights of the accused were compromised for the first seven months of trial when these facts were admitted. For almost the entirety of the prosecution case, these same facts – which were later deemed to be inconsistent with the rights of the accused – were admitted in the trial. One of the concerns noted by the Trial Chamber was the degree to which the onus shifted to the accused, and yet this was perhaps most keenly felt during the prosecution phase of the case where the accused would have to cross-examine prosecution witnesses to adduce evidence to rebut these facts. The concerns of the Trial Chamber, then, were too delayed to be properly addressed.

The prosecution sought to Appeal this decision, claiming that the decision 'affects the fair conduct of the proceedings' as it 'deprive[s] the Prosecution of its ability to rely on the proposed and previously granted adjudicated facts at this point of the trial'.[169] The prosecution argued that

> The decision affects the fair conduct of the proceedings in that the Prosecution has had to construct its case relying, to a large extent, on adjudicated facts. To deprive the Prosecution of its ability to rely on the proposed and previously granted adjudicated facts at this point of the trial is unfair.[170]

The Trial Chamber denied Certification to Appeal on the basis that, although the length of the proceedings might be extended, this would not

---

[167] Mark B Harmon, 'The Pre-Trial Process at the ICTY as a Means of Ensuring Expeditious Trials: A Potential Unrealised' (2007) 5 *JICJ* 377, 382.

[168] *Second Stanišić Decision on Judicial Notice* [45].

[169] *Prosecutor v Stanišić*, 'Prosecution's Request for Certification to Appeal the Decision Granting in Part Prosecution's Motions for Judicial Notice of Adjudicated Facts Pursuant to Rule 94(B)' (IT-08-91-T, 7 April 2010).

[170] Ibid. [9].

'significantly affect both the fair and the expeditious conduct of the proceedings'.[171] In doing so, the Trial Chamber noted that the prosecution was
wrong to have relied upon the adjudicated facts admitted in the first decision
as applicable in the joint case against both Stanišić and Župljanin because
ignoring the effect of the joinder on the admissibility of the facts 'could
not only have been unfair to the accused but also contrary to the existing
jurisprudence on Rule 94(B)'.[172] The Chamber continued that it was not
the decision, but rather the prosecution's reliance on the Trial Chambers
indications, 'that may have affected to some extent the fair conduct of the
proceedings'.[173] This, however, is rather disingenuous: the prosecution, of
course, could do nothing other than rely on the Trial Chamber's existing
orders.

On 26 May 2010, the prosecution applied to the Trial Chamber to add
a further fifty-three witnesses to its witness list 'in order to fill evidentiary
gaps left by the denied adjudicated facts'.[174] On the same day as denying
Certification to Appeal, the Trial Chamber ordered that forty-four of these
extra witnesses could testify, and should do so *viva voce*.[175] Accordingly, the
Chamber found, 'any unfairness that might have arisen from the context
in which the Impugned Decision was issued is now mitigated'.[176] The Trial
Chamber did not specify what particular unfairness this might have been,
or whether it particularly affected the prosecution or the accused – although
presumably the Trial Chamber was referring to the prosecution, as it was
the provision of extra prosecution witnesses which the Trial Chamber
granted on the basis that this mitigated 'any unfairness'. Thus, while the
Trial Chamber had originally cited fairness as the rationale for its first decision to reject adjudicated facts, this subsequent decision is an admission
that unfairness may have resulted from the first decision. It is difficult to

---

[171] *Prosecutor v Stanišić, Decision Denying the Prosecution's Request for Certification to Appeal
the 'Decision Granting in Part Prosecution's Motions for Judicial Notice of Adjudicated Facts
Pursuant to Rule 94(B)'* (IT-08-91-T, 14 July 2010) ('*Stanišić Decision Denying Certification to
Appeal*').

[172] Ibid. [13].

[173] Ibid.

[174] *Stanišić* Prosecution's Motion to Amend its 65 *ter* List; *Prosecutor v Stanišić*, 'Addendum
to Prosecution's Motion to Amend Its Rule 65 *ter* Witness List as a Result of the Trial
Chamber's 1 April 2010 Granting in Part Prosecution's Motions for Judicial Notice of
Adjudicated Facts Pursuant to Rule 94(B), with Confidential Annex' (IT-08-91, 16 June
2010).

[175] *Stanišić* Prosecution's Motion to Amend Its 65 *ter* List [15]; *Prosecutor v Stanišić, Decision
Granting in Part Prosecution's Motion to Amend its 65 ter Witness List as a Result of The Trial
Chamber's 1 April 2010 Decision Concerning Judicial Notice of Adjudicated Facts* (IT-08-91-T,
14 July 2010). Ultimately three months were added to the proceedings for the prosecution
to bring its additional witnesses: *Assessment and Report of Judge Robinson* (19 November 2010)
[28].

[176] *Stanišić Decision Denying Certification to Appeal* [15].

reconcile the fact that the decision was originally rationalised on the basis of fairness with the ultimate 'unfairness' of the decision.

At one level, these decisions demonstrate the incoherence of fairness, as described in Chapter Three, and how readily it can be invoked as a rationale for decision-making yet have little concrete content. At another level, these decisions show, again, that Trial Chambers can facilitate a disconnection between fairness and rights. The Trial Chamber did not examine the concerns relating to the rights of the accused arising from the Trial Chamber's decisions on the use of adjudicated facts – even while it invoked fairness and unfairness as the rationale for its decisions. 'Fairness' may be easily invoked as a basis for, or to justify, a decision, but rights may be challenged by the outcomes of these decisions. The relationship between fairness and rights is separated, and the rights of the accused may be negatively affected by the invocation of fairness.

E. FAIRNESS AND RIGHTS DISCONNECTED IN ADJUDICATED FACTS DECISIONS

This chapter has examined the relationships between fairness, the rights of an accused, and the use of adjudicated facts at the ICTY. I have examined how Chambers have used the concept of fairness when determining the admission of such evidence and how this relates to the rights of the accused. As the institution of the ICTY aged and more cases were finally resolved (passing through judgement and appeals processes), the number of facts established in trials grew. There was also a growing pressure to efficiently use resources and a view that repeatedly proving facts already well-established in previous trials was wasteful and inefficient. The problems with oral evidence have been set out in the preliminary parts of this chapter and are genuine issues that all parties and participants to trials grapple with. To address this, the ICTY has undergone an 'inquisitorial drift', which has involved a number of changes to allow greater amounts of testimonial evidence admitted in written form – including the admission of adjudicated facts. A similar drift can be seen at the ICC.

This inquisitorial drift has occurred by adding a variety of rules to permit this evidence to be adduced in written form, into a system that had been effectively adversarial, without adopting corresponding safeguards to ensure the procedural system operates in a coherent fashion. The use of adjudicated facts typifies this. Trial Chambers relied on fairness concerns initially to limit the use of adjudicated facts; then interpreted Rule 94(B) in a way that assuaged concerns about the undermining of fairness but expanded the rule beyond its literal meaning. The result has been that the admissibility requirements and the possibility of rebuttal of facts by the non-moving party are now part of the contemporary use of adjudicated facts. Thus, an emphasis on fairness has ironically led to the potential for more widespread use of adjudicated facts at the ICTY, and there has been a subsequent increase in the admission of these facts. Yet, as I have shown, the contemporary use of adjudicated facts has had detrimental implications for the rights of the accused to examine witnesses and to time and facilities to prepare their defence, as well as for the principle of equality of arms. In the *Karadžić*, *Mladić*, and *Stanišić and Župljanin* cases, we see that while Chambers consistently reference fairness and rights when making decisions on the admission of adjudicated facts, these decisions may still adversely affect the rights of the accused. As with Chapter Four, we see a challenge for Trial Chambers in reconciling fairness, rights and procedure. These findings are important also for the ICC, where the use of adjudicated facts may evolve further. The next chapter examines another mechanism for the admission of written evidence in place of oral testimony, in the complex cases of witness protection. We will similarly see issues of reconciling fairness, rights and procedure in this case study.

Chapter 6
Fairness, the rights of the accused and the protection of witnesses

One of the most dramatic areas in which the rights of the accused and the fairness of trials may be challenged is that of the protection of victims and witnesses. The Trial Chamber's obligation to 'ensure a trial is fair' has, as we have already seen, two particular aspects: the 'full respect for the rights of the accused' and the 'due regard for the protection of victims and witnesses'.[1] What happens when these elements – fairness, the rights of the accused, and the protection of victims and witnesses – come into conflict? How is fairness rhetorically used to mediate the rights of the accused and this protection of victims and witnesses – and what are the practical outcomes of using fairness in such a way? In this chapter, I examine the main mechanisms used by Chambers in order to ensure the safety of witnesses. Although there are a variety of protective measures, this chapter will particularly focus on procedural mechanisms of the use of delayed disclosure and redactions to disclosure, and the potential use of written evidence in place of oral evidence.

While the rights of the accused are adversely affected by protective measures for witnesses, this is both permissible under the relevant Statutes and required for these trials to continue. This case study is therefore unusual in that it provides a clear example where rights can justifiably be curtailed to protect trial fairness. Nonetheless, this is still a situation where there is considerable controversy about the appropriate weight to provide to fairness, rights and witness protection; and as I will show, several examples reveal an increasing extension of the protection of witnesses even in situations where the rights of the accused will be curtailed, with trial fairness provided as the reason to justify this and little consideration shown to the rights of the accused. In this chapter, I show that there has been a significant expansion – through jurisprudence, and then changes to the relevant *Rules of Procedure and Evidence* – to the use of redactions and limits on the provision of relevant disclosure, on the basis of witness protection, but where little regard has been provided to the rights of the accused. At the ICTY, we have seen this in an extension of the permissible time for redactions; at the ICC, this

---

[1] *Rome Statute of the International Criminal Court*, opened for signature 17 July 1998, 2187 UNTS 90 (entered into force 1 July 2002) ('*Rome Statute*') Art 64(2); SC Res 827, UN SCOR, 48th sess, 3217th mtg, UN Doc S/RES/827 (25 May 1993), as amended by SC Res 1877, UN SCOR, 64th sess, 6155th mtg, UN Doc S/RES/1877 (7 July 2009) ('*ICTY Statute*') Art 20.

is seen in the expansion of the redactions regime to 'innocent third parties'. In relation to the use of written testimony, again there has been significant expansion of this in the *Rules*, at both institutions, in order to allow written evidence in place of oral testimony in cases of witness intimidation; the relevant case law suggests a concerning approach by Trial Chambers to questions of the rights of the accused in relation to the use of this rule. Both of these procedural mechanisms – and their interpretation and use by Chambers – shows again the separability of fairness and rights, and the challenges for ensuring the rights of the accused in procedural decisions.

A. THE NEED FOR PROTECTION

The requirement to recognise the integral importance of the safety of victims and witnesses is articulated clearly in the *Statutes* of the courts and tribunals. For example, the *Statute* of the ICTY notes in Article 20 that a Trial Chamber 'will ensure that a trial is fair and expeditious and that pro-ceedings are conducted in accordance with the rules of procedure and evi-dence, with full respect for the rights of the accused and due regard for the protection of victims and witnesses'; this is followed by Article 21 entitled 'Rights of the Accused' and Article 22 on the 'Protection of Victims and Witnesses'. This structuring of the *Statute* demonstrates the importance of both the rights of the accused and the protection of victims and witnesses, and the requirement that Trial Chambers consider both. Article 22 states that the ICTY must provide, in its rules, for the protection of victims and witnesses, including measures to protect the victim's identity. Indeed, the Rules (and jurisprudence) do establish these measures, as we will see below. Similarly, the *Rome Statute* provides for the rights of the accused in Article 67, and the 'Protection of the victims and witnesses and their participation in the proceedings' in Article 68.

Ensuring the safety of witnesses is crucial for international criminal insti-tutions. At the most important and fundamental level, no person should face danger – possibly even death – for their cooperation with international criminal law and its processes. At a more prosaic and logistical level, despite the increasing move away from oral evidence at these courts and tribu-nals, witness appearance and testimony remain crucial in these trials. As Robert Cryer points out, this is for several reasons, including an attempt to satisfy 'the other aims' that have 'rightly or wrongly' been attached to international criminal law,[2] namely providing a voice to victims. Testifying

---

[2] Robert Cryer, 'Witness Tampering and International Criminal Tribunals' (2014) 27 *LJIL* 191, 191. See generally Sylvia Ntube Ngana, *The Position of Witnesses Before the International Criminal Court* (Brill Nijhoff, 2015); Guido Acquaviva and Mikaela Heikkilä, 'Protective and Special Measures for Witnesses' in Göran Sluiter et al. (eds), *International Criminal Procedure: Principles and Rules* (OUP, 2013); Patricia Wald, 'Dealing with Witnesses in War Crime Trials: Lessons from the Yugoslav Tribunal' (2002) 5 *YHRDLJ* 217.

is often thought to be cathartic for victims,[3] although it is also increasingly understood as often being retraumatising. Moreover, witness testimony can provide 'some level of theatre' to an otherwise dull legal process, and witnesses tend to provide emotive and powerful evidence that deeply impresses the judges and other observers.[4] Many of the reasons for witness appearance are set out in Chapter Five.

Yet while witness testimony remains crucial to international criminal trials, there are significant issues faced in obtaining this evidence. It is important to note at the outset that witness tampering includes many different forms of interference. Cryer has defined witness tampering as 'threats, both express and implicit, to witnesses and/or their families, as well as bribes and other inducements'.[5] As a result of these threats or inducements, witnesses may refuse to physically come to testify at all, they may omit important details from their testimony, or they may fabricate their testimony. As examples, they might attribute actions to people other than the defendant, provide an alibi to a defendant, testify that particular events did not occur at all – or indeed, they may falsely inculpate a defendant by testifying to acts that did not occur, incorrectly stating a defendant's presence at a location, or otherwise suggesting responsibility rested with a defendant when it did not. It is thus important to note that while the majority of attention is paid to the *suppression* of evidence, witness tampering can also be manifested in the *creation* of inaccurate evidence, such as in cases of witness bribery and coaching.[6] It is also important to note that witness tampering can be undertaken against either prosecution or defence witnesses. Therefore, witness interference is a term that could include, for example, inducements for the testimony of a prosecution witness, as well as intimidation and threats levelled at a defence witness (or vice versa).[7]

It is also important to recall that there may be situations where witnesses may not be directly tampered with but may still be reluctant to testify. Alleged perpetrators may continue to hold positions of power, and potential witnesses may fear retaliation.[8] This is even more complex in situations when threats may not come from the defendant but from 'societal pressures' in small, close-knit communities.[9] Indeed, defendants and their legal team

---

[3] Cryer (n 2) 191.

[4] Ibid. 191–2.

[5] Ibid. 192.

[6] Ibid. 193.

[7] On the intimidation of defence witnesses, see Jared Paul Marx, 'Intimidation of Defence Witnesses at the International Criminal Tribunals: Commentary and Suggested Legal Remedies' (2007) 7 *CJIL* 675.

[8] Mark Harmon and Fergal Gaynor, 'Prosecuting Massive Crimes with Primitive Tools: Three Difficulties Encountered by Prosecutors in International Criminal Proceedings' (2004) 2(2) *JICJ* 403, 407.

[9] Karim Khan and Caroline Buisman, 'Sitting on Evidence? Systemic Failings in the ICC

may be acting entirely ethically and in full compliance with the law, but witnesses may still be reluctant to testify. Moreover, allegations of threats to witnesses may have a chilling effect, whereby other witnesses will be reluctant to speak to investigators or to testify in court.

All these factors may mean that a Trial Chamber is less able to fulfil their ultimate objective in the trial process, namely reaching a determination on the guilt or otherwise of the accused. Without the relevant evidence, the prosecution may not be able to prove the case beyond a reasonable doubt; on the other hand, with the inclusion of falsely inculpatory evidence, an accused may be wrongly convicted. Witness tampering will also affect other aims that may have been applied to international criminal law (as examined in Chapter One).

In extreme cases, witness tampering can cause the collapse of trials. Recent years have seen several ICC trials end before judgment and not infrequently because of issues with prosecution witnesses. Knowing that they cannot prove the case beyond a reasonable doubt, the prosecution may voluntarily stop the case. For example, in withdrawing the charges against the accused in the *Muthaura* case at the ICC, prosecutor Fatou Bensouda noted that a 'critical witness against Mr Muthaura . . . recanted a significant part of his incriminating evidence . . . and . . . admitted accepting bribes from persons allegedly holding themselves out as representatives of both accused'.[10] It is, however, also worth recalling that in this case, the testimony of 'Witness 4' was relied upon to confirm the charges against Muthaura – indeed, Witness 4 was 'the principal source of evidence that supported the Prosecution's charges against Mr Muthaura at the confirmation stage', and 'there would not have been sufficient evidence to confirm the charges against Mr Muthaura without Witness 4's evidence'.[11] However, the Prosecution had failed to disclose to the Defence an asylum affidavit, where the Witness contradicts other statements made to the prosecution, particularly regarding his attendance at 'one of the key meetings in question', and moreover

---

Disclosure Regime – Time for Reform' in Carsten Stahn (ed) *The Law and Practice of the International Criminal Court* (OUP, 2015) 1029, 1054.

[10] *Prosecutor v Muthaura*, 'Prosecution Notification of the Withdrawal of Charges against Francis Kirimi Muthaura' (ICC-01/09-02/11-687, 11 March 2013); *Prosecutor v Muthaura, Decision on the withdrawal of charges against Mr Muthaura* (ICC-01/09-02/11, 18 March 2013). Similarly, in withdrawing the charges against Uhuru Kenyatta, Bensouda noted that 'several people who may have provided important evidence regarding Mr. Kenyatta's actions, have died, while others were too terrified to testify for the Prosecution' and 'key witnesses who provided evidence in this case later withdrew or changed their accounts' (Statement of the Prosecutor of the International Criminal Court, Fatou Bensouda, on the withdrawal of charges against Mr. Uhuru Muigai Kenyatta (5 December 2014)).

[11] *Prosecutor v Muthaura*, 'Public Redacted Version of the 25 February 2013 Consolidated Prosecution Response to the Defence Applications Under Article 64 of the Statue to Refer the Confirmation Decision Back to the Pre-Trial Chamber' (ICC-01/09-02/11, 25 February 2013) ('Muthaura Prosecution Response on Confirmation Decision') [44].

he 'provides evidence demonstrating that he could not have been present' at another meeting.[12] Such material is clearly exculpatory, and had been in the prosecution's possession for more than a year before the confirmation of charges hearing – but was disclosed to the defence only a year *after* the hearing.[13] The prosecution subsequently admitted that the affidavit 'could and should have been disclosed to the Defence prior to the confirmation hearing', and that 'the reasoning contained it its redactions application was insufficient in light of the potential significance of [the material] and provided the Single Judge with inadequate information'.[14] It was subsequent to this that the prosecutor withdrew the charges against Muthaura.

Other cases have also been controversial: for example, in the *Bemba* case – where the accused was acquitted on appeal but had been separately found guilty (alongside two members of his defence team and two other associates) of offences against the administration of justice, concerning the evidence of fourteen defence witnesses in the main trial.[15] Even in cases that proceed to full judgment and a guilty verdict, witness interference has been a live issue – such as in the *Lubanga* case, where there were 'significant allegations of witness tampering, intended both to incriminate and exculpate Lubanga', and affecting both prosecution and defence witnesses.[16] Indeed, witness interference has been a 'worrisome thread running through many ICC cases'.[17] Witness issues are also challenging at all other international criminal institutions. Given the widespread nature of these issues, and the potential for trials to be entirely undermined by witness interference, it is not an exaggeration to say that witness protection is an existential issue for the system of international criminal law.

Some argue that the nature of the crimes in these trials – emerging, as they do, from mass violence – will often 'expose witnesses to greater threats than might ordinarily be experienced in domestic jurisdictions'.[18] In international criminal trials, witness concerns are imbued with an additional level

---

[12] Karim A. A. Khan and Anand A. Shah, 'Defensive Practices: Representing Clients Before the International Criminal Court' (2013) 76 *LCP* 191, 209.

[13] Ibid. 210.

[14] *Muthaura* Prosecution Response on Confirmation Decision [37]–[38].

[15] *Prosecutor v Bemba et al, Public Redacted Version of Judgment Pursuant to Article 74 of the Statute* (ICC-01/05-01/03, 19 October 2016).

[16] Cryer (n 2) 196.

[17] Danya Chaikal, 'Recent Advancements and Remaining Gaps in Addressing the Witness Protection Challenge at the ICC', *International Criminal Justice Today* (17 April 2014), <https://www.international-criminal-justice-today.org/arguendo/recent-advancements-and-remaining-gaps-in-addressing-the-witness-protection-challenge-at-the-icc/> (last accessed 9 December 2021).

[18] Andrew Trotter, 'Witness Intimidation in International Trials: Balancing the Need for Protection Against the Rights of the Accused' (2012) *GWILR* 521, 521. See also Anne-Marie de Brouwer, 'The Problem of Witness Interference before International Criminal Tribunals' (2015) 15 *ICLR* 700.

of anxiety around safety and security, because the trials and institutions are often established in the context of armed conflict – a context where safety and security are already in danger. It is also true that international criminal institutions, lacking their own police and enforcement mechanisms, rely on domestic partners to undertake many of the logistics related to witnesses, which may leave such logistics vulnerable. For these reasons, it could be reasonably said that international criminal law has structural features which make it particularly susceptible to witness tampering.

Moreover, it is crucial to remember that the place of the victim-witness in these trials is not gender-neutral. Christine Chinkin has made a compelling argument that there is a feminist and equity perspective to the protection of victims, and of the relationship between victim protection and the rights of the accused. As she sets out,

> human rights standards have been defined by men in accordance with male assertions of what constitutes the most fundamental guarantees required by individuals', and this 'is highlighted in the conflict between the rights of the accused to a fair trial and the right of the victim to equality before the law and to be free from fear of further abuse. Women typically feature in a criminal trial as victims and witnesses, while more men than women appear as accused. It is not surprising that the guarantee of a fair trial is seen by many as more fundamental than the victim's interests, and those of other potential victims.[19]

This is particularly important given the jurisdiction of these institutions over gender-based crimes, including rape, alongside the 'long silence about the incidence of violent sexual abuse in armed conflict'.[20] For Chinkin, the progress of these institutions in prosecuting gender-based crimes 'will be prejudiced if fear prevents witnesses from giving their testimony'.[21] These are all important structural factors to keep in mind, and these show the great complexity of balancing the protection of witnesses with the rights of the accused and trial fairness in these trials.

B. PROTECTIVE MEASURES

In recognition of all the above, there are various measures available to Trial Chambers to protect witnesses and their testimony. The ICTY *Statute* states that the tribunal 'shall provide in its rules of procedure and evidence for the protection of victims and witnesses. Such protection measures shall include,

---

[19] Christine Chinkin, 'Due Process and Witness Anonymity' (1997) 91 *AJIL* 75, 78–9. See also Hilary Charlesworth and Christine Chinkin, *The Boundaries of International Law: A Feminist Analysis* (Manchester University Press, 2000) 324–9; Monroe Leigh, 'Witness Anonymity is Inconsistent with Due Process' (1997) 91 *AJIL* 80.

[20] Ibid. 79.

[21] Ibid.

but shall not be limited to, the conduct of *in camera* proceedings and the protection of the victim's identity.'[22] Under the *Rules*, a judge or Chamber may order 'appropriate measures for the privacy and protection of victims and witnesses, provided that the measures are consistent with the rights of the accused'.[23] They may do this either *proprio motu* or on the request of either party, the victim or witness concerned, or the Victims and Witnesses Section.[24]

Witness protection mechanisms can be understood as falling into two categories: in-court (procedural) or outside the court (non-procedural) measures.[25] In-court mechanisms include the use of pseudonym, facial or voice distortion, appearing in a private or closed session of court, or redacting the public record of testimony to ensure any identifying material is not broadcast. There are also procedural mechanisms to admit witness testimony in written form, where the witness's physical attendance at court cannot be obtained because of witness intimidation concerns (as we will see in greater detail below).[26] In addition, there are mechanisms outside the courtroom: delaying disclosure of witness materials to the accused, detaining the accused prior to trial,[27] and the work of Victims Units to support witnesses. Not infrequently, a combination of protective measures may be used. Moreover, both the ICTY and ICC have provisions for prosecutions to address alleged witness intimidation. At the ICC, article 70 of the Rome Statute provides for investigations and prosecutions for 'offenses against the administration of justice' – including 'Corruptly influencing a witness, obstructing or interfering with the attendance or testimony of a witness, retaliating against a witness for giving testimony or destroying, tampering with or interfering with the collection of evidence'.[28] The ICTY similarly has a provision for 'contempt of court' for interfering with the administration of justice in cases where a person 'threatens, intimidates, causes any injury or offers a bribe to, or otherwise interferes with, a witness who is giving, has given, or is about to give evidence in proceedings before a Chamber, or a potential witness'.[29]

Protective mechanisms are a common occurrence in international criminal trials. Almost one-third of witnesses at the ICTY have testified with some form of protective measures.[30] The most frequently used protection mecha-

---

[22] *ICTY Statute* Art 22.
[23] ICTY, *Rules of Procedure and Evidence*, Doc No IT/32/Rev.50 (adopted on 11 February 1994, amended 10 July 2015) ('*ICTY Rules*') r 75.
[24] Ibid.
[25] Romina Beqiri, 'Reflections on Certain Witness Protection Measures Under the Rome Statute of the International Criminal Court' (2017) 13 *ESJ* 342. See also Wald (n 2).
[26] See *ICTY Rules* r 92 *quinquies.*
[27] See generally Trotter (n 18).
[28] *Rome Statute* Art 70(c).
[29] *ICTY Rules* r 77 (iv).
[30] Approximately twenty-eight per cent of witnesses who testified between 1996–2013 had

nism was facial distortion with the addition of the use of a pseudonym, with ten per cent of witnesses requiring these protections; an additional approximately eight per cent have required facial and voice distortion as well as the provision of a pseudonym.[31] Around seven per cent of witnesses testified in closed court, either with or without a pseudonym.[32]

At the ICC, the Rome Statute provides that the Court 'shall take appropriate measures to protect the safety, physical and psychological well-being, dignity and privacy of victims and witnesses', and these measures 'shall not be prejudicial to or inconsistent with the rights of the accused and a fair and impartial trial'.[33] The measures include conducting proceedings in camera or allowing testimony by electronic or other means; and having the advice of the Victims and Witnesses Unit regarding 'appropriate protective measures, security arrangements, counselling and assistance'.[34] As we have already discussed, this part of the *Rome Statute* also allows for victim participation in trial.[35]

C. THE RELATIONSHIP BETWEEN WITNESS PROTECTION AND THE RIGHTS OF THE ACCUSED

This chapter will examine, in particular, the use of delayed disclosure as a protective measure, and the admission of written testimony in place of oral testimony from witnesses who have allegedly been subject to interference. These are measures available to Trial Chambers to avoid, mitigate and address alleged witness intimidation. Although less frequently used compared to other measures, these are areas that particularly demonstrate challenges for the rights of the accused. The rights of the accused especially affected are the rights to examine and cross-examine witnesses, to know the case against them, and to time and facilities to prepare a defence. The content of these rights has already been largely set out in Chapters Four and Five.

Many protective measures – using pseudonyms, distorting appearance, closing the court, or redacting the public record – are aimed towards protecting the identity of the witness from the *public*, but the use of delayed disclosure aims to withhold the identity of the witness from the *accused* (for a period of time). This poses particular issues for the rights of the accused.

some form of protective measures (ICTY, *Witness Statistics*, <https://www.icty.org/en/about /registry/witnesses/statistics> (last accessed 9 December 2021))

[31] Ibid.

[32] Ibid.

[33] *Rome Statute* Art 68. On witness testimony and protection generally at the ICC, see International Bar Association, 'Witnesses Before the International Criminal Court' (2013).

[34] *Rome Statute* Art 68 (4). See Markus Eikel, 'Witness Protection Measures at the International Criminal Court: Legal Framework and Emerging Practice' (2012) 23 CLF 97.

[35] *Rome Statute* Art 68(3).

Chapter Four has already established the importance of disclosure to the accused's rights to know the case and to 'time and facilities to prepare a defence'.[36] In a situation where the prosecution withholds the identity of a witness (and all identifying information) until a particular timeframe, the accused will have both more limited ability to know the case against them and to time and facilities to investigate and prepare their case. The reasons for this will be set out in greater detail below, in the section on delayed disclosure and redactions.

In situations where the prosecution seeks the admission of prior statements in place of oral testimony, the right of the accused 'to examine, or have examined, the witnesses against him'[37] may also be adversely affected. Again, this right has already been examined in some length in Chapter Five; and as was set out there, this is understood as an affirmation that an accused has a right to confront the witnesses against him or her.[38] The present chapter will examine this in relation to the insertion of new Rules which permit evidence going to the acts and conduct of the accused to be admitted to the trial even in the absence of any ability to cross-examine the witness. This is a significant difference from other provisions allowing the use of written evidence in place of oral testimony, as such provisions (including, for example, the use of adjudicated facts) cannot go to the acts or conduct of an accused. These new provisions (particularly Rule 92 *quinquies* at the ICTY and Rule 68(2)(d) at the ICC) may allow the written statements of witnesses who, for reason of 'improper interference', have failed to attend as a witness or have not given evidence in a material respect. It is perfectly plausible that under these provisions, crucial evidence regarding the conduct or acts of the accused could be admitted without any testing by the accused through cross-examination. On its face, this is clearly incompatible with the right of the accused to confront the witness against them; the question becomes how this operates in practice and whether it is justified.

D. FAIRNESS, RIGHTS, AND PROTECTION OF WITNESSES

As we have seen in previous chapters, where there is conflict in how to manage a trial issue – for example, between how different legal systems view a procedural mechanism and its operation in a *sui generis* procedural system – the court may revert to 'fairness' as an interpretative tool to assist

---

[36] *ICTY Statute* Art 21(4)(b); *Rome Statute* Art 67(1)(b).

[37] *Rome Statute* Art 67(1)(e); *ICTY Statute* Art 21(4)(e).

[38] Gideon Boas, *The Milošević Trial: Lessons for the Conduct of Complex International Criminal Proceedings* (CUP, 2007) 43. See also Eugene O'Sullivan and Deidre Montgomery, 'The Erosion of the Right to Confrontation under the Cloak of Fairness at the ICTY' (2010) 8 *JICJ* 511; Kweku Vanderpuye, 'Traditions in Conflict: The Internationalization of Confrontation' (2010) 43 *CILJ* 513; Megan A Fairlie, 'Due Process Erosion: The Diminution of Live Testimony at the ICTY' (2003) 34 *CWILJ* 47.

them in their decision-making or to justify a decision. In the case of witness protection, we see this emerge particularly strongly: fairness can be used as the 'mediating discourse' between the rights of the accused and the protection of victims and witnesses. There is a balance that occurs between the rights of the accused and the interests of the other parties, and fairness is the concept that regulates or oversees this balance. This, however, does not mean that the use of fairness as the mediator is straightforward.

Early in the life of the ICTY, the relationship between fairness, rights and victim protection was given significant analysis by the Trial Chamber in the *Tadić* case.[39] In that case, the Trial Chamber (by majority) agreed with the prosecution's argument that the Tribunal 'must interpret its provisions within its own context and determine where the balance lies between the accused's right to a fair . . . trial and the protection of the victims and witnesses within its unique legal framework'.[40] The 'unique legal framework' of the ICTY included the 'affirmative obligation to protect witnesses and victims' under Article 22 and Rules 69 and 75, and as a result, 'the safety of victims and witnesses must be balanced against the right of the accused to a fair trial'.[41] Moreover, the 'unique legal framework' was created in part due to the fact that the ICTY was established during armed conflict; as such, the Tribunal had decided, 'when preparing its Rules, to take into account the most conspicuous aspects of the armed conflict', including the 'terror and anguish among the civilian population' which the Judges feared would lead to 'many victims and witnesses [being] deterred from testifying . . . or would be concerned about the possible negative consequences that their testimony could have for themselves or their relatives'.[42] This, it was said, was 'particularly troubling' given the reliance of the prosecutions on eyewitness testimony.[43] Hence, article 21 of the ICTY Statute (the 'Rights of the Accused') must be 'interpreted within the context of the "object and purpose" and unique characteristics of the Statute. Among those unique considerations is the affirmative obligation to protect victims and witnesses'.[44]

In his separate opinion to that Decision, Judge Ninian Stephen noted that 'the problem is . . . how to respond to the very natural concern of witnesses while at the same time according justice to the accused and ensuring

---

[39] For more, see Anni Pues, 'A Victim's Right to a Fair Trial at the International Criminal Court? Reflections on Article 68(3)' (2015) 13 *JICJ* 951; Olivia Swaak-Goldman, 'The ICTY and the Right to a Fair Trial: A Critique of the Critics' (1997) 10(2) *LJIL* 215; Natasha Affolder, '*Tadić*, the Anonymous Witness and the Sources of International Procedural Law' (1997) 19 *MJIL* 445.

[40] *Prosecutor v Tadić, Decision on the Prosecutor's Motion Requesting Protective Measures for Victims and Witnesses* (IT-94-1-T, 10 August 1995) ('*Tadić Decision*') [27].

[41] Chinkin (n 19) 76.

[42] *Tadić Decision* [23].

[43] Ibid.

[44] Ibid. [26].

a fair trial'.[45] He acknowledges that throughout the relevant provisions of the Statute and the Rules, there is a 'tension' between the '"axiomatic" need to fully respect "unconditionally recognised standards of the rights of the accused" and the quite distinct need "to ensure the protection of victims and witnesses"'.[46] In particular (and as examined in Chapter Two), Judge Stephen noted the 'marked contrast' between the rights of the accused being provided 'full respect' and the protection of witnesses being provided 'due regard' in article 20 of the Statute.[47] He also noted the differences 'in both the tone and the substance' between article 21 (the rights of the accused) and article 22 (the protection of victims and witnesses).[48]

We can therefore see, in this decision and in the Separate Opinion, a distinct difference in approach as to how to use fairness to mediate the relationship between the rights of the accused and the interests of the witnesses. As with other examples that were examined in Chapter Three, we can conceive of this as being an early example of the 'rights-centred' and 'shared process-centred' divide. In the case of the protection of witnesses, the relationship between rights, interests and fairness is particularly complex and fraught, due to the high stakes involved – for the witness, their safety; for the accused, clear challenges for their rights; and for the trial process, real issues around the Chamber's ability to meet their key aim, to reach a forensic determination of the accused's guilt or innocence. As Yvonne McDermott points out, there is an important distinction

> between victims' participatory rights as 'status rights' and the human rights that are at issue when we discuss the witness's right to life [. . .] and the accused's right to a fair trial. Universally-accepted human rights should prevail over status rights, and when it comes to a clash between two human rights, the courts will have to strike a very delicate balance.[49]

In what follows, we see how this relationship and balance plays out in the context of delayed disclosure and redactions and the use of written evidence in place of oral testimony – and we see that frequently, the rights of the accused are not adequately considered in judicial decision-making to extend these mechanisms.

---

[45] *Prosecutor v Tadić*, 'Separate Opinion of Judge Stephen on the Prosecutor's Motion Requesting Protective Measures for Victims and Witnesses' (IT-94-1-T, 10 August 1995).

[46] Ibid.

[47] Ibid.

[48] Ibid.

[49] Yvonne McDermott, *Fairness in International Criminal Trials* (OUP, 2016) 120.

E. DELAYED DISCLOSURE AND REDACTIONS

There is an important relationship between the rights of the accused and their knowledge of the identity of witnesses against them. In particular, the right to 'examine, or have examined, the witnesses against him'[50] will be severely curtailed if the accused does not know the identity of the witness. It will be difficult to put this witness to proof or confront them – to interrogate their testimony for weaknesses that may raise a reasonable doubt; or to question the credibility of the witness and, therefore, of the reliability of their testimony. Moreover, as will be set out in greater detail below, an accused's right to 'time and facilities to prepare a defence' – especially their ability to conduct investigations – will be significantly adversely affected if they cannot access information about witnesses against them.

In this section, I set out the redaction process generally and its effect on the rights of the accused, before turning to how this is justified and undertaken at the ICTY and ICC, respectively. At both institutions, the use of redactions has been expanded significantly through judicial interpretation (and then at the ICTY, through subsequent changes to the *Rules*). The ICTY extended the timeframe for delayed disclosure significantly, from necessitating it to be completed prior to trial to the possibility (now frequently invoked) of it occurring throughout the trial. Initially, this change occurred in apparent contradiction with the wording of the provision in the *Rules*, and with little consideration paid to the rights of the accused. At the ICC, judicial interpretation has significantly expanded the categories of protected individuals, and again this occurred without proper consideration of how the rights of the accused would be affected.

Total witness anonymity is not common. At the ICTY, there has been one case of total witness anonymity – in the *Tadić* case – but this early exception has not been followed, and generally, there is no allowance of complete non-disclosure of a witness's identity at the trial stage.[51] While there has, so far, been no similar case of total witness anonymity at the ICC, the *Rome Statute* and Rules appear to leave open such a possibility,[52] and a 2008 Decision of the Trial Chamber in the *Lubanga* case also 'argued that preserving the anonymity of witnesses was compatible with the guarantee to a fair trial, as long as sufficient counterbalancing measures in favour of

---

[50] *ICTY Statute* Art 21(4)(e); *Rome Statute* Art 67(e).

[51] *Tadić Decision*. On witness anonymity generally, see Michael Kurth, 'Anonymous Witnesses before the International Criminal Court: Due Process in Dire Straits' in Carsten Stahn and Goran Sluiter (eds), *The Emerging Practice of the International Criminal Court* (Brill Nijhoff, 2009) 615.

[52] Kurth points out that while the drafters of the Rome Statute were aware of the precedent – and the controversy – of the *Tadić Decision*, they 'refrained from inserting any provision into the Statute or the RPE that allows the use of anonymous witnesses' (n 51, 626). Nonetheless, there appears to be some 'leeway' for ICC judges to adopt a similar position to that in the *Tadić Decision* and permit total anonymity (ibid. 628).

the Defence are adopted'.[53] It is, therefore, possible that the ICC may order cases of total witness anonymity in the future. However, thus far, the possibility raised by the *Lubanga* Trial Chamber more than a decade ago has not been used at the ICC.

Far more common is the delayed disclosure of the witness's name and other identifying material, particularly at the pre-trial stage, but potentially up to a point in the trial prior to the testimony of the witness. In such cases, the prosecution will generally disclose to the defence witness materials, such as witness statements, that have been carefully redacted to take out any identifying material. Redacted material may include, for example, a name, date of birth, place of birth, the identity of other individuals, particular locations, and so on. The full and unredacted witness materials will then be disclosed at a time set by the Trial Chamber. This protective mechanism of delayed disclosure has been 'extensively practiced' at the *ad hoc* tribunals;[54] and at the ICC, it has been said that the Court has 'adopted a permissive approach in authorising redactions', and that this is the case 'particularly by comparison with the *ad hoc* tribunals'.[55] It is therefore clear that the practice of redactions is widespread at both the ICTY and ICC.

Redactions obviously interact with the rights of the accused to know the case, to time and facilities to prepare their case, and to equality of arms. This is particularly clear with regards to the ability of the accused to investigate the material. Redactions are, by their nature, intended to ensure it is difficult for defence teams to investigate the information. Redactions are granted precisely because it is considered undesirable for the accused to be able to investigate the witness fully. Yet Caroline Buisman and David Hooper have provided an example of just how challenging this can be for defence teams:

> Protecting a witness's identity by redacting all references in the witness's statement that could possibly identify the witness or their family members and associates often leads to a situation in which the extent of blanked-out paragraphs results in an incomprehensible narrative, such as that "A met B at Y on X date."[56]

Investigating such material will be nearly impossible. Defence teams may have limited opportunities and budget to undertake field investigations of their own, and because it will often be difficult for defence teams to

---

[53] *Prosecutor v Lubanga*, *Decision on Victims Participation* (ICC-01/04-01/06, 18 January 2008). See Kurth (n 51) for analysis.

[54] Sangkul Kim, 'The Witness Protection Mechanism of Delayed Disclosure at the Ad Hoc International Criminal Tribunals' (2016) *JEAIL* 55

[55] Khan and Buisman (n 9) 1048. See also Nicholas Croquet, 'Implied External Limitations on the Right to Cross-Examine Prosecution Witnesses: The Tension Between a Means Test and a Balancing Test in the Appraisal of Anonymity Requests' (2010) 11 *MJIL* 27.

[56] Caroline Buisman and David Hooper, 'Defence Investigations and the Collection of Evidence' in Gentian Zyberi and Colleen Rohan (eds), *Defense Perspectives on International Criminal Justice* (CUP, 2018) 519, 532.

undertake field investigations during the trial, it may be that the defence must undertake the bulk of their defence investigations of prosecution witnesses before the trial commences – and thus before the disclosure has been 'unredacted'. Defence teams may, therefore, have to undertake field investigations without all the information they require on the witnesses – potentially wasting their time and resources or making the investigations less revealing or useful.

As time goes on, and the witness's appearance comes gradually closer, 'three or four versions of a particular statement' will be disclosed by the prosecution to the defence, each 'a little fuller and less redacted'.[57] Ultimately, the last things to be unredacted and disclosed will include 'the key names in the witness's narrative – names of persons met, places where events occurred, and family members and associates referred to, all of which are highly relevant to a defense investigation'.[58] This process, of gradually releasing material over the course of several disclosure batches, also means that:

> the same evidence may be disclosed to the Defence multiple times with different degrees of redactions. Effectively, the Defence may be required to review the same material three times before the . . . key information may be disclosed to the Defence and allows for full Defence investigations to take place at a very late stage in proceedings.[59]

At this point, then, defence lawyers may need to speak to potential witnesses or sources again to ask further questions about the now-disclosed material.[60] Khan and Buisman point out that this not only increases the burden on the limited defence budget, but it also runs the risk that witnesses or sources may no longer be available.[61] This is particularly problematic in situations where, for example, witnesses must be met outside the situation area, necessitating them to travel to a third country.[62] Ultimately, it is clear that the most useful information to the defence will be the last information to be revealed. While this may be appropriate, it is also important to note how this affects defence investigations and, therefore, the time and facilities they have to prepare their case.

Moreover, the process of requiring the defence to review the same material multiple times will inevitably consume defence time and facilities. One example can be found in the *Kenyatta* case. It is worth quoting the defence counsel's submissions on this point, at some length:

---

[57] Ibid. See also Guénaël Mettraux et al, *Expert Initiative Report on Promoting Effectiveness at the International Criminal Court* (2014) 115.

[58] Ibid.

[59] Mettraux et al. (n 57) 115.

[60] Khan and Buisman (n 9) 1050.

[61] Ibid.

[62] Ibid.

I'm going to take the witnesses 11 and 12, key witnesses which remain in this case relied upon by the Prosecution. The Prosecution has served 79 transcripts of evidence in respect of these two witnesses together. Out of the 1,415 pages, 1,021 pages were re-served lesser redacted and I can inform your Honours that from my personal experience of reading, re-reading, analysing and then of course preparing to segment the information that is necessary to be investigated, that this is not only an arduous task, but the fact of the lesser redaction makes it a task that must be repeated so that the key allegations are found and investigated properly in readiness for trial [. . .] From the Defence perspective in terms of preparation for trial, the practical task of firstly counsel reviewing the material, and your Honour can imagine 79 transcripts takes time, each of which may be between ten to 25 pages, once that task has been done, in the process of movement towards trial, the Prosecution has served the same material again to some extent with lesser redactions. So as counsel I need to go back through the material to see where the lesser redactions are and to review them within the context of the evidence that I had initially seen [. . .] So your Honour can imagine the onerous nature of which that task is in respect of the Defence preparations and the Defence resources that need to be employed to make sure that that work is conducted properly.[63]

This process has been described as 'overburden[ing] the already thinly stretched defence teams',[64] and defence lawyers have noted the process of redactions as being 'unwieldy and unmanageable'.[65] Defence counsel have complained about this process and have suggested that the Court 'does not appreciate the distinction between confidential disclosure to Defence counsel, who are bound by a Code of Professional Conduct, and disclosure to the public'.[66] Defence counsel have also complained that, on receiving unredacted materials, it is unclear as to why the redactions were considered necessary in the first place.[67] Ultimately, the whole process of imposing and lifting redactions has been described as 'cumbersome, lengthy, and resource-intensive'.[68]

At the ICC in particular, there is also little in the way of consistency between Chambers: various Chambers have adopted different processes for authorising redactions, and to lifting redactions at a later time.[69] This has resulted in 'inconsistent practice between Chambers', and consequently, this makes it more difficult for parties to 'anticipate how redactions will be addressed in advance and thus to manage their materials and resources

---

[63] As quoted in Khan and Shah (n 12) 214–5.
[64] Jenia Iontcheva Turner, 'Defence Perspectives on Fairness and Efficiency at the International Criminal Court' in Kevin Heller et al. (eds), *The Oxford Handbook of International Criminal Law* (OUP, 2020) 39, 56.
[65] Khan and Shah (n 12) 208.
[66] Mettraux et al (n 57) 115.
[67] Ibid.
[68] Khan and Shah (n 12) 200.
[69] Mettraux et al (n 57) 114.

accordingly'.[70] In some ICC cases, Chambers have adopted 'Redaction Protocols', which appear to have had a positive effect on case efficiency.[71]

(1) Delayed disclosure at the ICTY: the timing of the disclosure

The ICTY has two particular provisions for delayed disclosure: the first, Rule 53, is directed towards protecting the identity of the witness from the public; the second, Rule 69, is directed towards protecting the identity of the witness from the accused. Pursuant to Rule 69, in 'exceptional circumstances', either party 'may apply to a Judge or Trial Chamber to order the non-disclosure of the identity of a victim or witness who may be in danger or at risk until such person is brought under the protection of the Tribunal'.[72] However, the identity of the victim or witness must be disclosed within a time 'as determined by the Trial Chamber to allow adequate time for preparation of the Prosecution or Defence'.[73] It has been made clear that circumstances that may be sufficient for non-disclosure under Rule 53 (as towards the public) may not be sufficient for non-disclosure to the accused: any dangers that the witness may face from the public 'would not normally be sufficient to show that the witness may also be in danger or at risk if that witness's identity is disclosed only to the accused and the defence team'.[74]

The 'exceptional circumstances' required for redacting disclosure are an 'extreme nature of danger and risk that a victim or witness may face should it become known that he or she will testify'.[75] The prosecution must demonstrate specific evidence of an identifiable risk to the security and welfare of the particular witness or their family. The criteria for determining whether 'exceptional circumstances' should be used are (a) the objective likelihood that the witness will be subjected to interference or intimidation as a result of disclosure to the accused; (b) specific rather than general basis for the risk, relating to a particular witness; and (c) the length of time before the trial where the identity must be disclosed – the greater the length of time, the greater the possibility for interference.[76] Broad allegations 'of danger-

---

[70] Ibid.

[71] Ibid.

[72] *ICTY Rules*, r 69 (A).

[73] *ICTY Rules*, r 69 (C).

[74] *Prosecutor v Brđanin, Decision on Second Motion by Prosecution for Protective Measures* (IT-99-36, 27 October 2000) 18. See also *Prosecutor v Karadžić, Decision on Protective Measures for Witnesses* (IT-95-5/18-PT, 30 October 2008).

[75] Kim (n 54) 61.

[76] *Prosecutor v Karadžić, Decision on Prosecution's Motion for Delayed Disclosure for KDZ456, KDZ493, KDZ531 and KDZ532, and Variation of Protective Measures for KDZ489* (IT-95-5/18-PT, 5 June 2009) [11].

ous conditions for victims and witnesses in general' will not be sufficient to justify non-disclosure.[77]

The current wording of the provision – that the identity of the witness is disclosed to the accused 'within such time as determined by the Trial Chamber' – is the product of a significant amendment to the ICTY *Rules*. Rule 69 originally read that disclosure of the identity of the victim or witness would occur 'prior to the commencement of trial', but there is now no such requirement that disclosure of the witness identity must occur before trial. The Rule was changed in 2012.[78] This followed the same change at the International Criminal Tribunal for Rwanda's equivalent rule, a decade earlier in 2002.

However, the amendment to Rule 69 in 2012 reflected the practice of the Tribunal rather than signalling a real change in practice. Despite the literal reading of the previous version of Rule 69, in fact, Trial Chambers had interpreted this to allow delayed disclosure after the commencement of trial. For example, in 2002, the *Milošević* Trial Chamber decided that disclosure of unredacted witness material should be provided to the 'accused and his appointed associates not less than ten days, and in the case of the *amici curiae* not less than 30 days, *before the witness is expected to testify*'.[79] This 'appears to be an unequivocal violation of the pre-2012 version' of the Rule.[80] Indeed, as the Chamber itself noted, the measures were 'extraordinary in nature' and 'go beyond the normal ambit of Rule 69'.[81] The Chamber noted that this Rule is 'made subject to Rule 75', which permits the Chamber to take measures for the protection of victims and witnesses, as long as they are consistent with the rights of the accused;[82] the Chamber, therefore, noted that they would only grant such the requested order where 'justification is established' and that this would involve an enquiry into whether the measures 'are consistent with the rights of the accused'.[83] Hence, the Trial Chamber used Rule 75 (and its relationship to Rule 69) as

---

[77] *Prosecutor v Haradinaj, Decision on Second Haradinaj Motion to Lift Redactions of Protected Witness Statements* (IT-04-84-PT, 22 November 2006) [2]. This is different from at the ICTR, where generalised factors such as the security situation in Rwanda have been held to be sufficient: see *Prosecutor v Simba, Decision on Defence Request for Protection of Witnesses* (ICTR-01-76-I, 25 August 2004) [6].

[78] ICTY *Rules of Procedure and Evidence*, Doc No IT/32/Rev.48 (adopted on 11 February 1994, amended 19 November 2012).

[79] *Prosecutor v Milošević, Second Decision on Prosecution Motion for Protective Measures for Sensitive Source Witnesses* (IT-02-54-T, 18 June 2002) [10]; see also *Prosecutor v Milošević, Decision on Prosecution Motion to Amend Witness List and for Protective Measures for Sensitive Source Witnesses* (IT-02-54-T, 13 March 2003).

[80] Kim (n 54) 69–70.

[81] *Prosecutor v Milošević, Second Decision on Prosecution Motion for Protective Measures for Sensitive Source Witnesses* (IT-02-54-T, 18 June 2002) [10].

[82] Ibid. [9]

[83] Ibid. [10], [11].

a gateway to extend the non-disclosure period into the trial.[84] In theory, this should protect the rights of the accused, given the explicit provision for this in Rule 75. However, in this decision, the Chamber did not engage in any sustained examination of the rights of the accused and how such delayed disclosure might affect these rights; they simply noted that 'such orders are consistent with the rights of the accused' without any justification for this conclusion. We see here, then, that the Chamber uses the language of the rights of the accused to justify a decision that deliberately modifies a rule and where the rights of the accused do appear to be adversely affected.

This practice of 'rolling disclosure' of unredacted witness materials throughout the trial has hence become commonplace at the ICTY, even prior to the 2012 change to the *Rules*, which made this explicitly possible. The approach has been confirmed by the Appeals Chamber: for example, the Appeals Chamber has ruled that Rule 69(C) did not need to be 'interpreted as authorising delayed disclosure prior to the commencement of the trial only', and that

> the purpose of Rule 69(C) is to allow a Trial Chamber to grant those protective measures that are necessary to protect the integrity of its victims and witnesses, subject to the caveat that such measures are consistent with the right of the accused to have adequate time for the preparation of his defence. There is no rule that the rights of the defence to have adequate time for the preparation mandate that delayed disclosure be granted only with reference to the beginning of the trial. The matter rather falls under the discretion of the Trial Chamber.[85]

As a result, it was held that disclosure of the identities of three witnesses thirty days prior to their testimony was not an abuse of the Trial Chamber's discretion.[86] In that case, the Prosecutor had relied on ICTY and ICTR jurisprudence that showed that 'delayed disclosure of between 21 and 30 days prior to the witnesses' giving of evidence is consistent with the right of the defence to have sufficient time for the preparation of its case'.[87] Here, the prosecution relies on ICTR jurisprudence from 2001, 2004 and 2005, although it is worth remembering that the ICTR had, by 2002, already changed the wording of its equivalent rule. Again, the Appeals Chamber did not engage in any sustained examination regarding how the delayed disclosure would, in fact, affect the rights of the accused, instead deferring to the Trial Chamber's discretion.[88] Nonetheless, in light of this sustained jurisprudence and affirmation by the Appeals Chamber, it is now 'settled'

---

[84] See also Kim (n 54).

[85] *Prosecutor v Šešelj, Decisions on Vojislav Šešelj's Appeal Against the Trial Chamber's Oral Decision of 7 November 2007* (IT-03-67-AR73.6, 24 January 2008) [15].

[86] Ibid. [16].

[87] Ibid. [13] and the references cited there.

[88] Ibid. [15].

and 'well-established' practice of the ICTY that delayed disclosure of witness identity is permissible even after the trial commences.[89]

(2) Delayed disclosure at the ICC: categories of protected persons

At the ICC, given the confirmation stage of proceedings, there is a slightly different procedural framework. At the pre-trial stage, in cases where the disclosure of evidence 'may lead to the grave endangerment of the security of a witness or his or her family', the prosecutor may withhold that evidence or information 'and instead submit a summary thereof'.[90] This is relevant to 'any proceedings conducted prior to the commencement of the trial'.[91] As a result, anonymous witness summaries are accepted during the pre-trial phase, but witness identity must be disclosed to the Defence ahead of the trial itself. At the Confirmation Hearing, any anonymous witness statements will be given a lower probative value than other evidence,[92] and in deciding how to weigh such evidence, the Chamber will consider (*inter alia*) the reliability of the source and the Defence's ability to challenge the source. These measures must 'be exercised in a manner which is not prejudicial to or inconsistent with the rights of the accused to a fair and impartial trial',[93] and Chambers should only justify non-disclosure on a case-by-case basis and use the least restrictive measures available.[94] This has been described as a 'proportionality test'.[95]

Ahead of the trial phase of the case, the prosecution can apply to the Pre-Trial or Trial Chamber to be exempted from their general duty to disclose materials, where disclosure would jeopardise the safety and security of the victims or witnesses, or members of their families.[96] Moreover, the prosecution has been permitted to redact any identifying information of 'innocent

---

[89] *Prosecutor v Karadžić, Decision on Accused's Sixty-Sixth Disclosure Violation Motion* (IT-95-5/18-T, 8 February 2012) [20].

[90] *Rome Statute* Art 68(5).

[91] Ibid.

[92] See *Prosecutor v Abu Garda, Pre-Trial Chamber: Decision on the Confirmation of Charges* (ICC-02/05-02/09, 8 February 2010) [52]; *Prosecutor v Bemba, Pre-Trial Chamber: Decision Pursuant to Article 61(7)(a) and (b) of the Rome Statute on the Charges of the Prosecutor against Jean-Pierre Bemba Gombo* (ICC-01/05-01/08, 15 June 2009) [50]-[51].

[93] *Rome Statute* Art 68(5).

[94] *Prosecutor v Lubanga, Judgment on the Prosecutor's appeal against the decision of Pre-Trial Chamber I entitled 'Decision Establishing General Principles Governing Applications to Restrict Disclosure pursuant to Rule 81 (2) and (4) of the Rules of Procedure and Evidence'* (ICC-01/04-01/06-568, 13 October 2006) [36]-[37].

[95] See *Prosecutor v Lubanga, Judgment on the Appeal of Mr. Thomas Lubanga Dyilo Against the Decision of Pre-Trial Chamber I Entitled 'First Decision on the Prosecution Requests and Amended Requests for Redactions under Rule 81'* (ICC-01/04-01/06, 14 December 2006) [34]; see also Khan and Shah (n 12) 207–8.

[96] ICC, *Rules of Procedure and Evidence*, Doc No ICC-ASP/1/3 (adopted 9 September 2002) ('ICC Rules'), r 81(2) and (4), see also r 76.

third parties', or those persons who 'may be placed at risk as a result of the activities of the Court, but "who are not victims, current or prospective prosecution witnesses or sources, or members of their families"'.[97]

This was established by the Appeals Chamber (by majority) in the *Katanga* case in 2008. They found that redactions of the details of these 'innocent third parties' was permissible under Rule 81(4), but 'whether such non-disclosure should be authorised on the facts of an individual case will require a careful assessment by the Pre-Trial Chamber on a case-by-case basis, balancing the various interests at stake'.[98] This should involve a 'careful assessment' to 'ensure that any measures restricting the rights of the Defence that are taken to protect individuals at risk are strictly necessary and sufficiently counterbalanced by the procedures taken by the Pre-Trial Chamber'.[99] In coming to this decision, the Appeals Chamber noted that while the 'overriding principle is that full disclosure should be made', and that non-disclosure is the exception to his general rule,[100] nonetheless this right is 'not absolute' and 'the withholding of disclosure of information from the Defence is permissible so as to preserve the fundamental rights of another individual and that not every incident of non-disclosure automatically results in an unfair trial'.[101] The Appeals Chamber was confident that 'in circumstances in which the redaction sought would involve withholding exculpatory information which was required to be disclosed, or would result in "a manifest inequality of arms, with little, if any prospect for fair proceedings" the Pre-Trial Chamber would, no doubt, reject the application'.[102] A Pre-Trial Chamber must consider 'the danger that the disclosure of the identity of the person may cause; the necessity of the protective measure, including whether it is the least intrusive measure necessary to protect the person concerned; and the fact that any protective measures taken shall not be prejudicial to or inconsistent with the rights of the accused and a fair and impartial trial'.[103] The Pre-Trial Chamber should also consider, among other factors, 'the relevance of the information' to the Defence and whether 'the interests of the person potentially placed at risk outweigh those of the Defence' or, on the other hand, ether 'the information may be

---

[97] *Prosecutor v Katanga, Judgment on the appeal of the Prosecutor against the decision of Pre-Trial Chamber I entitled 'First Decision on the Prosecution Request for Authorisation to Redact Witness Statements'* (ICC-01/04-01/07 (OA) 13 May 2008) ('*Katanga Appeal Decision on Redactions*') [40].

[98] Ibid. [66].

[99] Ibid. [60].

[100] Ibid. [71]. See also *Prosecutor v Gbagbo, Judgment on the appeal of Mr Laurent Gbagbo against the oral decision on redactions of 29 November 2016* (ICC-02/11-01/15-915-Red OA9, 31 July 2017) ('*Gbagbo Appeals Decision on Redactions*').

[101] *Katanga Appeal Decision on Redactions* [62].

[102] Ibid.

[103] Ibid. [67], see also [71] and [72] for further details.

of assistance to the . . . suspect or may affect the credibility of the case of the Prosecutor'.[104] These points all direct the Pre-Trial Chamber, in their assessment, to consider the rights of the accused and trial fairness.

Nonetheless, the broad point remains that this decision means a large amount of information can be redacted – and therefore, the rights of the accused are adversely affected. As Karim Khan and Caroline Buisman point out, the categories of redactable material are now significant 'and have allowed the prosecution to redact identifying information of a large number of individuals'.[105] Indeed, the Appeals Chamber itself noted that given the nature of the crimes over which the Court has jurisdiction, 'affecting large numbers of persons including whole communities, the unfortunate yet unavoidable reality is that any number of persons may be exposed to risk through the activities of the Court'.[106] What the Chamber did not then consider was that this would mean a huge number of redactions, which would clearly adversely affect the ability of the accused to conduct their investigations (and therefore affect their time and facilities to prepare a defence), as well as to know the case against them.

The reality is that such wide categories mean that 'identifying information of any individual who has ever spoken to the prosecution, a prosecution witness, or a potential witness may be withheld from the defence'.[107] As a result, 'much of the evidence disclosed is heavily redacted and, thus, unintelligible because a great deal of related material is also redacted to prevent the persons whose protection is sought from being identified through indirect channels'.[108] It is common that entire pages are blacked out,[109] making it 'practically impossible' to analyse the material, and greatly impacting on the ability of the defence to conduct their own investigations.[110] It has been described as 'a sweeping and resource-intensive redaction regime that is highly prejudicial to the ability of the defense to analyze prosecution disclosure and conduct investigations'.[111] Khan and Buisman argue that the approach to redactions should be undertaken 'with more circumspection' and that 'too much material is redacted . . . and too few justifications are given' for these redactions.[112] At the Confirmation stage, which permits the use of anonymous summaries, Khan and Shah argue that this 'allows the prosecutor to submit and rely on anonymous summaries of witness evidence that may be significantly lacking in substance, coherence,

---

[104] Ibid. [72].
[105] Khan and Buisman (n 9) 1049.
[106] *Katanga Appeal Decision on Redactions* [45].
[107] Khan and Buisman (n 9) 1049.
[108] Ibid.
[109] Ibid.
[110] Ibid.
[111] Khan and Shah (n 12) 206.
[112] Khan and Buisman (n 9) 1049.

or both'.[113] Ultimately, these widespread redactions can be seen as 'prejudicial to the fair-trial rights of the accused in view of the significant time and investigatory opportunities lost as a result of the delayed lifting of these redactions'.[114]

Further details were provided in the *Gbagbo* case, where the Appeals Chamber ruled that when assessing whether redactions are justified, the Trial Chamber should not place any burden on the defence, but rather give the defence an opportunity to make submissions – including, potentially, on the impact that non-disclosure would have on the fairness of the proceedings.[115] Trial Chambers should also keep in mind that the defence will be at a disadvantage regarding making their case, given the inability to access the withheld information.[116] Again, the Appeals Chamber reiterated that non-disclosure is an exception to the general rule that full disclosure should be made.[117]

This Appeals Chamber jurisprudence was relied upon by the defence in the case of *Ruto and Sang*, when the prosecution applied to have delayed disclosure of two witnesses, thirty days before their testimony.[118] The defence set out how such delayed disclosure would affect their time and facilities to prepare their defence. The Trial Chamber ultimately did not allow this delayed disclosure, instead delaying disclosure until adequate protective measures were put in place for the witness. In their view, this 'strikes an appropriate balance between the need to ensure full disclosure to the Defence as early as possible and the concomitant need to ensure the safety of this witness', and they added that 'any further decision of the Chamber with regard to continued non-disclosure will be taken with full regard to the Defence entitlement to sufficient time and facilities to prepare its case'.[119] This is promising practice from the Trial Chamber here.

Despite such promising practice, however, other cases show the challenges for the Defence of the way rules 81(2) and (4) have been interpreted and applied. In the *Banda and Jerbo* case, 'all identifying details of persons who were present inside the AU base in Darfur in the period immediately prior to the attack on the base, which constitutes the core charge against the suspects, were withheld from the Defence for more than two years after the main disclosure was served'.[120] Khan and Buisman have written that this information was 'highly relevant to the Defence', but that disclosure was

---

[113] Khan and Shah (n 12) 200.

[114] Ibid. 208.

[115] *Gbagbo Appeals Decision on Redactions* [61].

[116] Ibid.

[117] Ibid.

[118] *Prosecutor v Ruto, Confidential redacted version of 'Decision on first prosecution application for delayed disclosure of witness identities'* (ICC-01/09-01/11, 4 January 2013).

[119] Ibid. [48].

[120] Khan and Buisman (n 9) 1049. See also Khan and Shah (n 12) 207.

only provided to the Defence 'after several months' effort was expended by the Defence on securing the same'.[121] Khan and Buisman argue that this was 'clearly relevant information', and that the delayed disclosure of this 'seriously jeopardized the Defence's investigations, especially in light of the fact that the Defence had no opportunity to visit the situation country', which meant Defence opportunities to investigate were already very limited. In their view, this means that the redactions were 'highly prejudicial to the fair trial rights of the suspects who were deprived of an opportunity to speak to potentially relevant sources'.[122]

All of the above has led Karim Khan and Anand Shah to argue that there is a 'reflexive, if not cavalier, attitude toward redactions by the ICC prosecution' and that this, matched with a 'wide scope and imposition of redactions at the ICC—beyond merely witnesses and their families', has 'resulted in a bureaucratic, overbroad, and resource-draining redaction regime. At its worst, such a regime risks resulting in a fundamental miscarriage of justice, and otherwise greatly hinders the work of the defense'.[123] We can see from the above that at the ICC, redactions have been expanded through case law to be extremely broad, and that this has challenged the defence's ability to ensure the accused's rights, in particular to time and facilities to prepare a defence and to know the evidence against them. There are examples of where Trial Chambers have been reluctant to authorise delayed disclosure, which is promising; but nonetheless, Trial Chamber practice is unclear and inconsistent. At the ICTY, redactions were also expanded through case law – to allow rolling disclosure into trials. In both situations of judicial expansion of the redaction regime, limited attention was paid to the rights of the accused in judicial decision-making: while rhetorically such rights were provided with some acknowledgement, there was no significant examination of how they would, in fact, be affected. This is concerning, and again shows the separability of fairness, rights and procedure.

F. WRITTEN EVIDENCE IN PLACE OF ORAL TESTIMONY

As we have seen above in Chapter Five, the *Rules* at both the ICC and ICTY have moved away from a principle of orality to allowing greater amounts of witness testimony to be admitted in writing. Of relevance in cases of alleged witness intimidation, there have been particular changes to the rules to now allow for written evidence to be admitted in place of oral testimony (even where the testimony goes to the acts and conduct of the accused), in cases of apparent witness interference. At the ICTY,

---

[121] Ibid.
[122] Ibid.
[123] Khan and Shah (n 12) 212.

Rule 92 *quinquies* was inserted into the *Rules* in December 2009; at the ICC, Rule 68(2)(d) was inserted in 2013.

The insertion of Rule 92 *quinquies* in the ICTY's *Rules* was a direct result of the situation in the *Haradinaj* and *Šešelj* cases, and came after a Working Group on Contempt Proceedings.[124] The Working Group, Rules Committee and the Judges 'all worked together in order to adopt' the Rule.[125] It was described by the President of the Tribunal as a 'procedural innovation' that would 'enable core proceedings to go forward even where there are attempts to interfere with the administration of justice.'[126] The provision – entitled 'Admission of Statements and Transcripts of Persons Subjected to Interference'– provides for a Trial Chamber to admit evidence from a witness in written form, either through a written witness statement or through a transcript of prior proceedings before the Tribunal. Unlike other rules that permit evidence to be admitted in writing (such as Rule 92 *bis*), the witness will not face cross-examination. Crucially, evidence admitted under Rule 92 *quinquies* may involve material that directly relates to 'the acts and conduct of the accused'.[127]

In order to be admitted, the material must satisfy various requirements. The Trial Chamber must be satisfied that the person has failed to attend as a witness 'or, having attended, has not given evidence at all or in a material respect'.[128] This quite extensive possibility appears to be a reaction to the proceedings in the *Haradinaj* case, where one witness did testify in the initial trial but whose testimony was felt by the prosecution to be incomplete.[129] Further, the Trial Chamber must be satisfied that this 'failure to attend or give evidence' was 'materially influenced by improper interference' such as threats or intimidation, that reasonable efforts have been made to secure the witness's attendance or to secure all material facts known to them, and that 'the interests of justice' are best served by admitting this evidence.[130]

Paragraph B of the provision outlines 'the interests of justice' in more detail, and notes that this includes an enquiry into the reliability of the statement or transcript, the apparent role of a party to the proceedings

---

[124] 'Report of the ICTY', UN Docs A/65/205 – S/2010/413 (30 July 2010) [23]. See also Megan Fairlie who notes that the 'rule was adopted at a time when the *Šešelj* trial had been delayed for nearly a year due to allegations of witness intimidation' (Megan Fairlie, 'The Abiding Problem of Witness Statements in International Criminal Trials' (2017) 50 *ILP* 75, 142).

[125] Statement by Judge Patrick Robinson, President of ICTY, to the Security Council on 18 June 2010 (18 June 2010) 3.

[126] Ibid.

[127] ICTY *Rules*, r 92 *quinquies* (B)(iii).

[128] ICTY *Rules*, r 92 *quinquies* (A)(i).

[129] See also Gideon Boas et al.(eds), *International Criminal Law Practitioner Library: Volume III, International Criminal Procedure* (CUP, 2011) 354 – suggesting that the rule was 'motivated by the difficulties in securing witnesses in the *Šešelj* and *Haradinaj* cases'; and Megan Fairlie (n 124) 142–3. See also *Prosecutor v Limaj*, Judgement (IT-03-66, 30 November 2005) [13].

[130] ICTY *Rules*, r 92 *quinquies* (A)(ii)–(iv).

(or someone acting on their behalf) in the 'improper interference', and whether the statement 'goes to proof of the acts and conduct of the accused as charged in the indictment'. This rule does not stipulate what may be required or examined with regard to the 'reliability' of the statement. Further, it does not indicate whether the statement or transcript must be signed (and witnessed) by the witness.

Even though the Rule was created in large part in response to the *Haradinaj* case, when a retrial was ordered in that case, the prosecution did not seek to rely on the Rule. In fact, there has only been one case where the prosecution sought to rely on 92 *quinquies* to admit a witness statement. In a decision in the *Karadžić* case, the Trial Chamber ruled that 92 *quinquies* cannot be applied retroactively in cases that were pending at the time the rule was adopted in December 2009, and thus, the prosecutor could not admit evidence in this case under Rule 92 *quinquies*.[131] Nonetheless, the Trial Chamber did provide some limited guidance on the use of the rule, stating that, in order for evidence to be admissible under Rule 92 *quinquies*, a witness's reluctance to testify must be genuine, and the extent of that fear must justify admitting the evidence without cross-examination, and that the interference 'must be improper, such as through intimidation or bribery'.[132] Given the lack of new cases at the MICT, it is unlikely any further use of Rule 92 *quinquies* will occur.

A similar Rule was inserted into the ICC framework in 2013, with the amendment to Rule 68 to include the new Rule 68(2)(d).[133] This provides that prior recorded testimony of a witness can be introduced to the Trial Chamber, even in the absence of the witness before the Trial Chamber, in cases where 'The prior recorded testimony comes from a person who has been subjected to interference.'[134] In such a case, the prior recorded testimony can only be introduced where

> the person has failed to attend as a witness or, having attended, has failed to give evidence with respect to a material aspect included in his or her prior recorded testimony; the failure of the person to attend or to give evidence has been materially influenced by improper interference, including threats, intimidation, or coercion; reasonable efforts have been made to secure the attendance of the person as a witness or, if in attendance, to secure from the witness all material facts known

---

[131] *Prosecutor v Karadžić, Decision on the Prosecution Motion to Admit the Prior Evidence of Milan Tupajic pursuant to Rule 92 quinquies* (IT-95-5/18-T 7 May 2012) [15].

[132] Ibid. [17].

[133] For more on Rule 68 generally, see Simon de Smet, 'All Roads Lead to Rome – Lifting the Veil on the ICC's Procedural Pluriformity' in Pavel Šturma (ed), *The Rome Statute of the ICC at Its Twentieth Anniversary: Achievements and Perspectives* (Brill Nijhoff, 2019); Hirad Abtahi and Shehzad Charania, 'Expediting the ICC Criminal Process: Striking the Right Balance between the ICC and States Parties' (2018) 18 *ICLR* 383.

[134] *ICC Rules*, r 68(2)(d).

to the witness; the interests of justice are best served by the prior recorded testimony being introduced; and the prior recorded testimony has sufficient indicia of reliability.[135]

Improper interference is defined as possibly relating to 'the physical, psychological, economic or other interests of the person'.[136] In cases where prior recorded testimony relates to 'completed proceedings for offences defined in article 70' – that is, cases of offences against the administration of justice on the basis of witness intimidation – the Court may consider adjudicated facts arising from those proceedings.[137] The Rule stipulates that if the prior recorded testimony 'goes to acts and conduct of an accused', this '*may* be a factor against its introduction, or part of it.'[138] This is unlike the ICTY's provision in 92 *quinquies*, and Fairlie has described this as a 'seemingly more rights-protective' provision.[139]

The application of this Rule was at issue in the *Ruto* case – the only case, to date, where this sub-rule has been examined (and indeed used, before being overturned by the Appeals Chamber). In that case, the prosecution sought the admission, through Rule 68(2)(d), of the prior statements of five witnesses. All were related to recanting witnesses. The prosecution also sought to tender an additional 210 attached items, of about 1,669 pages, 'as additional evidence of witness tampering'. This was in addition to twenty-one materials that had already been admitted to the trial previously, which had been admitted by the Trial Chamber 'upon the urging of the Prosecution to allow evidence of witness tampering to be exhibited in the course of the trial, in order to give the Chamber "a picture" of the extent of witness interference that would explain [witness] recantations'.[140]

The Trial Chamber admitted the prior statements of four witnesses under this rule, and rejected the fifth request on the basis that there was insufficient evidence of witness interference.[141] On Appeal, the evidence was excluded on the basis that this would have been a retrospective application of Rule 68(2)(d).[142] Thus, although it was eventually overturned, the

---

[135] *ICC Rules*, r 68(2)(d)(i).

[136] *ICC Rules*, r 68(2)(d)(ii).

[137] *ICC Rules*, r 68(2)(d)(iii).

[138] *ICC Rules*, r 68(2)(d)(iv), emphasis added.

[139] Fairlie (n 124) 145.

[140] *Prosecutor v Ruto, Decision on Prosecution Request for Admission of Prior Recorded Testimony* (19 August, 2015) ('*Ruto Decision on Prior Testimony*'), Separate, Partly Concurring Opinion of Judge Eboe-Osuji [6].

[141] *Ruto Decision on Prior Testimony*.

[142] *Prosecutor v Ruto, Judgment on the Appeals of Mr William Samoei Ruto and Joshua Arap Sang Against the Decision of Trial Chamber V(A) of 19 August 2015 entitled 'Decision on Prosecution Request for Admission of Prior Recorded Testimony'* (ICC-01/09-01/11-OA, 12 February 2016) ('*Ruto Appeal Decision*'). For more on this litigation, see Abtahi and Charania (n 133); Fairlie (n 124).

original decision nonetheless 'retains its value as potential (non-binding) precedent for future applications of the rule'.[143] Moreover, the question of retrospectivity of this Rule raises interesting and important points regarding how Trial and Appeals Chambers conceive of the rights of the accused, detriment and fairness, in considerations about the admission of evidence where there has been a question of witness interference.

The Trial Chamber decided that the Rule could be applied retrospectively, because they did not consider the amended Rule would be applied 'to the detriment' of the accused (as is proscribed under article 51(4) of the Rome Statute). In making this decision, the Chamber stated that the application of the amended Rule 68 could not be considered detrimental to the accused 'simply because it allows the Prosecution to request the admission of incriminatory evidence against the accused'.[144] Further, the Chamber held that because the Rule can be used by any party to a proceeding, it 'is a rule of neutral application' and 'is not inherently detrimental to the accused'.[145] In reaching that position, the Chamber did not consider the principle of orality and its general benefits, the rights of the accused (particularly to examine witnesses against them), or the principle of equality of arms (which, as we have seen previously, can have both formal and material aspects). While it would not be expected that a Chamber would find that the Rule itself was detrimental through examining fairness, rights and equality of arms, it may well have found that these factors were important when considering detriment and any retrospective application of the Rule. The simplistic reasoning of the Chamber in this regard leaves much to be desired.

Megan Fairlie also makes the point that while the Trial Chamber used ICTY jurisprudence 'to support its conclusion that the rule's reliability requirement can be met by a particularly modest showing', they also 'ignored an important point [of ICTY jurisprudence] in conjunction with this low reliability threshold: that there is a need for "cautious scrutiny" before admitting the statement of an unavailable witness that directly implicates the accused'.[146] Thus, the *Ruto* decision 'cites neither corroboration nor any other alternative guarantee of reliability in support of its decision to admit the statements', even though all of the four admitted statements in this decision addressed the acts and conduct of the accused.[147] Advancing this point further, it is thoroughly surprising that the rights of the implications on the rights of the accused – particularly the right to confrontation – are provided such short shrift in a situation where the relevance goes to the acts and conduct of the accused. Here, the 'interests of justice' test, for

---

143 Fairlie (n 124) 151.
144 Ruto Decision on Prior Testimony [24].
145 Ibid. [25].
146 Fairlie (n 124) 152.
147 Ibid.

the Chamber, was framed mainly in terms of the witnesses rather than any real examination of the position of the accused.

Indeed, the Appeals Chamber took a different approach, and ultimately overturned the Trial Chamber on this point. The Appeals Chamber found that applying the amended rule resulted in 'additional exceptions to the principle of orality and restrictions on the right to cross-examine witnesses'.[148] As a result, the admission of these statements under the amended Rule – which would not have been admissible under the previous formulation of the Rule – could be used against the accused in a judgement of conviction. Thus, the Appeals Chamber found that the application of the Rule 'negatively affected the overall position' of the accused, and the Trial Chamber had inappropriately applied the Rule 'to the detriment of the accused'.[149] This decision – which properly considered the rights of the accused in determining detriment – is far preferable to the Trial Chamber approach.

The above points relate significantly to the question of the retrospective application of the Rule, and therefore may be of limited assistance in future applications of the Rule. While the Court has not yet been called on again to make a decision in a case of alleged witness interference for the admission of statements under Rule 68(2)(d), there have been other cases where the Court has been asked to admit evidence going to the acts or conduct of an accused in situations where the witness has died or is otherwise unavailable, under Rule 68(2)(c).[150] In these cases, the Chamber has admitted the documents. Again, there has been little examination in these decisions of either fairness or the rights of the accused, and how these may be affected by statements that go to their acts or conduct, and for which there is no opportunity for cross-examination. Moreover, as Fairlie points out, under Rule 68(2)(c), evidence can be admitted even in cases where the alleged interference is not connected to the accused.[151] She argues, correctly, that it is 'unjust to saddle an accused with a trial that is less fair because of the conduct of others', particularly because the rationale for doing this is because of institutional weaknesses at the ICC.[152] The International Bar Association has noted that in *Ruto and Sang*, the Trial Chamber interpreted the rules 'in a broad and flexible manner' which, while 'consistent with the flexible approach to evidence allowed under the ICC framework', nonetheless has concerns,

---

[148] *Ruto Appeal Decision* [95].

[149] Ibid.

[150] *Prosecutor v Ntaganda, Decision on Prosecution Application Under Rule 68(2)(c) of the Rules for Admission of Prior Recorded Testimony of P-0022, P-0041 and P-0103* (ICC-01/04-02/06-1029, 20 November 2015); *Prosecutor v Bemba, Public Redacted Decision on 'Prosecution Submission of Evidence Pursuant to Rule 68(2)(c) of the Rules of Procedure and Evidence'* (ICC-01/05-01/13-1481-Red, 12 November 2015).

[151] Fairlie (n 124) 146.

[152] Ibid. 146–7.

particularly 'in relation to the fairness of trials'.[153] As a result, the IBA urges 'a cautious approach to the introduction of prior recorded testimony where it relates to unavailable and interfered-with witnesses',[154] and this should only occur 'in the most exceptional circumstances'.[155]

The approach so far of the ICC Trial Chamber is concerning, given the lack of consideration provided to the rights of the accused and the apparent balancing of the 'interests of justice' to the protection of witnesses (to the detriment of the rights of the accused). Here, again, we see the rights of the accused not adequately considered in a case where the fairness of the trial is clearly at issue. Thus, there is an obvious separation between fairness, rights and procedure in this approach.

G. CONCLUSIONS

The issue of witness protection and its correct relationship to trial fairness and the rights of the accused is perhaps the most thorny of procedural questions. Unlike other procedural issues, the lives and safety of witnesses are at issue here, which places this question as uniquely important. It is fundamentally wrong for witnesses to be placed in any unsafe situation because of their engagement with international criminal legal processes. International criminal procedure and international criminal trials must be able to keep these witnesses safe. The issue of witness protection is also particularly important given its clear links to the very existence of international criminal trials, which cannot proceed without witness evidence – and yet equally, should not be able to proceed to a verdict due to exculpatory evidence not being provided.

Moreover, unlike other procedural issues, it is clear from the wording of the statutes and rules that it is permissible for the rights of the accused to be adversely affected – in the name of trial fairness – in order to protect witness security. Nonetheless, the exact balance between trial fairness and the rights of the accused is still challenging. In cases at both the ICTY and ICC, we have seen an expansion of procedural mechanisms to protect witness security, with adverse implications for the rights of the accused – but frequently, Trial Chambers do not provide any real analysis of the relationships between trial fairness, rights and witness protection. This is obvious when we examine how the law in relation to redactions has been expanded in judicial decisions without any analysis by the Trial Chambers of the accused's rights. Changes to the rules to permit greater untested written evidence also show how little consideration is provided to the accused's rights even in situations where 'trial fairness' is invoked. Again, then, we see the

[153] International Bar Association, 'Evidence Matters in ICC Trials' (2016) 48–9.
[154] Ibid. 49.
[155] Ibid.

separability of fairness, rights and procedural decision-making. While in this case, diminution of the accused's rights may be warranted, it should still be carefully considered – yet these examples show that too often, it is not.

Conclusions
Closing the space between fairness and rights, and reimaging the future of international criminal law

In contemporary international criminal trials, the most fundamental guiding principles – those of fairness and rights – are divorced both from each other, and from procedural decisions. Indeed, I have shown how fairness has been rhetorically invoked to justify decisions that, nonetheless, have the effect of undermining the rights of the accused. Given the centrality of fairness and rights to international criminal law, this is a profound challenge for the system of law, its institutions and its processes. In these Conclusions, I want to tackle the question of what this tells us about international criminal law and its structural limitations and conditions of possibility. As I set out in the Introduction, this book has aimed to assist in the construction of a critical approach to procedural questions: to examine procedure in the context of international criminal law's biases and its economic, political, and social conditions and limitations.[1] In these Conclusions, I make the ultimate normative argument of this book: that there should be a renewed closeness between fairness and rights in the context of procedural decision-making in these trials. However, I want to also reiterate that even this claim is uncomfortable, given the possibilities and impossibilities of international criminal law.

A. THEMES AND FINDINGS OF THIS BOOK – THE SPACE BETWEEN THE PHOTOCOPIER AND THE ACQUITTAL

This book has interrogated the space where fairness, rights and procedure meet – or fail to do so. I have described this as 'the space between the photocopier and the acquittal'. The photocopier mentioned in the Introduction represents the problems that arise when fairness, rights and procedure are divergent. The acquittal demonstrates the possibility of what can happen when fairness, rights and procedure are integrated. I have demonstrated that fairness, rights and procedure currently fail to align at two levels: at the conceptual level (as demonstrated in Chapters One, Two and Three) and at the level of procedural decision-making (in Chapters Four, Five and Six). Yet, of course, it is not anticipated or hoped that any renewed association between fairness and rights will lead to an increase in acquittals – which,

[1] Mikael Baaz, 'Review Essay: Dissident Voices in International Criminal Law' (2015) 28 *LJIL* 673, 688.

as I have said, are not always (or even often) the appropriate conclusion in international criminal trials. However, it is hoped that this renewed close association between fairness, rights and procedure will have benefits for these trials in realising their proper aim: a forensic determination of the accused's guilt or innocence.[2]

This book has laid out some of the complexity of international criminal law: the uncertainty around what it aims to achieve; how its central and guiding ideas are nonetheless fundamentally contested and incoherent; and how this means that, at a practical level, its trial processes are also unpredictable. The uncertainty around international criminal law at the theoretical level – what it aims to do, and how it will achieve this, as examined in Chapters One, Two and Three – is replicated at the practical level of procedural decisions (as set out in Chapters Four, Five and Six).

Fairness and rights are central to international criminal trials and are a point of convergence between multiple stakeholders. Fairness and rights should also be closely aligned, at least in principle, in the context of procedural decision-making. Trial Chambers have a statutory responsibility to 'ensure that a trial is fair and expeditious and conducted with full respect for the rights of the accused and due regard for the protection of victims and witnesses' – a responsibility which explicitly links fairness and rights.[3] Chapters One and Two have set out these connections between fairness and rights.

Yet, as we have seen throughout this book, fairness and rights are separable, and indeed separated, in international criminal procedural decision-making. Appreciating fairness and rights as separate entities allows an examination of their differences, and how they interact. Fairness is the overarching requirement of the trial, rights particularise this and give the general requirement of fairness greater specificity, and procedural rules operationalise and ensure these rights. In other words, the rights of the accused are correctly seen to be a constitutive part of fairness. However, the lack of certainty about what else is required (beyond the rights of the accused) to ensure trial fairness is a key reason for the conceptual incoherence of fairness, as shown in Chapter Three. Other reasons for the incoherence of fairness include a conflict over who should be the main beneficiary of fairness in trials and a lack of certainty around how to ensure fairness in a *sui generis* procedural system. These areas expose the disagreement about how fairness and rights interact, and demonstrate the separability of fairness and rights.

---

[2] See Chapter One.

[3] SC Res 827, UN SCOR, 48th sess, 3217th mtg, UN Doc S/RES/827 (25 May 1993), as amended by SC Res 1877, UN SCOR, 64th sess, 6155th mtg, UN Doc S/RES/1877 (7 July 2009) Art 20 ('ICTY Statute'); *Rome Statute of the International Criminal Court*, opened for signature 17 July 1998, 2187 UNTS 90 (entered into force 1 July 2002) Art 64(2) ('*Rome Statute*').

Thus, the separation of fairness and rights emerges from, and adds to, the incoherence of fairness.

Indeed, this separability has led to fairness being invoked in ways that can challenge and even undermine the rights of the accused. The ascendancy of the shared process-centred approach to fairness has seen the interests of the prosecution, victims and even states protected, to the point of directly challenging the rights of the accused. This undermining of the accused's rights has been perpetrated under the guise of protecting trial fairness. We see this especially in the procedural case studies in Chapters Four, Five and Six.

If fairness and rights are separable and separated, the questions arise: *should* fairness and rights be closely connected? And if so, *why* should they be closely aligned? After all, it appears there are many who would argue that trial fairness and the rights of the accused should not be closely linked: the ascendancy of the shared-process approach to fairness (outlined in Chapter Three) is a testament to this. Perhaps if fairness and rights are separable, the ascendancy of a shared-process approach to fairness – where the rights of the accused are not necessarily seen as the primary consideration – is not a surprise nor, for some, a concern. However, while I have shown that there is a divide between fairness and rights in procedural matters, I now call for a renewed intimacy between them. Fairness and rights should be closely connected in international criminal trials, particularly when considering procedural matters.

The call for a greater alignment of fairness and rights has been building throughout this book. The book started, in Chapter One, with the argument that the accused should rightly be at the heart of the trial process. The discourse around the aims of international criminal law needs to be clarified in respect of the aims of the system of law, its institutions and its processes. These are better understood as three separate levels of analysis – capable of supporting different aims or of supporting the same aims in different ways. Thus, while the general system of international criminal law and the specific institution of the court or tribunal may have other aims, the aim of the trial itself must be to forensically determine the guilt or innocence of the accused. If we accept that the correct aim of international criminal trials is the determination of the accused's culpability, this aim becomes the core organising value for a trial's processes. It becomes a standard against which we must assess the success or otherwise of international criminal law, and it helps us to address the question of international criminal law's 'identity'.[4] Any conflicts between this aim and other aims (for example, the aims of the *system* of international criminal law, such as ending impunity or giving victims a meaningful voice) can be resolved by affording priority to the determination

---

[4] Carsten Stahn, 'Between "Faith" and "Facts": By What Standards Should We Assess International Criminal Justice?' (2012) 25 *LJIL* 251.

of the accused's culpability as the aim of the trial. This priority then guides procedural decision-making.

Identifying the forensic determination of the accused's culpability as the correct aim of international criminal trials has implications for the rights of the accused: they are integral to these trials. The rights of the accused take on an added resonance in a system of law that is animated by concerns of ending impunity and providing meaningful victim participation. Rights act as protector and equaliser for an accused whose culpability is the central concern of the trial process.[5] If rights are integral to a trial's aim, properly conceived, then fairness and rights should not be able to be traded off against each other. Yet as this book shows, it is possible to 'balance away' the accused's rights by invoking fairness in international criminal law. In the name of fairness, rights are undermined.

In Chapter Three, I argued that while fairness is considered central in international criminal law, there is little in the way of a shared understanding of fairness. I set out a taxonomy of the various perspectives of, and challenges to, fairness; and I demonstrated that there is a conceptual incoherence surrounding the concept of fairness. This incoherence makes the concept of fairness vulnerable – in particular, to being invoked in ways that may be contrary to what constitutes fairness (namely, the rights of the accused). The malleability of the concept of fairness, and the lack of shared understandings of fairness, leaves fairness without a strong foundation. This means that fairness can be invoked in argument by all trial participants and can be used as a rationale for any decision. Fairness operates as a normative ideal but does not have any real content or agreed meaning.

The incoherence of fairness at the conceptual level aligns with fairness being poorly invoked at the level of procedural decision-making in international criminal trials. Chapters Four, Five and Six show the incoherence of fairness in its application in matters of disclosure, the use of adjudicated facts, and the protection of witnesses. These chapters exposed the difficulties encountered in situations where fairness and rights are not considered to be intimately connected in procedural decision-making. In all these case studies, there is an identified gap between what Chambers say they are doing (protecting the trial's fairness) and what they are, in fact, doing (challenging the rights of the accused).

These case studies have also demonstrated just how difficult the practice of international criminal law is for all concerned. The judges face an unenviable task in ensuring 'that a trial is fair . . . and conducted with full respect for the rights of the accused'.[6] Defence lawyers, prosecution and victims' representatives are all challenged by the scale of these cases, their particular context (arising from mass atrocity and leaving victims and

---

[5] See Chapter Two.
[6] *ICTY Statute* Art 20; *Rome Statute* Art 64(2).

witnesses especially vulnerable), their resource constraints, and their multitude of supposed objectives. These structural features of international criminal law place real pressures on all parties and participants in the trial process. The emphasis of this book on the rights of the accused and the place of the defence is not a suggestion that the judges, prosecution, or victims have a comparatively easy experience. They are also challenged by these trials. Moreover, there may be no perfect way to resolve the issues exposed in the case studies. I have not attempted to 'solve' these issues and remain aware that they may be somewhat intractable – at least, for as long as criminal law is seen as the appropriate response to mass violence.

But a coherent appreciation of fairness is desirable – even required. Without a coherent understanding of fairness, fairness is unable to fulfil its promise of being a binding quality between otherwise divided communities of international criminal justice stakeholders, and any ability of fairness to set the standards for trials is compromised.[7] We must, therefore, pursue a coherent appreciation of fairness. The appropriate place to start is the only foundation fairness really enjoys – a close relationship with the rights of the accused. Although this is under challenge, it is time to renew the intimacy between fairness and rights, to move towards a conceptually coherent understanding of fairness. Without a strong understanding of how fairness and rights interlink, what each is, whom they are owed to, and how the rights of one party impact the fairness owed to another party, it is too easy to undermine fairness, rights, or both fairness and rights. Binding fairness and rights together will assist in a shared, and strong, understanding of fairness.

B. LOOKING TO THE FUTURE

This book has examined international criminal law and procedure at a particular point in time (2008–18) by analysing contemporary cases and procedural decision-making. What does this contemporary study suggest for future directions of the international criminal justice project? In particular, what might be the nature of a closer connection between fairness and rights in international criminal trials? There are several implications for how we might imagine international criminal trials if fairness and rights could be more closely aligned.

First, if we accept that the aim of the trial should be the determination of the individual's guilt or otherwise, and if we accept that fairness should be closely aligned with the rights of the accused, then these become the central organising principles of the trials. The forensic determination of an accused's culpability in a trial where rights are closely aligned to fairness would become the guiding value around which procedural decisions should

---

[7] See Chapter Two.

be made. In cases where the rights of the accused might conflict with the interests of victims or the prosecution, the rights of the accused would be given priority. An example would be ensuring victims are obliged to disclose potentially exculpatory material under their possession or control – either to the accused or at a minimum to the prosecution, who then would be obliged to disclose the material to the accused. This approach would ensure greater clarity about the organising values of international criminal trials and how such organising values are operationalised in the trial's processes.

Second, if we understand fairness and rights as being closely aligned, the conceptual incoherence of fairness would be ameliorated. There would, for example, be greater clarity around what fairness would look like for prosecutors and victims in these trials. The relationships between the trial participants and parties would be clearer and more easily managed by Trial Chambers. The expectations of prosecutors to a 'right to fairness' would be constrained, and it would be understood that prosecutors could not invoke a 'right to fairness' in a situation where the accused's rights would be adversely affected. Similarly, the role of victim participants would be further clarified. If victim participation was implemented in a way that defers to the determination of the accused's culpability in a way consistent with the accused's rights, this might also constrain some of the expectations around victim participation. Clarifying how 'fairness' to victims is limited in light of the rights of the accused may, in fact, ameliorate some of the challenges I have examined regarding how victims are treated in the process of these trials.[8]

Finally, an understanding of fairness as closely linked to the rights of the accused may ensure that, in procedural decision-making, fairness cannot be invoked in a way that undermines the rights of the accused. For example, in the *Stanišić* case,[9] the admission of adjudicated facts, and their subsequent rejection, could not be undertaken in a way that undermined the rights of the accused – particularly as it was rationalised on the basis of 'trial fairness'. In this case, the Trial Chamber should have acted more swiftly in its procedural decision-making, and should have rendered a decision as soon as it had any concerns about the rights of the accused being challenged by the use of adjudicated facts. Judges would also be encouraged to outline their decision-making regarding fairness and rights in greater detail and with more clarity. Throughout this book, we have witnessed numerous examples where 'fairness' has been invoked to justify decisions, but where there has been no sustained examination of the rights of the accused (and indeed, such rights were then adversely affected). This has been seen especially clearly in Chapter Six, where many of the decisions examined – even if justifiable on the basis of the need to protect witnesses – did not account for

---

[8] See Chapter One.
[9] See Chapter Five.

the rights of the accused and how these would be affected by the decisions. This is unacceptable and should be rectified.

There are numerous other benefits to rights being given greater emphasis. As this book has explained, rights do not exist in order to unfairly advantage the accused but to protect the accused from unjustified punishment, to protect the international rule of law, and to ensure the legitimacy of the system of law. Similarly, fairness will assist the Trial Chambers in both their procedural decision-making, and their decision on the ultimate question before them: the accused's culpability. Fairness will also act to legitimate the trial process and to assist the trial, institution and legal system to meet their aims.[10]

Nonetheless, I have not offered a proscriptive list for what can be done to improve international criminal law, or suggestions for judges, or policy solutions, or proposed amendments to the rules. That has not been my objective in this book. Instead, I hope that this book has been useful in showing some of the issues facing international criminal law, and posing the question of how international criminal law can best respond. Some readers may be uncomfortable by this, and ask the reasonable question, 'what now?' One potential response to such a question is my normative call for fairness and rights to be more closely aligned, and the possible implications of that realignment. But we can also interrogate this further.

C. REIMAGINATION?

How does this normative call fit within international criminal law's structural possibilities and impossibilities? One major structural feature of international criminal law, as I have set out, is its overarching aim as a system of law towards 'ending impunity' and convictions. This necessitates the normative call I have made for fairness and rights to be more strongly aligned. If rights are integral to trials that seek to determine the culpability of an accused, rights should not be able to be minimised in the name of trial fairness. This is particularly true in a system of law that values an end to impunity. Rather, fairness and rights should be interlocking. While some may call for fairness guarantees to be 'relaxed'[11] so that the system of international criminal justice can achieve its aim – namely, convictions – we must avoid this. Such a call may result in rights being minimised or traded away in a search for a conviction dressed up as 'fairness'.

Nonetheless, any attempt to 'improve' international criminal law is somewhat uncomfortable. To achieve a truly transformative moment,

---

[10] See Chapter Two.
[11] Mirjan Damaška, 'The Competing Visions of Fairness: The Basic Choice for International Criminal Tribunals' (2001) 36 *NCJILCR* 365; Mirjan Damaška, 'Reflections on Fairness in International Criminal Justice' (2012) 10 *JICJ* 611, 616.

those who think about international criminal law (scholars, advocates and students) should be focused on ending atrocities and the conditions that give rise to them– rather than simply on ending impunity or on strengthening criminal processes. Finalising this book in 2020, I am particularly aware of the current uprising we are witnessing in the police and prison abolition movements in domestic jurisdictions: the conversations, organising, and scholarship that has occurred particularly since the 1970s has gained new ground, as more people come to understand the structural causes of deviance and the links between capitalism, race, imperialism and criminal 'justice'. International criminal law, too, has deep connections to global capitalism, race and racism, and imperialism – and these connections tend to structure who and what is criminalised.[12] In holding individuals responsible for often collective violence, international criminal law also exonerates those political, economic and legal structures that create the conditions of criminality.[13] International criminal law's focus on particular types of core crimes disregards other types of harm.[14] International criminal law's jurisdictional limitations mean that certain states and people are often concentrated on, and others escape examination. International criminal law's hefty expenses could, surely, be redistributed into debt relief and addressing global inequalities. As a system of law, and in individual trials, international criminal law has shown itself to be too blunt an instrument to use to address a complicated world, and a complicated human nature that is capable of both good and evil; where individuals can be both victim and perpetrator, both responsible and constrained. In total, criminalisation has not proved itself capable of addressing the causes of mass violence, and indeed it appears structurally unable to do so.

International criminal law and procedure – both in scholarship and practice – has moved through several phases in a short space of time (at least if we accept the generally 'accepted history', of a 'moment' at Nuremburg, followed by relative lack of action and then a rapid acceleration in the

---

[12] See, e.g., Antony Anghie and B.S. Chimni, 'Third World Approaches to International Law and Individual Responsibility' (2003) 2 *CJIL* 77; John Reynolds and Sujith Xavier, '"The Dark Corners of the World": TWAIL and International Criminal Justice' (2016) 14 *JICJ* 959; Michelle Burgis-Kasthala, 'Scholarship as Dialogue? TWAIL and the Politics of Methodology' (2016) 14 *JICJ* 921; Randle C DeFalco and Frédéric Mégret, 'The Invisibility of Race at the ICC: Lessons from the US Criminal Justice System' (2019) 7(1) *LRIL* 55; Sophie Rigney, 'Distant Justice: The Impact of the International Criminal Court on African Politics (Book Review)' (2020) 31 *EJIL* 1157.

[13] Martti Koskenniemi, 'Between Impunity and Show Trials' (2002) 6 *Max Planck Yearbook of United Nations Law* 1; see also Tor Krever, 'International Criminal Law: An Ideology Critique' (2013) 26 *LJIL* 701; Immi Tallgren, 'Sensibility and Sense of International Criminal Law' (2002) 13 *EJIL* 561.

[14] Christine Schwöbel-Patel, 'The Core Crimes of International Criminal Law' in Kevin Heller et al. (eds), *The Oxford Handbook of International Criminal Law* (OUP, 2020); Burgis-Kasthala (n 12); Reynolds and Xavier (n 12).

1990s).[15] Much scholarship initially focused on bolstering the position of international criminal law, particularly given the concerns around ongoing atrocities and impunity and the perceived vulnerability of the entire legal system. The critical turn in the scholarship has started to question whether international criminal law is an unqualified good or whether its status is rather more complicated. Recent contributions have pointed out those connections to larger political and economic forces.[16] But largely, the scholarship – even the critical scholarship – has not yet taken this further to consider any form of abolition of international criminal law or 'what else might be possible'. This is entirely understandable: many scholars still believe in the promise and potential of the project and are wary of undermining or undoing the hard work that drove the (still very recent) gains. Nobody wishes to return to a system of impunity for mass violence. Nonetheless, it is possible to consider what else we could strive for, rather than advocating yet greater criminalisation and recourse to criminal law.

These are not easy questions. However, a dedication to structural justice demands that we think carefully about how to create the future and whether we want to invest more time and creative energy into a system of criminal law that has vast impossibilities. It is challenging to both advocate – as I do here – for improvements to the system of international criminal law and yet also carefully consider whether the system is even necessary or beneficial. There is some cognitive dissonance in this. But discussions of fairness and rights do prompt us to think about other possibilities for all the current stakeholders in international criminal law. This book has, I hope, shown that the current situation is not satisfactory, and alternatives – both large and small – need to be considered. It is increasingly incumbent on us to consider such possibilities. Just as abolition discussions at the domestic level focus on what else is possible – community-building, properly funded education, robust healthcare, rehabilitation – international criminal law needs to consider more deeply what a world could look like without any need for international criminal law. What is the utopia we are striving for? It is, surely, a future world without the need for international criminal trials at all. How do we get there? How do we build that future?

---

[15] Sarah Nouwen, 'Justifying Justice' in James Crawford and Martti Koskenniemi (eds), *The Cambridge Companion to International Law* (CUP, 2012) 327, 340. But see Kevin Heller and Gerry Simpson (eds), *The Hidden Histories of War Crimes Trials* (OUP, 2013); Emily Haslam, *The Slave Trade, Abolition, and the Long History of International Criminal Law: The Recaptive and the Victim* (Routledge, 2020).

[16] See particularly Krever (n 13); Kamari Maxine Clarke, 'We ask for justice, you give us law: The rule of law, economic markets, and the reconfiguration of victimhood', in Christian De Vos, Sara Kendall and Carsten Stahn (eds), *Contested Justice: The Politics and Practice of International Criminal Court Interventions* (CUP, 2015) 272; Burgis-Kasthala (n 12); Reynolds and Xavier (n 12).

Bibliography

BOOKS

Abtahi, Hirad and Gideon Boas (eds), *The Dynamics of International Criminal Justice* (Koninklijke Brill, 2006)

Arendt, Hannah, *Eichmann in Jerusalem: A Report of the Banality of Evil* (Penguin, 1963)

Besson, Samantha and John Tasioulas (eds), *Philosophy of International Law* (Oxford University Press, 2010)

Boas, Gideon et al (eds), *International Criminal Law Practitioner Library: Volume III, International Criminal Procedure* (Cambridge University Press, 2011)

Boas, Gideon, *The Milošević Trial: Lessons for the Conduct of Complex International Criminal Proceedings* (Cambridge University Press, 2007)

Cassese, Antonio (ed), *The Oxford Companion to International Criminal Justice* (Oxford University Press, 2009)

Cassese, Antonio, *International Criminal Law* (Oxford University Press, 2003)

Charlesworth, Hilary and Christine Chinkin, *The Boundaries of International Law: A Feminist Analysis* (Manchester University Press, 2000)

Clark, Janine Natalya, *International Trials and Reconciliation: Assessing the Impact of the International Criminal Tribunal for the Former Yugoslavia* (Routledge, 2014)

Clark, Phil, *Distant Justice: The Impact of the International Criminal Court on African Politics* (Cambridge University Press, 2018)

Clarke, Kamari Maxine, *Fictions of Justice: The International Criminal Court and the Challenge of Legal Pluralism in Sub-Saharan Africa* (Cambridge University Press, 2010)

Combs, Nancy, *Fact Finding Without Facts: The Uncertain Evidentiary Foundations of International Criminal Convictions* (Cambridge University Press, 2010)

Crawford, James and Martti Koskenniemi (eds), *The Cambridge Companion to International Law* (Cambridge University Press, 2012)

De Vos, Christian Sara Kendall and Carsten Stahn (eds), *Contested Justice: The Politics and Practice of International Criminal Court Interventions* (Cambridge University Press, 2015)

Douglas, Lawrence, *The Memory of Judgment: Making Law and History in the Trials of the Holocaust* (Yale University Press, 2000)

Drumbl, Mark, *Atrocity, Punishment and International Law* (Cambridge University Press, 2007)

Drumbl, Mark, *Reimagining Child Soldiers in International Law and Policy* (Oxford University Press, 2012)

Fedorova, Masha, *The Principle of Equality of Arms in International Criminal Proceedings* (Intersentia, 2012)

Fiori, Brando, *International Criminal Procedural Systems and Human Rights Law* (Wolf Legal, 2015)

Franck, Thomas, *Fairness in International Law and Institutions* (Oxford University Press, 1998)

Goss, Ryan, *Criminal Fair Trial Rights: Article 6 of the European Convention on Human Rights* (Oxford University Press, 2014)

Grey, Rosemary, *Prosecuting Sexual and Gender-Based Crimes at the International Criminal Court: Practice, Progress and Potential* (Cambridge University Press, 2019)

Hafetz, Jonathan, *Punishing Atrocities Through a Fair Trial* (Cambridge University Press, 2018)

Haslam, Emily, *The Slave Trade, Abolition, and the Long History of International Criminal Law: The Recaptive and the Victim* (Routledge, 2020)

Heinze, Alexander, *International Criminal Procedure and Disclosure* (Dunker & Humblodt, 2014)

Heller, Kevin et al (eds), *The Oxford Handbook of International Criminal Law* (Oxford University Press, 2020)

Heller, Kevin and Gerry Simpson (eds), *The Hidden Histories of War Crimes Trials* (OUP, 2013)

Henham, Ralph and Mark Findlay (eds), *Exploring the Boundaries of International Criminal Justice* (Ashgate, 2011)

International Military Tribunal, *The Trial of the Major War Criminals Before the International Military Tribunal* (International Military Tribunal, 1947) vol. 2

Jackson, John and Sarah Summers (eds), *Obstacles to Fairness in Criminal Proceedings: Individual Rights and Institutional Forms* (Hart, 2018)

Jackson, John, Máximo Langer and Peter Tillers (eds), *Crime, Procedure and Evidence in a Comparative and International Context: Essays in Honour of Professor Mirjan Damaška* (Hart Publishing, 2008)

Khan, Karim A. A., Caroline Buisman, and Christopher Gosnell (eds), *Principles of Evidence in International Criminal Justice* (Oxford University Press, 2010)

Klamberg, Mark, *Evidence in International Criminal Trials: Confronting Legal Gaps and the Reconstruction of Disputed Events* (Martinus Nijhoff, 2013)

Koskenniemi, Martti, *From Apology to Utopia: The Structure of International Legal Argument* (Cambridge University Press, 2005)

Leanza, Piero and Ondrej Pridal, *The Right to a Fair Trial: Article 6 of the European Convention on Human Rights* (Kluwer Law International, 2014)

McCormack, Timothy and Gerry Simpson (eds), *The Law of War Crimes: National and International Approaches* (Kluwer Law International, 1997)

McDermott, Yvonne, *Fairness in International Criminal Trials* (Oxford University Press, 2016)

Minow, Martha, *Between Vengeance and Forgiveness: Facing History after Genocide and Mass Violence* (Beacon Press, 1998)

Moffet, Luke, *Justice for Victims Before the International Criminal Court* (Routledge, 2014)

Ngana, Sylvia Ntube, *The Position of Witnesses Before the International Criminal Court* (Brill Nijhoff, 2015)

Nichols, Lionel, *The International Criminal Court and The End of Impunity in Kenya* (Springer, 2015)

Powderly, Joseph and Shane Darcy (eds), *Judicial Creativity at the International Criminal Tribunals* (Oxford University Press, 2010)

Ryngaert, Cedric (ed), *The Effectiveness of International Criminal Justice* (Intersentia, 2009)

Safferling, Christoph, *International Criminal Procedure* (Oxford University Press, 2012)

Safferling, Christoph, *Towards an International Criminal Procedure* (Oxford University Press, 2001)

Sarvarian, Arman Filippo Fontanelli, Rudy Baker and Vassilis Tzevelekos, *Procedural Fairness in International Courts and Tribunals* (British Institute of International and Comparative Law, 2015)

Schabas, William A, Yvonne McDermott and Niamh Hayes (eds), *The Ashgate Research Companion to International Criminal Law* (Ashgate, 2013)

Schwöbel, Christine (ed), *Critical Approaches to International Criminal Law* (Routledge, 2014)

Schwöbel-Patel, Christine, *Marketing Global Justice: The Political Economy of International Criminal Law* (Cambridge University Press, 2021)

Simpson, Gerry, *Law, War, and Crime* (Polity Press, 2007)

Sluiter, Göran and Sergey Vasiliev (eds), *International Criminal Procedure: Towards a Coherent Body of Law* (Cameron May, 2009)

Sluiter, Göran et al (eds), *International Criminal Procedure: Principles and Rules* (Oxford University Press, 2013)

Stahn, Carsten (ed), *The Law and Practice of the International Criminal Court: A Critical Account of Challenges and Achievements* (Oxford University Press, 2015)

Stahn, Carsten, *A Critical Introduction to International Criminal Justice* (Cambridge University Press, 2018)

Swart, Bert, Alexander Zahar and Göran Sluiter (eds), *The Legacy of the International Criminal Tribunal for the Former Yugoslavia* (Oxford University Press, 2011)

Thakur, Ramesh and Peter Malcontent (eds), *From Sovereign Impunity to International Accountability: The Search for Justice in a World of States* (United Nations University Press, 2004)

Van Sliedregt, Elies and Sergey Vasiliev (eds), *Pluralism in International Criminal Law* (Oxford University Press, 2014)

Vriend, Koen, *Avoiding a Full Criminal Trial: Fair Trial Rights, Diversions and Shortcuts in Dutch and International Criminal Proceedings* (Springer, 2016)

Wheeler, Caleb H, *The Right to be Present at Trial in International Criminal Law* (Brill, 2018)

Widdar, Elmar, *A Fair Trial at the International Criminal Court? Human Rights Standards and Legitimacy* (Peter Lang 2016)

Wilson, Richard Ashby, *Writing History in International Criminal Trials* (Cambridge University Press, 2011)

Zappalà, Salvatore, *Human Rights in International Criminal Proceedings* (Oxford University Press, 2003)

Zyberi, Gentian and Colleen Rohan (eds), *Defense Perspectives on International Criminal Justice* (Cambridge University Press, 2018)

ARTICLES AND CHAPTERS IN EDITED VOLUMES

Abtahi, Hirad and Shehzad Charania, 'Expediting the ICC Criminal Process: Striking the Right Balance between the ICC and States Parties' (2018) 18 *International Criminal Law Review* 383

Acquaviva, Guido and Mikaela Heikkilä, 'Protective and Special Measures for Witnesses' in Göran Sluiter et al (eds), *International Criminal Procedure: Principles and Rules* (Oxford University Press, 2013)

Affolder, Natasha, '*Tadić*, the Anonymous Witness and the Sources of International Procedural Law' (1997) 19 *Michigan Journal of International Law* 445

Ahronovitz, Michelle, 'Guilty Until Proven Innocent: International Prosecutorial Failure to Disclose Exculpatory Evidence' (2017) 48 *University of the Pacific Law Review* 343

Akhaven, Payam, 'The Rise, and Fall, and Rise, of International Criminal Justice' (2013) 11 *Journal of International Criminal Justice*, 527

Ambos, Kai, 'Fairness and Expediency in International Criminal Procedure', in John Jackson and Sarah Summers, *Obstacles to Fairness in Criminal Proceedings: Individual Rights and Institutional Forms* (Hart, 2018) 179

Anghie, Antony and B. S. Chimni, 'Third World Approaches to International Law and Individual Responsibility' (2003) 2 *Chinese Journal of International Law* 77

Anoushirvani, Sara, 'The Future of the International Criminal Court: The Long Road to Legitimacy Begins with the Trial of Thomas Lubanga Dyilo' (2010) 22 *Pace International Law Review* 213

Baaz, Mikael and Mona Lilja, 'Using International Criminal Law to Resist Transitional Justice: Legal Rupture in the Extraordinary Chambers in the Courts of Cambodia' (2016) 2 *Conflict and Society* 142

Baaz, Mikael, 'Review Essay: Dissident Voices in International Criminal Law' (2015) 28 *Leiden Journal of International Law* 673

Beqiri, Romina, 'Reflections on Certain Witness Protection Measures Under the Rome Statute of the International Criminal Court' (2017) 13 *European Scientific Journal* 342

Bonomy, Iain, 'The Reality of Conducting a War Crimes Trial' (2007) 5 *Journal of International Criminal Justice* 348

Bourgon, Stéphane, 'Procedural Problems Hindering Expeditious and Fair Justice' (2004) 2 *Journal of International Criminal Justice* 526

Brouwer, Anne-Marie de, 'The Problem of Witness Interference before International Criminal Tribunals' (2015) 15 *International Criminal Law Review* 700

Buisman, Caroline and David Hooper, 'Defence Investigations and the Collection of Evidence' in Gentian Zyberi and Colleen Rohan (eds), *Defense Perspectives on International Criminal Justice* (Cambridge University Press, 2018) 519

Büngener, Lars, 'Disclosure of Evidence' in Christoph Safferling (ed), *International Criminal Procedure* (Oxford University Press, 2012) 374

Burgis-Kasthala, Michelle, 'Scholarship as Dialogue? TWAIL and the Politics of Methodology' (2016) 14 *Journal of International Criminal Justice* 921

Caianiello, Michele, 'Disclosure before the ICC: The Emergence of a New Form of Policies Implementation System in International Criminal Justice?' (2010) 10 *International Criminal Law Review* 23

Carayon, Gaelle and Jonathan O'Donohue, 'The International Criminal Court's Strategies in Relation to Victims' (2017) 15 *Journal of International Criminal Justice* 567

Charlesworth, Hilary, 'International Law: A Discipline of Crisis' (2002) 65 *Modern Law Review* 377

Chenivesse, Pascal and Christopher Piranio, 'What Price Justice? On the Evolving Notion of "Right to a Fair Trial" from Nuremberg to The Hague' (2011) 24 *Cambridge Review of International Affairs* 403

Chinkin, Christine, 'Due Process and Witness Anonymity' (1997) 91 *American Journal of International Law* 75

Clarke, Kamari Maxine, 'Refiguring the Perpetrator: Culpability, History and International Criminal Law's Impunity Gap' (2015) 19 *International Journal of Human Rights* 592

Clarke, Kamari Maxine, 'We ask for justice, you give us law: The rule of law, economic markets, and the reconfiguration of victimhood' in Christian De Vos, Sara Kendall and Carsten Stahn (eds), *Contested Justice: The Politics and Practice of International Criminal Court Interventions* (Cambridge University Press, 2015) 272

Clarke, Kamari, 'The Rule of Law Through its Economies of Appearances: The Making of the African Warlord' (2011) 18 *Indiana Journal of Global Legal Studies* 7

Combs, Nancy, 'Deconstructing the Epistemic Challenges to Mass Atrocity Prosecutions' (2018) 75 *Washington and Lee Law Review* 223

Crawford, James, 'The ILC Adopts a Statute for an International Criminal Court' (1995) 89 *American Journal of International Law* 404

Cronin-Furman, Kate and Amanda Taub, 'Lions and Tigers and Deterrence, Oh My: Evaluating Expectations of International Criminal Justice' in William A Schabas, Yvonne McDermott and Niamh Hayes (eds), *The Ashgate Research Companion to International Criminal Law* (Ashgate, 2013) 435

Cronin-Furman, Kate, 'Managing Expectations: International Criminal Trials and the Prospects for Deterrence of Mass Atrocity' (2013) 7(3) *International Journal of Transitional Justice* 434

Croquet, Nicholas, 'Implied External Limitations on the Right to Cross-Examine Prosecution Witnesses: The Tension Between a Means Test and a Balancing Test in the Appraisal of Anonymity Requests' (2010) 11 *Melbourne Journal of International Law* 27

Cryer, Robert, 'Witness Tampering and International Criminal Tribunals' (2014) 27 *Leiden Journal of International Law* 191

Damaška, Mirjan 'Negotiated Justice in International Criminal Courts' (2004) 2 *Journal of International Criminal Justice* 1018

Damaška, Mirjan, 'Problematic Features of International Criminal Procedure' in Antonio Cassese (ed), *The Oxford Companion to International Criminal Justice* (Oxford University Press, 2009) 175

Damaška, Mirjan, 'Reflections on Fairness in International Criminal Justice' (2012) 10 *Journal of International Criminal Justice* 611

Damaška, Mirjan, 'The Competing Visions of Fairness: The Basic Choice for International Criminal Tribunals' (2001) 36 *North Carolina Journal of International Law and Commercial Regulation* 365

Damaška, Mirjan, 'The International Criminal Court Between Aspiration and Achievement' (2009) 14 *UCLA Journal of International Law & Foreign Affairs* 19

Damaška, Mirjan, 'The Uncertain Fate of Evidentiary Transplants: Anglo-American and Continental Experiments' (1997) 45 *American Journal of Comparative Law* 839

Damaška, Mirjan, 'What is the Point of International Criminal Justice?' (2008) 83 *Chicago-Kent Law Review* 329

De Vos, Christian M, '*Prosecutor v Lubanga*: "Someone Who Comes between One Person and Another": *Lubanga*, Local Cooperation and the Right to a Fair Trial' (2011) 12 *Melbourne Journal of International Law* 217

DeFalco, Randle C and Frédéric Mégret, 'The Invisibility of Race at the ICC: Lessons from the US Criminal Justice System' (2019) 7(1) *London Review of International Law* 55

Dieckmann, Jens and Marie O'Leary, 'The Role of Defense Counsel in Pre-Trial' in Gentian Zyberi and Colleen Rohan (eds), *Defense Perspectives on International Criminal Justice* (Cambridge University Press, 2018) 237

Drumbl, Mark, 'Collective Violence and Individual Punishment: The Criminality of Mass Atrocity' (2005) 99 *Northwestern University Law Review* 593

Drumbl, Mark, 'Pluralising International Criminal Justice' (2005) 103 *Michigan Law Review* 101

Drumbl, Mark, 'The Curious Criminality of Mass Atrocity' in Elies van Sliedregt and Sergey Vasiliev (eds), *Pluralism in International Criminal Law* (Oxford University Press, 2014) 68

Drumbl, Mark, 'Victims who Victimise' (2016) 4(2) *London Review of International Law* 217

Eikel, Markus, 'Witness Protection Measures at the International Criminal Court: Legal Framework and Emerging Practice' (2012) 23 *Criminal Law Forum* 97

Ellis, Mark S, 'Achieving Justice before the International War Crimes Tribunal' (2000) 7 *Duke Journal of Comparative and International Criminal Law* 519

Engle, Karen, 'Anti-Impunity and the Turn to Criminal Law in Human Rights Law and Advocacy' (2015) 100 *Cornell Law Review* 1070

Eser, Albin, 'Procedural Structure and Features of International Criminal Justice: Lessons from the ICTY' in Bert Swart, Alexander Zahar and Göran Sluiter (eds), *The Legacy of the International Criminal Tribunal for the Former Yugoslavia* (Oxford University Press, 2011) 108

Fairlie, Megan A, 'Due Process Erosion: The Diminution of Live Testimony at the ICTY' (2003) 34 *California Western International Law Journal* 47

Fairlie, Megan, 'The Abiding Problem of Witness Statements in International Criminal Trials' (2017) 50 *International Law and Politics* 75

Fedorova, Masha, 'The Principle of Equality of Arms in International Criminal Proceedings' in Gentian Zyberi and Colleen Rohan (eds), *Defense Perspectives on International Criminal Justice* (Cambridge University Press, 2018) 204

Fedorova, Masha, Sten Verhoeven and Jan Wouters, 'Safeguarding the Rights of Suspects and Accused Persons in International Criminal Proceedings' in Cedric Ryngaert (ed), *The Effectiveness of International Criminal Justice* (Intersentia, 2009) 55

Fletcher, Laurel, 'Refracted Justice: The Imagined Victim and the International Criminal Court' in Christian De Vos, Sara Kendall and Carsten Stahn (eds), *Contested Justice: The Politics and Practice of International Criminal Court Interventions* (Cambridge University Press, 2015) 302

Gaynor, Fergal, 'Uneasy Partners — Evidence, Truth and History in International Trials' (2012) 10 *Journal of International Criminal Justice* 1257

Gibson, Kate and Cainnech Lussiaà-Berdou, 'Disclosure of Evidence' in Karim Khan, Caroline Buisman and Christopher Gosnell (eds), *Principles of Evidence in International Criminal Justice* (Oxford University Press, 2010) 306

Grover, Leena, 'A Call to Arms: Fundamental Dilemmas Confronting the Interpretation of Crimes in the Rome Statute of the International Criminal Court' (2010) 21(3) *European Journal of International Law* 543

Guilfoyle, Douglas, 'Lacking Conviction: Is the International Criminal Court Broken?' 20(2) *Melbourne Journal of International Law* (2019) 401

Gut, Till, Stefan Kirsch, Daryl Mundis and Melinda Taylor, 'Defence Issues', in Göran Sluiter et al (eds), *International Criminal Procedure: Rules and Principles* (Oxford University Press, 2013) 1202

Guy-Smith, Gregor, 'Developing a Case Theory and a Defence Strategy', in Gentian Zyberi and Colleen Rohan (eds), *Defense Perspectives on International Criminal Justice* (Cambridge University Press, 2018) 385

Harmon, Mark and Fergal Gaynor, 'Prosecuting Massive Crimes with Primitive Tools: Three Difficulties Encountered by Prosecutors in International Criminal Proceedings' (2004) 2(2) *Journal of International Criminal Justice* 403

Harmon, Mark B, 'The Pre-Trial Process at the ICTY as a Means of Ensuring Expeditious Trials: A Potential Unrealised' (2007) 5 *Journal of International Criminal Justice* 377

Haslam, Emily and Rod Edmunds, 'Whose Number is it Anyway? Common Legal Representation, Consultations, and the 'Statistical Victim'' (2017) 15 *Journal of International Criminal Justice* 931

Heinze, Alexander, 'Bridge over Troubled Water – a Semantic Approach to Purposes and Goals in International Criminal Justice' (2018) 18 *International Criminal Law Review* 929

Heller, Kevin Jon, '"A Stick to Hit the Accused With": The Legal Recharacterization of Facts under Regulation 55' in Carsten Stahn (ed), *The Law and Practice of the*

International Criminal Court: A Critical Account of Challenges and Achievements (Oxford University Press, 2015) 981

Heller, Kevin Jon, 'The Shadow Side of Complementarity: The Effect of Article 17 of the *Rome Statute* on National Due Process' (2006) *Criminal Law Forum* 255

Heller, Kevin, 'Radical Complementarity' (2016) 14(3) *Journal of International Criminal Justice* 637

Jackson, John, 'Finding the Best Epistemic Fit for International Criminal Tribunals: Beyond the Adversarial-Inquisitorial Dichotomy' (2009) 7 *Journal International Criminal Justice* 17

Jackson, John, 'The Effect of Human Rights on Criminal Evidentiary Process: Towards Convergence, Divergence or Realignment?' (2005) 68 *Modern Law Review* 737

Jackson, John, 'Transnational Faces of Justice: Two Attempts to Build Common Standards Beyond National Boundaries' in John Jackson, Máximo Langer and Peter Tillers (eds), *Crime, Procedure and Evidence In A Comparative And International Context: Essays In Honour of Professor Mirjan Damaška* (Hart Publishing, 2008) 221

Jacobs, Dov, 'Neither here nor there: the position of the defence in International Criminal Trials', in Kevin Heller et al (eds), *The Oxford Handbook of International Criminal Law* (Oxford University Press, 2020) 67

Jacobs, Dov, 'Sitting on the Wall, Looking in: Some Reflections on the Critique of International Criminal Law' (2015) 28 *Leiden Journal of International Law* 1

Jalloh, Charles Chernor and Amy DiBella, 'Equality of Arms in International Criminal Law: Continuing Challenges' in William A Schabas, Yvonne McDermott and Niamh Hayes (eds), *The Ashgate Research Companion to International Criminal Law* (Ashgate, 2013) 251

Johnson, Scott T, 'On the Road to Disaster: The Rights of the Accused and the International Criminal Tribunal for the Former Yugoslavia' (1998) 10 *International Legal Perspective* 111

Jørgensen, Nina, 'Judicial Notice', in Karim Khan, Caroline Buisman, Christopher Gosnell (eds) *Principles of Evidence in International Criminal Justice* (Oxford University Press, 2010) 695

Katzman, Rachel, 'The Non-Disclosure of Confidential Exculpatory Evidence and the *Lubanga* Proceedings: How the ICC Defence System Affects the Accused's Right to a Fair Trial' (2009) 8 *Northwestern Journal of International Human Rights* 77

Kay, Stephen, 'The Move from Oral to Written Evidence' (2004) 2 *Journal of International Criminal Justice* 495

Keïta, Xavier-Jean, 'Disclosure of Evidence in the Law and Practice of the ICC' (2016) 16 *International Criminal Law Review* 1018

Kendall, Sara and Sarah Nouwen, 'Representational Practices at the International Criminal Court: The Gap Between Juridified and Abstract Victimhood' (2013) 76 *Law and Contemporary Problems* 235

Kendall, Sara, 'Commodifying Global Justice: Economics of Accountability at the International Criminal Court' (2015) 13 *Journal of International Criminal Justice* 113

Kendall, Sara, 'Critical Orientations: A Critique of International Criminal Court

Practice' in Christine Schwöbel (ed), *Critical Approaches to International Criminal Law* (Routledge, 2014) 59

Khan, Karim A. A. and Anand A. Shah, 'Defensive Practices: Representing Clients Before the International Criminal Court' (2013) 76 *Law and Contemporary Problems* 191

Khan, Karim and Caroline Buisman, 'Sitting on Evidence? Systemic Failings in the ICC Disclosure Regime – Time for Reform' in Carsten Stahn (ed) *The Law and Practice of the International Criminal Court* (Oxford University Press, 2015) 1029

Killean, Rachel and Luke Moffett, 'Victim Legal Representation before the ICC and the ECCC' (2017) 15(4) *Journal of International Criminal Justice* 713

Kim, Sangkul, 'The Witness Protection Mechanism of Delayed Disclosure at the Ad Hoc International Criminal Tribunals' (2016) *Journal of East Asia and International Law* 55

Klamberg, Mark, 'Epistemological Controversies and Evaluation of Evidence in International Criminal Trials', in Kevin Heller et al. (eds), *The Oxford Handbook of International Criminal Law* (Oxford University Press, 2020) 450

Klamberg, Mark, 'What Are the Objectives of International Criminal Procedure? Reflections on the Fragmentation of a Legal Regime' (2010) 79 *Nordic Journal of International Law* 279

Koskenniemi, Martti, 'Between Impunity and Show Trials' (2002) 6 *Max Planck Yearbook of United Nations Law* 1

Kress, Claus, 'The Procedural Law of the International Criminal Court in Outline: Anatomy of a Unique Compromise' (2003) 1 *Journal of International Criminal Justice* 603

Krever, Tor, 'International Criminal Law: An Ideology Critique' (2013) 26 *Leiden Journal of International Law* 701

Kurth, Michael, 'Anonymous Witnesses before the International Criminal Court: Due Process in Dire Straits' in Carsten Stahn and Goran Sluiter (eds), *The Emerging Practice of the International Criminal Court* (Brill Nijhoff, 2009) 615

Kuschnik, Bernhard, 'International Criminal Due Process in the Making: New Tendencies in the Proceedings Before the ICC' (2009) 9 *International Criminal Law Review* 157

Kwon, O-Gon, 'The Challenge of an International Criminal Trial as Seen from the Bench' (2007) 5 *Journal of International Criminal Justice* 360

Langer, Máximo, 'The Rise of Managerial Judging in International Criminal Law' (2005) 53 *American Journal of Comparative Law* 835

Leigh, Monroe, 'Witness Anonymity is Inconsistent with Due Process' (1997) 91 *American Journal of International Law* 80

Leyh, Brianne McGonigle, 'Pragmatism over Principles: The International Criminal Court and a Human Rights-Based Approach to Judicial Interpretation' (2018) 41 *Fordham International Law Journal* 697

Luban, David, 'Fairness to Rightness: Jurisdiction, Legality, and the Legitimacy of International Criminal Law' in Samantha Besson and John Tasioulas (eds), *Philosophy of International Law* (Oxford University Press, 2010) 569

Mariniello, Triestino and Paolo Lobba, 'The Cross-Fertilisation Rhetoric in

Question: Use and Abuse of the European Court's Jurisprudence by International Criminal Tribunals' (2015) 84 *Nordic Journal of International Law* 363

Marx, Jared Paul, 'Intimidation of Defence Witnesses at the International Criminal Tribunals: Commentary and Suggested Legal Remedies' (2007) 7 *Chicago Journal of International Law* 675

Majzub, Diba 'Peace or Justice?: Amnesties and the International Criminal Court' (2002) 3(2) *Melbourne Journal of International Law* 247

McAuliffe, Pádraig and Christine Schwöbel-Patel, 'Disciplinary Matchmaking: Critics of International Criminal Law Meet Critics of Liberal Peacebuilding' (2018) 16(5) *Journal of International Criminal Justice* 985

McDermott, Yvonne, 'International Criminal Procedure and the False Promise of an Ideal Model of Fairness' in John Jackson and Sarah Summers, *Obstacles to Fairness in Criminal Proceedings: Individual Rights and Institutional Forms* (Hart, 2018) 191

McDermott, Yvonne, 'Rights in Reverse: A Critical Analysis of Fair Trial Rights under International Criminal Law' in William A Schabas, Yvonne McDermott and Niamh Hayes (eds), *The Ashgate Research Companion to International Criminal Law* (Ashgate, 2013) 165

McDermott, Yvonne, 'Strengthening the Evaluation of Evidence in International Criminal Trials' (2017) 17 *International Criminal Law Review* 682

McDermott, Yvonne, 'The Admissibility and Weight of Written Witness Testimony in International Criminal Law: A Socio-Legal Analysis' (2013) 26 *Leiden Journal of International Law* 971

McIntyre, Gabrielle, 'Equality of Arms — Defining Human Rights in the Jurisprudence of the International Criminal Tribunal for the Former Yugoslavia' (2003) 16 *Leiden Journal of International Law* 269

Mégret, Frédéric 'The Legacy of the ICTY as Seen through Some of Its Actors and Observers' (2011) 3 *Goettingen Journal of International Law* 1011

Mégret, Frédéric and Marika Giles Samson, 'Holding the Line on Complementarity in Libya: The Case for Tolerating Flawed Domestic Trials' (2013) 11 *Journal of International Criminal Justice* 571

Mégret, Frédéric, 'Beyond "Fairness": Understanding the Determinants of International Criminal Procedure' (2009) 14 *UCLA Journal of International Law and Foreign Affairs* 37

Mégret, Frédéric, 'The Anxieties of International Criminal Justice' (2016) 29(1) *Leiden Journal of International Law* 197

Mégret, Frédéric, 'The Strange Case of the Victim Who Did Not Want Justice' (2018) 12 *International Journal of Transitional Justice* 444

Mégret, Frédéric, 'What Sort of Global Justice is "International Criminal Justice"?' (2015) 13(1) *Journal of International Criminal Justice* 77

Meron, Theodor, 'Procedural Evolution in the ICTY' (2004) 2 *Journal of International Criminal Justice* 520

Mistry, Hemi, 'The Significance of Institutional Culture in Enhancing the Validity of International Criminal Tribunals' (2017) 17(4) *International Criminal Law Review* 703

Moffett, Luke and Clara Sandoval, 'Tilting at windmills: Reparations and the International Criminal Court' (2021) *Leiden Journal of International Law* 1

Moffett, Luke, 'Reparations for victims at the International Criminal Court: a new way forward?' (2017) 21(9) *International Journal of Human Rights* 1204

Morrissey, Peter, 'Applied Rights in International Criminal Law: Defence Counsel and the Right to Disclosure' in Gideon Boas, William A Schabas and Michael P Scharf (eds), *International Criminal Justice: Legitimacy and Coherence* (Edward Elgar, 2012) 68

Negri, Stefania, 'The Principle of "Equality of Arms" and the Evolving Law of International Criminal Procedure' (2005) 5 *International Criminal Law Review* 513

Nice, Geoffrey and Philippe Vallières-Roland, 'Procedural Innovations in War Crimes Trials' (2005) 3 *Journal of International Criminal Justice* 354

Nicholson, Joanna, '"Too High", "Too Low", or "Just Fair Enough"? Finding Legitimacy Through the Accused's Right to a Fair Trial' (2019) 17(2) *Journal of International Criminal Justice* 351

Nouwen, Sarah and Wouter Werner, 'Monopolising Global Justice: International Criminal Law as Challenge to Human Diversity' (2015) 13 *Journal of International Criminal Justice* 157

Nouwen, Sarah, 'Justifying Justice' in James Crawford and Martti Koskenniemi (eds), *The Cambridge Companion to International Law* (Cambridge University Press, 2012) 327

O'Sullivan, Eugene and Deidre Montgomery, 'The Erosion of the Right to Confrontation under the Cloak of Fairness at the ICTY' (2010) 8 *Journal of International Criminal Justice* 511

Ohlin, Jens David, 'A Meta-Theory of International Criminal Procedure: Vindicating the Rule of Law' (2009) 14 *Journal of International and Foreign Affairs* 77

Orford, Anne, 'International Law and the Populist Moment: A Comment on Martti Koskenniemi's Enchanted by the Tools? International Law and Enlightenment' (2020) 35 *American University International Law Review* 427

Pena, Mariana and Gaelle Carayon, 'Is the ICC Making the Most of Victim Participation?' (2013) 7 *International Journal of Transitional Justice* 518

Pena, Mariana, 'Victim Participation at the International Criminal Court: Achievements Made and Challenges Lying Ahead' (2010) 16 *ILSA Journal of International & Comparative Law* 497

Powderly, Joseph, 'International Criminal Justice in an Age of Perpetual Crisis' (2019) 32 *Leiden Journal of International Law* 1

Pues, Anni, 'A Victim's Right to a Fair Trial at the International Criminal Court? Reflections on Article 68(3)' (2015) 13 *Journal of International Criminal Justice* 951

Reynolds, John and Sujith Xavier, '"The Dark Corners of the World": TWAIL and International Criminal Justice' (2016) 14 *Journal of International Criminal Justice* 959

Rigney, Sophie, '"The Words Don't Fit You": Recharacterisation of The Charges, Trial Fairness, and *Katanga*' (2014) 15 *Melbourne Journal of International Law* 515

Rigney, Sophie, 'Distant Justice: The Impact of the International Criminal Court on African Politics (Book Review)' (2020) 31(3) *European Journal of International Law* 1157

Rigney, Sophie, 'Postcard from the ICTY: Examining International Criminal Law's Narratives', in Daniel Joyce and Jessie Hohmann (eds) *International Law's Objects* (Oxford University Press, 2018) 366

Rigney, Sophie, 'You Start to Feel Really Alone: Defence Lawyers and Narratives of International Criminal Law in Film' (2018) 6(1) *London Review of International Law* 97

Robinson, Darryl, 'International Criminal Law as Justice' (2013) 11(2) *Journal of International Criminal Justice* 699

Robinson, Darryl, 'Inescapable Dyads: Why the International Criminal Court Cannot Win' (2015) 28 *Leiden Journal of International Law* 323

Robinson, Patrick, 'Fair but Expeditious Trials' in Hirad Abtahi and Gideon Boas (eds), *The Dynamics of International Criminal Justice* (Brill, 2006) 169

Robinson, Patrick, 'Rough Edges in the Alignment of Legal Systems in the Proceedings at the ICTY' (2005) 3 *Journal of International Criminal Justice* 1037

Robinson, Patrick, 'The Right to a Fair Trial in International Law, with Specific Reference to the Work of the ICTY' (2009) 3 *Berkeley Journal of International Law Publicist* 1

Rohan, Colleen 'Ethical Standards in the practice of international criminal law', in Gentian Zyberi and Colleen Rohan (eds), *Defense Perspectives on International Criminal Justice* (Cambridge University Press, 2018) 41

Rohan, Colleen, 'Protecting the Rights of the Accused in International Criminal Proceedings: Lip Service or Affirmative Action?' in William A Schabas, Yvonne McDermott and Niamh Hayes (eds), *The Ashgate Research Companion to International Criminal Law* (Ashgate, 2013) 289

Roth, Robert and Françoise Tulkens (eds), 'Symposium: The Influence of the European Court of Human Rights' Case Law on (International) Criminal Law' (2011) 9 *Journal of International Criminal Justice* 571

Sadat, Leila, 'Prosecutor v. Jean-Pierre Bemba Gombo' (2019) 113(2) *American Journal of International Law* 353

Sander, Barrie, 'The Expressive Turn of International Criminal Justice: A Field in Search of Meaning' (2019) 32 *Leiden Journal of International Law* 851

Sander, Barrie, 'The Method is the Message: Narrative Authority and Historical Contestation in International Criminal Courts' (2018) 10 *Melbourne Journal of International Law* 299

Sander, Barrie, 'Unveiling the Historical Function of International Criminal Courts: Between Adjudicative and Sociopolitical Justice' (2018) 12(2) *International Journal of Transitional Justice* 334

Schabas, William A, 'Balancing the Rights of the Accused with the Imperatives of Accountability' in Ramesh Thakur and Peter Malcontent (eds), *From Sovereign Impunity to International Accountability: The Search for Justice in a World of States* (United Nations University Press, 2004) 154

Schabas, William, 'Synergy or Fragmentation? International Criminal Law and the European Convention on Human Rights' (2011) 9 *Journal of International Criminal Justice* 609

Schrag, Minna, 'Lessons Learned from the ICTY Experience: Notes for the ICC Prosecutor' (2004) 2 *Journal of International Criminal Justice* 427

Schwöbel, Christine, 'The Market and Marketing Culture of International Criminal Law' in Christine Schwöbel (ed), *Critical Approaches to International Criminal Law* (Routledge, 2014) 279

Schwöbel-Patel, Christine, 'The "Ideal" Victim of International Criminal Law' (2018) 29(3) *European Journal of International Law* 703

Schwöbel-Patel, Christine, 'The Core Crimes of International Criminal Law' in Kevin Heller et al. (eds), *The Oxford Handbook of International Criminal Law* (2020, OUP)

Sehmi, Anushka, '"Now that we have no voice, what will happen to us?" Experiences of Victim Participation in the Kenyatta Case' (2018) 16 *Journal of International Criminal Justice* 571

Shany, Yuval, 'Assessing the effectiveness of International Courts: A Goal-based Approach' (2012) 106 *American Journal of International Law* 225

Simpson, Gerry, 'War Crimes: A Critical Introduction' in Timothy McCormack and Gerry Simpson (eds), *The Law of War Crimes: National and International Approaches* (Kluwer Law International, 1997) 1

Skilbeck, Rupert, 'Frankenstein's Monster: Creating a New International Procedure' (2010) 8 *Journal of International Criminal Justice* 451

Smet, Simon De, 'All Roads Lead to Rome – Lifting the Veil on the ICC's Procedural Pluriformity' in Pavel Šturma (ed), *The Rome Statute of the ICC at Its Twentieth Anniversary: Achievements and Perspectives* (2019, Brill Nijhoff) 193

Smet, Simon De, 'The International Criminal Standard of Proof at the ICC — Beyond Reasonable Doubt or Beyond Reason?' in Carsten Stahn (ed), *The Law and Practice of the International Criminal Court: A Critical Account of Challenges and Achievements* (Oxford University Press, 2015) 861

Stahn, Carsten, 'Between "Faith" and "Facts": By What Standards Should We Assess International Criminal Justice?' (2012) 25 *Leiden Journal of International Law* 251

Stahn, Carsten, 'Modification of the Legal Characterisation of Facts in the ICC System: A Portrayal of Regulation 55' (2005) 16 *Criminal Law Forum* 1

Stolk, Sofia, 'The Victim, the International Criminal Court and the Search for Truth: On the Interdependence and Incompatibility of Truths about Mass Atrocity' (2015) 13 *Journal of International Criminal Justice* 973

Swaak-Goldman, Olivia, 'The ICTY and the Right to a Fair Trial: A Critique of the Critics' (1997) 10(2) *Leiden Journal of International Law* 215

Swart, Bert, 'Damaška and the Faces of International Criminal Justice' (2008) 6 *Journal of International Criminal Justice* 87

Swart, Bert, 'International Criminal Justice and Models of Traditional Process' in Göran Sluiter and Sergey Vasiliev (eds), *International Criminal Procedure: Towards a Coherent Body of Law* (Cameron May, 2009) 93

Swoboda, Sabine, 'The ICC Disclosure Regime — A Defence Perspective' (2008) 19 *Criminal Law Forum* 449

Tallgren, Immi, 'Sensibility and Sense of International Criminal Law' (2002) 13 *European Journal of International Law* 561

Tallgren, Immi, 'We Did It? The Vertigo of Law and Everyday Life at the Diplomatic Conference on the Establishment of an International Criminal Court' (1999) 12 *Leiden Journal of International Law* 683)

Tolbert, David and Fergal Gaynor, 'International Tribunals and the Right to a Speedy Trial: Problems and Possible Remedies' (2009) 27 *Law in Context* 33

Trechsel, Stefan, 'Rights in Criminal Proceedings under the *ECHR* and the *ICTY Statute* — A Precarious Comparison' in Bert Swart, Alexander Zahar and Göran Sluiter (eds), *The Legacy of the International Criminal Tribunal for the Former Yugoslavia* (Oxford University Press, 2011) 149

Trechsel, Stefan, 'Why Must Trials be Fair?' (1997) 31 *Israel Law Review* 94

Trotter, Andrew, 'Witness Intimidation in International Trials: Balancing the Need for Protection Against the Rights of the Accused' (2012) *George Washington International Law Review* 521

Turner, Jenia Iontcheva, 'Defence Perspectives on Fairness and Efficiency at the International Criminal Court', in Kevin Heller et al (eds), *Oxford Handbook of International Criminal Law* (Oxford University Press, 2020) 39

Van Sliedregt, Elies 'International Criminal Law: Over studied and Underachieving?' (2016) 29 *Leiden Journal of International Law* 1

Van Sliedregt, Elies and Sergey Vasiliev, 'Pluralism: A New Framework for International Criminal Justice' in Elies van Sliedregt and Sergey Vasiliev (eds), *Pluralism in International Criminal Law* (Oxford University Press, 2014)

Van Sliedregt, Elies, 'Introduction: Common Civility – International Criminal Law as Cultural Hybrid' (2011) 24 *Leiden Journal of International Law* 389

Van Sliedregt, Elies, 'The Curious Case of International Criminal Liability' (2012) 10 *Journal of International Criminal Justice* 1171

Vanderpuye, Kweku 'Traditions in Conflict: The Internationalization of Confrontation' (2010) 43 *Cornell International Law Journal* 513

Vasiliev, Sergey, 'International Criminal Tribunals in the Shadows of Strasbourg and Politics of Cross-Fertilization' (2015) 84 *Nordic Journal of International Law* 371

Vasiliev, Sergey, 'On trajectories and destinations of international criminal law scholarship' (2015) 28(4) *Leiden Journal of International Law* 701

Vasiliev, Sergey, 'The Crises and Critiques of International Criminal Justice', in Kevin Heller et al. (eds), *The Oxford Handbook of International Criminal Law* (Oxford University Press, 2020) 626

Vasiliev, Sergey, 'Victim Participation Revisited — What the ICC is Learning about Itself' in Carsten Stahn (ed), *The Law and Practice of the International Criminal Court: A Critical Account of Challenges and Achievements* (Oxford University Press, 2015) 1133

Vogler, Richard, 'Making International Criminal Procedure Work: From Theory to Practice' in Ralph Henham and Mark Findlay (eds), *Exploring the Boundaries of International Criminal Justice* (Ashgate, 2011) 105

Wald, Patricia, 'The International Criminal Tribunal for the Former Yugoslavia Comes of Age: Some Observations on Day-to-Day Dilemmas of an International Court' (2001) 5 *Washington University Journal of Law and Policy* 87

Wald, Patricia, 'Dealing with Witnesses in War Crime Trials: Lessons from the Yugoslav Tribunal' (2002) 5 *Yale Human Rights and Development Law Journal* 217

Warbrick, Colin, 'International Criminal Courts and Fair Trial' (1998) 3 *Journal of Armed Conflict Law* 45

Wheeler, Caleb H 'The Scales of Justice: Balancing the Goals of International Criminal Trials' (2019) 30 *Criminal Law Forum* 145

Wilson, R A, 'Judging History: The Historical Record of the International Criminal Tribunal for the former Yugoslavia' (2005) 27 *Human Rights Quarterly* 908

Woolaver, Hannah and Emma Palmer, 'Challenges to the Independence of the International Criminal Court from the Assembly of States Parties' (2017) 15(4) *Journal of International Criminal Justice* 641

Wyngaert, Christine Van den, 'Victims before International Criminal Courts: Some Views and Concerns of an ICC Trial Judge' (2011) 44 *Case Western Reserve Journal of International Law* 475

Zappalà, Salvatore, 'The Rights of Victims v the Rights of the Accused' (2010) 8 *Journal of International Criminal Justice* 137

Zolo, Danilo, 'Peace Through Criminal Law?' (2004) 2 *Journal of International Criminal Justice* 727

THESES

McDermott, Yvonne, *The Right to a Fair Trial in International Criminal Law* (PhD Thesis, National University of Ireland Galway, 2013)

Vasiliev, Sergey, *International Criminal Trials: A Normative Framework* (PhD Thesis, University of Amsterdam, 2014)

TREATIES

Rome Statute of the International Criminal Court, opened for signature 17 July 1998, 2187 UNTS 90 (entered into force 1 July 2002)

International Covenant on Civil and Political Rights, opened for signature on 16 December 1966, 999 UNTS 171 (entered into force 23 March 1976)

UNITED NATIONS SECURITY COUNCIL RESOLUTIONS

Statute of the International Criminal Tribunal for the Former Yugoslavia, SC Res 827, UN SCOR, 48th sess, 3217th mtg, UN Doc S/RES/827 (25 May 1993), as amended by SC Res 1877, UN SCOR, 64th sess, 6155th mtg, UN Doc S/RES/1877 (7 July 2009)

INSTRUMENTS

ICC, *Regulations of the Court*, Doc No ICC-BD/01-01-04 (adopted 26 May 2004)

ICC, *Rules of Procedure and Evidence*, Doc No ICC-ASP/1/3 (adopted 9 September 2002)

ICTY, *Rules of Procedure and Evidence*, Doc No IT/32/Rev.13 (adopted on 11 February 1994, amended 10 July 1998)

ICTY, *Rules of Procedure and Evidence*, Doc No IT/32/Rev.19 (adopted on 11 February 1994, amended 19 January 2001)

ICTY, *Rules of Procedure and Evidence*, Doc No IT/32/Rev.48 (adopted on 11 February 1994, amended 19 November 2012)

ICTY, *Rules of Procedure and Evidence*, Doc No IT/32/Rev.50 (adopted on 11 February 1994, amended 10 July 2015)

JUDGMENTS

'Judgement of the Nuremberg International Military Tribunal 1946' (1947) 41 *American Journal of International Law* 172

Attorney General (Israel) v Eichmann (1961) 36 ILR 5

ICTY – Trial

Prosecutor v Haradinaj, Public Judgement with Confidential Annexes (IT-04-84bis-T, 29 November 2012)

Prosecutor v Limaj, Judgement (IT-03-66, 30 November 2005)

Prosecutor v Prlić, Judgement (IT-04-74-T, 29 May 2013)

Prosecutor v Šešelj, Judgement (IT-03-67-T, 31 March 2016)

Prosecutor v Sikirica, Sentencing Judgment (IT-95-8, 13 November 2001)

Prosecutor v Mladić, Judgement (IT-09-92-T, 22 November 2017)

ICTY and MICT – Appeals

Prosecutor v Haradinaj, Judgement (IT-04-84-A, 19 July 2010)

Prosecutor v Haradinaj, Corrigendum to Judgement of 19 July 2010 (IT-04-84-A, 23 July 2010)

Prosecutor v Karadžić, Judgement (MICT-13-55-A, 20 March 2019)

Prosecutor v Kordić, Judgement (IT-95-14/2-A, 17 December 2004)

Prosecutor v Krstić, Judgement (IT-98-33-A, 19 April 2004)

Prosecutor v Perišić, Judgement (IT-04-18-A, 28 February 2013)

Prosecutor v Šainović, Judgement (IT-05-87-A, 23 January 2014)

Prosecutor v Tadić, Appeal Judgement on Allegations of Contempt Against Prior Counsel, Milan Vujin (IT-94-1-A-AR77, 27 February 2001)

Prosecutor v Tadić, Judgement (IT-94-1-A, 15 July 1999)

ICC – Trial

Prosecutor v Katanga, Jugement rendu en application de l'article 74 du Statut (ICC-01/04-01/07, 7 March 2014)

Prosecutor v Lubanga, Judgment pursuant to Article 74 of the Statute (ICC-01/04-01/06, 14 March 2012)

Prosecutor v Ngudjolo, Judgment pursuant to Article 74 of the Statute (ICC-01/04-02/12, 18 December 2012)

Prosecutor v Bemba, Public Redacted Version of Judgment Pursuant to Article 74 of the Statute (ICC-01/05-01/03, 19 October 2016)

ICC – Appeals

Prosecutor v Bemba Gombo, Judgment on the appeal of Mr Jean-Pierre Bemba Gombo against Trial Chamber III's "Judgment pursuant to Article 74 of the Statute" (ICC-01/05-01/08-3636-Red, 8 June 2018)

Prosecutor v Gbagbo, Delivery of Decision (ICC-02/11-01/15, 16 January 2019)

Prosecutor v Gbagbo, Reasons for Oral Decision of 15 January 2019 on the Requête de la Défense de Laurent Gbagbo afin qu'un jugement d'acquittement portant sur toutes les charges soit prononcé en faveur de Laurent Gbagbo et que sa mise en liberté immédiate soit ordonnée, and on the Blé Goudé Defence No Case to Answer Motion (ICC-02/11-01/15, 16 July 2019)

Prosecutor v Ngudjolo, Judgment on the Prosecutor's Appeal against the Decision of Trial Chamber II entitled 'Judgment Pursuant to Article 74 of the Statute' (ICC-01/04-02/12A, 27 February 2015)

PROCEDURAL DECISIONS AND ORDERS

International Criminal Tribunal for the Former Yugoslavia

Prosecutor v Blaskić (IT-95-14-A) (Appeals Chamber)
Decision on the Appellant's Motions for the Production of Material, Suspension or Extension of the Briefing Schedule, and Additional Filings (26 September 2000)

Prosecutor v Brđanin (IT-99-36) (Trial Chamber)
Decision on Second Motion by Prosecution for Protective Measures (27 October 2000)

Prosecutor v Delalić (IT-96-21-T) (Trial Chamber)
Decision on the Motion to Allow Witnesses K, L and M to Give Their Testimony by Means of Video-Link Conference (28 May 1997)

Prosecutor v Halilović (IT-01-48-T) (Trial Chamber)
Decision on Motion for Enforcement of Court Order re Electronic Disclosure Suite (27 July 2005)

Prosecutor v Haradinaj (IT-04-84-PT) (Pre-Trial Chamber)
Decision on Second Haradinaj Motion to Lift Redactions of Protected Witness Statements (22 November 2006)

Prosecutor v Haradinaj (IT-04-84bis-T) (Trial Chamber)
Decision on Joint Defence Motion for Relief from Rule 68 Violations by the Prosecution and for Sanctions to be Imposed Pursuant to Rule 68bis (12 October 2011)
Decision on Prosecutor's Motion for Reconsideration of Relief Ordered Pursuant to Rule 68Bis (27 March 2012)

Prosecutor v Karadžić (IT-95-5/18-PT) (Pre-Trial Chamber)
Decision on Protective Measures for Witnesses (30 October 2008)
Decision on Prosecution's Motion for Delayed Disclosure for KDZ456, KDZ493, KDZ531 and KDZ532, and Variation of Protective Measures for KDZ489 (5 June 2009)

Prosecutor v Karadžić (IT-95-05/18-T) (Trial Chamber)
Order Following on Status Conference and Appended Work Plan (6 April 2009)
Decision on Motion on Modalities of Rule 66 (A)(ii) Disclosure (27 April 2009)
Decision on the Accused's Holbrooke Agreement Motion (8 July 2009)
Decision on Third Prosecution Motion for Judicial Notice of Adjudicated Facts (9 July 2009)
Decision on Accused's Application for Certification to Appeal Decision on Rule 92 Quater (Witness KDZ198) (31 August 2009)
Decision on Second Prosecution Motion for Judicial Notice of Adjudicated Facts (9 October 2009)
Decision on Accused's Motion to Set Deadlines for Disclosure (1 October 2009)
Decision on Accused's Motion to Preclude Evidence or to Withdraw Adjudicated Facts (31 March 2010)
Decision on Motion for Stay of Proceedings (8 April 2010)
Decision on Accused's Second Motion for Finding Disclosure Violation and for Remedial Measures (17 June 2010)
Decision on the Accused's Motion for Additional Time to Prepare Cross-Examination of Momčilo Mandić (2 July 2010)
Decision on Accused's Third, Fourth, Fifth and Sixth Motions for Finding Disclosure Violation and for Remedial Measures (20 July 2010)
Decision on Accused's Seventh and Eighth Motions for Finding Disclosure Violation and for Remedial Measures (18 August 2010)
Decision on Accused's Ninth and Tenth Motions for Finding Disclosure Violation and for Remedial Measures (26 August 2010)
Decision on Accused's Eleventh to Fifteenth Motions for Finding of Disclosure Violation and for Remedial Measures (24 September 2010)
Decision on Accused's Seventeenth Motion for Finding Disclosure Violation and for Remedial Measures (29 September 2010)
Decision on Accused's Eighteenth to Twenty-First Disclosure Violation Motions (2 November 2010)
Decision on Accused's Twenty-Second, Twenty-Fourth and Twenty-Sixth Disclosure Violation Motions (11 November 2010)
Decision on Accused's Twenty-Seventh Disclosure Violation Motion (17 November 2010)
Decision on Prosecution's Request for Reconsideration of Trial Chamber's 11 November 2010 Decision (10 December 2010)

Decision on Accused's Seventeenth Bis and Twenty-Eighth Disclosure Violation Motions (16 December 2010)

Decision on Accused's Twenty-Ninth Disclosure Violation Motions (11 January 2011)

Decision on Accused's Thirtieth and Thirty-First Disclosure Violation Motions (February 2011)

Decision on Accused's Thirty-Second, Thirty-Third, Thirty-Fifth and Thirty-Sixth Disclosure Violation Motion (24 February 2011)

Decision on Accused's Thirty-Seventh to Forty-Second Disclosure Violation Motions (29 March 2011)

Decision on Prosecution Request for Certification to Appeal Decision on Accused's Thirty-Seventh to Forty-Second Disclosure Violation Motions (7 April 2011)

Decision on Accused's Forty-Third to Forty-Fifth Disclosure Violation Motion (8 April 2011)

Decision on Accused's Forty-Seventh Motion for Finding of Disclosure Violation and for Further Suspension of Proceedings (10 May 2011)

Decision on Accused's Forty-Ninth and Fiftieth Disclosure Violation Motions (30 June 2011)

Decision on Accused's Fifty-First and Fifty-Second Disclosure Violation Motions (7 July 2011)

Decision on Accused's Fifty-Third and Fifty-Fourth Disclosure Violation Motions (22 July 2011)

Decision on Accused's Sixty-Fifth Disclosure Violation Motion (12 January 2012)

Decision on Accused's Sixty-Sixth Disclosure Violation Motion (8 February 2012)

Public Redacted Version of 'Decision on Accused's Sixty-Seventh and Sixty-Eight Disclosure Violation Motions' Issued on 1 March 2012 (1 March 2012)

Decision on the Prosecution Motion to Admit the Prior Evidence of Milan Tupajic pursuant to Rule 92 quinquies (7 May 2012)

Decision on Accused's Motion for New Trial for Disclosure Violations (3 September 2012)

Decision on Time Allocated to the Accused for the Presentation of His Case (19 September 2012)

Prosecutor v Karadžić (IT-95-05/18-AR73.10) (Appeals Chamber)
Decision on Appeal from Decision on Duration of Defence Case (29 January 2013)

Prosecutor v Kordić (IT-95-14/2-AR73.5) (Appeals Chamber)
Decision on Appeal regarding Statement of a Deceased Witness (21 July 2000)
Decision on Appeal regarding the Admission into Evidence of Seven Affidavits and One Formal Statement (18 September 2000)

Prosecutor v Kordić (IT-95-14/2) (Trial Chamber)
Decision on Appellant's Notice and Supplemental Notice of Prosecution's Non-Compliance with its Disclosure Obligations under Rule 68 of the Rules (11 February 2004)

Prosecutor v Krajišnik (IT-00-39-PT) (Trial Chamber)

Decision on Prosecution Motions of Judicial Notices of Adjudicated Facts and for Admission of Written Statements of Written Statements of Witnesses pursuant to Rule 92bis (28 February 2003)

Prosecutor v Lukić (No IT-98-32/1-T) (Trial Chamber)

Decision on Milan Lukić's Motion to Suppress Testimony for Failure of Timely Disclosure (3 November 2008)

Prosecutor v Milošević (IT-02-54-AR73.5) (Appeals Chamber)

Decision on the Prosecution's Interlocutory Appeal Against the Trial Chamber's 10 April 2003 Decision on Prosecution Motion for Judicial Notice of Adjudicated Facts (28 October 2003)

Prosecutor v Milošević (IT-02-54-T) (Trial Chamber)

Second Decision on Prosecution Motion for Protective Measures for Sensitive Source Witnesses (18 June 2002)

Decision on Prosecution Motion to Amend Witness List and for Protective Measures for Sensitive Source Witnesses (13 March 2003)

Final Decision on Prosecution Motion for Judicial Notice of Adjudicated Facts (16 December 2003)

Reasons for Decision on Assignment of Defence Counsel (22 September 2004)

Decision in Relation to Severance, Extension of Time and Rest (12 December 2005)

Prosecutor v Mladić (IT-09-92-T) (Trial Chamber)

Decision on Defence Motion for a Fair Trial and the Presumption of Innocence or, in the alternative, a Mistrial (4 July 2016)

Decision on Submissions Relative to the Proposed "EDS" Method of Disclosure (26 June 2012)

Prosecutor v Mladić (IT-09-92-A) (Appeals Chamber)

Decision on Defence Interlocutory Appeal Against the Trial Chamber's Decision on EDS Disclosure Methods (28 November 2013)

Decision on Interlocutory Appeal Against Decision on Defence Motion for a Fair Trial and the Presumption of Innocence (27 February 2017)

Decision on Ratko Mladić's Appeal Against the Trial Chamber's Decisions on the Prosecution Motion for Judicial Notice of Adjudicated Facts (12 November 2013)

Prosecutor v Perišić (IT-04-81-A) (Appeals Chamber)

Decision on Motion for Reconsideration (20 March 2014)

Prosecutor v Popović (IT-05-88-T) (Trial Chamber)

Decision on Prosecution Motion for Judicial Notice of Adjudicated Facts with Annex (26 September 2006)

Prosecutor v Prlić (IT-04-74-A) (Appeals Chamber)
*Decision on Joint Defence Interlocutory Appeal against the Trial Chamber's Oral Decision
    of 8 May 2006 relating to Cross Examination by Defence and Association of Defence
    Counsel's Request for Leave to File an Amicus Curiae Brief* (4 July 2006)
*Decision on Prosecution Appeal Concerning the Trial Chamber's Ruling Reducing Time for
    the Prosecution Case* (6 February 2007)
*Decision on Appeals Against Decision Admitting Transcript of Jadranko Prlić's Questioning
    into Evidence* (23 November 2007)

Prosecutor v Šešelj (IT-03-67-PT) (Pre-Trial)
Decision on Form of Disclosure (4 July 2006)

Prosecutor v Šešelj (IT-03-67-T)
*Decision on Defence Motion For Disqualification of Judge Frederick Harhoff and Report to
    the Vice-President* (28 August 2013)
Order Assigning a Judge pursuant to Rule 15 (31 October 2013)

Prosecutor v Šešelj (IT-03-67-AR73.6) (Appeals Chamber)
*Decisions on Vojislav Šešelj's Appeal Against the Trial Chamber's Oral Decision of
    7 November 2007* (24 January 2008)

**Prosecutor v Stanišić and Simatović (Trial Chamber) (IT-03-69-PT) (Pre-Trial
    Chamber)**
Decision on Defence Motion to Receive Hard Copies of Rule 66 Material (11 March
    2005)
Decision Pursuant to Rule 73 bis(D) (4 February 2008)

Prosecutor v Stanišić (IT-04-79-PT) (Pre-Trial Chamber)
Decision on Judicial Notice (14 December 2007)

Prosecutor v Stanišić (IT-08-91-T) (Trial Chamber)
*Decision Granting in Part the Prosecution's Motions for Judicial Notice of Adjudicated Facts
    Pursuant to Rule 94(B)* (1 April 2010)
*Decision Granting in Part Prosecution's Motion to Amend Its 65 ter Witness List as a Result
    of the Trial Chamber's 1 April 2010 Decision Concerning Judicial Notice of Adjudicated
    Facts* (14 July 2010)
*Decision Denying the Prosecution's Request for Certification to Appeal the 'Decision
    Granting in Part Prosecution's Motions for Judicial Notice of Adjudicated Facts pursuant
    to Rule 94(B)'* (14 July 2010)

Prosecutor v Tadić (IT-94-1-T) (Trial Chamber)
*Decision on the Prosecutor's Motion Requesting Protective Measures for Victims and
    Witnesses* (10 August 1995)
*Separate Opinion of Judge Stephen on the Prosecutor's Motion Requesting Protective Measures
    for Victims and Witnesses* (10 August 1995)

Prosecutor v Tolimir (IT-05-88/2-PT) (Pre-Trial)
Decision on Prosecution Motion for Judicial Notice of Adjudicated Facts Pursuant to Rule 94(B) (17 December 2009)

International Criminal Court

Prosecutor v Abu Garda (ICC-02/05-02/09) (Pre-Trial Chamber)
Decision on the Confirmation of Charges (8 February 2010)

Prosecutor v Banda & Jerbo (ICC-02/05-03/09) (Appeals Chamber)
Judgment on the Defence Appeal for the Disclosure of Documents (28 August 2013)

Prosecutor v Bemba (ICC-01/05-01/08) (Trial Chamber)
Decision on the Evidence Disclosure System and Setting a Timetable for Disclosure between the Parties (31 July 2008)
Decision Giving Notice to the Parties and Participants that the Legal Characterisation of the Facts May Be Subject to Change in Accordance with Regulation 55(2) of the Regulations of the Court (21 September 2008)
Public Redacted Decision on 'Prosecution Submission of Evidence Pursuant to Rule 68(2)(c) of the Rules of Procedure and Evidence' (12 November 2015)

Prosecutor v Bemba (ICC-01/05-01/08) (Pre-Trial Chamber)
Decision pursuant to Article 61(7)(a) and (b) of the Rome Statute on the Charges of the Prosecutor against Jean-Pierre Bemba Gombo (15 June 2009)

Prosecutor v Gaddafi (ICC-01/11-01/11) (Pre-Trial Chamber)
Decision on the Admissibility of the Case against Saif Al-Islam Gaddafi (31 May 2013)
Decision on the Admissibility of the Case against Abdullah Al-Senussi (11 October 2013)

Prosecutor v Gaddafi (ICC-01/11-01/11) (Appeals Chamber)
Judgment on the Appeal of Libya against the Decision of Pre-Trial Chamber I of 31 May 2013 entitled 'Decision on the Admissibility of the Case against Saif Al-Islam Gaddafi' (21 May 2014)

Prosecutor v Gbagbo (ICC-02/11-01/15) (Appeals Chamber)
Judgment on the appeal of Mr Laurent Gbagbo against the oral decision on redactions of 29 November 2016 (31 July 2017)

Prosecutor v Katanga (ICC-01/04-01/07) (Pre-Trial Chamber)
Decision on the Set of Procedural Rights Attached to Procedural Status of Victims at the Pre-Trial Stage of a Case (13 May 2008)
Decision on Article 54(3)(e) Documents Identified as Potentially Exculpatory or Otherwise Material to the Defence's Preparation for the Confirmation Hearing (20 June 2008)

Prosecutor v Katanga (ICC-01/04-01/07) (Trial Chamber)
Decision on the Modalities of Victim Participation at Trial (22 January 2010)
Decision on the Implementation of Regulation 55 of the Regulations of the Court and Severing the Charges against the Accused Persons (21 November 2012)
Décision relative à la peine (article 76 du Statut) (23 May 2014)

Prosecutor v Katanga (ICC-01/04-01/07) (Appeals Chamber)
Judgment on the appeal of the Prosecutor against the decision of Pre-Trial Chamber I entitled "First Decision on the Prosecution Request for Authorisation to Redact Witness Statements" (13 May 2008)
Judgment on the Appeal of Mr Katanga against the Decision of the Trial Chamber II of 22 January 2010 entitled 'Decision on the Modalities of Victim Participation at Trial (16 July 2010)

Prosecutor v Kenyatta (ICC-01/09-02/11) (Pre-Trial Chamber)
Decision on the Confirmation of Charges Pursuant to Article 61(7)(a) and (b) of the Rome Statute (23 January 2012)
Decision on the Withdrawal of Charges Against Mr Kenyatta (13 March 2015)

Prosecutor v Lubanga (ICC-01/04-01/06) (Pre-Trial Chamber)
Decision on the Final System of Disclosure and the Establishment of a Timetable (15 May 2006)

Prosecutor v Lubanga (ICC-01/04-01/06) (Trial Chamber)
Decision on Victim's Participation (18 January 2008)
Decision on the Defence and Prosecution Requests for Leave to Appeal the Decision on Victims' Participation of 18 January 2008 (26 February 2008)
Decision on the Consequences of Non-Disclosure of Exculpatory Materials Covered by Article 54(3)(e) Agreements and the Application to Stay the Prosecution of the Accused, Together with Certain other Issues Raised at the Status Conference on 10 June 2008 (13 June 2008)
Judgment on Appeals of the Prosecutor and the Defence against Trial Chamber I's Decision on Victims' Participation of 18 January 2008 (11 July 2008)
Prosecutor v Lubanga Decision on the Defence Application for Disclosure of Victims Applications (21 January 2009)
Decision Giving Notice to the Parties and Participants that the Legal Characterisation of the Facts May be Subject to Change in accordance with Regulation 55(2) of the Regulations of the Court (14 July 2009)

Prosecutor v Lubanga (ICC-01/04-01/06) (Appeals Chamber)
Judgment on the Prosecutor's appeal against the decision of Pre-Trial Chamber I entitled 'Decision Establishing General Principles Governing Applications to Restrict Disclosure pursuant to Rule 81 (2) and (4) of the Rules of Procedure and Evidence' (13 October 2006)

Judgment on the Appeal of Mr Thomas Lubanga Dyilo against the Decision on the Defence Challenge to the Jurisdiction of the Court pursuant to Article 19(2)(a) of the Statute of 3 October 2006 (14 December 2006)

Judgment on the Appeal of Mr. Thomas Lubanga Dyilo Against the Decision of Pre-Trial Chamber I Entitled "First Decision on the Prosecution Requests and Amended Requests for Redactions under Rule 81" (14 December 2006)

Judgment on the Appeals of Mr Lubanga Dyilo and the Prosecutor Against the Decision of Trial Chamber I of 14 July 2009 Entitled 'Decision Giving Notice to the Parties and Participants that the Legal Characterisation of the Facts May Be Subject to Change in Accordance with Regulation 55(2) of the Regulations of the Court' (8 December 2009)

Prosecutor v Mbarushimana (ICC-01/04-01/10) (Pre-Trial Chamber)
Decision on the Confirmation of Charges (16 December 2011)

Prosecutor v Muthaura (ICC-01/09-02/11) (Pre-Trial Chamber)
Decision on the withdrawal of charges against Mr Muthaura (18 March 2013)
Public Redacted Version of the 25 February 2013 Consolidated Prosecution Response to the Defence Applications Under Article 64 of the Statue to Refer the Confirmation Decision Back to the Pre-Trial Chamber (25 February 2013)

Prosecutor v Ntaganda (ICC-01/04-02/06) (Trial Chamber)
Decision on Prosecution Application Under Rule 68(2)(c) of the Rules for Admission of Prior Recorded Testimony of P-0022, P-0041 and P-0103 (20 November 2015)

Prosecutor v Ruto ICC-01/09-01/11 (Pre-Trial Chamber)
Decision on the Confirmation of Charges Pursuant to Article 61(7)(a) and (b) of the Rome Statute (23 January 2012)

Prosecutor v Ruto ICC-01/09-01/11 (Trial Chamber)
Confidential redacted version of 'Decision on first prosecution application for delayed disclosure of witness identities' (4 January 2013)
Decision on the Prosecution's Request for Admission of Documentary Evidence (10 June 2014)
Decision on Prosecution Request for Admission of Prior Recorded Testimony (19 August 2015)
Decision on Defence Applications for Judgments of Acquittal (5 April 2016)

Prosecutor v Ruto (ICC-01/09-01/11-OA) (Appeals Chamber)
Judgment on the Appeals of Mr William Samoei Ruto and Joshua Arap Sang Against the Decision of Trial Chamber V(A) of 19 August 2015 entitled 'Decision on Prosecution Request for Admission of Prior Recorded Testimony' (12 February 2016)

Situation in the Democratic Republic of the Congo (ICC-01/04) (Pre-Trial Chamber)
Decision on the Application for Participation in Proceedings of VPRS1, VPRS 2-3-4-5-6 (17 January 2006)

Decision on the Prosecutor's Application for leave to appeal the Chamber's Decision of 17 January 2006 on the Applications for Participation in the Proceedings of VPRS 1, VPRS 2, VPRS 3, VPRS 4, VPRS 5 and VPRS 6 (31 March 2006)

Situation in Uganda (ICC-02/04-01/05) (Pre-Trial Chamber)
Decision on the Prosecutor's Applications for Leave to Appeal dated the 15th of March 2006 and to Suspend or Stay Consideration of Leave to Appeal Dated the 11th day of March 2006 (10 July 2006)
Decision on the Prosecution's Application for Leave to Appeal the Decision on Victims' Applications for Participation a/001/06, a/0064/06 to a/0070/06, a/0104/06 and a/0111/06 to a/0127/06 (19 December 2007)

International Criminal Tribunal for Rwanda

Prosecutor v Karemera (ICTR-98-44-AR73(C)) (Appeals Chamber)
Decision on Prosecutor's Interlocutory Appeal of Decision on Judicial Notice (ICTR, 16 June 2006)

Prosecutor v Simba (ICTR-01-76-I) (Trial Chamber)
Decision on Defence Request for Protection of Witnesses (25 August 2004)

MOTIONS

International Criminal Tribunal for the Former Yugoslavia

Prosecutor v Haradinaj (IT-04-84-A) (Appeals Chamber)
'Prosecution Appeal Brief' (16 July 2008)

Prosecutor v Haradinaj (IT-04-84bis-T) (Trial Chamber)
'Motion for Reconsideration of Relief Ordered Pursuant to Rule 68*bis*' (26 October 2011)
'Lahi Brahimaj's Response to Motion for Reconsideration of Relief Ordered Pursuant to Rule 68*bis*' (27 October 2011)
'Defence Response on Behalf of Ramush Haradinaj to Motion for Reconsideration of Relief Ordered Pursuant to Rule 68*bis*' (9 November 2011)

Prosecutor v Karadžić (IT-95-05/18-PT) (Pre-Trial Chamber)
'First Prosecution Motion for Judicial Notice of Adjudicated Facts' (27 October 2008)
'Second Prosecution Motion for Judicial Notice of Adjudicated Facts and Corrigendum to First Prosecution Motion of Judicial Notice of Adjudicated Facts' (16 March 2009)

Prosecutor v Karadžić (IT-95-05/18-T) (Trial Chamber)
'Accused's Motion for Disclosure of Rule 68 Material' (6 February 2009)

'Third Prosecution Motion for Judicial Notice of Adjudicated Facts' (6 April 2009)

'Motion on Modalities of Rule 66 (A)(ii) Disclosure' (14 April 2009)

'Response to Third Prosecution Motion for Judicial Notice of Adjudicated Facts and Motion for List of Witnesses to be Eliminated' (29 May 2009)

'Fourth Prosecution Motion for Judicial Notice of Adjudicated Facts' (25 August 2009)

'Motion to Set Deadlines for Disclosure' (9 September 2009)

'Fifth Prosecution Motion for Judicial Notice of Adjudicated Facts' (14 December 2009)

'Motion For Stay of Proceedings: Violation of Burden of Proof and Presumption of Innocence' (1 April 2010)

'Second Motion for Finding Disclosure Violation and for Remedial Measures' (14 May 2010)

'Prosecution Request for Certification to Appeal Decision on Accused's Thirty-Seventh to Forty-Second Disclosure Violation Motions' (1 April 2011)

'Prosecution Response to Motion for New Trial for Disclosure Violations' (7 August 2012)

'Motion for New Trial for Disclosure Violations' (13 August 2012)

'Defence Submission Pursuant to Rule 65 *ter* and Related Motions' (27 August 2012)

'Appeal from Decision on Duration of Appeals Case' (12 October 2012)

'96th Motion for Finding of Disclosure Violation and for Exclusion of Evidence' (11 December 2014)

'108th Motion for Finding of Disclosure Violation and for Remedial Measures' (14 March 2016)

Prosecutor v Karadžić **(IT-95-05/18-T) (Appeals Chamber)**
'Prosecution Request for Reconsideration of Trial Chamber's 11 November 2010 Decision' (1 December 2010)

Prosecutor v Karadžić **(MICT-13-55-A) (MICT Appeals Chamber)**
'Radovan Karadžić's Appeal Brief' (23 December 2016)

Prosecutor v Mladić **(IT-09-92-AR73.1) (Appeals Chamber)**
'Defense Interlocutory Appeal Brief Against the Trial Chamber Decisions on the Prosecution Motion for Judicial Notice of Adjudicated Facts' (4 July 2012)

Prosecutor v Perišić **(Appeals Chamber, IT-04-81-A)**
'Motion for Reconsideration' (3 February 2014)

Prosecutor v Prlić **(Trial Chamber, IT-04-74)**
'Prosecution Appeal Concerning the Trial Chamber's Ruling Dated 13 November 2006 Reducing Time for the Prosecution Case' (30 November 2006)

Prosecutor v Stanišić (IT-04-79-PT) (Pre-Trial Chamber)
'Prosecution's Motion for Judicial Notice of Facts of Common Knowledge and Adjudicated Facts, with Annex' (31 August 2006)
'Prosecution's Second Motion for Judicial Notice of Adjudicated Facts, with Revised and Consolidated Annex' (10 May 2007)
'Prosecution's Third Motion for Judicial Notice of Adjudicated Facts, with Annex' (25 January 2008)
'Prosecution's Fourth Motion for Judicial Notice of Adjudicated Facts, with Annex' (24 April 2008)

Prosecutor v Stanišić (IT-08-91-PT) (Pre-Trial Chamber)
'Prosecution's Request and Notice regarding Application of Adjudicated Facts to Stojan Župljanin, with Annex' (23 February 2009)
'Prosecution's Fifth Motion for Judicial Notice of Adjudicated Facts, With Annex' (21 August 2009)
'Prosecution's Sixth Motion for Judicial Notice of Adjudicated Facts, With Annex' (2 February 2010)
'Prosecution's Request for Certification to Appeal the Decision Granting in Part Prosecution's Motions for Judicial Notice of Adjudicated Facts Pursuant to Rule 94(B)' (7 April 2010)

Prosecutor v Stanišić (IT-08-91) (Trial Chamber)
'Prosecution's Motion to Amend its Rule 65 *ter* Witness List as a Result of the Trial Chamber's 1 April 2010 Granting in Part Prosecution's Motions for Judicial Notice of Adjudicated Facts Pursuant to Rule 94(B)', with Confidential Annex (26 May 2010)
'Addendum to Prosecution's Motion to Amend its Rule 65 *ter* Witness List as a Result of the Trial Chamber's 1 April 2010 Granting in Part Prosecution's Motions for Judicial Notice of Adjudicated Facts Pursuant to Rule 94(B), with Confidential Annex' (16 June 2010)
'Prosecution's Notice Pursuant to the Trial Chamber's Decision Granting in Part Prosecution's Motion to Amend its 65 *ter* Witness List, with Confidential Annex' (21 July 2010)
'Prosecution's Notice of Timings for Rule 92 *bis* Witnesses with Confidential Annexes A and B' (19 August 2010)

International Criminal Court

Prosecutor v Gaddafi (ICC-01/11-01/11) (Pre-Trial Chamber)
'Application on behalf of the Government of Libya pursuant to Article 19 of the ICC Statute' (1 May 2012)

Prosecutor v Gaddafi (ICC-01/11-01/11) (Appeals Chamber)
'The Government of Libya's Appeal against Pre-Trial Chamber I's *'Decision on the Admissibility of the Case against Saif Al-Islam Gaddafi'*' (7 June 2013)

'Document in Support of the Government of Libya's Appeal against the *Decision on the Admissibility of the Case against Saif Al-Islam Gaddafi*' (24 June 2013)

Prosecutor v Katanga (ICC-01/04-01/07) (Trial Chamber)
'Application to Determine the Modalities of the Participation of Victims at the Trial Stage' (13 January 2009)

Prosecutor v Ngudjolo (ICC-01/04-02/12 A) (Appeals Chamber)
'Second Public Redacted Version of "Prosecution's Document in Support of Appeal against the 'Jugement rendu en application de l'article 74 du Statut'" (19 March 2013)
'Prosecution's Appeal of Judgment' (3 April 2013)

Prosecutor v Muthaura (ICC-01/09-02/11-687)
'Prosecution Notification of the Withdrawal of Charges against Francis Kirimi Muthaura' (11 March 2013)

Prosecutor v Kenyatta (ICC-01/09-02/11-983)
'Notice of withdrawal of the charges against Uhuru Muigai Kenyatta' (5 December 2014)

TRANSCRIPTS
Prosecutor v Katanga (ICC-01/04-01/07) (Trial Chamber)
Transcript of Proceedings of 18 October 2011
Transcript of Proceedings of 19 October 2011

REPORTS, COMMENTS AND LETTERS
Amnesty International, 'Amnesty International's Position on Proposals to Amend the ICC Rules of Procedure and Evidence at the Thirteenth Session of the Assembly of States Parties' (Report, Amnesty International, 5 August 2014)

Amnesty International, 'Recommendations to the Twelfth Session of the Assembly of States Parties (20 to 28 November 2013)' (Report, Amnesty International, November 2013)

Assembly of States Parties to the Rome Statute of the International Criminal Court, Report of the Working Group on Amendments, ICC Doc ICC-ASP/12/44 (24 October 2013)

Assembly of States Parties to the Rome Statute of the International Criminal Court, Report on the Review of the Organizational Structure of the Registry, ICC Doc ICC-ASP/13/26 (28 October 2014)

Assembly of States Parties to the Rome Statute of the International Criminal Court, Report of the Working Group on Amendments, ICC Doc ICC-ASP/13/31 (7 December 2014)

Assembly of States Parties to the Rome Statute of the International Criminal Court, Report of the Bureau on Study Group on Governance, ICC Doc ICC-ASP/13/28 (28 November 2014)

Butler, Richard, 'Srebrenica Military Narrative (Revised) Operation "Krivaja 95"'

International Bar Association, 'Fairness at the International Criminal Court' (August 2011)

International Bar Association, 'IBA ICC Programme Legal Opinion: Rule 68 Proposal' (12 November 2013)

International Bar Association, 'Evidence Matters in ICC Trials' (2016)

International Bar Association, 'Witnesses Before the International Criminal Court' (2013)

Koskenniemi Martti, 'International Law and the Far-Right: Reflections on Law and Cynicism' Fourth Annual Asser Institute Lecture, <https://www.asser.nl/upload/documents/20191121T165243-Koskenniemi_web.pdf> (last accessed 9 December 2021)

Mettraux, Guénaël et al., *Expert Initiative Report on Promoting Effectiveness at the International Criminal Court* (2014)

Schense, Jennifer and Linda Carter (eds), *Two Steps Forward, One Step Back: The Deterrent Effect of International Criminal Tribunals* (International Nuremberg Principles Academy, 2016)

Statement by Judge Patrick Robinson, President of ICTY, to the Security Council on 18 June 2010 (18 June 2010)

Assessment and Report of Judge Theodor Meron, President of the International Tribunal for the Former Yugoslavia, Provided to the Security Council pursuant to Paragraph 6 of Security Council Resolution 1534 (2004), and Covering the Period from 15 November 2011 to 22 May 2012, UN Doc S/2012/354 (23 May 2012)

Assessment and Report of Judge Patrick Robinson, President of the International Tribunal for the Former Yugoslavia, Provided to the Security Council pursuant to Paragraph 6 of Security Council Resolution 1534 (2004), Covering the Period from 15 May 2010 to 15 November 2010, UN Doc S/2010/588 (19 November 2010)

Report of the United Nations Secretary-General, Submitted to the Security Council 3 May 1993, Pursuant to Operative Paragraph 2 of Security Council Resolution 808, UN Doc S/25704 (3 May 1993)

'Report of the ICTY', UN Docs A/65/205 – S/2010/413 (30 July 2010)

United Nations Economic and Social Commission on Human Rights, *Report of the Independent Expert to Update the Set of Principles to Combat Impunity*, E/CN.4/2005/102/Add.1 (8 February 2005)

INTERNET SOURCES

Amann, Diane Marie, 'In Bemba and Beyond, Crimes Adjudged to Commit Themselves' on *EJILTalk!* (13 June 2018) <https://www.ejiltalk.org/in-bemba-and-beyond-crimes-adjudged-to-commit-themselves/> (last accessed 9 December 2021)

Amnesty International, 'DRC/ICC: Katanga Found Guilty of War Crimes and Crimes Against Humanity' (7 March 2014) <http://amnesty.org/en/news/drcicc-katanga-found-guilty-war-crimes-and-crimes-against-humanity-2014-03-07> (last accessed 20 March 2020)

Amnesty International, 'Public Statement: ICC Decision to Allow Abdullah al-Senussi to Stand Trial in Libya 'Deeply Alarming' Amidst Overwhelming Security Vacuum' (24 July 2014) <https://www.amnesty.org/download/Documents/8000/ior530082014en.pdf> (last accessed 9 December 2021)

Bouwknegt, Thijs, 'Gbagbo: An Acquittal Foretold' on *Justiceinfo.net* (31 January 2019) <https://www.justiceinfo.net/en/tribunals/icc/40156-gbagbo-an-acquittal-foretold.html> (last accessed 9 December 2021)

Coalition for the ICC, 'Qualified welcome for ICC's Katanga conviction' (20 March 2014) <https://www.coalitionfortheicc.org/news/20140320/qualified-welcome-iccs-katanga-conviction> (last accessed 9 December 2021)

Chaikal, Danya, 'Recent Advancements and Remaining Gaps in Addressing the Witness Protection Challenge at the ICC', International Criminal Justice Today (17 April 2014) <https://www.international-criminal-justice-today.org/arguendo/recent-advancements-and-remaining-gaps-in-addressing-the-witness-protection-challenge-at-the-icc/> (last accessed 9 December 2021)

Drumbl, Mark, 'The Ongwen Trial at the ICC: Tough Questions on Child Soldiers' on *Open Democracy* (14 April 2015) <https://www.opendemocracy.net/openglobalrights/mark-drumbl/ongwen-trial-at-icc-tough-questions-on-child-soldiers> (last accessed 9 December 2021)

Easterday, Jennifer, 'A Closer Look at Regulation 55 at the ICC' on *International Justice Monitor* (28 May 2013) <http://www.ijmonitor.org/2013/05/a-closer-look-at-regulation-55-at-the-icc/> (last accessed 9 December 2021)

Goldstone, Richard, 'Acquittals by the International Criminal Court' on *EJILTalk!* (18 January 2019) <https://www.ejiltalk.org/acquittals-by-the-international-criminal-court/> (last accessed 9 December 2021)

Heinze, Alexander, 'Some Reflections on the Bemba Appeals Chamber Judgment' on *Opinio Juris* (18 June 2018) <http://opiniojuris.org/2018/06/18/some-reflections-on-the-bemba-appeals-chamber-judgment/> (last accessed 9 December 2021)

Heller, Kevin, 'Another Terrible Day for the OTP' on *Opinio Juris* (8 March 2014) <http://opiniojuris.org/2014/03/08/another-terrible-day-otp/> (last accessed 9 December 2021)

Heller, Kevin, 'The Final Nail in the ICTY's Coffin' on *Opinio Juris* (16 December 2013) <http://opiniojuris.org/2013/12/16/final-nail-ictys-coffin/> (last accessed 9 December 2021)

Human Rights Watch, 'Libya: ICC Judges Reject Sanussi Appeal' (24 July 2014) <https://www.hrw.org/news/2014/07/24/libya-icc-judges-reject-sanussi-appeal> (last accessed 9 December 2021)

ICC, 'Statement of the Prosecutor of the International Criminal Court, Fatou Bensouda, at the opening of Trial in the case against Dominic Ongwen' (4 December 2016) <https://www.icc-cpi.int//Pages/item.aspx?name=2016-12-06-otp-stat-ongwen> (last accessed 9 December 2021)

ICC, 'Statement of the Prosecutor of the International Criminal Court, Fatou Bensouda, on the withdrawal of charges against Mr. Uhuru Muigai Kenyatta' (5 December 2014) <https://www.icc-cpi.int/Pages/item.aspx?name=otp-statement-05-12-2014-2> (last accessed 9 December 2021)

ICTY, *About the ICTY* <https://www.icty.org/en/about> (last accessed 9 December 2021)

ICTY, *Witness Statistics* <https://www.icty.org/en/about/registry/witnesses/statistics> (last accessed 9 December 2021)

Jacobs, Dov, 'Partial Retrial Ordered in Haradinaj' on *Spreading the Jam* (21 July 2010) <http://dovjacobs.com/2010/07/21/partial-retrial-ordered-in-haradinaj/> (last accessed 9 December 2021)

Jacobs, Dov, 'The ICC Katanga Judgment: A Commentary (Part 3): Some Final Thoughts on its Legacy' on *Spreading the Jam* (12 March 2014) <http://dovjacobs.com/2014/03/12/the-icc-katanga-judgment-a-commentary-part-3-some-final-thoughts-on-its-legacy/> (last accessed 9 December 2021)

Jordash, Wayne, 'Fairness of Karadzic Trial in Question' (4 October 2010) *International Justice Tribune* (online) <http://www.rnw.nl/international-justice/article/fairness-karadzic-trial-question> (last accessed 19 July 2013)

Karnavas, Michael, 'The Reversal of Bemba's Conviction: What Went Wrong or Right?' (19 June 2018) <http://michaelgkarnavas.net/blog/2018/06/19/bemba-reversal/> (last accessed 9 December 2021)

Mégret, Frédéric, 'International Criminal Law: A New Legal Hybrid?' (2003) <http://papers.ssrn.com/sol3/papers.cfm?abstract_id=1269382> (last accessed 9 December 2021)

Milanovic, Marko, 'Breaking: Judge Harhoff Disqualified from the Seselj Case' on *EJIL Talk!* (28 August 2013) <http://www.ejiltalk.org/breaking-judge-harhoff-disqualified-from-the-seselj-case/> (last accessed 9 December 2021)

No Peace Without Justice, 'Libya: NPWJ and NRPTT Welcome ICC Ruling on the Al-Senussi Case, which Heralds New Potential for Justice and Strengthening Human Rights Protection' (24 July 2014) <http://www.npwj.org/ICC/Libya-NPWJ-and-NRPTT-welcome-ICC-ruling-Al-Senussi-case-which-heralds-new-potential-justice-and-> (last accessed 9 December 2021)

O'Donohue, Jonathan and Sophie Rigney, 'The ICC Must Consider Fair Trial Concerns in Determining Libya's Application to Prosecute Saif al-Islam Gaddafi Nationally' on *EJIL Talk!* (8 June 2012) <http://www.ejiltalk.org/the-icc-must-consider-fair-trial-concerns-in-determining-libyas-application-to-prosecute-saif-al-islam-gaddafi-nationally/> (last accessed 9 December 2021)

Powderly, Joseph and Niamh Hayes, 'The Bemba Appeal: A Fragmented Appeals Chamber Destablises the Law and Practice of the ICC' on *PhD Studies in Human Rights* (26 June 2018) <https://humanrightsdoctorate.blogspot.com/2018/06/the-bemba-appeal-fragmented-appeals.html> (last accessed 9 December 2021)

Rigney, Sophie, 'The Deep Fractures in International Justice' on *New Matilda* (4 June 2013) <https://newmatilda.com/2013/06/04/deep-fractures-international-justice/> (last accessed 9 December 2021)

Rigney, Sophie, 'Yugoslav Tribunal's Reputation under Threat' on *New Matilda* (23 September 2013) <https://newmatilda.com/2013/09/23/yugoslav-tribunals-reputation-under-threat> (last accessed 9 December 2021)

Sadat, Leila, 'Fiddling While Rome Burns? The Appeals Chamber's Curious Decision in Prosecutor v Jean-Pierre Bemba Gombo' on *EJILTalk!* (12 June 2018) <https://www.ejiltalk.org/fiddling-while-rome-burns-the-appeals-chambers-curious-decision-in-prosecutor-v-jean-pierre-bemba-gombo/> (last accessed 9 December 2021)

Whiting, Alex, 'Guest Post: The ICC's Last Days? Not So Fast' on *Spreading the Jam* (20 March 2014) <http://dovjacobs.com/2014/03/20/guest-post-the-iccs-end-days-not-so-fast/> (last accessed 9 December 2021)

Women's Initiatives for Gender Justice, 'Partial Conviction of Katanga by ICC, Acquittals for Sexual Violence and Use of Child Soldiers' (7 March 2014) <http://www.iccwomen.org/images/Katanga-Judgement-Statement-corr.pdf> (last accessed 9 December 2021)

INTERVIEWS

Interview with Judge A (The Hague, 31 May 2013)
Interview with Danya Chaikal (The Hague, 23 May 2013)
Interview with Judge Adrian Fulford (London, 5 June 2014)
Interview with Joanna Korner (London, 21 May 2013)
Interview with Judge Justice Bakone Moloto (The Hague, 27 May 2013)
Interview with Judge Howard Morrison (The Hague, 29 May 2013)
Interview with Peter Robinson (The Hague, 2 May 2013)
Interview with Colleen Rohan and Gregor Guy-Smith (The Hague, 8 May 2013)
Interview with Stefan Trechsel (The Hague, 28 May 2013)
Interview with Judge X (The Hague, 14 May 2013)

Index